THE ARIANS

OF THE

FOURTH CENTURY

THE WORKS OF

CARDINAL JOHN HENRY NEWMAN

BIRMINGHAM ORATORY

MILLENNIUM EDITION

VOLUME IV

SERIES EDITOR

JAMES TOLHURST DD

THE ARIANS
OF THE
FOURTH CENTURY

BY

JOHN HENRY CARDINAL NEWMAN

with an Introduction and Notes by

ROWAN WILLIAMS

Gracewing.

NOTRE DAME

First published in 1833
Published in the Birmingham Millennium Oratory Edition in 2001
jointly by

Gracewing
2 Southern Avenue
Leominster
Herefordshire HR6 0QF

University of Notre Dame Press
310 Flanner Hall
Notre Dame
IN 46556 USA

Library of Congress Cataloging-in-Publication Data

Newman, John Henry, 1801–1890.
The Arians of the fourth century/by John Henry Newman; with an introduction and notes by Rowan Williams.
p. cm. – (The works of Cardinal John Henry Newman; v. 4)
"The text here reproduced is basically that revised by Newman in 1871 for the third edition"–P.
Includes bibliographical references.
ISBN 0-268-02012-4 (cl.)
1. Arianism. I. Williams, Rowan, 1950 II. Title.

BT1350.N4 2001
273'.4–dc21 2001037333

UK ISBN 0 85244 448 6
US ISBN 0-268-02012-4

Additional typesetting by Action Publishing Technology Ltd, Gloucester, GL1 5SR
Printed in England by MPG Books Ltd, Bodmin, PL31 1EG

CONTENTS

PART II. HISTORICAL.

CHAPTER III.

THE ECUMENICAL COUNCIL OF NICAEA, IN THE REIGN OF CONSTANTINE.

CHAPTER IV.

COUNCILS IN THE REIGN OF CONSTANTIUS.

APPENDIX.

NOTE ON THE TEXT

The text here reproduced is basically that revised by Newman in 1871 for the third edition, incorporating numerous minor stylistic improvements, and two more substantial alterations reflecting Newman's changed ecclesiastical allegiance. The Appendices were added in this edition. The third edition was reprinted in 1895, with one small extra note (p. 420; c.f. p. 422), and is photographically reproduced in this present edition.

INTRODUCTION

Newman is not the first author to have ended up writing a book very different from the one he had originally envisaged. *The Arians of the Fourth Century* has its origins in a correspondence between Newman and Hugh James Rose in early 1831 about the possibility of a textbook on the Thirty-Nine Articles of the Church of England – part of the steadily developing campaign among High Churchmen at the time to revive serious theological study among Anglican clergy.[1] The publishing house of Rivington's, which had been prominent in the production of High Church periodical and other literature from early in the century were now proposing a 'Theological Library' of volumes designed to defend and advance

[1] *Letters and Diaries of John Henry Newman* II, p. 321; on the anxieties of the High Church party at the time and the concern to promote good theology, see Peter B. Nockles, *The Oxford Movement in Context. Anglican High Churchmanship 1760–1857*, Cambridge, 1994, pp. 273–274.

the High Church perspective.[2] The initial idea was that Newman should write a study of the Articles designed for this series, but as the correspondence with Rose continued, both agreed that there was a necessary preliminary job to be done in the shape of a history of the Councils of the early and mediaeval Church. By the end of June, Newman was working hard at the background to the Council of Nicaea, the first ecclesiastical gathering to be recognised as a 'general' or 'ecumenical' council. It had been convened in 325 by the emperor Constantine to deal with the controversies around the Alexandrian priest, Arius, whose teaching was regarded as compromising the Church's acknowledgment of true and full divinity at work in the person of Jesus of Nazareth. But as the book grew, questions of method and fundamental principle in the history of doctrine preoccupied Newman more and more; the book began to change its character quite radically. As it neared completion, the editors of the Theological Library became more and more anxious about the direction it was taking, and in October 1832 Rose and his fellow editor, W. R. Lyall had decided that the book was unsuitable for inclusion in the series.[3] Rivington's published it as an independent volume; but the decision of 1832 was

[2] On the role of Rivington's, see Nockles, op.cit., p. 271. The present writer's article, 'Newman's *Arians* and the Question of Method in Doctrinal History', *Newman After a Hundred Years*, ed. Ian Ker and Alan G. Hill, Oxford, 1990, pp. 263–285, refers by an oversight to this proposed library as the 'Library of Anglo-Catholic Theology', a different and later project (p. 264). Pp. 264–273 give further details of the process of the composition of the *Arians*.

[3] *Letter and Diaries of John Henry Newman* III, pp. 104–105, 112–113 for Lyall's criticisms.

significant. Newman could not be presented to the theological world as an entirely safe representative of High Church orthodoxy.

What lay behind this, and what was wrong, from the viewpoint of Lyall and Rose, with Newman's argument? Part of the fascination of this too much neglected work is the way it precariously holds together a strongly conservative agenda, grounded in the specific political and church-political struggles of the early 1830s, with a disturbingly radical view of the history of theology – or rather, how Newman, in a way prophetic of much of his later work, recognises that a 'traditionalist' cause can sometimes be plausibly defended only by adopting utterly untraditional methods and looking for new structures of understanding. As he was to say so often, in varying phrases later in his career, saying the same thing *now* as was said *then* may involve you in saying something apparently novel.[4]

There is no doubt of Newman's conservative intention (and it is clearly evident in the book). He is writing for a situation in which High Church Anglicans, after a brief period of relatively strong influence at the very beginning of the nineteenth century, believed, accurately enough, that English society was going through a rapid and (to them) unwelcome transformation; it was ceasing to be even nominally a Christian body, governed by the

[4] For the background, see especially Owen Chadwick, *From Bossuet to Newman*, Cambridge, 1957, chs. 4 and 5. Chadwick charts how the question had begun to be raised earlier (see e.g., pp. 79–80), but his work as a whole (though it does not examine the precise way in which the *Arians* treats the issue) reinforces how novel the *Arians* discussion was as a matter of primarily historical argument.

doctrines of a particular church. Worse, these changes were regarded by the governments of the day as a tacit licence to remove from the Church itself its own doctrinal standards and disciplinary independence. Recent scholarship[5] has successfully challenged the conventional picture of an eighteenth-century Church of England sunk in corruption and inactivity, indifferent about doctrine and enslaved to political interests. From the middle of the eighteenth century onwards, the intellectually serious and powerful voices in the national Church were 'orthodox' – doctrinally conservative, devotionally disciplined, committed to the vision of a unified social order under a divinely authorised monarchy. They were not 'Erastians', believing in the subordination of Church to state; but they did believe that the monarch had been given a guardianship over the Church of the nation: the monarch's privilege and responsibility was to secure the orthodoxy of the Church and to support its enactments.[6] As many of the apologists of the period insisted, this did not mean that the monarch had the right to define doctrines that the Church was then bound to accept, simply that the Church's self-definition was assured by the backing of the supreme authority in the state. Thus is was quite defensible for the key institutions of society (including the universities) to be controlled in the Church's interest by the

[5] Taking its cue above all from J.C.D. Clark's brilliant study, *English Society 1688–1832*.

[6] Nockles, *The Oxford Movement in Context*, ch. 1, especially pp. 44–53 and 63–67, is of great help in clarifying this; see also J.H.L. Rowlands, *Church, State and Society: the Attitudes of John Keble, Richard Hurrell Froude and John Henry Newman, 1827–1845*, Worthing, 1989.

Crown. The monarch guaranteed the organic unity of the realm as a Christian body, and a Christian body of a specific kind – episcopally governed, independent of the Papacy, bound by scripture and creeds and by the disciplined practice of the sacraments. It would make no sense for the monarch to permit or encourage alternative teachings and convictions among the governing classes (intellectual and political). Hence the disabilities imposed on Protestant Nonconformists and Roman Catholics. Their convictions (the High Churchmen would have said) were respected, they were not actively persecuted; but they lived in a society which explicitly recognised another theological or ideological base for its coherence and legitimacy, and must therefore abide by the consequences of this.[7]

The ecclesiastical upheavals of the 1830s

Such was the predominant view among those who saw themselves as 'orthodox' at the opening of the nineteenth century. It had a great deal in common with the model of Church and society developed by Richard Hooker at the end of the sixteenth century,[8] and had survived the huge political and dynastic upheavals of the late seventeenth and early eighteenth centuries. It had with some difficulty come to terms

[7] See e.g., Clark, *English Society 1688–1832*, p. 352, Nockles, op.cit., p. 92.

[8] For an accessible and reliable survey, see the Introduction to Richard Hooker, *Of the Laws of Ecclesiastical Polity* (Preface, Book I and Book VIII), ed. A.S. McGrade, Cambridge, 1989; a recent very creative discussion is Debra Shuger, '"Societie Supernaturall": The Imagined Community of Hooker's *Lawes*' in *Richard Hooker and the Construction of Christian Community*, ed. A.S. McGrade, Tempe, Arizona, 1997, pp. 307–329.

with the 1688 Revolution and with the arrival of the Hanoverians. Its theological solidity has often been underrated – a trend beginning with the Oxford Movement itself, many of whose leaders, Newman included, thought that it had proved itself impotent and inadequate to meet the challenges of a new situation. It was very much in the interests of the Tractarians – as of any vigorous new movement – to emphasise the faults in what had gone before so as to appear more clearly as a fresh response to problems that others had failed to solve. For the new challenges had arrived with unexpected and rather brutal clarity. Between 1828 and 1834, the franchise had been extended (in a way seen as threatening the exclusively Anglican character of Parliament), the civil disabilities of Roman Catholics had been removed and the Anglican monopoly in public life, not least in the ancient universities, had been decisively weakened; the suppression of a number of Irish bishoprics in 1833, which provoked Keble's famous Assize Sermon on 'National Apostasy' had demonstrated that government could no longer be relied upon to endorse the polity of the Church of England, but retained the right to interfere in the Church's structures. The overwhelming majority of the bishops during these years had supported the extension of the rights of Protestant Dissenters and had been at best ineffectual and lukewarm in their resistance to Catholic Emancipation; a substantial minority had backed the Reform Bill of 1832. In short, the confessional character of English society had not only been shattered, it had been surrendered with hardly a shot fired from the Church's chief pastors.

Jonathan Clark, the leading revisionist historian of eighteenth- and early nineteenth-century British ideology, notes the 'smooth, bland, and ultimately anti-intellectual norm' of the bishops of the period,[9] and speaks of 'a final and sudden betrayal from within'.[10] This was certainly how High Church theologians and essayists perceived matters in the early 1830s: the bishops had apparently no understanding that the interest of the Church could not be identified with the interest of the government of the day (however strongly supported by popular, or populist, pressure). They had been seduced by the idea of a national *religiosity* that could ally itself with democratic aspirations, without insisting upon dogmatic orthodoxy; but the classical Anglican position had nothing to do with conserving a religiously flavoured morality for the nation, everything to do with the legal maintenance of a highly specific set of doctrinal commitments. If even the bishops had become so illiterate about the nature of the Church they were supposed to lead and represent, there was urgent need for a campaign of theological education. Well before the Oxford Tracts began to appear, the High Church group had begun to marshal a response: and, as we have seen, the invitation to Newman to write a theological textbook was part of this response.

The agenda implied in all this is still very plainly evident in the book as we have it. Newman, despite some rather strained expressions of confidence 'in the piety, prudence, and varied graces of our Spiritual Rulers' (p. 394; the reader familiar with Newman

[9] Clark, *English Society 1688–1832*, p. 408.
[10] Ibid., p. 409.

may well suspect a note of irony), does not lose opportunities of describing the sad weaknesses of fourth-century bishops – 'The orthodox majority of Bishops divines, ... timorously or indolently, kept in the background', he writes of one critical period (p. 294). Those who proved insufficiently aware of the dangers of heresy have something to be said in their favour, compared with outright apostates; they were 'men of correct and exemplary life, and earnest according to their views' (p. 300). But their naivety, ignorance or spiritual laziness helped to perpetuate the cancer of false teaching; at best, such prelates fell victim to sophistical argument, at worst they proved cowards in the face of imperial threats (pp. 308, 310–11, 315, 316–7, 359). Clark's charges of blandness and anti-intellectualism against the bishops of the 1830s are precisely Newman's charges against the fourth-century bishops who confusedly, even if not with deliberate apostate intent, sought a middle way between truth and falsehood.

So far, Newman's High Church patrons would have agreed. They may have been less sure about those passages in which Newman expresses reservations about the very idea of state endorsement for the Church. His pages on Constantine and Constantine's legacy (especially pp. 243–4) are profoundly sceptical of the capacity of any ordinary political managers to understand what Christian unity really means: not a socially useful consensus or a tolerant pluralism, but a spiritual reality that arises out of zeal for truth (with all the risk of division which that brings). Religious controversy, unwelcome or incomprehensible to the secular ruler (and the secular public) represents 'the history of truth in its first stage of trial, when it aims at being "pure," before it is "peaceable"' (p. 244). In other words, you can never be sure that a sovereign will be a lastingly reliable ally in the defence of orthodox confession. There were High Churchmen who were moving towards some such scepticism; but there is a difference between bewailing the failure or betrayal of an ideal and questioning the very basis of that ideal. Newman was stepping over a significant boundary; and when, a few pages later (pp. 257–9), he elaborated his theory of the Church as 'necessarily a political power or party', independent of and relating very critically to civil government, he was articulating a theology that was by no means easy to reconcile with the traditional High Church position. To repeat the point made earlier: it was *not* that the older position entailed subservience to some alien body called 'the state'. In the society of the baptised, civil power sanctioned and protected belief, as defined by the organs of teaching within that society. Newman is moving towards a view of the state as indeed at least a potentially alien thing – towards a theory of the state as intrinsically secular, a system of human organisation with which the Church is in constant struggle and negotiation. It seeks to convince the state and to defend its doctrines; where the state gives rights to the Church, the Church properly fights for their maintenance. But the picture is a great deal more restless and conflictual than any traditional High Churchman could readily have allowed. Of course, such a reader might have said, the civil government is fallible and may at times betray or persecute; then the believer is called to what we should call non-violent resistance, and what classical Anglicans called (misleadingly to modern ears) 'passive obedience'.[11] The end of Newman's brief polemic on this (p. 259) speaks of the Church's ultimate 'sanction' being simply to oblige the state to make martyrs. This is in itself not far from the 'passive resistance' principle; but, read in context, it gives no indication of what a traditionalist would have taken for granted – that there is an expected *norm* of 'baptised' civil authority.

The disciplina arcani

However, this was not the issue that aroused most anxiety among Newman's first readers. He discusses at some length (especially on pp. 44–56) the *disciplina arcani* of the early Church, particularly as evidenced in Alexandria. Patristic catechesis, he claims, was carefully graded, beginning with general principles to do with God's existence and the moral law, advancing to more specific instruction in the creed, but reserving until after baptism a full exposition of the mysteries concerned with salvation, sacramental theology and the trinitarian character of God (p. 45). This is contrasted polemically with nineteenth-century evangelical practice, preaching the doctrine of the atonement in the hope of awakening the conscience

[11] Clark, *English Society 1688–1832*, pp. 141–161 for some background; c.f. pp. 224–228. There is, in Orthodox Anglican political thought no right, against a divinely sanctioned government, of active resistance, rebellion; but there is a significant distinction between active obedience, co-operating with the demands of authority, and passive obedience, being subject to the laws when they require a penalty for non-co-operation. The precise degree to which non-co-operation might be defended was an occasion of some dispute, not least because of the legacy of the dynastic upheaval of 1688.

before any general instruction is considered. Newman, defensibly enough, observes that what the New Testament has to say about Christian instruction bears relatively little relation to this modern habit. But the point of the whole discussion is to help explain why theologians who lived and died before the Council of Nicaea so often used language that might by an unsympathetic reader be thought as compatible with 'Arianism' as with the Creed of Nicaea. Naturally, pre-Nicene language is not always clear, since these doctrinal issues were not publicly debated, and indeed not even explicitly taught except to the mature initiate. When we understand this, we shall also see the inadequacy of appeal to the Bible alone to settle doctrinal questions (pp. 50–51). Before the Arian crisis, the doctrine of the Trinity was believed and understood; but it was not publicly and decisively formulated, because you could – so to speak – trust those to whom something of its depths were imparted to receive it with the right degree of spiritual humility and prayerfulness.

Thus Newman argues, with conscious paradox, that 'the highest state of Christian communion' in the abstract is what exists prior to any credal formulation or doctrinal test: '... when confessions do not exist, the mysteries of divine truth, instead of being exposed to the gaze of the profane and uninstructed, are kept hidden in the bosom of the Church ... and reserved by a private teaching, through the channel of her ministers, as rewards in due measure and season, for those who are prepared to profit by them;' (p. 37). The obligation to reduce doctrine to authoritative formulae, and to examine the utterances of pastors and teachers to square them with declared orthodoxy, is a sign of spiritual loss or degeneracy (e.g. pp. 179–80). There is no way of avoiding this, once challenges of a certain kind are raised: pp. 156–78 set out with great learning and subtlety what the pre-Nicene Fathers said about the Trinity, pointing out at every step the ambiguity of their language, especially if severed from a shared ecclesial and spiritual experience. When heretics arose who were 'tone-deaf' to the spiritual depth of this earlier idiom, the Church could defend its teaching only by defining, and in some senses narrowing, the language of a more innocent age.

This is where Newman's High Church colleagues felt most alarm, alarm expressed in the correspondence from Archdeacon Lyall late in 1832, already referred to,[12] and echoed in some reviews and comments after publication (there was a particularly sharp critique of Newman's handling of the historical evidence for 'secret tradition' from the Bishop of Lincoln, John Kaye, one of the leading patristic scholars of the day and a moderate but convinced High Churchman of the older school).[13] There were two kinds of problem. At the surface level, there is real confusion in Newman's text: it is not clear whether he is saying that a full and satisfactory doctrine of the Trinity was actually believed and taught in the pre-Nicene period, but only to the spiritual elite; or that there was no adequate verbal account of this doctrine, although its

[12] Above, n.3; Williams, 'Newman's *Arians*', pp. 272–273.

[13] Kaye had sent comments to Hugh James Rose, who relayed them to Newman. See *Letters and Diaries of John Henry Newman* IV, p. 169, n.1; Williams, 'Newman's *Arians*' art.cit., pp. 273–274 (where Kaye is mistakenly called Bishop of Norwich).

essence was believed and taught; or that the language of the earlier period was correct but intermixed with metaphorical extravagance or unexamined idioms so that the unreflective reader may be misled. Different passages suggest these in turn; and, as Kaye observed, the evidence for a developed system of graded catechesis such as Newman takes for granted can only really be drawn from the *post*-Nicene era, and is not wholly universal and schematic even then.

But the deeper problem was with the very notion of secret or unexpressed tradition. Lyall wrote to Rose that 'a "secret tradition" is not tradition at all', and this sums up the anxieties of orthodox High Church theologians. Newman is apparently granting that pre-Nicene formulations actually *are* compatible with something other than Nicene orthodoxy (indeed, Newman criticises earlier Anglican scholars like Bishop Bull for failing to come clean about this).[14] But this undermines one of the most fundamental concerns of traditional High Church theology, the battle on two fronts that had been waged by the apologists and doctrinal historians of the seventeenth and early eighteenth centuries in particular. On the one hand, Anglicans were faced with radical Protestants who claimed that the doctrine of the Trinity was the product of a corruption of the gospel by philosophy, or of authoritarian priestcraft and ecclesiastical

[14] Note particularly the comments on Bull in the second appendix to the present work (pp. 416–422), and c.f. Chadwick, *From Bossuet to Newman*, p. 122 and the note to this on p. 232 referring to R.H. Broker's dissertation, *The Influence of Bull and Petavius on Cardinal Newman's theory of the development of Christian doctrine*, Rome 1938. C.f. also remarks by Newman in a letter of 1831 to Samuel Rickards (*Letters and Diaries of John Henry Newman* II, p. 371).

tyranny, or of both together. There were sufficient articulate and combative 'Arians' in Britain between 1650 and 1750 to justify the anxiety of High Church thinkers; for them, it was axiomatic that pre-Nicene writers had not only believed what later Christians came to believe but had also expressed their beliefs in a form acceptable to such later Christians. The extensive and fierce controversies around these matters have lately been the subject of an excellent monograph by Maurice Wiles.[15] But there was a further danger, the second front which had to be defended. Some Roman Catholic scholars, above all the doyen of French doctrinal historians, Denis Petau, often referred to as Petavius, were happy to steal the clothes of anti-Trinitarian polemicists, agreeing that pre-Nicene theology often was rather a conceptual mess. The confusions of this theology only reinforced the need to recognise a single, dependable teaching authority (the Papacy); in the earliest Church, all positive doctrine was in process of winning recognition, so that you could see the development of credal orthodoxy advancing hand-in-hand with the development of clear papal authority.[16]

For a Rose or a Lyall, therefore, Newman was admitting a Trojan Horse into the Anglican citadel. The classical Anglican appeal to the 'undivided Church' is less plausible if the undivided Church actually has a history, if not of conflict, then at least of trial

[15] *Archetypal Heresy. Arianism Through the Centuries*, Oxford, 1996. For Wiles's discussion of Newman's *Arians*, see pp. 165–173. On earlier attitudes to 'Arianism' in England and the Church of England, see also Clark, *English Society 1688–1832*, pp. 279–289.

[16] See Chadwick, *From Bossuet to Newman*, pp. 58–60, 215–216; Williams, 'Newman's *Arians*', pp. 277–278.

and error in its utterances. A High Church Anglican apologist would have wanted to know how we could persuade anyone to believe in the Trinity if we were unable to be confident that the belief had been there from the beginning. Newman's text in fact offers an implicit response to such a challenge. Yes, belief had been there from the start, but the language of Christians had taken time to catch up with the fullness of what was believed; in an era when Christian commitment was radical and deep, and there was a proper spiritual formation for members of the Church, it was simply the case that those who needed to understand *did* understand. Furthermore, theological language, though unsystematic in this early age, had had its own ways of correcting misunderstanding by its variety and fluidity; it was never mortgaged to one set of images, even though it dealt with images rather than formulae (we shall be looking further at this later on). God's providence allowed conflict to arise so that any remaining unclarity might be overcome; but this was not without cost. Yet the High Church critic might still come back and object that where *language* was unclear, we simply could not be sure about what people meant; if the pre-Nicenes didn't know exactly what to say about the Trinity, how could we possibly know what they thought, except by an appeal to a shared spiritual sense that might look dangerously subjective or esoteric? The only other option would have to be what Petavius argued: you might never know exactly how orthodox a second-century writer was, but you could know what the true mind of the Church as a whole was through its magisterium.

Certainly Newman is walking a tightrope, and we

can see the germs of the *Essay on Development* pretty plainly. What is different in the *Arians*, though, is the pervasive sense that it is, in the abstract, better not to define mysteries, that the Church is most itself when it feels no need to prescribe formulae, because Christians can trust one another's spiritual discernment. Nor do we find in this earlier work any real hint of the search for general *principles* of development; there is no *a priori* element in the discussion of doctrinal history. The effect is a strikingly intense rhetoric of initiation, revealed-but-concealed mystery, the holy community guarding its integrity against a hostile world. And we can imagine our High Church commentator observing that this was exactly what was to be expected from Newman's rhetoric elsewhere about Church and State. Orthodoxy has become more of a quality of spiritual life than a public system by which a community may govern itself. If you hold Newman's view of the Church, the legal privileges of the Church of England, with the ideology that went with them, could hardly be at the top of a polemical agenda. Stephen Thomas, in his discussion of Newman's attitudes to heresy, rightly notes that 'Newman's treatment of Arianism reflects the transition from the pre-1832 situation, in which it was not necessarily *party*-political to defend Establishment, to the new situation, after Reform, in which an ecclesiastical *party* had to be created in the Church of England'.[17] Relating this to the argument of Peter Nockles's outstanding work on the High Church tradition, it is possible to see how the fate of Tractarianism within the Church of England was

[17] Stephen Thomas, *Newman and Heresy*, Cambridge 1991, p. 61.

virtually sealed in advance by what might be seen as Newman's allying of 'orthodoxy' not with a policy for the whole national Church, but with the nurturing of a particular style and spirituality within it.[18] Lyall's unhappiness about Newman on the *disciplina arcani* was ultimately a political concern, and a well-founded one; though whether Newman's own final resolution of his difficulties by – in effect – accepting something very like Petavius's logic was the only available outcome will still be matter for debate, if you are uneasy about the *a priori* arguments for a single visible teaching authority, or about the historical defensibility of seeing credal and papal clarifications advancing in step.

It should be plain by now that this book is a highly sophisticated contribution to a very specific debate in the early 1830s, and that it is anything but a bland textbook (anyone expecting textbooks from Newman at any point in his career was doomed to disappointment or worse). Its importance in tracing Newman's own evolution has often been underrated; and, as I have argued at length elsewhere, it succeeds in establishing a new set of possibilities for doctrinal history, in that it gives a real *theological* valuation to the processes of intellectual history and does not attempt to deny that the accurate perception of Christian truth is shaped by conflict.[19] But how far does it succeed in its explicit task of charting those processes as they occurred? The answer must be, very poorly. As a guide to the theological or ecclesiastical history of the fourth century, the book cannot be sensibly recommended. Its virtue is in the questions it raises, not the answers it provides. It is

[18] Nockles, *The Oxford Movement in Context*, pp. 319ff.

[19] Williams, 'Newman's *Arians*', especially pp. 268–271, 282–285.

emphatically a powerful and original essay, questioning received wisdom on a number of major topics; but Newman's own perspectives and proposals are often flawed by a colossally over-schematic treatment and a carelessness in detail. There are, of course, areas in which he was no more astray than any other writer of the period, where insufficient textual evidence or critical analysis was available; but his Procrustean treatment of what evidence there was on several key matters remains a problem.

Antioch and Alexandria

Central to his presentation is a thesis about the theological styles of Antioch and Alexandria in the early Church, a thesis deliberately opposed to a quite widespread seventeenth- and eighteenth-century consensus. Both Catholic writers like Petavius or Maimbourg and Protestants like Mosheim (a major source for Newman, and a precursor of later nineteenth-century Protestant methodology in doctrinal history)[20] agreed that early Christian theology had been adversely affected by what we should now call Middle Platonism and Neoplatonism, and that this baleful influence had been especially active in Alexandria. An adequate theology would have to distance itself from such philosophising, either by settling into the authorised propositions of Catholic dogma or by returning to a scriptural and pre-metaphysical innocence. The

[20] On Maimbourg, see Wiles, *Archetypal Heresy*, ch. 3; on Mosheim, Williams, 'Newman's *Arians*', pp. 279–282, and the article on him by N. Bonwetsch in *Realencyclopädiae für Protestantische Theologie und Kirche* xiii (1903), pp. 502–506. Mosheim's anticipation of some characteristic perspectives in Harnack bears more examination.

teachings of Arius, a presbyter of Alexandria, were very much what you might expect from a mind formed in the intellectual climate of the city, with ambiguous figures like Clement and Origen in the background, theologians with a strong Platonising bent and a commitment to allegorical interpretation of Scripture.

Newman repudiates this picture with vehemence. If there is a root of all evil to be identified, let it be sought in Antioch. Why? Chiefly because, Newman claims, the Antiochene Church, or indeed, as he will sometimes say, the Syrian Church as a whole, was fatally compromised with Judaism, constantly liable to read the Bible in a literalist fashion which weakened the witness to Christ of the allegorical or mystical interpretation, and to deny or obscure the doctrine of God's full and unequivocal incarnate presence in Christ. Prior to the crisis provoked by Arius, the most overt denial of Christ's divinity by a 'mainstream' theologian was in the teaching of Paul of Samosata, Bishop of Antioch and (Newman believed) protégé of the Palmyrene queen Zenobia, a Jewish convert. Arius's bishop, Alexander, accuses him of renewing the heresy of Paul; Arius lets us know that he and some of his allies had been pupils of the exegete Lucian of Antioch, friend (Newman believed) of Paul. Later Antiochene theology minimised the full involvement of the divine Son in the life of the earthly Jesus, and was duly condemned by later councils. The prosecution rests.

Unfortunately, this account is deeply flawed. Newman makes one composite monster out of hugely diverse material, ranging from the second to the fifth or even sixth centuries, and some of his exposition, in the text and in the long appendix from the

Development essay on 'The Syrian School', shows signs of strain as he attempts to fit into one pattern the diversity of theologies he deals with. He certainly overlooks one central fact – that, after Nicaea, the most ferocious opposition to the teachings of Arius regularly came from West Syria.[21] Scholarship in recent decades has decisively rejected the idea of a connection between 'Arianism' and literalist exegesis.[22] Despite the accusations of enemies, Arius's theology and that of Paul of Samosata were poles apart. Paul, it appears, was at best ambigous about the real and independent existence of the heavenly Son or Word of God, and had a Christology centering upon grace and inspiration; Arius was completely committed to the idea of an independent pre-existent heavenly person who subsequently became the subject of the human experiences associated with Jesus – therefore a heavenly person who could doubt and suffer, therefore a heavenly person who was not God in the strict sense.[23] These are very distinct agendas. Arius may have studied with Lucian, and Lucian may

[21] Eustathius, Bishop of Antioch at the time of Nicaea, was a consistent opponent of Arius, and suffered for his convictions. On the whole issue, see (with some caution) D.S. Wallace-Hadrill, *Christian Antioch. A Study of early Christian thought in the East*, Cambridge, 1982, ch. 4.

[22] The decisive study is M. Simonetti, 'Le origini dell' Arianesimo', *Rivista di storia e letteratura religiosa* 7 (1971), pp. 317–330; on the whole question of 'literal' and 'non-literal' exegesis, an oustanding recent study is Frances Young, *Biblical Exegesis and the Formation of Christian Culture*, Cambridge, 1997.

[23] Frederick Norris, 'Paul of Samosata: *Procurator Ducenarius*', *Journal of Theological Studies*, n.s. 35 (1984), pp. 50–70, offers a reliable guide to current assessment of Paul. On Arius's theology in general, see R. Williams, *Arius: Heresy and Tradition*, London, 1987, especially Part II, and R.P.C. Hanson, *The Search for the Christian Doctrine of God: The Arian Controversy*, Edinburgh, 1988.

(though we do not really know) have been more literalist than some others in his biblical interpretation; but nothing bears out an association between Paul and Lucian.[24] Newman's 'Antioch' is an ideal type not an historical reality.

It is the type of a theology dictated by human wisdom, human desire, the reluctance to be humble before revelation. Alexandria, the home of true theology, is characterised by reverence, by the expectation that the Bible will always be deeply mysterious, working through elusive symbolism over a lifetime of contemplation; this is a theology giving priority to God. Newman's purpose in terms of the 1830s was evidently to challenge any English assimilation of German critical scholarship and doctrinal revisionism (his source, Mosheim, though belonging to an earlier generation, would already have shown signs of rationalist infidelity, and Newman goes out of his way to counter Mosheim's assumptions, even when following his narrative and borrowing his vocabulary). For the contemporary reader, though, the hardest aspect of this to read sympathetically is the quite virulent anti-Judaism that pervades the argument. Judaism too becomes an 'ideal type', a 'carnal, self-indulgent religion' (p. 18), clearly opposed to the spiritual and ascetical faith of Alexandrian Christianity. One modern writer[25] has also noted Newman's fascination with the role of Queen Zenobia in Paul of Samosata's

[24] The issue was dealt with authoritatively by G. Bardy, *Recherches sur Saint Lucien d'Antioche et son ecole*, Paris, 1936. See also Wallace-Hadrill, op.cit., pp. 81–88.

[25] Professor Virginia Burrus, in a paper delivered to the 1999 Oxford International Conference on Patristic Studies, as yet unpublished.

career (a role whose historicity is now generally challenged by scholarship): it is as if Antioch is overshadowed by a kind of mythical femininity. The false theology of Syria is 'female' – sensual, preoccupied with appearance rather than reality (hence the literalism in interpreting Scripture), incapable of rational detachment from the self-interested deliverances of unaided human intellect (there is a powerful sermon of Pusey's on sins of the intellect in theology),[26] incapable of fortitude and spiritual heroism. Spiritually speaking, men are from Alexandria, women from Antioch.

This may be an over-mischievous reading (though not by any means implausible if you examine Newman's language with care, in the early chapters especially). But what is plain is that a very rigid structure has been allowed to dictate Newman's narrative and analysis. Alexandria must be beyond reproach; and so Antioch must be practically without redeeming features. It must be covertly 'Jewish', and therefore antithetical to Christianity. Newman raises the question of whether the 'Eclectic' philosophy, as he calls it, following Mosheim in his description of what we should call early Neoplatonism, was an influence on Arius and his followers, but concludes that it was probably not (though it did leave its mark on Eusebius of Caesarea). However, 'Eclecticism'

[26] 'The Responsibility of the Intellect in Matters of Faith', preached in the University Church, Oxford, on Advent Sunday 1872, and included in Pusey's *Eight Sermons Preached Before the University of Oxford Between 1864–1876, and a Sermon Preached at the Opening of the Chapel of Keble College*, Oxford and London, 1878. Despite the difference in date, this gives a useful amplification as to the attitudes shared by Newman and Pusey to the 'natural' intellect.

gives him, as Stephen Thomas notes, another mythical structure to oppose to true religion: like Judaism, this philosophy is deaf and blind to mystery; and – worse – it conceals its true import, using words in sophistical and misleading senses. It is just like the anti-supernaturalist religion of incipient liberal Protestantism in Germany, beginning to infect the English universities (see p. 87, for example, for an explicit comparison between 'Eclecticism' and German 'Neologism').[27]

The doctrine of the Trinity

But for all Newman's appeals to reverence and obedience in theology, we should credit him also with a serious attempt to give intellectual coherence to the trinitarian faith he is defending. He does not simply put before us a pre-Nicene fuzz of reverential vagueness and a post-Nicene dogmatic precision that has lost some of its soul. Section III of ch.II, 'The Ecclesiastical Doctrine of the Trinity' (pp. 156–78) is a significant essay on the origins of Trinitarian theology, and a serious attempt to consider the implications of granting that language about the Trinity alters in the early centuries. The doctrine of divine generation is conveyed not only through the central revealed vocabulary about Father and Son, but through a plethora of metaphors (wellspring and stream, fire kindling fire, and so on; p. 162), whose purpose is partly, by their very profusion, to prevent us taking any one of them literally or in isolation. What is at

[27] 'Neologism' seems to have been coined by conservative Anglicans to describe liberal German theology of the period; Newman's source for this vocabulary is Rose.

work is what has been called an 'ecology' of doctrinal language: within the whole system of Christian speech, words receive their proper sense, balanced by others, qualified and nuanced by their neighbours. But heresy forces the Christian to analyse language more than he would otherwise want or need to. Early doctrinal language had spoken unselfconsciously of the Son as serving or obeying the Father. This had posed no problem, because the early theologians took equally unselfconsciously for granted the unity of living nature between Father and Son. Of course the Father was 'greater', prior to the Son as origin; but the Son is still 'internal to the Divine Mind', no more a different agent than the human will is a different 'thing' from the human reason. However, they also attempted to offset the possible anthropomorphic resonances of the word 'Son', which undoubtedly *could* suggest a separate agent, by their use of language about 'Logos' or 'Sophia'. This in turn could weaken belief in the real personality of the Second Person of the Trinity; hence the need to insist that this divine 'reason' or 'wisdom' existed in 'hypostasis', real subsistence. This early theology, in other words, maintains orthodoxy by a constant process of self-correction, the endlessly mobile, circling reference of metaphor to metaphor, one balancing another.

In the chapter that follows (pp. 179–200), Newman defends the orthodox intention of the pre-Nicenes by pointing out that post-Nicenes can use similarly ambiguous language at times without their doctrinal probity being called in question (see especially p. 198). If we put together the post-Nicene balancing of such language by adherence to the definitive agreed formula and the pre-Nicene ecology of complementary, balancing imagery, we can see that orthodoxy is never, before or after Nicaea, just a matter of getting one set of formulae right. And if we turn to the Appendices which Newman added to the later editions, especially Notes 2 and 4, we can see further illustration of Newman's concern to understand patristic language in its widest possible linguistic context. We cannot simply assume that we know what any one set of words means in isolation, let alone concluding from our analysis that such and such a writer is 'really' heretical, or that Arius's theology was shared by this or that pre-Nicene divine. It is an unexpected echo of Wittgenstein and kindred philosophers of language: to find meaning, look for use, use in the global context of a system of speech.

In other words, Newman's appeal to reverential humility before doctrinal mystery is not a commendation of blind or bland acceptance. Pre-Nicene theology was intensely aware of the mystery with which it dealt, but this meant that it was a fertile, imaginative affair, seeking and finding correctives to any one narrowing form of words by exploring another; not in shapeless chaos, but in a way clearly disciplined by the priorities manifest in the language of the Bible. Our imagined High Church critic would not, after all, be wholly correct to suppose that Newman was reducing the criteria for doctrinal continuity to an elusive inner sensibility. By sidestepping the rather sterile controversies about whether the pre-Nicene theologians had conformed to the requirements of later orthodoxy or not, Newman was able to make a substantive point about how theological language works, a point still well worth pondering. Do some of the bitternesses and anxieties in current theology about (for example) gender bias in traditional theological language have at least something to do with an isolation of formulae from practice, from the fluid, cross-referential process Newman sees in early theology, so that literalist interpretations are the point from which both liberal and conservative begin? Does the difficulty some moderns have with aspects of Chalcedonian Christology have to do with a weakening or confusion in aspects of piety towards Christ, so that the conceptual filigree of the classical definition seems empty because few understand its motivation?

But the putative High Church reader of 1833 might be forgiven for some residual doubts; and the contemporary reader, High Church or not, might likewise register some questions. In 1833, the *Arians*, more (probably) than its author realised, set out an agenda for the Church of England that would dramatically change its character. By stressing the Church's character as a 'political' entity in its own right, Newman takes a decisive step towards the social dualism that his predecessors and patrons deplored. He accepts in advance that the bishops will not be able to guarantee the privileges of the old Church of England; what is needed is a revival of the integrity of the patristic church. We cannot go back to the pious intensity of the pre-Nicene Church in every respect, but we can learn from it where the pulse of true theology beats. Even when we have been obliged to define and to impose external tests, we must not forget that orthodoxy is a matter of obedience to what exceeds our grasp. Thus the only integrity worth saving in the Church is ultimately that of the spirit, which all external tests must serve. No national polity can secure this.

But to the extent that this meant that the Church of England as a national institution receded, giving way to a community devoted to spiritual pedagogy, it condemned the national institution to a degree of incoherence. Without the clear principle of support from the confessional state, the Christian prince, the Church of England was bound to become an uneasy alliance of private pious associations. John Shelton Reed[28] has chronicled the deeply ironic way in which the interests of Anglo-Catholics and of liberals in the nineteenth-century church coincided; both needed a sort of inner space in the established church where their own priorities could be cultivated. In a word, Newman's *Arians* helped to create 'Anglicanism' – that troubled and complex family of attempts to define a reformed Catholicism without the benefit of state endorsement, developing among the ruins of the High Church project for the maintenance of a confessional society. Loss and gain, no doubt (in an appropriately Newmanesque phrase). But the contemporary student might want to add that perhaps more of that older aspiration might be salvaged from Newman's picture than Newman himself realised. Picking up the idea of an 'ecology' of doctrine, we might want to ask whether the notion of mutually referential balances should

[28] John Shelton Reed, *Glorious Battle. The Cultural Politics of Victorian Anglo-Catholicism*, Nashville, Tennessee, 1996; London, 1998, especially ch. 14.

not include what is shown in individual and corporate life within the community. Continuity of teaching may also be continuity of the criteria for recognising holy lives. But holy lives, especially as lived in community, pose challenges of a public kind; they make bids for the 'public square', they set out to persuade and include. Even if the protection of establishment disappears, the Church may not have to accept a role as just a self-protecting minority. And common work on the definitions of holiness is one of the things that goes rather beyond the situation of mutual tolerance or (more often) subdued and irresoluble domestic warfare between contending styles of piety in the Anglican family.

This is to go beyond our text, of course. For Newman, the composition of this book was a stage not towards a fresh definition of Anglican identity, but towards a systematic typology of doctrinal change, focused on a contemporary and personal authority, the magisterium of the Roman Catholic Church. In reading the work, we have to keep in mind both what it made possible for the later Newman and what it opened up, inchoately and unwittingly, for the theological culture of the Church of England. Newman regarded the book in later life with some real embarrassment;[29] but it is a good deal more interesting and significant than either he or the majority of more recent Newman

[29] See *Letters and Diaries of John Henry Newman* XXIII, p. 46; XXV, p. 197; XXVIII, p. 172; XXX, p. 105. He declined to undertake a full-scale revision on the grounds that he would need to rewrite the entire work *ab initio*.

scholars allow. Stephen Thomas calls it, not without reason, 'Newman's first novel', shot through as it is with a powerful sense of individual pathos and herosim.[30] But it is also Newman's first essay in what was so much his own and his central contribution to modern theological, thinking: the neglected questions of method and discourse, which more conventional (even if more accurate) works on doctrinal history had not addressed.

[30] Thomas, *Newman and Heresy*, p. 43. Thomas rightly draws attention to the importance for Newman (who writes about it in the *Apologia*) of Joseph Milner's 1816 *History of the Church of Christ*, a dramatic and 'edifying' record of the patristic period (pp. 45ff.); it also seems likely that Milner, who had read Mosheim and uses the same vocabulary as Mosheim in describing Neoplatonism as 'the Eclectic philosophy' (p. 48), may have been the first to draw Newman's attention to the German historian.

CHAPTER I.

SCHOOLS AND PARTIES IN AND ABOUT THE ANTE-NICENE CHURCH, CONSIDERED IN THEIR RELATION TO THE ARIAN HERESY.

SECTION I.

THE CHURCH OF ANTIOCH.

IT is proposed in the following pages to trace the outlines of the history of Arianism, between the first and the second General Councils. These are its natural chronological limits, whether by Arianism we mean a heresy or a party in the Church. In the Council held at Nicæa, in Bithynia, A.D. 325, it was formally detected and condemned. In the subsequent years it ran its course, through various modifications of opinion, and with various success, till the date of the second General Council, held A.D. 381, at Constantinople, when the resources of heretical subtilty being at length exhausted, the Arian party was ejected from the Catholic body, and formed into a distinct sect, exterior to it. It is during this period, while it still maintained its hold upon the creeds and the government of the Church, that it especially invites the attention of the student in ecclesiastical history. Afterwards, Arianism presents nothing new in its doctrine, and is only remarkable as becoming the animating principle of a second series of persecutions, when the barbarians of the North, who were infected with it, possessed themselves of the provinces of the Roman Empire.

The line of history which is thus limited by the two first Ecumenical Councils, will be found to pass through a variety of others, provincial and patriarchal, which form easy and intelligible breaks in it, and present the heretical doctrine in the various stages of its impiety. These, accordingly, shall be taken as cardinal points for our narrative to rest upon;—and it will matter little in the result, whether it be called a history of the Councils, or of Arianism, between the eras already marked out.

However, it is necessary to direct the reader's attention in the first place, to the state of parties and schools, in and about the Church, at the time of its rise, and to the sacred doctrine which it assailed, in order to obtain a due insight into the history of the controversy; and the discussions which these subjects involve, will occupy a considerable portion of the volume. I shall address myself without delay to this work; and, in this chapter, propose first to observe upon the connexion of Arianism with the Church of Antioch, and upon the state and genius of that Church in primitive times. This shall be the subject of the present section: in those which follow, I shall consider its relation towards the heathen philosophies and heresies then prevalent; and towards the Church of Alexandria, to which, though with very little show of reasoning, it is often referred. The consideration of the doctrine of the Trinity shall form the second chapter.

I.

During the third century, the Church of Antioch was more or less acknowledged as the metropolis of Syria, Cilicia, Phœnicia, Comagene, Osrhoene, and Mesopotamia, in which provinces it afterwards held patriarchal sway[1]. It had been the original centre of Apostolical missions among the heathen[2]; and claimed St. Peter himself for its first bishop, who had been succeeded by Ignatius, Theophilus, Babylas, and others of sacred memory in the universal Church, as champions and martyrs of the faith[3]. The secular importance of the city added to the influence which accrued to it from the religious associations thus connected with its name, especially when the Emperors made Syria the seat of their government. This ancient and celebrated Church, however, is painfully conspicuous in the middle of the century, as affording so open a manifestation of the spirit of Antichrist, as to fulfil almost literally the prophecy of the Apostle in his second Epistle to the Thessalonians[4]. Paulus, of Samosata, who was raised to the see of Antioch not many years after the martyrdom of Babylas, after holding the episcopate for ten years, was deposed by a Council of eastern bishops, held in that city A.D. 272, on the ground of his heretical notions concerning the nature of Christ. His original calling seems to have been that of a sophist[5]; how he obtained admit-

[1] Bingham, Antiq. ix. 1.

[2] Acts xi., xiii., xiv.

[3] Vide Tillemont, Mem. vol. i. &c.

[4] Vide Euseb. vii. 30.

[5] Mosheim, de Reb. ante Constant. sæc. iii. § 35.

tance into the clerical order is unknown; his elevation, or at least his continuance in the see, he owed to the celebrated Zenobia[6], to whom his literary attainments, and his political talents, may be supposed to have recommended him. Whatever were the personal virtues of the Queen of the East, who is said to have been a Jewess by birth or creed, it is not surprising that she was little solicitous for the credit or influence of the Christian Church within her dominions. The character of Paulus is consigned to history in the Synodal Letter of the bishops, written at the time of his condemnation[7]; which, being circulated through the Church, might fairly be trusted, even though the high names of Gregory of Neocæsarea and Firmilian were not found in the number of his judges. He is therein charged with a rapacity, an arrogance, a vulgar ostentation and desire of popularity, an extraordinary profaneness, and a profligacy, which cannot but reflect seriously upon the Church and clergy which elected, and so long endured him. As to his heresy, it is difficult to determine what were his precise sentiments concerning the Person of Christ, though they were certainly derogatory of the doctrine of His absolute divinity and eternal existence. Indeed, it is probable that he had not any clear view on the solemn subject on which he allowed himself to speculate; nor had any wish to make proselytes, and form a party in the

[6] He was raised to the episcopate at the commencement of Odenatus's successes against Sapor (Tillemont, Mem. vol. iv. Chronol.). In the years which followed, he held a civil magistracy with his ecclesiastical dignity; in the temporalities of which, moreover, he was upheld by Zenobia, some years after his formal deposition by the neighbouring bishops. (Basnag. Annal. A.D. 269, § 6.)

[7] Euseb. Hist. vii. 30.

Church[8]. Ancient writers inform us that his heresy was a kind of Judaism in doctrine, adopted to please his Jewish patroness[9]; and, if originating in this motive, it was not likely to be very systematic or profound. His habits, too, as a sophist, would dispose him to employ himself in attacks upon the Catholic doctrine, and in irregular discussion, rather than in the sincere effort to obtain some definite conclusions, to satisfy his own mind or convince others. And the supercilious spirit, which the Synodal letter describes as leading him to express contempt for the divines who preceded him at Antioch, would naturally occasion incaution in his theories, and a carelessness about guarding them from inconsistencies, even where he perceived them. Indeed, the Primate of Syria had already obtained the highest post to which ambition could aspire, and had nothing to labour for; and having, as we find, additional engagements as a civil magistrate, he would still less be likely to covet the barren honours of an heresiarch. A sect, it is true, was formed upon his tenets, and called after his name, and has a place in ecclesiastical history till the middle of the fifth century; but it never was a considerable body, and even as early as the date of the Nicene Council had split into parties, differing by various shades of heresy from the orthodox faith[1]. We shall have a more correct notion, then, of the heresy of

[8] Mosheim, de Reb. ante Const. § 35, n. 1. [For the opinions of Paulus. vide Athan, Tr. p, 175.]

[9] Athan. Epist. ad Monachos, § 71. Theod. Hær. ii. 8. Chrysost. in Joann. Hom. 7, but Philastr. Hær. § 64, says that Paulus docuit Zenobiam judaizare.

[1] Tillemont, Mem. vol. iv. p. 126. Athan. in Arianos, iv. 30.

Paulus, if we consider him as the founder of a school rather than of a sect, as encouraging in the Church the use of those disputations and sceptical inquiries, which belonged to the Academy and other heathen philosophies, and as scattering up and down the seeds of errors, which sprang up and bore fruit in the generation after him. In confirmation of this view, which is suggested by his original vocation, by the temporal motives which are said to have influenced him, and by his inconsistencies, it may be observed, that his intimate friend and fellow-countryman, Lucian, who schismatized or was excommunicated on his deposition, held heretical tenets of a diametrically opposite nature, that is, such as were afterwards called Semi-Arian, Paulus himself advocating a doctrine which nearly resembled what is commonly called the Sabellian.

More shall be said concerning Paulus of Samosata presently; but now let us advance to the history of this Lucian, a man of learning[2], and at length a martyr, but who may almost be considered the author of Arianism. It is very common, though evidently illogical, to attribute the actual rise of one school of opinion to another, from some real or supposed similarity in their respective tenets. It is thus, for instance, Platonism, or again, Origenism, has been assigned as the actual source from which Arianism was derived. Now, Lucian's doctrine is known to have been precisely the same as that species of Ari-

[2] He was distinguished in biblical literature, as being the author of a third edition of the Septuagint. Vide Tillemont, Mem. vol. v. p. 202, 203. Du Pin, cent. iii.

anism afterwards called Semi-Arianism[3]; but it is not on that account that I here trace the rise of Arianism to Lucian. There is an historical, and not merely a doctrinal connexion between him and the Arian party. In his school are found, in matter of fact, the names of most of the original advocates of Arianism, and all those who were the most influential in their respective Churches throughout the East:—Arius himself, Eusebius of Nicomedia, Leontius, Eudoxius, Asterius, and others, who will be familiar to us in the sequel; and these men actually appealed to him as their authority, and adopted from him the party designation of Collucianists[4]. In spite of this undoubted connexion between Lucian and the Arians, we might be tempted to believe, that the assertions of the latter concerning his heterodoxy, originated in their wish to implicate a man of high character in the censures which the Church directed against themselves, were it not undeniable, that during the times of the three bishops who successively followed Paulus, Lucian was under excommunication. The Catholics too, are silent in his vindication, and some of them actually admit his unsoundness in faith[5]. However, ten or fifteen years before his martyrdom, he was reconciled to the

[3] Bull, Baronius, and others, maintain his orthodoxy. The Semi-Arians adopted his creed, which is extant. Though a friend, as it appears, of Paulus, he opposed the Sabellians (by one of whom he was at length betrayed to the heathen persecutors of the Church), and this opposition would lead him to incautious statements of an Arian tendency. Vide below, Section v. Epiphanius (Ancor. 33) tells us, that he considered the Word in the Person of Christ as the substitute for a human soul.

[4] Theod. Hist. i. 5. Epiph. Hær. lxix. 6. Cave, Hist. Literar. vol. i. p. 201.

[5] Theod. Hist. i. 4.

Church; and we may suppose that he then recanted whatever was heretical in his creed: and his glorious end was allowed to wipe out from the recollection of Catholics of succeeding times those passages of his history, which nevertheless were so miserable in their results in the age succeeding his own. Chrysostom's panegyric on the festival of his martyrdom is still extant, Ruffinus mentions him in honourable terms, and Jerome praises his industry, erudition, and eloquence in writing[6].

Such is the historical connexion at the very first sight between the Arian party and the school of Antioch[7]: corroborative evidence will hereafter appear, in the similarity of character which exists between the two bodies. At present, let it be taken as a confirmation of a fact, which Lucian's history directly proves, that Eusebius the historian, who is suspected of Arianism, and his friend Paulinus of Tyre, one of its first and principal supporters, though not pupils of Lucian, were more or less educated, and the latter ordained at Antioch[8]; while in addition to the Arian bishops at Nicæa already mentioned, Theodotus of Laodicea, Gregory of Berytus, Narcissus of Neronias, and two others, who were all supporters of Arianism at the Council, were all situated within the ecclesiastical influence, and some of them in the vicinity of Antioch[9]; so that (besides Arius himself), of thirteen, who according to Theodoret, arianized at the Council, nine are referable to the Syrian patriarchate. If we continue the history of the controversy, we have fresh

6 Vide Tillemont, Mem. vol. v.

7 [Vide Appendix, *Syrian School.*]

8 Vales. de Vit. Euseb. et ad Hist. x. i.

9 Tillemont, Mem. vol. vi. p. 276.

evidence of the connexion between Antioch and Arianism. During the interval between the Nicene Council and the death of Constantius (A.D. 325—361), Antioch is the metropolis of the heretical, as Alexandria of the orthodox party. At Antioch, the heresy recommenced its attack upon the Church after the decision at Nicæa. In a Council held at Antioch, it first showed itself in the shape of Semi-Arianism, when Lucian's creed was produced. There, too, in this and subsequent Councils, negotiations on the doctrine in dispute were conducted with the Western Church. At Antioch, lastly, and at Tyre, a suffragan see, the sentence of condemnation was pronounced upon Athanasius.

2.

Hitherto I have spoken of individuals as the authors of the apostasy which is to engage our attention in the following chapters; but there is reason to fear that men like Paulus were but symptoms of a corrupted state of the Church. The history of the times gives us sufficient evidence of the luxuriousness of Antioch; and it need scarcely be said, that coldness in faith is the sure consequence of relaxation of morals[1]. Here, however, passing by this consideration, which is too obvious to require dwelling upon, I would rather direct the reader's attention to the particular form which the Antiochene corruptions seem to have assumed, viz., that of Judaism[2]; which at that time, it must be

[1] [Vide a remarkable passage in Origen, on the pomp of the Bishops of his day, quoted by Neander, Hist. vol. ii. p. 330, Bohn.]

[2] [Lengerke, de Ephræm. Syr. p, 64. traces the literal interpretation, which was the characteristic of the school of Antioch, to the example of the Jews.]

recollected, was the creed of an existing nation, acting upon the Church, and not merely, as at this day, a system of opinions more or less discoverable among professing Christians.

The fortunes of the Jewish people had experienced a favourable change since the reign of Hadrian. The violence of Roman persecution had been directed against the Christian Church; while the Jews, gradually recovering their strength, and obtaining permission to settle and make proselytes to their creed, at length became an influential political body in the neighbourhood of their ancient home, especially in the Syrian provinces which were at that time the chief residence of the court. Severus (A.D. 194) is said to have been the first to extend to them the imperial favour, though he afterwards withdrew it. Heliogabalus, and Alexander, natives of Syria, gave them new privileges; and the latter went so far as to place the image of Abraham in his private chapel, among the objects of his ordinary worship. Philip the Arabian continued towards them a countenance, which was converted into an open patronage in the reign of Zenobia. During the Decian persecution, they had been sufficiently secure at Carthage, to venture to take part in the popular ridicule which the Christians excited; and they are even said to have stimulated Valerian to his cruelties towards the Church[3].

But this direct hostility was not the only, nor the most formidable means of harassing their religious enemies, which their improving fortunes opened upon them. With their advancement in wealth and im-

[3] Basnage, Hist. des Juifs, vi. 12. Tillemont, Hist. des Emper. iii. iv.

portance, their national character displayed itself under a new exterior. The moroseness for which they were previously notorious, in great measure disappears with their dislodgment from the soil of their ancestors; and on their re-appearance as settlers in a strange land, those festive, self-indulgent habits, which, in earlier times, had but drawn on them the animadversion of their Prophets, became their distinguishing mark in the eyes of external observers[4]. Manifesting a rancorous malevolence towards the zealous champions of the Church, they courted the Christian populace by arts adapted to captivate and corrupt the unstable and worldly-minded. Their pretensions to magical power gained them credit with the superstitious, to whom they sold amulets for the cure of diseases; their noisy spectacles attracted the curiosity of the idle, who weakened their faith, while they disgraced their profession, by attending the worship of the Synagogue. Accordingly there was formed around the Church a mixed multitude, who, without relinquishing their dependence on Christianity for the next world, sought in Judaism the promise of temporal blessings, and a more accommodating rule of life than the gospel revealed. Chrysostom found this evil so urgent at Antioch in his day, as to interrupt his course of homilies on the heresy of the Anomœans, in order to direct his preaching against the seductions to which his hearers were then exposed, by the return of the Jewish festivals[5]. In another

[4] Vide Gibbon, Hist. ch. xvi. note 6. Chrysost. in Judæos, i. p. 386—388, &c.

[5] Chrysost. in Judæos, i. p. 389, &c. [Jerome speaks of a law of Valens:—"ne quis vitulorum carnibus vesceretur, utilitati agriculturæ providens, et pessimam *judaizantis vulgi* emendans consuetudinem." Adv. Jovinian. ii. 7.]

part of the empire, the Council of Illiberis found it necessary to forbid a superstitious custom, which had been introduced among the country people, of having recourse to the Jews for a blessing on their fields. Afterwards, Constantine made a law against the intermarriage of Jews and Christians; and Constantius confiscated the goods of Christians who lapsed to Judaism[6]. These successive enactments may be taken as evidence of the view entertained by the Church of her own danger, from the artifices of the Jews. Lastly, the attempt to rebuild the temple in Julian's reign, was but the renewal of a project on their part, which Constantine had already frustrated, for reinstating their religion in its ancient ritual and country[7].

Such was the position of the Jews towards the primitive Church, especially in the patriarchate of Antioch; which, I have said, was their principal place of settlement, and was at one time under the civil government of a Judaizing princess, the most illustrious personage of her times, who possessed influence enough over the Christian body to seduce the Metropolitan himself from the orthodox faith.

3.

But the evidence of the existence of Judaism, as a system, in the portion of Christendom in question, is

[6] Bingham, Antiq. xvi. 6. Basnage, Hist. des Juifs, vi. 14.

[7] Chrysost, in Judæos, iii. p. 435. [Vide Chrysost. in Matth. Hom. 43, where he says that in Julian's time, "they ranged themselves with the heathen and courted their party." He proceeds to say that "in all their other evil works they surpass their predecessors, in sorceries, magic arts, impurities." Oxford Transl.]

contained in a circumstance which deserves our particular attention; the adoption, in those parts, of the quarto-deciman rule of observing Easter, when it was on the point of being discontinued in the Churches of Proconsular Asia, where it had first prevailed.

It is well known that at the close of the second century, a controversy arose between Victor, Bishop of Rome, and Polycrates, Bishop of Ephesus, concerning the proper time for celebrating the Easter feast, or rather for terminating the ante-paschal fast. At that time the whole of Christendom, with the exception of Proconsular Asia (a district of about two hundred miles by fifty), and its immediate neighbourhood[8], continued the fast on to the Sunday after the Jewish Passover, which they kept as Easter Day as we do now, in order that the weekly and yearly commemorations of the Resurrection might coincide. But the Christians of the Proconsulate, guided by Jewish custom, ended the fast on the very day of the paschal sacrifice, without regarding the actual place held in the week by the feast, which immediately followed; and were accordingly called Quarto-decimans[9]. Victor felt the inconvenience of this want of uniformity in the celebration of the chief Christian festival; and was urgent, even far beyond the bounds of charity, and the rights of his see, in his endeavour to obtain the compliance of the Asiatics. Polycrates, who was primate of the Quarto-deciman Churches, defended their peculiar custom by a statement which is plain and unexceptionable. They had received their rule, he said, from St. John and St.

[8] Euseb. Hist. v. 23—25, and Vales. ad loc.

[9] Exod. xii. 6. Vide Tillemont, Mem. vol. iii. p. 629, &c.

Philip the Apostles, Polycarp of Smyrna, Melito of Sardis, and others; and deemed it incumbent on them to transmit as they had received. There was nothing Judaistic in this conduct; for, though the Apostles intended the Jewish discipline to cease with those converts who were born under it, yet it was by no means clear, that its calendar came under the proscription of its rites. On the other hand, it was natural that the Asian Churches should be affectionately attached to a custom which their first founders, and they inspired teachers, had sanctioned.

But the case was very different, when Churches, which had for centuries observed the Gentile rule, adopted a custom which at the time had only existence among the Jews. The Quarto-decimans of the Proconsulate had come to an end by A.D. 276; and, up to that date, the Antiochene provinces kept their Easter feast in conformity with the Catholic usage[1]; yet, at the time of the Nicene Council (fifty years afterwards), we find the Antiochenes the especial and solitary champions of the Jewish rule[2]. We can scarcely doubt that they adopted it in imitation of the Jews who were settled among them, who are known to have influenced them, and who about that very date, be it observed, had a patroness in Zenobia, and, what was stranger, had almost a convert in the person of the Christian Primate. There is evidence, moreover, of the actual growth of the custom in the Patriarchate at the end of the third century; which

[1] Tillemont, Mem. vol. iii. p. 48, who conjectures that Anatolius of Laodicea was the author of the change. But changes require predisposing causes.

[2] Athan. ad Afros, § 2.

well agrees with the hypothesis of its being an innovation, and not founded on ancient usage. And again (as was natural, supposing the change to begin at Antioch), at the date of the Nicene Council, it was established only in the Syrian Churches, and was but making its way with incomplete success in the extremities of the Patriarchate. In Mesopotamia, Audius began his schism with the characteristic of the Quarto-deciman rule, just at the date of the Council[3]; and about the same time, Cilicia was contested between the two parties, as I gather from the conflicting statements of Constantine and Athanasius, that it did, and that it did not, conform to the Gentile custom[4]. By the same time, the controversy had reached Egypt also. Epiphanius refers to a celebrated, contest, now totally unknown, between one Crescentius and Alexander, the first defender of the Catholic faith against Arianism[5].

It is true that there was a third Quarto-deciman school, lying geographically between the Proconsulate and Antioch, which at first sight might seem to have been the medium by which the Jewish custom was conveyed on from the former to the latter; but there is no evidence of its existence till the end of the fourth century. In order to complete my account of the Quarto-decimans, and show more fully their relation to the Judaizers, I will here make mention of it; though, in doing so, I must somewhat digress from the main subject under consideration.

[3] Epiph. Hær. lxx. § 1.

[4] Athan. ad Afros, supra. Socr. Hist. i. 9, where, by the bye, the Proconsulate is spoken of as conforming to the general usage; so as clearly to distinguish between the two Quarto-deciman schools.

[5] Epiph. ibid. § 9.

The portion of Asia Minor, lying between the Proconsulate and the river Halys, may be regarded, in the Ante-Nicene times, as one country, comprising the provinces of Phrygia, Galatia, Cappadocia, and Paphlagonia, afterwards included within the Exarchate of Cæsarea; and was then marked by a religious character of a peculiar cast. Socrates, speaking of this district, informs us, that its inhabitants were distinguished above other nations by a strictness and seriousness of manners, having neither the ferocity of the Scythians and Thracians, nor the frivolity and sensuality of the Orientals[6]. The excellent qualities, however, implied in this description, were tarnished by the love of singularity, the spirit of insubordination and separatism, and the gloomy spiritual pride which their history evidences. St. Paul's Epistle furnishes us with the first specimen of this unchristian temper, as evinced in the conduct of the Galatians[7], who, dissatisfied with the exact evangelical doctrine, aspired to some higher and more availing system than the Apostle preached to them. What the Galatians were in the first century, Montanus and Novatian became in the second and third; both authors of a harsh and arrogant discipline, both natives of the country in question[8], and both meeting with special success in that country, although the schism of the latter was organized at Rome, of which Church he was a presbyter. It was, moreover, the peculiarity, more or less, of both Montanists and Novatians in those parts, to differ from the general Church as to the time of

[6] Socrat. Hist. iv. 28, cf, Epiph. Hær. xlviii. 14 [and xlvii. 1].

[7] [Jerome calls the Galatians "ad intelligentiam tardiores, vecordes," and speaks of their "stoliditas barbara," in Galat. lib. ii. præf.]

[8] Vales, ad loc. Socr. [Philostorg. viii. 15.]

observing Easter[9]; whereas, neither in Africa nor in Rome did the two sects dissent from the received rule[1]. What was the principle or origin of this irregularity, does not clearly appear; unless we may consider as characteristic, what seems to be the fact, that when their neighbours of the Proconsulate were Quarto-decimans, they (in the words of Socrates) "shrank from feasting on the Jewish festival[2]," and after the others had conformed to the Gentile rule, they, on the contrary, openly judaized[3]. This change in their practice, which took place at the end of the fourth century, was mainly effected by a Jew, of the name of Sabbatius, who becoming a convert to Christianity, rose to the episcopate in the Novatian Church. Sozomen, in giving an account of the transaction, observes that it was a national custom with the Galatians and Phrygians to judaize in their observance of Easter. Coupling this remark with Eusebius's mention of Churches in the neighbourhood of the Proconsulate, as included among the Quarto-decimans whom Victor condemned[4], we may suspect that the perverse spirit which St. Paul reproves in his Epistle, and which we have been tracing in its Montanistic and Novatian varieties, still lurked in those parts in its original judaizing form, till after a course of years it was accidentally brought out by circumstances upon the public scene of ecclesiastical history. If further evidence of the connexion of the Quarto-

[9] Socrat. Hist. v. 22. Sozom. Hist. vii. 18.

[1] Tertull. de Jejun. 14. Vales. ad Sozom. vii. 18. Socrat. Hist. v. 21.

[2] Valesius ad. loc. applies this differently.

[3] Socrat. Hist. v. 21.

[4] Eusb. Hist. ut supra.

deciman usage with Judaism be required, I may refer to Constantine's Nicene Edict, which forbids it, among other reasons, on the ground of its being Jewish[5].

4.

The evidence, which has been adduced for the existence of Judaism in the Church of Antioch, is not without its bearing upon the history of the rise of Arianism. I will not say that the Arian doctrine is the direct result of a judaizing practice; but it deserves consideration whether a tendency to derogate from the honour due to Christ, was not created by an observance of the Jewish rites, and much more, by that carnal, self-indulgent religion, which seems at that time to have prevailed in the rejected nation. When the spirit and morals of a people are materially debased, varieties of doctrinal error spring up, as if self-sown, and are rapidly propagated. While Judaism inculcated a superstitious, or even idolatrous dependence on the mere casualties of daily life, and gave license to the grosser tastes of human nature, it necessarily indisposed the mind for the severe and unexciting mysteries, the large indefinite promises, and the remote sanctions, of the Catholic faith; which fell as cold and uninviting on the depraved imagination, as the doctrines of the Divine Unity and of implicit trust in the unseen God, on the minds of the early Israelites. Those who were not constrained by the message of mercy, had time attentively to consider the intellectual difficulties which were the medium of its communication, and heard but "a hard saying" in what was sent from heaven as "tidings of

[5] Theod. Hist. i. 10.

great joy." "The mind," says Hooker, "feeling present joy, is always marvellously unwilling to admit any other cogitation, and in that case, casteth off those disputes whereunto the intellectual part at other times easily draweth. . . The people that are said in the sixth of John to have gone after our Lord to Capernaum . . leaving Him on the one side of the sea of Tiberias, and finding Him again as soon as they themselves by ship were arrived on the contrary side . . as they wondered, so they asked also, 'Rabbi, when camest Thou hither?' The Disciples, when Christ appeared to them in a far more strange and miraculous manner, moved no question, but rejoiced greatly in what they saw . . The one, because they enjoyed not, disputed; the other disputed not, because they enjoyed[6]."

It is also a question, whether the mere performance of the rites of the Law, of which Christ came as anti-type and repealer, has not a tendency to withdraw the mind from the contemplation of the more glorious and real images of the Gospel; so that the Christians of Antioch would diminish their reverence towards the true Saviour of man, in proportion as they trusted to the media of worship provided for a time by the Mosaic ritual. It is this consideration which accounts for the energy with which the great Apostle combats the adoption of the Jewish ordinances by the Christians of Galatia, and which might seem excessive, till vindicated by events subsequent to his own day[7]. In the Epistle addressed to them, the

[6] Eccles. Pol. v. 67.

[7] [Eusebius says, that St. Paul detected humanitarianism in the Galatian Judaism. Contr. Marcell. i. 1, p. 7.]

Judaizers are described as men labouring under an irrational fascination, fallen from grace, and self-excluded from the Christian privileges[8]; when in appearance they were but using, what on the one hand might be called mere external forms, and on the other, had actually been delivered to the Jews on Divine authority. Some light is thrown upon the subject by the Epistle to the Hebrews, in which it is implied throughout, that the Jewish rites, after their Antitype was come, did but conceal from the eye of faith His divinity, sovereignty, and all-sufficiency. If we turn to the history of the Church, we seem to see the evils in actual existence, which the Apostle anticipated in prophecy; that is, we see, that in the obsolete furniture of the Jewish ceremonial, there was in fact retained the pestilence of Jewish unbelief, tending (whether directly or not, at least eventually) to introduce fundamental error respecting the Person of Christ.

Before the end of the first century, this result is disclosed in the system of the Cerinthians and the Ebionites. These sects, though more or less infected with Gnosticism, were of Jewish origin, and observed the Mosaic Law; and whatever might be the minute peculiarities of their doctrinal views, they also agreed in entertaining Jewish rather than Gnostic conceptions of the Person of Christ[9]. Ebion, especially, is characterised by his Humanitarian creed; while on the other hand, his Judaism was so notorious, that Tertullian does not scruple to describe him as virtually the object of the Apostle's censure in his Epistle to the Galatians[1].

[8] Socrat. Hist. v. 22.

[9] Burton, Bamp. Lect, notes 74. 82.

[1] Tertull. de Præscript. Hæret. c. 33, p. 243.

The Nazarenes are next to be noticed;—not for the influence they exercised on the belief of Christians, but as evidencing, with the sects just mentioned, the latent connection between a judaizing discipline and heresy in doctrine. Who they were, and what their tenets, has been a subject of much controversy. It is sufficient for my purpose—and so far is undoubted—that they were at the same time "zealous of the Law" and unsound in their theology[2]; and this without being related to the Gnostic families: a circumstance which establishes them as a more cogent evidence of the real connexion of ritual with doctrinal Judaism than is furnished by the mixed theologies of Ebion and Cerinthus[3]. It is worth observing that their declension from orthodoxy appears to have been gradual; Epiphanius is the first writer who includes them by name in the number of heretical sects[4].

[2] Burton, Bampt. Lect., note 84.

[3] For the curious in ecclesiastical antiquity, Mosheim has elicited the following account of their name and sect (Mosheim de Reb. Christ. ante Constant. Sæcul. ii. § 38, 39). The title of Nazarene he considers to have originally belonged to the body of Jewish converts, taken by them with a reference to Matt. ii. 23, while the Gentiles at Antioch assumed the Greek appellation of Christians. As the Mosaic ordinances gradually fell into disuse among the former, in process of time it became the peculiar designation of the Church of Jerusalem; and that Church in turn throwing off its Jewish exterior in the reign of Hadrian, on being unfairly subjected to the disabilities then laid upon the rebel nation, it finally settled upon the scanty remnant, who considered their ancient ceremonial to be an essential part of their present profession. These Judaizers, from an over-attachment to the forms, proceeded in course of time, to imbibe the spirit of the degenerate system; and ended in doctrinal views not far short of modern Socinianism.

[4] Burton, Bampt. Lect., note 84. Considering the Judaism of the Quarto-decimans after Victor's age, is it impossible that he may have suspected that the old leaven was infecting the Churches of Asia? This

5.

Such are the instances of the connexion between Judaism and theological error, previously to the age of Paulus, who still more strikingly exemplifies it. First, we are in possession of his doctrinal opinions, which are grossly humanitarian; next we find, that in early times they were acknowledged to be of Jewish origin; further, that his ceremonial Judaism also was so notorious that one author even affirms that he observed the rite of circumcision[5]: and lastly, just after his day we discover the rise of a Jewish usage, the Quarto-deciman, in the provinces of Christendom, immediately subjected to his influence.

It may be added that this view of the bearing of Judaism upon the sceptical school afterwards called Arian is countenanced by frequent passages in the writings of the contemporary Fathers, on which no stress, perhaps, could fairly be laid, were not their

will explain and partly excuse his earnestness in the controversy with them. It must be recollected that he witnessed, in his own branch of the Church, the rise of the first simply humanitarian school which Christianity had seen, that of Theodotus, Artemas, &c. (Euseb. Hist. v. 28), the latter of whom is charged by Alexander with reviving the heresy of the judaizing Ebion (Theod. Hist., i. 4); [while at the same time at Rome Blastus was introducing the Quarto-deciman rule]. Again, Theodotus, Montanus, and Praxeas, whose respective heresies he was engaged in combating, all belonged to the neighbourhood of the Proconsulate, where there seems to have been a school, from which, Praxeas derived his heresy (Theod. Hær. iii. 3); while Montanism, as its after history shows, contained in it the seeds, both of the Quarto-deciman and Sabellian errors (Tillemont, Mem. vol. ii. p. 199.205. Athan. in Arian. ii. 43). It may be added that the younger Theodotus is suspected of Montanism (Tillemont. Mem. vol. iii. p. 277).

[5] Philastr. Hær. § 64. [Epiphanius denies that the Paulianists circumcised. Hær. lxv. 2. It is remarkable that the Arian Whiston looked favourably on the rite. Biograph. Brit. p. 4213.]

meaning interpreted by the above historical facts[6]. Moreover, in the popular risings which took place in Antioch and Alexandria in favour of Arianism, the Jews sided with the heretical party[7]; evincing thereby, not indeed any definite interest in the subject of dispute, but a sort of spontaneous feeling, that the side of heresy was their natural position; and further, that its spirit, and the character which it created, were congenial to their own. Or, again, if we consider the subject from a different point of view, and omitting dates and schools, take a general survey of Christendom during the first centuries, we shall find it divided into the same two parties, both on the Arian and the Quarto-deciman questions; Rome and Alexandria with their dependencies being the champions of the Catholic tradition in either controversy, and Palestine, Syria, and Asia Minor, being the strongholds of the opposition. And these are the two questions which occasioned the deliberations of the Nicene Fathers.

However, it is of far less consequence, as it is less certain, whether Arianism be of Jewish origin, than whether it arose at Antioch: which is the point principally insisted on in the foregoing pages. For in proportion as it is traced to Antioch, so is the charge of originating it removed from the great Alexandrian School, upon which various enemies of our Apostolical Church have been eager to fasten it. In corroboration of what has been said above on this subject, I here add the words of Alexander, in his letter to the Church of

[6] Athan. de Decret. 2. 27; Sentent. Dionys. 3, 4; ad Episc. Æg. 13; de fug, 2; in Arian. iii. 27, and *passim*. Chrysost. Hom. in Anomœos and in Judæos. Theod. Hist. i. 4. Epiphan. Hær. lxix. 79.

[7] Basnage, Hist. des Juifs, vi. 41.

Constantinople, at the beginning of the controversy; which are of themselves decisive in evidence of the part, which Antioch had, in giving rise to the detestable blasphemy which he was combating.

"Ye are not ignorant," he writes to the Constantinopolitan Church concerning Arianism, "that this rebellious doctrine belongs to Ebion and Artemas, and is in imitation of Paulus of Samosata, Bishop of Antioch, who was excommunicated by the sentence of the Bishops assembled in Council from all quarters. Paulus was succeeded by Lucian, who remained in separation for many years during the time of three bishops. . . . Our present heretics have drunk up the dregs of the impiety of these men, and are their secret offspring; Arius and Achillas, and their party of evil-doers, incited as they are to greater excesses by three Syrian prelates, who agree with them . . . Accordingly, they have been expelled from the Church, as enemies of the pious Catholic teaching; according to St. Paul's sentence, 'If any man preach any other Gospel unto you than that ye have received, let him be anathema[8].'"

[8] Theod. Hist. i. 4. [Simeon, Bishop of Beth-Arsam, in Persia, A.D. 510—525, traces the genealogy of Paulianism and Nestorianism from Judaism thus:—Caiaphas to Simon Magus; Simon to Ebion; Ebion to Artemon; Artemon to Paul of Somosata; Paul to Diodorus; Diodorus to Theodore; Theodore to Nestorius. Asseman. Bibl. Orient. t. i. p. 347.]

SECTION II.

THE SCHOOLS OF THE SOPHISTS.

As Antioch was the birth-place, so were the Schools of the Sophists the place of education of the heretical spirit which we are considering. In this section, I propose to show its disputatious character, and to refer it to these Schools as the source of it.

The vigour of the first movement of the heresy, and the rapid extension of the controversy which it introduced, are among the more remarkable circumstances connected with its history. In the course of six years it called for the interposition of a General Council; though of three hundred and eighteen bishops there assembled, only twenty-two, on the largest calculation and, as it really appears, only thirteen, were after all found to be its supporters. Though thus condemned by the whole Christian world, in a few years it broke out again; secured the patronage of the imperial court, which had recently been converted to the Christian faith; made its way into the highest dignities of the Church; presided at her Councils, and tyrannized over the majority of her members who were orthodox believers.

Now, doubtless, one chief cause of these successes is found in the circumstance, that Lucian's pupils were brought together from so many different places, and were promoted to posts of influence in so many parts of the Church. Thus Eusebius, Maris, and Theognis, were bishops of the principal sees of Bithynia; Menophantes was exarch of Ephesus; and Eudoxius was one of the Bishops of Comagene. Other causes will hereafter appear in the secular history of the day; but here I am to speak of their talent for disputation, to which after all they were principally indebted for their success.

It is obvious, that in every contest, the assailant, as such, has the advantage of the party assailed; and that, not merely from the recommendation which novelty gives to his cause in the eyes of bystanders, but also from the greater facility in the nature of things, of finding, than of solving objections, whatever be the question in dispute. Accordingly, the skill of a disputant mainly consists in securing an offensive position, fastening on the weaker points of his adversary's case, and then not relaxing his hold till the latter sinks under his impetuosity, without having the opportunity to display the strength of his own cause, and to bring it to bear upon his opponent; or, to make use of a familiar illustration, in causing a sudden run upon his resources, which the circumstances of time and place do not allow him to meet. This was the artifice to which Arianism owed its first successes[1]. It owed them to the circumstance of its being (in its original form) a sceptical rather than a dogmatic

[1] ἀναπηδῶσι γὰρ ὡς λυσσητῆρες κῦνες εἰς ἐχθρῶν ἄμυναν. Epiph. Hær lxix. 15. Vide the whole passage.

teaching; to its proposing to inquire into and reform the received creed, rather than to hazard one of its own. The heresies which preceded it, originating in less subtle and dexterous talent, took up a false position, professed a theory, and sunk under the obligations which it involved. The monstrous dogmas of the various Gnostic sects pass away from the scene of history as fast as they enter it. Sabellianism, which succeeded, also ventured on a creed; and vacillating between a similar wildness of doctrine, and a less imposing ambiguity, soon vanished in its turn[2]. But the Antiochene School, as represented by Paulus of Samosata and Arius, took the ground of an assailant, attacked the Catholic doctrine, and drew the attention of men to its difficulties, without attempting to furnish a theory of less perplexity or clearer evidence.

The arguments of Paulus (which it is not to our purpose here to detail) seem fairly to have overpowered the first of the Councils summoned against him (A.D. 264), which dissolved without coming to a decision[3]. A second, and (according to some writers) a third, were successfully convoked, when at length his subtleties were exposed and condemned; not, however, by the reasonings of the Fathers of the Council themselves, but by the instrumentality of one Malchion, a presbyter of Antioch, who, having been by profession a Sophist, encountered his adversary with his own arms[4]. Even in yielding, the arts of

[2] Vide § 5, infra. [Gregory Naz. speaks of a γαλήνη after these heresies, and before Arianism. Orat. xxv. 8.]

[3] Euseb. Hist. vii. 28. Cave, Hist. Literar. vol. I. p. 158.

[4] [σφόδρα καταπολεμοῦνται οἱ πολέμιοι, ὅταν τοῖς αὐτῶν ὅπλοις χρώμεθα κατ' αὐτῶν. Socr. iii. 16.]

Paulus secured from his judges an ill-advised concession, the abandonment of the celebrated word *homoüsion (consubstantial)*, afterwards adopted as the test at Nicæa; which the orthodox had employed in the controversy, and to which Paulus objected as open to a misinterpretation[5]. Arius followed in the track thus marked out by his predecessor. Turbulent by character, he is known in history as an offender against ecclesiastical order, before his agitation assumed the shape which has made his name familiar to posterity[6]. When he betook himself to the doctrinal controversy, he chose for the first open avowal of his heterodoxy the opportunity of an attack upon his diocesan, who was discoursing on the mystery of the Trinity to the clergy of Alexandria. Socrates, who is far from being a partisan of the Catholics, informs us that Arius being well skilled in dialectics sharply replied to the bishop, accused him of Sabellianism, and went on to *argue* that "*if* the Father begat the Son, certain conclusions would follow," and so proceeded. His heresy, thus founded in a syllogism, spread itself by instruments of a kindred character. First, we read of the excitement which his reasonings produced in Egypt and Lybia; then of his letters addressed to Eusebius and to Alexander, which display a like pugnacious and almost satirical spirit; and then of his verses composed for the use of the populace in ridicule of the orthodox doctrine[7]. But afterwards, when the heresy was arraigned before the Nicene

[5] Bull. Defens. Fid. Nic. ii. i. § 9—14.

[6] Epiph. Hær. lxix. 2.

[7] Socr. i. 5, 6. Theod. Hist. i. 5. Epiphan. Hær. lxix. 7, 8. Philostorg. ii. 2. Athan. de Decret. 16.

Council, and placed on the defensive, and later still, when its successes reduced it to the necessity of occupying the chairs of theology, it suffered the fate of the other dogmatic heresies before it; split, in spite of court favour, into at least four different creeds, in less than twenty years[8]; and at length gave way to the despised but indestructible truth which it had for a time obscured.

Arianism had in fact a close connexion with the existing Aristotelic school. This might have been conjectured, even had there been no proof of the fact, adapted as that philosopher's logical system confessedly is to baffle an adversary, or at most to detect error, rather than to establish truth[9]. But we have actually reason, in the circumstances of its history, for considering it as the off-shoot of those schools of inquiry and debate which acknowledged Aristotle as their principal authority, and were conducted by teachers who went by the name of Sophists. It was in these schools that the leaders of the heretical body were educated for the part assigned them in the troubles of the Church. The oratory of Paulus of Samosata is characterized by the distinguishing traits of the scholastic eloquence in the descriptive letter of the Council which condemned him; in which, moreover, he is stigmatized by the most disgraceful title to which a Sophist was exposed by the degraded exercise

[8] Petav. Dogm. Theol. t. ii. i. 9 and 10.

[9] "Omnem vim venenorum suorum in dialectica disputatione constituunt, quæ philosophorum sententia definitur non adstruendi vim habere, sed studium destruendi. Sed non in dialectica complacuit Deo salvum facere populum suum." Ambros. de Fide, i. 5. [§ 42.]

of his profession[1]. The skill of Arius in the art of disputation is well known. Asterius was a Sophist by profession. Aetius came from the School of an Aristotelian of Alexandria. Eunomius, his pupil, who re-constructed the Arian doctrine on its original basis, at the end of the reign of Constantius, is represented by Ruffinus as "pre-eminent in dialectic power[2]." At a later period still, the like disputatious spirit and spurious originality are indirectly ascribed to the heterodox school, in the advice of Sisinnius to Nectarius of Constantinople, when the Emperor Theodosius required the latter to renew the controversy with a view to its final settlement[3]. Well versed in theological learning, and aware that adroitness in debate was the very life and weapon of heresy, Sisinnius proposed to the Patriarch, to drop the use of dialectics, and merely challenge his opponents to utter a general anathema against all such Ante-Nicene Fathers as had taught what they themselves now denounced as false doctrine. On the experiment being tried, the heretics would neither consent to be tried by the opinions of the ancients, nor yet dared condemn those whom "all the people counted as prophets." "Upon this," say the historians who record the story, "the Emperor perceived that they rested their cause on their dialectic skill, and not on the testimony of the early Church[4]."

Abundant evidence, were more required, could be

[1] σοφιστὴς καὶ γοής, a juggler. Vide Cressol. Theatr. Rhetor. i. 13. iii. 17.

[2] Petav. Theol. prolegom. iii. 3. Baltus, Defense des Peres, ii. 19. Brucker. vol. iii. p. 288. Cave, Hist. Literar. vol. 1.

[3] Bull, Defens. Fid. Nic. Epilog.

[4] Socr. Hist. v. 10. Soz. Hist. vii. 12.

added to the above, in proof of the connexion of the Arians with the schools of heathen disputation. The two Gregories, Basil, Ambrose, and Cyril, protest with one voice against the dialectics of their opponents; and the sum of their declarations is briefly expressed by a writer of the fourth century, who calls Aristotle the Bishop of the Arians[5]

2.

And while the science of argumentation provided the means, their practice of disputing for the sake of exercise or amusement supplied the temptation, of assailing received opinions. This practice, which had long prevailed in the Schools, was early introduced into the Eastern Church[6]. It was there employed as a means of preparing the Christian teacher for the controversy with unbelievers. The discussion sometimes proceeded in the form of a lecture delivered by the master of the school to his pupils; sometimes in that of an inquiry, to be submitted to the criticism of his hearers; sometimes by way of dialogue, in which opposite sides were taken for argument-sake. In some cases, it was taken down in notes by the bystanders, at the time; in others committed to writing by the parties engaged in it[7]. Necessary

[5] Petav. Dogm. Theol. supra. Brucker, vol. iii. pp. 324. 352, 353. Epiph. Hær. lxix. 69. [Vigil. Thaps. contr. Eutych. i. 2.]

[6] The art was called ἐριστική; and the actual discussion, γυμνασία. Cressol. Theatr. Rhet. ii. 3. [Vide also Athan. Tr. p. 44, e. Also a remarkable instance in Ernesti from Origen, ap Lumper, t. 10, p. 148. Contrasted with γυμναστικοὶ λόγοι were ἀγωνιστικοὶ, *in earnest*, according to Sextus Empiricus, vide Hypot. i. 33, p. 57, with Fabricius's note.]

[7] Dodw. Diss. in Iren. v. 14. Socr. Hist. i. 5.

as these exercises would be for the purpose designed, yet they were obviously open to abuse, though moderated by ever so orthodox and strictly scriptural a rule, in an age when no sufficient ecclesiastical symbol existed, as a guide to the memory and judgment of the eager disputant. It is evident, too, how difficult it would be to secure opinions or arguments from publicity, which were but hazarded in the confidence of Christian friendship, and which, when viewed apart from the circumstances of the case, lent a seemingly deliberate sanction to heterodox novelties. Athanasius implies[8], that in the theological works of Origen and Theognostus, while the orthodox faith was explicitly maintained, nevertheless heretical tenets were discussed, and in their place more or less defended, by way of exercise in argument. The countenance thus accidentally given to the cause of error is evidenced in his eagerness to give the explanation. But far greater was the evil, when men destitute of religious seriousness and earnestness engaged in the like theological discussions, not with any definite ecclesiastical object, but as a mere trial of skill, or as a literary recreation ; regardless of the mischief thus done to the simplicity of Christian morals, and the evil encouragement given to fallacious reasonings and sceptical views. The error of the ancient Sophists had consisted in their indulging without restraint or discrimination in the discussion of practical topics, whether religious or political, instead of selecting such as might exercise, without demoralizing, their minds. The rhetoricians of Christian times intro-

[8] Athan. de Decret. 25 and 27. [He says the same of Marcellus in his defence, Apol. contr. Ar. 47.]

duced the same error into their treatment of the highest and most sacred subjects of theology. We are told, that Julian commenced his opposition to the true faith by defending the heathen side of religious questions, in disputing with his brother Gallus[9]; and probably he would not have been able himself to assign the point of time at which he ceased merely to take a part, and became earnest in his unbelief. But it is unnecessary to have recourse to particular instances, in order to prove the consequences of a practice so evidently destructive of a reverential and sober spirit.

Moreover, in these theological discussions, the disputants were in danger of being misled by the unsoundness of the positions which they assumed, as elementary truths or axioms in the argument. As logic and rhetoric made them expert in proof and refutation, so there was much in other sciences, which formed a liberal education, in geometry and arithmetic, to confine the mind to the contemplation of material objects, as if these could supply suitable tests and standards for examining those of a moral and spiritual nature; whereas there are truths foreign to the province of the most exercised intellect, some of them the peculiar discoveries of the improved moral sense (or what Scripture terms "*the Spirit*"), and others still less on a level with our reason, and received on the sole authority of Revelation. Then, however, as now, the minds of speculative men were impatient of ignorance, and loth to confess that the laws of truth and falsehood, which their experience of this world furnished, could not at once be applied to

[9] Greg. Nazianz. Orat. iii. 27. 31. [iv. 30.]

measure and determine the facts of another. Accordingly, nothing was left for those who would not believe the incomprehensibility of the Divine Essence, but to conceive of it by the analogy of sense; and using the figurative terms of theology in their literal meaning as if landmarks in their inquiries, to suppose that then, and then only, they steered in a safe course, when they avoided every contradiction of a mathematical and material nature. Hence, canons grounded on physics were made the basis of discussions about possibilities and impossibilities in a spiritual substance, as confidently and as fallaciously, as those which in modern times have been derived from the same false analogies against the existence of moral self-action or free-will. Thus the argument by which Paulus of Samosata baffled the Antiochene Council, was drawn from a sophistical use of the very word *substance*, which the orthodox had employed in expressing the scriptural notion of the unity subsisting between the Father and the Son[1]. Such too was the mode of reasoning adopted at Rome by the Artemas or Artemon, already mentioned, and his followers, at the end of the second century. A contemporary writer, after saying that they supported their "God-denying apostasy" by syllogistic forms of argument, proceeds, "Abandoning the inspired writings, they devote themselves to geometry, as becomes those who are of the earth, and speak of the earth, and are ignorant of Him who is from above. Euclid's treatises, for instance, are zealously studied by some of them; Aristotle and Theophrastus are objects of their admiration; while Galen may be

[1] Bull, Defens. F. N. ii. 1. § 10.

said even to be adored by others. It is needless to declare that such perverters of the sciences of unbelievers to the purposes of their own heresy, such diluters of the simple Scripture faith with heathen subtleties, have no claim whatever to be called believers.[2]" And such is Epiphanius's description of the Anomœans, the genuine offspring of the original Arian stock. "Aiming," he says, "to exhibit the Divine Nature by means of Aristotelic syllogisms and geometrical data, they are thence led on to declare that Christ cannot be derived from God[3]."

3.

Lastly, the absence of an adequate symbol of doctrine increased the evils thus existing, by affording an excuse and sometimes a reason for investigations, the necessity of which had not yet been superseded by the authority of an ecclesiastical decision. The traditionary system, received from the first age of the Church, had been as yet but partially set forth in authoritative forms; and by the time of the Nicene Council, the voices of the Apostles were but faintly heard throughout Christendom, and might be plausibly disregarded by those who were unwilling to hear. Even at the beginning of the third century, the disciples of Artemas boldly pronounced their heresy to be apostolical, and maintained that all the bishops of Rome had held it till Victor inclusive[4], whose episcopate was but a few years before their own time. The progress of unbelief naturally led them on to disparage, rather than to appeal to their predecessors; and to trust their cause to their own

[2] Euseb. Hist. v. 28. [3] Epiph. Hær. p. 809. [4] Euseb. ibid.

ingenuity, instead of defending an inconvenient fiction concerning the opinions of a former age. It ended in teaching them to regard the ecclesiastical authorities of former times as on a level with the uneducated and unenlightened of their own days. Paulus did not scruple to express contempt for the received expositors of Scripture at Antioch; and it is one of the first accusations brought by Alexander against Arius and his party, that "they put themselves above the ancients, and the teachers of our youth, and the prelates of the day; considering themselves alone to be wise, and to have discovered truths, which had never been revealed to man before them[5]."

On the other hand, while the line of tradition, drawn out as it was to the distance of two centuries from the Apostles, had at length become of too frail a texture, to resist the touch of subtle and ill-directed reason, the Church was naturally unwilling to have recourse to the novel, though necessary measure, of imposing an authoritative creed upon those whom it invested with the office of teaching. If I avow my belief, that freedom from symbols and articles is abstractedly the highest state of Christian communion, and the peculiar privilege of the primitive Church[6], it is not from any tenderness towards that proud impatience of control in which many exult, as in a virtue: but first, because technicality and formalism

[5] Theod. Hist. i. 4. ["Solæ in contemptu sunt divinæ literæ, quæ nec suam scholam nec magistros habeant, et de quibus peritissimè disputare se credat, qui nunquam didicit." Facund. p. 581. ed. Sirm.; vide also, p. 565.]

[6] ["Non eguistis literâ, qui spiritu abundabatis, etc. Ubi sensus conscientiæ periclitatur, illic litera postulatur." Hilar. de Syn. 63. Vide the Benedictine note.]

are, in their degree, inevitable results of public confessions of faith; and next, because when confessions do not exist, the mysteries of divine truth, instead of being exposed to the gaze of the profane and uninstructed, are kept hidden in the bosom of the Church, far more faithfully than is otherwise possible; and reserved by a private teaching, through the channel of her ministers, as rewards in due measure and season, for those who are prepared to profit by them; for those, that is, who are diligently passing through the successive stages of faith and obedience. And thus, while the Church is not committed to declarations, which, most true as they are, still are daily wrested by infidels to their ruin; on the other hand, much of that mischievous fanaticism is avoided, which at present abounds from the vanity of men, who think that they can explain the sublime doctrines and exuberant promises of the Gospel, before they have yet learned to know themselves and to discern the holiness of God, under the preparatory discipline of the Law and of Natural Religion. Influenced, as we may suppose, by these various considerations, from reverence for the free spirit of Christian faith, and still more for the sacred truths which are the objects of it, and again from tenderness both for the heathen and the neophyte, who were unequal to the reception of the strong meat of the full Gospel, the rulers of the Church were dilatory in applying a remedy, which nevertheless the circumstances of the times imperatively required. They were loth to confess, that the Church had grown too old to enjoy the free, unsuspicious teaching with which her childhood was blest; and that her disciples must, for the future, calculate and reason before they spoke and acted. So much was this the case, that in the Council of Antioch (as has been said), on the objection of Paulus, they actually withdrew a test which was eventually adopted by the more experienced Fathers at Nicæa; and which, if then sanctioned, might, as far as the Church was concerned, have extinguished the heretical spirit in the very place of its birth.—Meanwhile, the adoption of Christianity, as the religion of the empire, augmented the evil consequences of this omission, excommunication becoming more difficult, while entrance into the Church was less restricted than before.

SECTION III.

THE CHURCH OF ALEXANDRIA.

As the Church of Antioch was exposed to the influence of Judaism, so was the Alexandrian Church characterized in primitive times by its attachment to that comprehensive philosophy, which was reduced to system about the beginning of the third century, and then went by the name of the New Platonic, or Eclectic. A supposed resemblance between the Arian and the Eclectic doctrine concerning the Holy Trinity, has led to a common notion that the Alexandrian Fathers were the medium by which a philosophical error was introduced into the Church; and this hypothetical cause of a disputable resemblance has been apparently evidenced by the solitary fact, which cannot be denied, that Arius himself was a presbyter of Alexandria. We have already seen, however, that Arius was educated at Antioch; and we shall see hereafter that, so far from being favourably heard at Alexandria, he was, on the first promulgation of his heresy, expelled the Church in that city, and obliged to seek refuge among his Collucianists of Syria. And it is manifestly the opinion of Athanasius, that he was but the pupil or the tool of deeper men[1], probably of Eusebius of Nicomedia,

[1] Athan. oc Decr. Nic. 8. 20; ad Monach. 66; de Synod. 22.

who in no sense belongs to Alexandria. But various motives have led theological writers to implicate this celebrated Church in the charge of heresy. Infidels have felt a satisfaction, and heretics have had an interest, in representing that the most learned Christian community did not submit implicitly to the theology taught in Scripture and by the Church; a conclusion, which, even if substantiated, would little disturb the enlightened defender of Christianity, who may safely admit that learning, though a powerful instrument of the truth in right hands, is no unerring guide into it. The Romanists[2], on the other hand, have thought by the same line of policy to exalt the Apostolical purity of their own Church, by the contrast of unfaithfulness in its early rival; and (what is of greater importance) to insinuate both the necessity of an infallible authority, by exaggerating the errors and contrarieties of the Ante-Nicene Fathers, and the fact of its existence, by throwing us, for exactness of doctrinal statement, upon the decisions of the subsequent Councils. In the following pages, I hope to clear the illustrious Church in question of the grave imputation thus directed against her from opposite quarters: the imputation of considering the Son of God by nature inferior to the Father, that is, of platonizing or arianizing. But I have no need to profess myself her disciple, though, as regards the doctrine in debate, I might well do so; and, instead of setting about any formal defence, I will merely place before the reader the general principles of her

[2] [As to the charges made against Petavius, vide Bull, Defens. N. F. procem.; Budd. Isagog. p. 580; Bayle, Dict. (Petau.); Brucker, Phil. t. iii. p. 345.]

teaching, and leave it to him to apply them, as far as he judges they will go, in explanation of the language, which has been the ground of the suspicions against her.

I.

St. Mark, the founder of the Alexandrian Church, may be numbered among the personal friends and associates of that Apostle, who held it to be his especial office to convert the heathen; an office, which was impressed upon the community formed by the Evangelist, with a strength and permanence unknown in the other primitive Churches. The Alexandrian may peculiarly be called the Missionary and Polemical Church of Antiquity. Situated in the centre of the accessible world, and on the extremity of Christendom, in a city which was at once the chief mart of commerce, and a celebrated seat of both Jewish and Greek philosophy, it was supplied in especial abundance, both with materials and instruments prompting to the exercise of Christian zeal. Its catechetical school, founded (it is said) by the Evangelist himself, was a pattern to other Churches in its diligent and systematic preparation of candidates for baptism; while other institutions were added of a controversial character, for the purpose of carefully examining into the doctrines revealed in Scripture, and of cultivating the habit of argument and disputation[3]. While the internal affairs of the community were administered by its bishops, on these academical bodies, as subsidiary to the divinely-sanctioned system, devolved the defence and propagation of the faith, under the

[3] Cave, Hist. Literar. vol. i. p. 80.

presidency of laymen or inferior ecclesiastics. Athenagoras, the first recorded master of the catechetical school, is known by his defence of the Christians, still extant, addressed to the Emperor Marcus. Pantænus, who succeeded him, was sent by Demetrius, at that time bishop, as missionary to the Indians or Arabians. Origen, who was soon after appointed catechist at the early age of eighteen, had already given the earnest of his future celebrity, by his persuasive disputations with the unbelievers of Alexandria. Afterwards he appeared in the character of a Christian apologist before an Arabian prince, and Mammæa, the mother of Alexander Severus, and addressed letters on the subject of religion to the Emperor Philip and his wife Severa; and he was known far and wide in his day, for his indefatigable zeal and ready services in the confutation of heretics, for his various controversial and critical writings, and for the number and dignity of his converts[4].

Proselytism, then, in all its branches, the apologetic, the polemical, and the didactic, being the peculiar function of the Alexandrian Church, it is manifest that the writings of its theologians would partake largely of an exoteric character. I mean, that such men would write, not with the openness of Christian familiarity, but with the tenderness or the reserve with which we are accustomed to address those who do not sympathize with us, or whom we fear to mislead or to prejudice against the truth, by precipitate disclosures of its details. The example of the inspired writer of the Epistle to the Hebrews was their authority for making a broad distinction between the doctrines

[4] Philipp. Sidet. fragm. apud Dodw. in Iren. Huet. Origen.

suitable to the state of the weak and ignorant, and those which are the peculiar property of a baptized and regenerate Christian. The Apostle in that Epistle, when speaking of the most sacred Christian verities, as hidden under the allegories of the Old Testament, seems suddenly to check himself, from the apprehension that he was divulging mysteries beyond the understanding of his brethren ; who, instead of being masters in Scripture doctrine, were not yet versed even in its elements, needed the nourishment of children rather than of grown men, nay, perchance, having quenched the illumination of baptism, had forfeited the capacity of comprehending even the first elements of the truth. In the same place he enumerates these elements, or foundation of Christian teaching[5], in contrast with the esoteric doctrines which the "long-exercised habit of moral discernment" can alone appropriate and enjoy, as follows ;—repentance, faith in God, the doctrinal meaning of the right of baptism, confirmation as the channel of miraculous gifts, the future resurrection, and the final separation of good and bad. His first Epistle to the Corinthians contains the same distinction between the carnal or imperfect and the established Christian, which is laid down in that addressed to the Hebrews. While maintaining that in Christianity is contained a largeness of wisdom, or (to use human language) a profound philosophy, fulfilling those vague conceptions of greatness, which had led the aspiring intellect of the heathen sages to shadow forth their unreal systems, he at the same time insists

[5] Hebr. v. 11; vi. 6. τὰ στοιχεῖα τῆς ἀρχῆς τῶν λογίων τοῦ θεοῦ. ὁ τῆς ἀρχῆς τοῦ Χριστοῦ λόγος.

upon the impossibility of man's arriving at this hidden treasure all at once, and warns his brethren, instead of attempting to cross by a short path from the false to the true knowledge, to humble themselves to the low and narrow portal of the heavenly temple, and to become fools, that they might at length be really wise. As before, he speaks of the difference of doctrine suited respectively to neophytes and confirmed Christians, under the analogy of the difference of food proper for the old and young; a difference which lies, not in the arbitrary will of the dispenser, but in the necessity of the case, the more sublime truths of Revelation affording no nourishment to the souls of the unbelieving or unstable.

Accordingly, in the system of the early catechetical schools, the *perfect*, or men in Christ, were such as had deliberately taken upon them the profession of believers; had made the vows, and received the grace of baptism; and were admitted to all the privileges and the revelations of which the Church had been constituted the dispenser. But before reception into this full discipleship, a previous season of preparation, from two to three years, was enjoined, in order to try their obedience, and instruct them in the principles of revealed truth. During this introductory discipline, they were called *Catechumens*, and the teaching itself *Catechetical*, from the careful and systematic examination by which their grounding in the faith was effected. The matter of the instruction thus communicated to them, varied with the time of their discipleship, advancing from the most simple principle of Natural Religion to the peculiar doctrines of the Gospel, from moral truths to the Christian mysteries. On their first admission they were denominated *hearers*, from the leave granted them to attend the reading of the Scriptures and sermons in the Church. Afterwards, being allowed to stay during the prayers, and receiving the imposition of hands as the sign of their progress in spiritual knowledge, they were called *worshippers.* Lastly, some short time before their baptism, they were taught the Lord's Prayer (the peculiar privilege of the regenerate), were entrusted with the knowledge of the Creed, and, as destined for incorporation into the body of believers, received the titles of *competent* or *elect*[6]. Even to the last, they were granted nothing beyond a formal and general account of the articles of the Christian faith; the exact and fully developed doctrines of the Trinity and the Incarnation, and still more, the doctrine of the Atonement, as once made upon the cross, and commemorated and appropriated in the Eucharist, being the exclusive possession of the serious and practised Christian. On the other hand, the chief subjects of catechisings, as we learn from Cyril[7], were the doctrines of repentance and pardon, of the necessity of good works, of the nature and use of baptism, and the immortality of the soul;—as the Apostle had determined them.

The exoteric teaching, thus observed in the Catechetical Schools, was still more appropriate, when the Christian teacher addressed himself, not to the instruction of willing hearers, but to controversy or public preaching. At the present day, there are very many sincere Christians, who consider that the evangelical

[6] τέλειοι; ἀκροώμενοι, or audientes; γονυκλίνοντες, or εὐχόμενοι; competentes, electi, or φωτιζομενοι. Bingham, Antiq. book x. Suicer. Thes. in verb, κατηχέω.

[7] Bingham, ibid.

doctrines are the appointed instruments of conversion, and, as such, exclusively attended with the Divine blessing. In proof of this position, with an inconsistency remarkable in those who profess a jealous adherence to the inspired text, and are not slow to accuse others of ignorance of its contents, they appeal, not to Scripture, but to the stirring effects of this (so-called) Gospel preaching, and to the inefficiency, on the other hand, of mere exhortations respecting the benevolence and mercy of God, the necessity of repentance, the rights of conscience, and the obligation of obedience. But it is scarcely the attribute of a generous faith, to be anxiously inquiring into the consequences of this or that system, with a view to decide its admissibility, instead of turning at once to the revealed word, and inquiring into the rule there exhibited to us. God can defend and vindicate His own command, whatever it turn out to be ; weak though it seem to our vain wisdom, and unworthy of the Giver ; and that His course in this instance is really that which the hasty religionist condemns as if the theory of unenlightened formalists, is evident to careful students of Scripture, and is confirmed by the practice of the Primitive Church.

As to Scripture, I shall but observe, in addition to the remarks already made on the passages in the Epistles to the Corinthians and Hebrews, that no one sanction can be adduced thence, whether of precept or of example, in behalf of the practice of stimulating the affections, such as gratitude or remorse, by means of the doctrine of the Atonement, in order to the conversion of the hearers ;—that, on the contrary, it is its uniform method to connect the Gospel with Natural Religion, and to mark out obedience to the moral law as the ordinary means of attaining to a Christian faith, the higher evangelical truths, as well as the Eucharist, which is the visible emblem of them, being received as the reward and confirmation of habitual piety;—that, in the preaching of the Apostles and Evangelists in the Book of Acts, the sacred mysteries are revealed to individuals in proportion to their actual religious proficiency; that the first principles of righteousness, temperance, and judgment to come, are urged upon Felix; while the elders of Ephesus are reminded of the divinity and vicarious sacrifice of Christ, and the presence and power of the Holy Spirit in the Church;—lastly, that among those converts, who were made the chief instruments of the first propagation of the Gospel, or who are honoured with especial favour in Scripture, none are found who had not been faithful to the light already given them, and were not distinguished, previously to their conversion, by a strictly conscientious deportment. Such are the divine notices given to those who desire an apostolical rule for dispensing the word of life; and as such, the ancient Fathers received them. They received them as the fulfilment of our Lord's command, not to give that which is holy to dogs, nor to cast pearls before swine; a text cited by Clement and Tertullian[8], among others, in justification of their cautious distribution of sacred truth. They also considered this caution as the result of the most truly charitable consideration for those whom they addressed, who were likely to be perplexed, not converted, by the sudden exhibition of the whole evangelical scheme. This is the doctrine of Theodoret, Chrysostom, and others, in their com-

[8] Ceillier, Apol. des Pères, ch. ii. Bingh. Antiq. x. 5.

ments upon the passage in the Epistle to the Hebrews[9]. "Should a catechumen ask thee what the teachers have determined, (says Cyril of Jerusalem) tell nothing to one who is without. For we impart to thee a secret and a promise of the world to come. Keep safe the secret for Him who gives the reward. Listen not to one who asks, 'What harm is there in my knowing also?' Even the sick ask for wine, which, unseasonably given, brings on delirium; and so there come two ills, the death of the patient and the disrepute of the physician." In another place he says, "All may hear the Gospel, but the glory of the Gospel is set apart for the true disciples of Christ. To all who could hear, the Lord spake, but in parables; to His disciples He privately explained them. What is the blaze of Divine glory to the enlightened, is the blinding of unbelievers. These are the secrets which the Church unfolds to him who passes on from the catechumens, and not to the heathen. For we do not unfold to a heathen the truths concerning Father, Son, and Holy Spirit; nay, not even in the case of catechumens, do we clearly explain the mysteries, but we frequently say many things indirectly, so that believers who have been taught may understand, and the others may not be injured[1]."

The work of St. Clement, of Alexandria, called Stromateis, or Tapestry-work, from the variety of its contents, well illustrates the Primitive Church's method of instruction, as far as regards the educated portion of the community. It had the distinct object of interesting and conciliating the learned heathen who

[9] Suicer. Thes. in verb. στοιχεῖον,

[1] Cyril. Hieros. ed. Milles, præf. § 7 catech. vi. 16.

perused it; but it also exemplifies the peculiar caution then adopted by Christians in teaching the truth,—their desire to rouse the moral powers to internal voluntary action, and their dread of loading or formalizing the mind. In the opening of his work, Clement speaks of his miscellaneous discussions as mingling truth with philosophy; "or rather," he continues, "involving and concealing it, as the shell hides the edible fruit of the nut." In another place he compares them, not to a fancy garden, but to some thickly-wooded mountain, where vegetation of every sort, growing promiscuously, by its very abundance conceals from the plunderer the fruit trees, which are intended for the rightful owner. "We must hide," he says, "that wisdom, spoken in mystery, which the Son of God has taught us. Thus the Prophet Esaias has his tongue cleansed with fire, that he may be able to declare the vision; and our ears must be sanctified as well as our tongues, if we aim at being recipients of the truth. This was a hindrance to my writing; and still I have anxiety, since Scripture says, 'Cast not your pearls before swine;' for those pure and bright truths, which are so marvellous and full of God to goodly natures, do but provoke laughter, when spoken in the hearing of the many[2]." The Fathers considered that they had the pattern as well as the recommendation of this method of teaching in Scripture itself[3].

2.

This self-restraint and abstinence, practised at least

[2] Strom. i. 1. 12; v. 3; vi. 1; vii, 18.

[3] "Bonæ sunt in Scripturis sacris mysteriorum profunditates, quæ ob hoc teguntur, ne vilescant; ob hoc quæruntur, ut exerceant; ob hoc autem aperiuntur, ut pascant." August. in Petav. præf. in Trin. i. 5.

partially, by the Primitive Church in the publication of the most sacred doctrines of our religion, is termed, in theological language, the *Disciplina Arcani;* concerning which a few remarks may here be added, not so much in recommendation of it (which is beside my purpose), as to prevent misconception of its principle and limits.

Now, first, it may be asked, How was any secrecy practicable, seeing that the Scriptures were open to every one who chose to consult them? It may startle those who are but acquainted with the popular writings of this day, yet, I believe, the most accurate consideration of the subject will lead us to acquiesce in the statement, as a general truth, that the doctrines in question have never been learned merely from Scripture. Surely the Sacred Volume was never intended, and is not adapted, to teach us our creed; however certain it is that we can prove our creed from it, when it has once been taught us[4], and in spite of individual producible exceptions to the general rule. From the very first, that rule has been, as a matter of fact, that the Church should teach the truth, and then should appeal to Scripture in vindication of its own teaching. And from the first, it has been the error of heretics to neglect the information thus provided for them, and to attempt of themselves a work to which they are unequal, the eliciting a systematic doctrine from the scattered notices of the truth which Scripture contains. Such men act, in the solemn concerns of religion, the part of the self-sufficient natural

[4] Vide Dr. Hawkins's original and most conclusive work on Unauthoritative Tradition, which contains in it the key to a number of difficulties which are apt to perplex the theological student.

philosopher, who should obstinately reject Newton's theory of gravitation, and endeavour, with talents inadequate to the task, to strike out some theory of motion by himself. The insufficiency of the mere private study of Holy Scripture for arriving at the exact and entire truth which Scripture really contains, is shown by the fact, that creeds and teachers have ever been divinely provided, and by the discordance of opinions which exists wherever those aids are thrown aside; as it is also shown by the very structure of the Bible itself. And if this be so, it follows that, while inquirers and neophytes in the first centuries lawfully used the inspired writings for the purposes of morals and for instruction in the rudiments of the faith, they still might need the teaching of the Church as a key to the collection of passages which related to the mysteries of the Gospel, passages which are obscure from the necessity of combining and receiving them all.

A more plausible objection to the existence of this rule of secrecy in the Early Church arises from the circumstance, that the Christian Apologists openly mention to the whole world the sacred tenets which have been above represented as the peculiar possession of the confirmed believer. But it must be observed, that the writers of these were frequently laymen, and so did not commit the Church as a body, nor even in its separate authorities, to formal statement or to theological discussion. The great duty of the Christian teacher was to unfold the sacred truths in due order, and not prematurely to insist on the difficulties, or to apply the promises of the Gospel; and if others erred in this respect, still it remained a duty to him.

And further, these disclosures are not so conclusive as they seem to be at first sight ; the approximations of philosophy, and the corruptions of heresy, being so considerable, as to create a confusion concerning the precise character of the ecclesiastical doctrine. Besides, in matter of fact, some of the early apologists themselves, as Tatian, were tainted with heretical opinions.

But in truth, it is not the actual practice of the Primitive Church, which I am concerned with, so much as its principle. Men often break through the rules, which they set themselves for the conduct of life, with or without good reason. If it was the professed principle of the early teachers, to speak exoterically to those who were without the Church, instances of a contrary practice but prove their inconsistency ; whereas the fact of the existence of the principle answers the purpose which is the ultimate aim of these remarks, viz. it accounts for those instances in the teaching of the Alexandrians, whether many or few, and whether extant or not in writing, in which they were silent as regards the mysterious doctrines of Christianity. Indeed it is evident, that anyhow the *Disciplina Arcani* could not be observed for any long time in the Church. Apostates would reveal its doctrines, even if these escaped in no other way. Perhaps it was almost abandoned, as far as men of letters were concerned, after the date of Ammonius ; indeed there are various reasons for limiting its strict enforcement to the end of the second century. And it is plain, that during the time when the sacred doctrines were passing into the stock of public knowledge, Christian controversialists would be in a difficulty how to conduct themselves, what to deny, explain or complete, in the popular notions of their creed; and they would consequently be betrayed into inconsistencies of statement, and vary in their method of disputing.

The *Disciplina Arcani* being supposed, with these limitations, to have had a real existence, I observe further, in explanation of its principle, that the elementary information given to the heathen or catechumen was in no sense undone by the subsequent secret teaching, which was in fact but the filling up of a bare but correct outline. The contrary theory was maintained by the Manichees, who represented the initiatory discipline as founded on a fiction or hypothesis, which was to be forgotten by the learner as he made progress in the real doctrine of the gospel[5]; somewhat after the manner of a school in the present day, which supposes conversion to be effected by an exhibition of free promises and threats, and an appeal to our moral capabilities, which after conversion are discovered to have no foundation in fact. But "Far be it from so great an Apostle," says Augustine, speaking of St. Paul, "a vessel elect of God, an organ of the Holy Ghost, to be one man when he preached, another when he wrote, one man in private, another in public. He was made all to all men, not by the craft of a deceiver, but from the affection of a sympathizer, succouring the diverse diseases of souls with the diverse emotions of compassion; to the little ones dispensing the lesser doctrines, not false ones, but the higher mysteries to the perfect, all of them, however, true, harmonious, and divine[6]."

[5] August. in Advers. Leg. et Proph. lib. ii.

[6] Mosheim, de Caus. Supp. Libror. § 17. I do not find it in this exact form in Augustine's treatise; vide in Advers. Leg. et Proph. lib. ii. 4. 6. &c.

Next, the truths reserved for the baptized Christian were not put forward as the arbitrary determinations of individuals, as the word of man, but rather as an apostolical legacy, preserved and dispensed by the Church. Thus Irenæus when engaged in refuting the heretics of his age, who appealed from the text of Scripture to a sense independent of it, as the test between truth and falsehood in its contents, says, "We know the doctrine of our salvation through none but those who have transmitted to us the gospel, first proclaiming it, then (by God's will) delivering it to us in the Scriptures, as a basis and pillar of our faith. Nor dare we affirm that their announcements were made previously to their attaining perfect knowledge, as some presume to say, boasting that they set right the Apostles[7]." He then proceeds to speak of the clearness and cogency of the traditions preserved in the Church, as containing that true wisdom of the perfect, of which St. Paul speaks, and to which the Gnostics pretended. And, indeed, without formal proofs of the existence and the authority in primitive times of an Apostolical Tradition, it is plain that there must have been such tradition, granting that the Apostles conversed, and their friends had memories, like other men. It is quite inconceivable that they should not have been led to arrange the series of revealed doctrines more systematically than they record them in Scripture, as soon as their converts became exposed to the attacks and misrepresentations of heretics; unless they were forbidden so to do, a supposition which cannot be maintained. Their statements thus occasioned would be preserved, as a matter of course; together

[7] Iren. iii. 1. Vide also Tertull. de Præscr. Hæret. 22.

with those other secret but less important truths, to which St. Paul seems to allude, and which the early writers more or less acknowledge, whether concerning the types of the Jewish Church, or the prospective fortunes of the Christian[8]. And such recollections of apostolical teaching would evidently be binding on the faith of those who were instructed in them; unless it can be supposed, that, though coming from inspired teachers, they were not of divine origin.

However, it must not be supposed, that this appeal to Tradition in the slightest degree disparages the sovereign authority and sufficiency of Holy Scripture, as a record of the truth. In the passage from Irenæus above cited, Apostolical Tradition is brought forward, not to supersede Scripture, but in conjunction with Scripture, to refute the self-authorized, arbitrary doctrines of the heretics. We must cautiously distinguish, with that Father, between a tradition supplanting or perverting the inspired records, and a corroborating, illustrating, and altogether subordinate tradition. It is of the latter that he speaks, classing the traditionary and the written doctrine together, as substantially one and the same, and as each equally opposed to the profane inventions of Valentinus and Marcion.

Lastly, the secret tradition soon ceased to exist even in theory. It was authoritatively divulged, and perpetuated in the form of symbols according as the successive innovations of heretics called for its publication. In the creeds of the early Councils, it may be considered as having come to light, and so ended; so that whatever has not been thus authenticated, whether

[8] Mosheim, de Reb. ante Const. sæc. ii. § 34.

it was prophetical information, or comment on the past dispensations[9], is, from the circumstances of the case, lost to the Church. What, however, was then (by God's good providence) seasonably preserved, is in some sense of apostolical authority still; and at least serves the chief office of the early traditions, viz. that of interpreting and harmonizing the statements of Scripture.

3.

In the passages lately quoted from Clement and Cyril, mention was made by those writers of a mode of speaking, which was intelligible to the well-instructed, but conveyed no definite meaning to ordinary hearers. This was the Allegorical Method; which well deserves our attention before we leave the subject of the *Disciplina Arcani*, as being one chief means by which it was observed. The word *allegorizing* must here be understood in a wide signification; as including in its meaning, not only the representation of truths, under a foreign, though analogous exterior, after the manner of our Lord's parables, but the practice of generalizing facts into principles, of adumbrating greater truths under the image of lesser, of implying the consequences or the basis of doctrines in their correlatives, and altogether those instances of thinking, reasoning, and teaching, which depend upon the use of propositions which are abstruse, and of connexions which are obscure, and which, in the case of uninspired authors, we consider profound, or poetical, or enthusiastic, or illogical, according to our opinion of those by whom they are exhibited.

[9] 2 Thes. ii. 5. 15. Heb. v. 11.

This method of writing was the national peculiarity of that literature in which the Alexandrian Church was educated. The hieroglyphics of the ancient Egyptians mark the antiquity of a practice, which, in a later age, being enriched and diversified by the genius of their Greek conquerors, was applied as a key both to mythological legends, and to the sacred truths of Scripture. The Stoics were the first to avail themselves of an expedient which smoothed the deformities of the Pagan creed. The Jews, and then the Christians, of Alexandria, employed it in the interpretation of the inspired writings. Those writings themselves have certainly an allegorical structure, and seem to countenance and invite an allegorical interpretation; and in consequence, they have been referred by some critics to one and the same heathen origin, as if Moses first, and then St. Paul, borrowed their symbolical system respectively from the Egyptian and the Alexandrian philosophy.

But it is more natural to consider that the Divine Wisdom used on the sublimest of all subjects, media, which we spontaneously select for the expression of solemn thought and elevated emotion; and had no especial regard to the practice in any particular country, which afforded but one instance of the operation of a general principle of our nature. When the mind is occupied by some vast and awful subject of contemplation, it is prompted to give utterance to its feelings in a figurative style; for ordinary words will not convey the admiration, nor literal words the reverence which possesses it; and when, dazzled at length with the great sight, it turns away for relief, it still catches in every new object which it encounters, glimpses of its former vision, and colours its whole range of thought with this one abiding association. If, however, others have preceded it in the privilege of such contemplations, a well-disciplined piety will lead it to adopt the images which they have invented, both from affection for what is familiar to it, and from a fear of using unsanctioned language on a sacred subject. Such are the feelings under which a deeply impressed mind addresses itself to the task of disclosing even its human thoughts; and this account of it, if we may dare to conjecture, in its measure applies to the case of a mind under the immediate influence of inspiration. Certainly, the matter of Revelation suggests some such hypothetical explanation of the structure of the books which are its vehicle; in which the divinely-instructed imagination of the writers is ever glancing to and fro, connecting past things with future, illuminating God's lower providences and man's humblest services by allusions to the relations of the evangelical covenant, and then in turn suddenly leaving the latter to dwell upon those past dealings of God with man, which must not be forgotten merely because they have been excelled. No prophet ends his subject: his brethren after him renew, enlarge, transfigure, or reconstruct it; so that the Bible, though various in its parts, forms a whole, grounded on a few distinct doctrinal principles discernible throughout it; and is in consequence intelligible indeed in its general drift, but obscure in its text; and even tempts the student, if I may so speak, to a lax and disrespectful interpretation of it. History is made the external garb of prophecy, and persons and facts become the figures of heavenly things. I need only refer, by way of instance, to the delineation of Abraham as the type of the accepted worshipper of God ; to the history of the brazen serpent ; to the prophetical bearing of the "call of Israel out of Egypt ;" to the personification of the Church in the Apostolic Epistles as the reflected image of Christ ; and, further, to the mystical import, interpreted by our Lord Himself, of the title of God as the God of the Patriarchs. Above all other subjects, it need scarcely be said, the likeness of the promised Mediator is conspicuous thoughout the sacred volume as in a picture : moving along the line of the history, in one or other of His destined offices, the dispenser of blessings in Joseph, the inspired interpreter of truth in Moses, the conqueror in Joshua, the active preacher in Samuel, the suffering combatant in David, and in Solomon the triumphant and glorious king.

Moreover, Scripture assigns the same uses to this allegorical style, which were contemplated by the Fathers when they made it subservient to the *Disciplina Arcani ;* viz. those of trying the earnestness and patience of inquirers, discriminating between the proud and the humble, and conveying instruction to believers, and that in the most permanently impressive manner, without the world's sharing in the knowledge. Our Lord's remarks on the design of his own parables, is a sufficient evidence of this intention.

Thus there seemed every encouragement, from the structure of Scripture, from the apparent causes which led to that structure, and from the purposes to which it was actually applied by its Divine Author, to induce the Alexandrians to consider its text as primarily and directly the instrument of an allegorical teaching. And since it sanctions the principle of allegorizing by its own example, they would not consider themselves confined within the limits of the very instances which it supplies, because of the evident spiritual drift of various passages which, nevertheless, it does not interpret spiritually; thus to the narrative contained in the twenty-second chapter of Genesis, few people will deny an evangelical import, though the New Testament itself nowhere assigns it. Yet, on the other hand, granting that a certain liberty of interpretation, beyond the precedent, but according to the spirit of Scripture, be allowable in the Christian teacher, still few people will deny, that some rule is necessary as a safeguard against its abuse, in order to secure the sacred text from being explained away by the heretic, and misquoted and perverted by weak or fanatical minds. Such a safeguard we shall find in bearing cautiously in mind this consideration: viz. that (as a general rule), every passage of Scripture has some one definite and sufficient sense, which was prominently before the mind of the writer, or in the intention of the Blessed Spirit, and to which all other ideas, though they might arise, or be implied, still were subordinate. It is this true meaning of the text, which it is the business of the expositor to unfold. This it is, which every diligent student will think it a great gain to discover; and, though he will not shut his eyes to the indirect and instructive applications of which the text is capable, he never will so reason as to forget that there is one sense peculiarly its own. Sometimes it is easily ascertained, sometimes it can be scarcely conjectured; sometimes it is contained in the literal sense of the words employed, as in the historical parts ; sometimes it is the allegorical, as in our Lord's parables ; or sometimes the secondary sense may be more important in after ages than the original, as in the instance of the Jewish ritual ; still in all cases (to speak generally) there is but one main primary sense, whether literal or figurative ; a regard for which must ever keep us sober and reverent in the employment of those allegorisms, which, nevertheless, our Christian liberty does not altogether forbid.

The protest of Scripture against all careless expositions of its meaning, is strikingly implied in the extreme reserve and caution, with which it unfolds its own typical signification ; for instance, in the Mosaic ritual no hint was given of its undoubted prophetical character, lest an excuse should be furnished to the Israelitish worshipper for undervaluing its actual commands. So, again, the secondary and distinct meaning of prophecy, is commonly hidden from view by the veil of the literal text, lest its immediate scope should be overlooked ; when that is once fulfilled, the recesses of the sacred language seem to open, and give up the further truths deposited in them. Our Lord, probably, in the prophecy recorded in the Gospels, was not careful (if I may so express myself) that His disciples should distinguish between His final and immediate coming ; thinking it a less error that they should consider the last day approaching, than that they should forget their own duties in the contemplation of the future fortunes of the Church. Nay, even types fulfilled, if they be historical, seem sometimes purposely to be left without the sanction of an interpretation, lest we should neglect the instruction still conveyed in a literal narrative. This accounts for the silence observed concerning the evangelical import, to which I have already referred, of the sacrifice of Isaac, which contains a definite and permanent moral lesson, as a matter of fact, however clear may be its further meaning as emblematical of our Lord's sufferings on the cross. In corroboration of this remark, let it be observed, that there seems to have been in the Church a traditionary explanation of these historical types, derived from the Apostles, but kept among the secret doctrines, as being dangerous to the majority of hearers[1]; and certainly St. Paul, in the Epistle to the Hebrews, affords us an instance of such a tradition, both as existing and as secret (even though it be shown to be of Jewish origin), when, first checking himself and questioning his brethren's faith, he communicates, not without hesitation, the evangelical scope of the account of Melchisedec, as introduced into the book of Genesis.

As to the Christian writers of Alexandria, if they erred in their use of the Allegory, their error did not lie in the mere adoption of an instrument which Philo or the Egyptian hierophants had employed (though this is sometimes made the ground of objection), for Scripture itself had taken it out of the hands of such authorities. Nor did their error lie in the mere circumstance of their allegorizing Scripture, where Scripture gave no direct countenance; as if we might not interpret the sacred word for ourselves, as we interpret the events of life, by the principles which itself supplies. But they erred, whenever and as far as they carried their favourite rule of exposition

[1] Vide Mosheim, de Reb. Ant. Const. sæc. ii. § 34. Rosenmuller, Hist. Interpr. iii. 2. § 1.

beyond the spirit of the canon above laid down, so as to obscure the primary meaning of Scripture, and to weaken the force of historical facts and doctrinal declarations; and much more, if at any time they degraded the inspired text to the office of conveying the thoughts of uninspired teachers on subjects not sacred.

And, as it is impossible to draw a precise line between the use and abuse of allegorizing, so it is impossible also to ascertain the exact degree of blame incurred by individual teachers who familiarly indulge in it. They may be faulty as commentators, yet instructive as devotional writers; and their liberty in interpretation is to be regulated by the state of mind in which they address themselves to the work, and by their proficiency in the knowledge and practice of Christian duty. So far as men use the language of the Bible (as is often done in poems and works of fiction) as the mere instrument of a cultivated fancy, to make their style attractive or impressive, so far, it is needless to say, they are guilty of a great irreverence towards its Divine Author. On the other hand, it is surely no extravagance to assert that there are minds so gifted and disciplined as to approach the position occupied by the inspired writers, and therefore able to apply their words with a fitness, and entitled to do so with a freedom, which is unintelligible to the dull or heartless criticism of inferior understandings. So far then as the Alexandrian Fathers partook of such a singular gift of grace (and Origen surely bears on him the tokens of some exalted moral dignity), not incited by a capricious and presumptuous imagination, but burning with that vigorous faith, which, seeing God in all things, does and suffers all for His sake, and, while filled with the contemplation of His supreme glory, still discharges each command in the exactness of its real meaning, in the same degree they stand not merely excused, but are placed immeasurably above the multitude of those who find it so easy to censure them.—And so much on the Allegory, as the means of observing the *Disciplina Arcani.*

4.

The same method of interpretation was used for another purpose, which is more open to censure. When Christian controversialists were urged by objections to various passages in the history of the Old Testament, as derogatory to the Divine Perfections or to the Jewish saints, they had recourse to an allegorical explanation by way of answer. Thus Origen spiritualizes the account of Abraham's denying his wife, the polygamy of the Patriarchs, and Noah's intoxication[2]. It is impossible to defend such a mode of interpretation, which seems to imply a want of faith in those who had recourse to it. Doubtless this earnestness to exculpate the saints of the elder covenant is partly to be attributed to a noble jealousy for the honour of God, and a reverence for the memory of those who, on the whole, rise in their moral attainments far above their fellows, and well deserve the confidence in their virtue which the Alexandrians manifest. Yet God has given us rules of right and wrong, which we must not be afraid to apply in estimating the conduct of even the best of mere men;

[2] Heut. Origen. p. 171, Rosenmuller supra. [On this subject, vide a striking passage in Facundus, Def. Tr. Cap. xii. 1, pp. 568-9.]

though errors are thereby detected, the scandal of which we ourselves have to bear in our own day. So far must be granted in fairness; but some have gone on to censure the principle itself which this procedure involved: viz. that of representing religion, for the purpose of conciliating the heathen, in the form most attractive to their prejudices: and, as it was generally received in the Primitive Church, and the considerations which it involves are not without their bearings upon the doctrinal question in which we shall be presently engaged, I will devote some space here to the examination of it.

The mode of arguing and teaching in question which is called *economical*[3] by the ancients, can scarcely be disconnected from the *Disciplina Arcani*, as will appear by some of the instances which follow, though it is convenient to consider it by itself. If it is necessary to contrast the two with each other, the one may be considered as withholding the truth, and the other as setting it out to advantage. The Economy is certainly sanctioned by St. Paul in his own conduct. To the Jews he became as a Jew, and as without the Law to the heathen[4]. His behaviour at Athens is the most remarkable instance in his history of this method of acting. Instead of uttering any invective against their Polytheism, he began a discourse upon the Unity of the Divine Nature; and then proceeded to claim the altar[5],

[3] *κατ' οἰκονομίαν.*

[4] [On the economies of St. Peter and St. Paul, vide Lardner's Heathen Test. ch. xxxvii. 7.

[5] [Vide this argument in the mouth of Dionysius (in Euseb. Hist. vii. 11, *οὐ πάντες πάντας*, &c.) as his plea for liberty of worship, with the neat retort of the Prefect.]

consecrated in the neighbourhood to the unknown God, as the property of Him whom he preached to them, and to enforce his doctrine of the Divine Immateriality, not by miracles, but by argument, and that founded on the words of a heathen poet. This was the example which the Alexandrians set before them in their intercourse with the heathen, as may be shown by the following instances.

Theonas, Bishop of Alexandria (A.D. 282—300), has left his directions for the behaviour of Christians who were in the service of the imperial court. The utmost caution is enjoined them, not to give offence to the heathen emperor. If a Christian was appointed librarian, he was to take good care not to show any contempt for secular knowledge and the ancient writers. He was advised to make himself familiar with the poets, philosophers, orators, and historians, of classical literature; and, while discussing their writings, to take incidental opportunities of recommending the Scriptures, introducing mention of Christ, and by degrees revealing the real dignity of His nature[6].

The conversion of Gregory of Neocæsarea, (A.D. 231) affords an exemplification of this procedure in an individual case. He had originally attached himself to the study of rhetoric and the law, but was persuaded by Origen, whose lectures he attended, to exchange these pursuits, first for science, then for philosophy, then for theology, so far as right notions concerning religion could be extracted from the promiscuous

[6] Rose's Neander, Eccl. Hist. vol. i. p. 145. "Insurgere poterit Christi mentio, explicabitur paullatim ejus sola divinitas." Tillem. Mem. vol. iv. p. 240, 241.

writings of the various philosophical sects. Thus, while professedly teaching him Pagan philosophy, his skilful master insensibly enlightened him in the knowledge of the Christian faith. Then leading him to Scripture, he explained to him its difficulties as they arose; till Gregory, overcome by the force of truth, announced to his instructor his intention of exchanging the pursuits of this world for the service of God[7].

Clement's Stromateis (A.D. 200), a work which has already furnished us with illustrations of the Alexandrian method of teaching, was written with the design of converting the learned heathen, and pursues the same plan which Origen adopted towards Gregory. The author therein professes his wish to blend together philosophy and religion, refutes those who censure the former, shows the advantage of it, and how it is to be applied. This leading at once to an inquiry concerning what particular school of philosophy is to be held of divine origin, he answers in a celebrated passage, that all are to be referred thither as far as they respectively inculcate the principles of piety and morality, and none, except as containing the portions and foreshadowings of the truth. "By philosophy," he says, "I do not mean the Stoic, nor the Platonic, nor the Epicurean and Aristotelic, but all good doctrine in every one of the schools, all precepts of holiness combined with religious knowledge. All this, taken together, or the *Eclectic*, I call *philosophy*: whereas the rest are mere forgeries of the human

[7] This was Origen's usual method, vide Euseb. Eccl. Hist. vi. 18. He has signified it himself in these words: *γυμνάσιον μέν φαμεν εἶναι τῆς ψυχῆς τὴν ἀνθρωπίνην σοφίαν, τέλος δὲ τὴν θείαν.* Contr. Cels. vi. 13.

intellect, and in no respect to be accounted divine[8]." At the same time, to mark out the peculiar divinity of Revealed Religion, he traces all the philosophy of the heathen to the teaching of the Hebrew sages, earnestly maintaining its entire subserviency to Christianity, as but the love of that truth which the Scriptures really impart.

The same general purpose of conciliating the heathen, and (as far as might be,) indulging the existing fashions to which their literature was subjected, may be traced in the slighter compositions[9] which the Christians published in defence of their religion[1], being what in this day might be called pamphlets, written in imitation of speeches after the manner of Isocrates, and adorned with those graces of language which the schools taught, and the inspired Apostle has exhibited in his Epistle to the Hebrews. Clement's Exhortation to the Gentiles is a specimen of this style of writing; as also those of Athenagoras and Tatian, and that ascribed to Justin Martyr.

Again :— the last-mentioned Father supplies us with an instance of an economical relinquishment of a sacred doctrine. When Justin Martyr, in his argument with the Jew Trypho, (A.D. 150.) finds himself unable to convince him from the Old Testament of the divinity of Christ, he falls back upon the doctrine of His divine Mission, as if this were a point

[8] Clem. Strom. i. 7.

[9] λόγοι. [Such are those (Pagan) of Maximus Tyrius. Three sacred narratives of Eusebius Emesenus are to be found at Vienna. Augusti has published one of them: Bonn, 1820. Vide Lambec. Bibl. Vind. iv. p. 286.]

[1] Dodwell in Iren. Diss. vi. § 14. 16.

indisputable on the one hand, and on the other, affording a sufficient ground, from which to advance, when expedient, to the proof of the full evangelical truth[2]. In the same passage, moreover, as arguing with an unbeliever, he permits himself to speak without an anathema of those (the Ebionites) who professed Christianity, and yet denied Christ's divinity. Athanasius himself fully recognizes the propriety of this concealment of the doctrine on a fitting occasion, and thus accounts for the silence of the Apostles concerning it, in their speeches recorded in the book of Acts, viz. that they were unwilling, by a disclosure of it, to prejudice the Jews against those miracles, the acknowledgment of which was a first step towards their receiving it[3].

Gregory of Neocæsarea (A.D. 240—270), whose conversion by Origen has already been adduced in illustration, furnishes us in his own conduct with a similar but stronger instance of an economical concealment of the full truth. It seems that certain heretical teachers, in the time of Basil, ascribed to Gregory, whether by way of censure or in self-defence, the Sabellian view of the Trinity; and, moreover, the belief that Christ was a creature. The occasion of these statements, as imputed to him, was a *vivâ voce* controversy with a heathen, which had been taken down in writing by the bystanders. The charge of Sabellianism is refuted by Gregory's extant writings; both imputations, however, are answered by St. Basil,

[2] Vide Bull, Judic. Eccl. vi. 7.

[3] Athan. de Sent. Dionys. 8. Theodoret, Chrysostom, and others say the same. Vide Suicer. Thesaurus, verb στοιχεῖον, and Whitby on Heb. v. 12.

and that, on the principle of controversy which I have above attempted to describe. "When Gregory," he says, "declared that the Father and Son were two in our conception of them, one in *hypostasis*, he spoke not as teaching doctrine, but as arguing with an unbeliever, viz. in his disputation with Ælianus; but this distinction our heretical opponents could not enter into, much as they pride themselves on the subtlety of their intellect. Even granting there were no mistakes in taking the notes (which, please God, it is my intention to prove from the text as it now stands), it is to be supposed, that he did not think it necessary to be very exact in his doctrinal terms, when employed in converting a heathen; but in some things, even to concede to his feelings, that he might gain him over to the cardinal points. Accordingly, you may find many expressions there, of which heretics now take great advantage, such as 'creature,' 'made,' and the like So again, many statements which he has made concerning the Incarnation, are referred to the Divine Nature of the Son by those who do not skilfully enter into his meaning; as, indeed, is the very expression in question which they have circulated[4]."

I will here again instance a parallel use of the Economy on the part of Athanasius himself, and will avail myself of the words of the learned Petavius "Even Athanasius," he says, "whose very gift it was, above all other Fathers, to possess a clear and accurate knowledge of the Catholic doctrine concerning the Trinity, so that all succeeding antagonists of Arianism may be truly said to have derived their

[4] Basil. Epist. ccx. § 5.

powers and their arguments from him, even this keen and vigilant champion of orthodoxy, in arguing with the Gentiles for the Divinity and incarnation of the Word, urges them with considerations drawn from their own philosophical notions concerning Him. Not that he was ignorant how unlike orthodoxy, and how like Arianism, such notions were, but he bore in mind the necessity of favourably disposing the minds of the Gentiles to listen to his teaching; and he was aware that it was one thing to lay the rudiments of the faith in an ignorant or heathen mind, and another to defend the faith against heretics, or to teach it dogmatically. For instance, in answering their objection to the Divine Word having taken flesh, which especially offended them, he bids them consider whether they are not inconsistent in dwelling upon this, while they themselves believe that there is a Divine Word, the presiding principle and soul of the world, through the movements of which He is visibly displayed; 'for what (he asks) does Christianity say more than that the Word has presented Himself to the inspection of our senses by the instrumentality of a body?' And yet it is certain that the Father and the pervading Word of the Platonists, differed materially from the Sacred Persons of the Trinity, as we hold the doctrine, and Athanasius too, in every page of his writings[5]."

There are instances in various ways of the economical method, that is, of accommodation to the feelings and prejudices of the hearer, in leading him to the

[5] Petav. de Trin. ii. præf. 3, § 5. [abridged and re-arranged. Vide ibid. iii. 1, § 6. Vide also Euseb. contr. Marcell. ii. 22, p. 140; iii. 3. pp. 161, 2].

reception of a novel or unacceptable doctrine. It professes to be founded in the actual necessity of the case; because those who are strangers to the tone of thought and principles of the speaker, cannot at once be initiated into his system, and because they must begin with imperfect views; and therefore, if he is to teach them at all, he must put before them large propositions, which he has afterwards to modify, or make assertions which are but parallel or analogous to the truth, rather than coincident with it. And it cannot be denied that those who attempt to speak at all times the naked truth, or rather the commonly-received expression of it, are certain, more than other men, to convey wrong impressions of their meaning to those who happen to be below them, or to differ widely from them, in intelligence and cast of mind. On the other hand, the abuse of the Economy in the hands of unscrupulous reasoners, is obvious. Even the honest controversialist or teacher will find it very difficult to represent without misrepresenting, what it is yet his duty to present to his hearers with caution or reserve. Here the obvious rule to guide our practice is, to be careful ever to maintain substantial truth in our use of the economical method. It is thus we lead forward children by degrees, influencing and impressing their minds by means of their own confined conceptions of things, before we attempt to introduce them to our own; yet at the same time modelling their thoughts according to the analogy of those to which we mean ultimately to bring them. Again, the information given to the blind man, that scarlet was like the sound of a trumpet, is an instance of an unexceptionable economy, since it was as true as it could be under the circumstances of the case, conveying a substantially correct impression as far as it went.

In applying this rule to the instances above given, it is plain that Justin, Gregory, or Athanasius, were justifiable or not in their Economy, according as they did or did not practically mislead their opponents. Merely to leave a man in errors which he had independently of us, or to abstain from removing them, cannot be blamed as a fault, and may be a duty; though it is so difficult to hit the mark in these perplexing cases, that it is not wonderful, should these or other Fathers have failed at times, and said more or less than was proper. Again, in the instances of St. Paul, Theonas, Origen, and Clement, the doctrine which their conduct implies, is the Divinity of Paganism; a true doctrine, though the heathen whom they addressed would not at first rightly apprehend it. But I am aware that some persons will differ from me here, and others will be perplexed about my meaning. So let this be a reserved point, to be considered when we have finished the present subject.

The Alexandrian Father who has already been quoted, accurately describes the rules which should guide the Christian in speaking and acting economically. "Being fully persuaded of the omnipresence of God," says Clement, "and ashamed to come short of the truth, he is satisfied with the approval of God, and of his own conscience. Whatever is in his mind, is also on his tongue; towards those who are fit recipients, both in speaking and living, he harmonizes his profession with his thoughts. He both thinks and speaks the truth; except when careful treatment is necessary, and then, as a physician for the good of his patients, he will lie, or rather utter a lie, as the Sophists say. For instance, the noble Apostle circumcised Timothy, while he cried out and wrote down, 'Circumcision availeth not.' . . Nothing, however, but his neighbour's good will lead him to do this. . . He gives himself up for the Church, for the friends whom he hath begotten in the faith for an ensample to those who have the ability to undertake the high office *(economy)* of a religious and charitable teacher, for an exhibition of truth in his words, and for the exercise of love towards the Lord[6]."

Further light will be thrown upon the doctrine of the Economy, by considering it as exemplified in the dealings of Providence towards man. The word occurs in St. Paul's Epistle to the Ephesians, where it is used for that series of Divine appointments viewed as a whole, by which the Gospel is introduced and realized among mankind, being translated in our version "*dispensation.*" It will evidently bear a wider sense, embracing the Jewish and patriarchal dispensations, or any Divine procedure, greater or less, which consists of means and an end. Thus it is applied by the Fathers, to the history of Christ's humiliation, as exhibited in the doctrines of His incarnation, ministry, atonement, exaltation, and mediatorial sovereignty, and, as such distinguished from the "*theologia*" or the collection of truths relative to His personal indwelling in the bosom of God. Again, it might with equal fitness be used for the general system of provi-

[6] Clem. Strom. vii. 8, 9 (abridged). [Vide Plat. Leg. ii. 8, οὔποτε ψεύδεται, κἂν ψεῦδος λέγῃ. Sext. Empir. adv. Log. p. 378, with notes T and U. On this whole subject, vide the Author's "Apologia," notes F and G, pp. 343—363.]

dence by which the world's course is carried on; or, again, for the work of creation itself, as opposed to the absolute perfection of the Eternal God, that internal concentration of His Attributes in self-contemplation, which took place on the seventh day, when He rested from all the work which He had made. And since this everlasting and unchangeable quiescence is the simplest and truest notion we can obtain of the Deity, it seems to follow, that strictly speaking, all those so-called Economies or dispensations, which display His character in action, are but condescensions to the infirmity and peculiarity of our minds, shadowy representations of realities which are incomprehensible to creatures such as ourselves, who estimate everything by the rule of association and arrangement, by the notion of a purpose and plan, object and means, parts and whole. What, for instance, is the revelation of general moral laws, their infringement, their tedious victory, the endurance of the wicked, and the "winking at the times of ignorance," but an "*Economia*" of greater truths untold, the best practical communication of them which our minds in their present state will admit? What are the phenomena of the external world, but a divine mode of conveying to the mind the realities of existence, individuality, and the influence of being on being, the best possible, though beguiling the imagination of most men with a harmless but unfounded belief in matter as distinct from the impressions on their senses? This at least is the opinion of some philosophers, and whether the particular theory be right or wrong, it serves as an illustration here of the great truth which we are considering. Or what, again, as others hold, is the popular argument from final causes but an "*Economia*" suited to the practical wants of the multitude, as teaching them in the simplest way the active presence of Him, who after all dwells intelligibly, prior to argument, in their heart and conscience? And though on the mind's first mastering this general principle, it seems to itself at the moment to have cut all the ties which bind it to the universe, and to be floated off upon the ocean of interminable scepticism; yet a true sense of its own weakness brings it back, the instinctive persuasion that it must be intended to rely on something, and therefore that the information given, though philosophically inaccurate, must be practically certain; a sure confidence in the love of Him who cannot deceive, and who has impressed the image and thought of Himself and of His will upon our original nature. Here then we may lay down with certainty as a consolatory truth, what was but a rule of duty when we were reviewing the Economies of man; viz. that whatever is told us from heaven, is true in so full and substantial a sense, that no possible mistake can arise practically from following it. And it may be added, on the other hand, that the greatest risk will result from attempting to be wiser than God has made us, and to outstep in the least degree the circle which is prescribed as the limit of our range. This is but the duty of implicit faith in Him who knows what is good for us, and who has ordained that in our practical concerns intellectual ability should do no more than enlighten us in the difficulties of our situation, not in the solutions of them. Accordingly, we may safely admit the first chapter of the book of Job, the twenty-second of the first book of Kings, and other passages of Scripture, to be *Economies*, that is, representations conveying substantial truth in the form in which we are best able to receive it; and to be accepted by us and used in their literal sense, as our highest wisdom, because we have no powers of mind equal to the more philosophical determination of them. Again, the Mosaic Dispensation was an Economy, simulating (so to say) unchangeableness, when from the first it was destined to be abolished. And our Blessed Lord's conduct on earth abounds with the like gracious and considerate condescension to the weakness of His creatures, who would have been driven either to a terrified inaction or to presumption, had they known then as afterwards the secret of His Divine Nature.

I will add two or three instances, in which this doctrine of the Divine Economies has been wrongly applied; and I do so from necessity, lest the foregoing remarks should seem to countenance errors, which I am most desirous at all times and every where to protest against.

For instance, the Economy has been employed to the disparagement of the Old Testament Saints; as if the praise bestowed on them by Almighty God were but economically given, that is, with reference to their times and circumstances; their real insight into moral truth being possibly below the average standard of knowledge in matters of faith and practice received among nations rescued from the rude and semi-savage state in which they are considered to have lived. And again, it has been even supposed, that injunctions, as well as praise, have been thus given them, which an enlightened age is at liberty to criticize ; for instance, the command to slay Isaac has sometimes been viewed as an economy, based upon certain received ideas in Abraham's day, concerning the innocence and merit of human sacrifice. It is enough to have thus disclaimed participation in these theories, which of course are no objection to the general doctrine of the Economy, unless indeed it could be shown, that those who hold a principle are answerable for all the applications arbitrarily made of it by the licentious ingenuity of others.

Again, the principle of the Economy has sometimes been applied to the interpretation of the New Testament. It has been said, for instance, that the Epistle to the Hebrews does not state the simple truth in the sense in which the Apostles themselves believed it, but merely as it would be palatable to the Jews. The advocates of this hypothesis have proceeded to maintain, that the doctrine of the Atonement is no part of the essential and permanent evangelical system. To a conscientious reasoner, however, it is evident, that the structure of the Epistle in question is so intimately connected with the reality of the expiatory scheme, that to suppose the latter imaginary, would be to impute to the writer, not an economy (which always preserves substantial truth), but a gross and audacious deceit.

A parallel theory to this has been put forward by men of piety among the Predestinarians, with a view of reconciling the inconsistency between their faith and practice. They have suggested, that the promises and threats of Scripture are founded on an economy, which is needful to effect the conversion of the elect, but clears up and vanishes under the light of the true spiritual perception, to which the converted at length attain. This has been noticed in another connexion, and will here serve as one among many illustrations which might be given, of the fallacious application of a true principle. And so much upon the *Economia.*

5.

A question was just now reserved, as interfering with the subject then before us. In what sense can it be said, that there is any connection between Paganism and Christianity so real, as to warrant the preacher of the latter to conciliate idolaters by allusion to it? St. Paul evidently connects the true religion with the existing systems which he laboured to supplant, in his speech to the Athenians in the Acts, and his example is a sufficient guide to missionaries now, and a full justification of the line of conduct pursued by the Alexandrians, in the instances similar to it; but are we able to account for his conduct, and ascertain the principle by which it was regulated? I think we can; and the exhibition of it will set before the reader another doctrine of the Alexandrian school, which it is as much to our purpose to understand, and which I shall call *the divinity of Traditionary Religion.*

We know well enough for practical purposes what is meant by Revealed Religion; viz. that it is the doctrine taught in the Mosaic and Christian dispensations, and contained in the Holy Scriptures, and is from God in a sense in which no other doctrine can be said to be from Him. Yet if we would speak correctly, we must confess, on the authority of the Bible itself, that all knowledge of religion is from

Him, and not only that which the Bible has transmitted to us. There never was a time when God had not spoken to man, and told him to a certain extent his duty. His injunctions to Noah, the common father of all mankind, is the first recorded fact of the sacred history after the deluge. Accordingly, we are expressly told in the New Testament, that at no time He left Himself without witness in the world, and that in every nation He accepts those who fear and obey Him. It would seem, then, that there is something true and divinely revealed, in every religion all over the earth, overloaded, as it may be, and at times even stifled by the impieties which the corrupt will and understanding of man have incorporated with it. Such are the doctrines of the power and presence of an invisible God, of His moral law and governance, of the obligation of duty, and the certainty of a just judgment, and of reward and punishment, as eventually dispensed to individuals; so that Revelation, properly speaking, is an universal, not a local gift; and the distinction between the state of Israelites formerly and Christians now, and that of the heathen, is, not that we can, and they cannot attain to future blessedness, but that the Church of God ever has had, and the rest of mankind never have had, authoritative documents of truth, and appointed channels of communication with Him. The word and the Sacraments are the characteristic of the elect people of God; but all men have had more or less the guidance of Tradition, in addition to those internal notions of right and wrong which the Spirit has put into the heart of each individual.

This vague and uncertain family of religious truths, originally from God, but sojourning without the sanction of miracle, or a definite home, as pilgrims up and down the world, and discernible and separable from the corrupt legends with which they are mixed, by the spiritual mind alone, may be called the *Dispensation of Paganism*, after the example of the learned Father already quoted[7]. And further, Scripture gives us reason to believe that the traditions, thus originally delivered to mankind at large, have been secretly re-animated and enforced by new communications from the unseen world; though these were not of such a nature as to be produced as evidence, or used as criteria and tests, and roused the attention rather than informed the understandings of the heathen. The book of Genesis contains a record of the Dispensation of Natural Religion, or Paganism, as well as of the patriarchal. The dreams of Pharaoh and Abimelech, as of Nebuchadnezzar afterwards, are instances of the dealings of God with those to whom He did not vouchsafe a written revelation. Or should it be said, that these particular cases merely come within the range of the Divine supernatural Governance which was in their neighbourhood,—an assertion which requires proof,—let the book of Job be taken as a less suspicious instance of the dealings of God with the heathen. Job was a pagan in the same sense in which the Eastern nations are Pagans in the present day. He lived among idolaters[8], yet he and his friends had cleared themselves from the superstitions with which the true creed was beset; and while one of them was

[7] Clement says, Τὴν φιλcσοφίαν Ἕλλησιν οἷον διαθήκην οἰκείαν δεδόσθαι, ὑποβάθραν οὖσαν τῆς κατὰ Χριστὸν φιλοσοφίας. Strom vi. p. 648.

[8] Job xxxi. 26—28.

divinely instructed by dreams[9], he himself at length heard the voice of God out of the whirlwind, in recompense for his long trial and his faithfulness under it[1]. Why should not the book of Job be accepted by us, as a gracious intimation given us, who are God's sons, for our comfort, when we are anxious about our brethren who are still "scattered abroad" in an evil world; an intimation that the Sacrifice, which is the hope of Christians, has its power and its success, wherever men seek God with their whole heart?—If it be objected that Job lived in a less corrupted age than the times of ignorance which followed, Scripture, as if for our full satisfaction, draws back the curtain farther still in the history of Balaam. There a bad man and a heathen is made the oracle of true divine messages about doing justly, and loving mercy, and walking humbly; nay, even among the altars of superstition, the Spirit of God vouchsafes to utter prophecy[2]. And so in the cave of Endor, even a saint was sent from the dead to join the company of an apostate king, and of the sorceress whose aid he was seeking[3]. Accordingly, there is nothing unreasonable in the notion, that there may have been heathen poets and sages, or sibyls again, in a certain extent divinely illuminated, and organs through whom religious and moral truth was conveyed to their countrymen; though their knowledge of the Power from whom the gift came, nay, and their perception of the gift as existing in themselves, may have been very faint or defective.

[9] Ibid. iv. 13, &c.

[1] Job xxxviii. 1; xlii. 10, &c. [Vide also Gen. xli. 45. Exod. iii. 1. Jon. i. 5—16.]

[2] Numb. xxii.—xxiv. Mic. vi. 5–8.

[3] 1 Sam. xxviii. 14.

This doctrine, thus imperfectly sketched, shall now be presented to the reader in the words of St. Clement. "To the Word of God," he says, "all the host of angels and heavenly powers is subject, revealing, as He does, His holy office (*economy*), for Him who has put all things under Him. Wherefore, His are all men; some actually knowing Him, others not as yet: some as friends" (Christians), "others as faithful servants" (Jews), "others as simply servants" (heathen). "He is the Teacher, who instructs the enlightened Christian by mysteries, and the faithful labourer by cheerful hopes, and the hard of heart with His keen corrective discipline; so that His providence is particular, public, and universal. . He it is who gives to the Greeks their philosophy by His ministering Angels . . for He is the Saviour not of these or those, but of all. . . His precepts, both the former and the latter, are drawn forth from one fount; those who were before the Law, not suffered to be without law, those who do not hear the Jewish philosophy, not surrendered to an unbridled course. Dispensing in former times to some His precepts, to others philosophy, now at length, by His own personal coming, He has closed the course of unbelief, which is henceforth inexcusable; Greek and barbarian" (that is, Jew) "being led forward by a separate process to that perfection which is through faith[4]."

If this doctrine be scriptural, it is not difficult to determine the line of conduct which is to be observed by the Christian apologist and missionary. Believing God's hand to be in every system, so far forth as it is true (though Scripture alone is the depositary of His

[4] Clem. Strom. vii. 2.

unadulterated and complete revelation), he will, after St. Paul's manner, seek some points in the existing superstitions as the basis of his own instructions, instead of indiscriminately condemning and discarding the whole assemblage of heathen opinions and practices; and he will address his hearers, not as men in a state of actual perdition, but as being in imminent danger of "the wrath to come," because they are in bondage and ignorance, and probably under God's displeasure, that is, the vast majority of them are so in fact; but not necessarily so, from the very circumstance of their being heathen. And while he strenuously opposes all that is idolatrous, immoral, and profane, in their creed, he will profess to be leading them on to perfection, and to be recovering and purifying, rather than reversing the essential principles of their belief.

A number of corollaries may be drawn from this view of the relation of Christianity to Paganism, by way of solving difficulties which often perplex the mind. For example, we thus perceive the utter impropriety of ridicule and satire as a means of preparing a heathen population for the reception of the truth. Of course it is right, soberly and temperately, to expose the absurdities of idol-worship; but sometimes it is maintained that a writer, such as the infamous Lucian, who scoffs at an established religion altogether, is the suitable preparation for the Christian preacher,—as if infidelity were a middle state between superstition and truth. This view derives its plausibility from the circumstance that in drawing out systems in writing, to erase a false doctrine is the first step towards inserting the true. Accordingly, the mind is often compared to a tablet or paper: a state of it is contemplated of absolute freedom from all prepossessions and likings for one system or another, as a first step towards arriving at the truth; and infidelity represented as that candid and dispassionate frame of mind, which is the desideratum. For instance, at the present day, men are to be found of high religious profession, who, to the surprise and grief of sober minds, exult in the overthrow just now of religion in France, as if an unbeliever were in a more hopeful state than a bigot, for advancement in real spiritual knowledge. But in truth, the mind never can resemble a blank paper, in its freedom from impressions and prejudices. Infidelity is a positive, not a negative state; it is a state of profaneness, pride, and selfishness; and he who believes a little, but encompasses that little with the inventions of men, is undeniably in a better condition than he who blots out from his mind both the human inventions, and that portion of truth which was concealed in them.

Again: it is plain that the tenderness of dealing, which it is our duty to adopt towards a heathen unbeliever, is not to be used towards an apostate. No *economy* can be employed towards those who have been once enlightened, and have fallen away. I wish to speak explicitly on this subject, because there is a great deal of that spurious charity among us which would cultivate the friendship of those who, in a Christian country, speak against the Church or its creeds. Origen and others were not unwilling to be on a footing of intercourse with the heathen philosophers of their day, in order, if it were possible, to lead them into the truth; but deliberate heretics and apostates, those who had known the truth, and rejected it, were objects of their abhorrence, and were avoided from the truest charity to them. For what can be said to those who already know all we have to say? And how can we show our fear for their souls, nay, and for our own steadfastness, except by a strong action? Thus Origen, when a youth, could not be induced to attend the prayers of a heretic of Antioch whom his patroness had adopted, from a loathing[5], as he says, of heresy. And St. Austin himself tells us, that while he was a Manichee, his own mother would not eat at the same table with him in her house, from her strong aversion to the blasphemies which were the characteristic of his sect[6]. And Scripture fully sanctions this mode of acting, by the severity with which such unhappy men are spoken of, on the different occasions when mention is made of them[7].

Further; the foregoing remarks may serve to show us, with what view the early Church cultivated and employed heathen literature in its missionary labours; viz. not with the notion that the cultivation, which literature gives, was any substantial improvement of our moral nature, but as thereby opening the mind, and rendering it susceptible of an appeal; nor as if the heathen literature itself had any direct connexion with the matter of Christianity, but because it contained in it the scattered fragments of those original traditions which might be made the means of introducing a student to the Christian system, being the ore in which the true metal was found. The account above given of the conversion of Gregory is a proof of this.

[5] βδελυττόμενος. Eus. Hist. vi. 2 [vii. 7, Eulog. ap. Phot. p. 861]

[6] Bingham, Antiq. xvi. 2, § 11.

[7] Rom. xvi. 17. 2 Thess. iii. 14. 2 John 10, 11, &c.

The only danger to which the Alexandrian doctrine is exposed, is that of its confusing the Scripture Dispensations with that of Natural Religion, as if they were of equal authority; as if the Gospel had not a claim of acceptance on the conscience of all who heard it, nor became a touchstone of their moral condition; and as if the Bible, as the Pagan system, were but partially true, and had not been attested by the discriminating evidence of miracles. This is the heresy of the Neologians in this day, as it was of the Eclectics in primitive times; as will be shown in the next section. The foregoing extract from Clement shows his entire freedom from so grievous an error; but in order to satisfy any suspicion which may exist of his using language which may have led to a more decided corruption after his day, I will quote a passage from the sixth book of his Stromateis, in which he maintains the supremacy of Revealed Religion, as being in fact the source and test of all other religions; the extreme imperfection of the latter; the derivation of whatever is true in these from Revelation; the secret presence of God in them, by that Word of Life which is directly and bodily revealed in Christianity; and the corruption and yet forced imitation of the truth by the evil spirit in such of them, as he wishes to make pass current among mankind.

"Should it be said that the Greeks discovered philosophy by human wisdom," he says, "I reply, that I find the Scriptures declare all wisdom to be a divine gift: for instance, the Psalmist considers wisdom to be the greatest of gifts, and offers this petition, 'I am thy servant, make me wise.' And does not David ask for illumination in its diverse functions, when he says

'Teach me goodness, discipline, and knowledge, for I have believed Thy precepts'? Here he confesses that the Covenants of God are of supreme authority, and vouchsafed to the choice portion of mankind. Again, there is a Psalm which says of God, 'He hath not acted thus with any other nation, and His judgments He hath not revealed to them;' where the words, 'He hath not done *thus*,' imply that He hath indeed done somewhat, but not *thus*. By using *thus* he contrasts their state with our superiority; else the Prophet might simply have said, 'He hath not acted with other nations,' without adding *thus*. The prophetical figure, 'The Lord is over many waters,' refers to the same truth; that is, a Lord not only of the different covenants, but also of the various methods of teaching, which lead to righteousness, whether among the Gentiles or the Jews. David also bears his testimony to this truth, when he says in the Psalm, 'Let the sinners be turned into hell, all the nations which *forget* God; that is, they forget whom they formerly remembered, they put aside Him whom they knew before they forgot. It seems then there was some dim knowledge of God even among the Gentiles.. They who say that philosophy originates with the devil, would do well to consider what Scripture says about the devil's being transformed into an Angel of light. For what will he do then? it is plain he will prophesy. Now if he prophesies as an Angel of light, of course he will speak what is true. If he shall prophesy angelic and enlightened doctrine, he will prophesy what is profitable also; that is, *at the time when* he is thus changed in his apparent actions, far different as he is at bottom in his real apostasy. For how would he deceive except by craftily leading on the inquirer *by means of truth*, to an intimacy with himself, and so at length seducing him into error? . . Therefore philosophy is not false, though he who is thief and liar speaks truth by a change in his manner of acting. . . The philosophy of the Greeks, limited and particular as it is, contains the rudiments of that really perfect knowledge which is beyond this world, which is engaged in intellectual objects, and upon those more spiritual, which eye hath not seen, nor ear heard, nor the heart of man conceived, before they were made clear to us by our Great Teacher, who reveals the holy of holies, and still holier truths in an ascending scale, to those who are genuine heirs of the Lord's adoption[8]."

6.

What I have said about the method of teaching adopted by the Alexandrian, and more or less by the other primitive Churches, amounts to this; that they on principle refrained from telling unbelievers all they believed themselves, and further, that they endeavoured to connect their own doctrine with theirs, whether Jewish or pagan, adopting their sentiments and even their language, as far as they lawfully could. Some instances of this have been given; more will follow, in the remarks which I shall now make upon the influence of Platonism on their theological language.

The reasons, which induced the early Fathers to avail themselves of the language of Platonism, were various. They did so, partly as an *argumentum ad hominem;* as if the Christian were not professing in the doctrine of the Trinity a more mysterious tenet,

[8] Strom. vi. 8.

than that which had been propounded by a great heathen authority; partly to conciliate their philosophical opponents; partly to save themselves the arduousness of inventing terms, where the Church had not yet authoritatively supplied them; and partly with the hope, or even belief, that the Platonic school had been guided in portions of its system by a more than human wisdom, of which Moses was the unknown but real source. As far as these reasons depend upon the rule of the Economy, they have already been considered; and an instance of their operation given in the exoteric conduct of Athanasius himself, whose orthodoxy no one questions. But the last reason given, their suspicion of the divine origin of the Platonic doctrine, requires some explanation.

It is unquestionable that, from very early times, traditions have been afloat through the world, attaching the notion of a Trinity, in some sense or other, to the First Cause. Not to mention the traces of this doctrine in the classical and the Indian mythologies, we detect it in the Magian hypothesis of a supreme and two subordinate antagonist deities in Plutarch's Trinity of God, matter, and the evil spirit, and in certain heresies in the first age of the Church, which, to the Divine Being and the Demiurgus, added a third original principle, sometimes the evil spirit, and sometimes matter [9]. Plato has adopted the same general notion; and with no closer or more definite approach to the true doctrine. On the whole, it seems reasonable to infer, that the heathen world possessed traditions too ancient to be rejected, and too sacred to

[9] Cudworth, Intell. Syst. i. 4, § 13, 16. Beausobre, Hist. de Manich. iv. 6, § 8, &c.

be used in popular theology. If Plato's doctrine bears a greater apparent resemblance to the revealed truth than that of others, this is owing merely to his reserve in speaking on the subject. His obscurity allows room for an ingenious fancy to impose a meaning upon him. Whether he includes in his Trinity the notion of a First Cause, its active energy, and the influence resulting from it; or again, the divine substance as the source of all spiritual beings from eternity, the divine power and wisdom as exerted in time in the formation of the material world, and thirdly, the innumerable derivative spirits by whom the world is immediately governed, is altogether doubtful. Nay, even the writers who revived his philosophy in the third and fourth centuries after Christ, and embellished the doctrine with additions from Scripture, discover a like extraordinary variation in their mode of expounding it. The Maker of the world, the *Demiurge*, considered by Plato sometimes as the first, sometimes as the second principle, is by Julian placed as the second, by Plotinus as the third, and by Proclus as the fourth, that is, the last of three subordinate powers, all dependent on a First, or the One Supreme Deity [1]. In truth, speculations, vague and unpractical as these, made no impression on the minds of the heathen philosophers, perhaps as never being considered by them as matters of fact, but as allegories and metaphysical notions, and accordingly, caused in them no solicitude or diligence to maintain consistency in their expression of them.

But very different was the influence of the ancient theory of Plato, however originated, when it came in

[1] Petav. Theol. Dogm. tom. ii. i. 1, § 5.

contact with believers in the inspired records, who at once discerned in it that mysterious Doctrine, brought out as if into bodily shape and almost practical persuasiveness, which lay hid under the angelic manifestations of the Law and the visions of the Prophets. Difficult as it is to determine the precise place in the sacred writings, where the Divine Logos or Word was first revealed, and how far He is intended in each particular passage, the idea of Him is doubtless seated very deeply in their teaching. Appearing first as if a mere created minister of God's will, He is found to be invested with an ever-brightening glory, till at length we are bid fall down as before the personal Presence and consubstantial Representative of the one God. Those then, who were acquainted with the Sacred Volume, possessed in it a key, more or less exact according to their degree of knowledge, for that aboriginal tradition which the heathen ignorantly but piously venerated, and were prompt in appropriating the language of philosophers, with a changed meaning, to the rightful service of that spiritual kingdom, of which a divine personal mediation was the great characteristic. In the books of Wisdom and Ecclesiasticus, and much more, in the writings of Philo, the Logos of Plato, which had denoted the divine energy in forming the world, or the Demiurge, and the previous all-perfect incommunicable design of it, or the Only-begotten, was arrayed in the attributes of personality, made the instrument of creation, and the revealed Image of the incomprehensible God. Amid such bold and impatient anticipations of the future, it is not wonderful that the Alexandrian Jews outstepped the truth which they hoped to appropriate; and that intruding into things not seen as yet, with the confidence of prophets rather than of disciples of Revelation, they eventually obscured the doctrine when disclosed, which we may well believe they loved in prospect and desired to honour. This remark particularly applies to Philo, who associating it with Platonic notions as well as words, developed its lineaments with so rude and hasty a hand, as to separate the idea of the Divine Word from that of the Eternal God; and so perhaps to prepare the way for Arianism [2].

Even after this Alexandrino-Judaic doctrine had been corrected and completed by the inspired Apostles St. Paul and St. John, it did not lose its hold upon the Fathers of the Christian Church, who could not but discern in the old Scriptures, even more clearly than their predecessors, those rudiments of the perfect truth which God's former revelations concealed; and who in consequence called others, (as it were,) to gaze upon these both as a prophetical witness in confutation of unbelief, and in gratitude to Him who had wrought so marvellously with His Church. But it followed from the nature of the case, that, while they thus traced with watchful eyes, under the veil of the literal text, the first and gathering tokens of that Divine Agent who in fulness of time became their Redeemer, they were led to speak of Him in terms

[2] This may be illustrated by the theological language of the Paradise Lost, which, as far as the very words go, is conformable both to Scripture and the writings of the early Fathers, but becomes offensive as being dwelt upon as if it were literal, not figurative. It is scriptural to say that the Son went forth from the Father to create the worlds; but when this is made the basis of a scene or pageant, it borders on Arianism. Milton has made Allegory, or the Economy, *real*. Vide infra, ch. ii. § 4, fin.

short of that full confession of His divine greatness, which the Gospel reveals, and which they themselves elsewhere unequivocally expressed, especially as living in times before the history of heresy had taught them the necessity of caution in their phraseology. Thus, for instance, from a text in the book of Proverbs[3], which they understood to refer to Christ, Origen and others speak of Him as "created by the Lord in the beginning, before His works of old;" meaning no more than that it was He, the true Light of man, who was secretly intended by the Spirit, and mystically (though incompletely) described, when Solomon spoke of the Divine Wisdom as the instrument of God's providence and moral governance. In like manner, when Justin speaks of the Son as the minister of God, it is with direct reference to those numerous passages of the Old Testament, in which a ministering angelic presence is more or less characterized by the titles and attributes of Divine Perfection[4]. And, in the use of this emblematical diction they were countenanced (not to mention the Apocalypse) by the almost sacred authority of the platonizing books of Wisdom and Ecclesiasticus; works so highly revered by the Alexandrian Church as to be put into the hands of Catechumens as a preparation for inspired Scripture, contrary to the discipline observed in the neighbouring Church of Jerusalem[5].

The following are additional instances of Platonic language in the early Fathers; though the reader will scarcely perceive at first sight what is the fault in

[3] Prov. viii. 22, Κύριος ἔκτισεν. *Septuag.*

[4] Justin. Apol. i. 63. Tryph. 56, &c.

[5] Bingh. Antiq. x. 1. § 7.

them, unless he happens to know the defective or perverse sense in which philosophy or heresy used them[6]. For instance, Justin speaks of the Word as "fulfilling the Father's will." Clement calls Him[7] "the Thought or Reflection of God;" and in another place, "the Second Principle of all things," the Father Himself being the First. Elsewhere he speaks of the Son as an "all-perfect, all-holy, all-sovereign, all-authoritative, supreme, and all-searching nature, reaching close upon the sole Almighty." In like manner Origen speaks of the Son as being "the immediate Creator, and as it were, Artificer of the world;" and the Father, "the Origin of it, as having committed to His Son its creation." A bolder theology than this of Origen and Clement is adopted by five early writers connected with very various schools of Christian teaching; none of whom, however, are of especial authority in the Church[8]. They explained the Scripture doctrine of the generation of the Word to mean, His manifestation at the beginning of the world as distinct from God; a statement, which, by weakening the force of a dogmatic formula which implies our Lord's Divine Nature, might perhaps lend some accidental countenance after their day to the Arian denial of it. These subjects will come before us in the next chapter.

I have now, perhaps, sufficiently accounted for the apparent liberality of the Alexandrian School; which,

[6] Petav. Theol. Dogm. tom. ii. I. 3, 4.

[7] ἐννόημα.

[8] Theophilus of Antioch (A.D. 168); Tatian, pupil of Justin Martyr (A.D. 169); Athenagoras of Alexandria (A.D. 177); Hippolytus, the disciple

notwithstanding, was strict and uncompromising, when its system is fairly viewed as a whole, and with reference to its objects, and as distinct from that rival and imitative philosophy, to be mentioned in the next section, which rose out of it at the beginning of the third century, and with which it is by some writers improperly confounded. That its principles were always accurately laid, or the conduct of its masters nicely adjusted to them, need not be contended ; or that they opposed themselves with an exact impartiality to every form of error which assailed the Church ; or that they duly entered into and soundly applied the Jewish Scriptures ; or that in conducting the Economy they were altogether free from an ambitious imitation of the Apostles, nobly conceived indeed, but little becoming uninspired teachers. It may unreluctantly be confessed, wherever it can be proved, that their exoteric professions at times affected the purity of their esoteric doctrine, though this remark scarcely applies to their statements on the subject of the Trinity ; and that they indulged a boldness of inquiry, such as innocence prompts, rashness and irreverence corrupt, and experience of its mischievous consequences is alone able to repress. Still all this, and much more than this, were it to be found, weighs as nothing against the mass of testimonies producible from extant documents in favour of the real orthodoxy of their creed. Against a multitude of the very strongest and most explicit declarations of the divinity of Christ, some of which will be cited in their proper

of Irenæus and friend of Origen (A.D. 222) : and the Author who goes under the name of Novatian (A. D. 250). [This is Bull's view ; for that maturely adopted by the author, vide his "Theological Tracts."]

place, but a very few apparent exceptions to the strictest language of technical theology can be gathered from their writings, and these are sufficiently explained by the above considerations. And further, such is the high religious temper which their works exhibit, as to be sufficient of itself to convince the Christian inquirer, that they would have shrunk from the deliberate blasphemy with which Arius in the succeeding century assailed and scoffed at the awful majesty of his Redeemer.

Origen, in particular, that man of strong heart, who has paid for the unbridled freedom of his speculations on other subjects of theology, by the multitude of grievous and unfair charges which burden his name with posterity, protests, by the forcible argument of a life devoted to God's service, against his alleged connexion with the cold disputatious spirit, and the unprincipled domineering ambition, which are the historical badges of the heretical party. Nay, it is a remarkable fact that it was he who discerned the heresy[9] outside the Church on its first rise, and actually gave the alarm, sixty years before Arius's day.

[9] "The Word," says Origen, "being the Image of the Invisible God, must Himself be invisible. Nay, I will maintain further, that as being the Image He is eternal, as the God whose Image He is. For when was that God, whom St. John calls the Light, destitute of the Radiance of His incommunicable glory, so that a man may dare to ascribe a beginning of existence to the Son? . . . Let a man, who dares to say that the Son is not from eternity, consider well, that this is all one with saying, Divine Wisdom had a beginning, or Reason, or Life." Athan. de Decr. Nic. § 27. Vide also his περὶ ἀρχῶν (if Ruffinus may be trusted), for his denouncement of the still more characteristic Arianisms of the ἦν ὅτε οὐκ ἦν and the ἐξ οὐκ ὄντων. [On Origen's disadvantages, vide Lumper Hist. t. x. p. 406, &c.]

Here let it suffice to set down in his vindication the following facts, which may be left to the consideration of the reader;—first, that his habitual hatred of heresy and concern for heretics were such, as to lead him, even when left an orphan in a stranger's house, to withdraw from the praying and teaching of one of them, celebrated for his eloquence, who was in favour with his patroness and other Christians of Alexandria; that all through his long life he was known throughout Christendom as the especial opponent of false doctrine, in its various shapes; and that his pupils, Gregory, Athenodorus, and Dionysius, were principal actors in the arraignment of Paulus, the historical forerunner of Arius;—next, that his speculations, extravagant as they often were, related to points not yet determined by the Church, and, consequently, were really, what he frequently professed them to be, inquiries;—further, that these speculations were for the most part ventured in matters of inferior importance, certainly not upon the sacred doctrines which Arius afterwards impugned, and in regard to which even his enemy Jerome allows him to be orthodox;—that the opinions which brought him into disrepute in his lifetime concerned the creation of the world, the nature of the human soul, and the like;—that his opinions, or rather speculations, on these subjects, were imprudently made public by his friends;—that his writings were incorrectly transcribed even in his lifetime, according to his own testimony;—that after his death, Arian interpolations appear to have been made in some of his works now lost, upon which the subsequent Catholic testimony of his heterodoxy is grounded;—that, on the other hand, in his extant works, the doctrine of the Trinity is clearly avowed, and in particular, our Lord's Divinity energetically and variously enforced ;—and lastly, that in matter of fact, the Arian party does not seem to have claimed him, or appealed to him in self-defence, till thirty years after the first rise of the heresy, when the originators of it were already dead, although they had showed their inclination to shelter themselves behind celebrated names, by the stress they laid on their connexion with the martyr Lucian[1]. But if so much can be adduced in exculpation of Origen from any grave charge of heterodoxy, what accusation can be successfully maintained against his less suspected fellow-labourers in the polemical school ? so that, in concluding this part of the subject, we may with full satisfaction adopt the judgment of Jerome :—" It may be that they erred in simplicity, or that they wrote in another sense, or that their writings were gradually corrupted by unskilful transcribers ; or certainly, before Arius, like 'the sickness that destroyeth in the noon-day,' was born in Alexandria, they made statements innocently and incautiously, which are open to the misinterpretation of the perverse[2]."

[1] Huet. Origen. lib. i. lib.ii. 4. § 1. Bull, Defens. F. N. ii. 9. Waterland's Works, vol. iii. p. 322. Baltus, Défense des Ss. Pères, ii. 20 Tillemont, Mem. vol. iii. p. 259. Socrat. Hist. iv. 26. Athanasius notices the change in the Arian polemics, from mere disputation to an appeal to authority, in his De Sent. Dionys. § 1, written about A.D. 354. οὐδὲν οὔτ' εὔλογον οὔτε πρὸς ἀπόδειξιν ἐκ τῆς θείας γραφῆς ῥητὸν ἐχούσης τῆς αἱρέσεως αὐτῶν, ἀεὶ μὲν προφάσεις ἀναισχύντους ἐπορίζοντο καὶ σοφίσματα πιθανά· νῦν δὲ καὶ διαβάλλειν τοὺς πατέρας τετολμήκασι.

[2] Apolog. adv. Ruffin. ii. Oper. vol. ii. p. 149.

SECTION IV.

THE ECLECTIC SECT.

THE words of St. Jerome, with which the last section closed, may perhaps suggest the suspicion, that the Alexandrians, though orthodox themselves, yet incautiously prepared the way for Arianism by the countenance they gave to the use of the Platonic theological language. But, before speculating on the medium of connexion between Platonism and Arianism, it would be well to ascertain the existence of the connexion itself, which is very doubtful, whether we look for it in history, or in the respective characters of the parties professing the two doctrines; though it is certain that Platonism, and Origenism also, became the excuse and refuge of the heresy when it was condemned by the Church. I proceed to give an account of the rise and genius of Eclecticism, with the view of throwing light upon this question; that is, of showing its relation both to the Alexandrian Church and to Arianism.

I.

The Eclectic philosophy is so called from its professing to select the better parts of the systems invented before it, and to digest these into one consistent doctrine. It is doubtful where the principle of it originated, but it is probably to be ascribed to the Alexandrian Jews. Certain it is, that the true faith never could come into contact with the heathen philosophics, without exercising its right to arbitrate between them, to protest against their vicious or erroneous dogmas, and to extend its countenance to whatever bore an exalted or a practical character. A cultivated taste would be likely to produce among the heathen the same critical spirit which was created by real religious knowledge; and accordingly we find in the philosophers of the Augustan and the succeeding age, an approximation to an eclectic or syncretistic system, similar to that which is found in the writings of Philo. Some authors have even supposed, that Potamo, the original projector of the school based on this principle, flourished in the reign of Augustus; but this notion is untenable, and we must refer him to the age of Severus, at the end of the second century[1]. In the mean time, the Christians had continued to act upon the discriminative view of heathen philosophy which the Philonists had opened; and, as we have already seen, Clement, yet without allusion to particular sect or theory, which did not exist till after his day, declares himself the patron of the Eclectic principle. Thus we are introduced to the history of the School which embodied it.

Ammonius, the contemporary of Potamo, and virtually the founder of the Eclectic sect, was born of

[1] Brucker, Hist. Phil. per. ii. part i. 2, § 4. [Vide Fabric. Bibl. Græc. 3. v. p. 680, ed. Harles.]

Christian parents, and educated as a Christian in the catechetical institutions of Alexandria, under the superintendence of Clement or Pantænus. After a time he renounced, at least secretly, his belief in Christianity; and opening a school of morals and theology on the stock of principles, esoteric and exoteric, which he had learned in the Church, he became the founder of a system really his own, but which by a dexterous artifice he attributed to Plato. The philosophy thus introduced into the world was forthwith patronized by the imperial court, both at Rome and in the East, and spread itself in the course of years throughout the empire, with bitter hostility and serious detriment to the interests of true religion; till at length, obtaining in the person of Julian a second apostate for its advocate, it became the authorized interpretation and apology for the state polytheism. It is a controverted point whether or not Ammonius actually separated from the Church. His disciples affirm it; Eusebius, though not without some immaterial confusion of statement, denies it[2]. On the whole, it is probable that he began his teaching as a Christian, and but gradually disclosed the systematic infidelity on which it was grounded. We are told expressly that he bound his disciples to secrecy, which was not broken till they in turn became lecturers in Rome, and were led one by one to divulge the real doctrines of their master[3]; nor can we otherwise account for the fact of Origen having attended him for a time, since he who refused to hear Paulus of Antioch, even when dependent on the patroness of

[2] Euseb. Hist. Eccl. vi. 19.

[3] Brucker, ibid.

that heretic, would scarcely have extended a voluntary countenance to a professed deserter from the Christian faith and name.

This conclusion is confirmed by a consideration of the nature of the error substituted by Ammonius for the orthodox belief; which was in substance what in these times would be called *Neologism*, a heresy which, even more than others, has shown itself desirous and able to conceal itself under the garb of sound religion, and to keep the form, while it destroys the spirit, of Christianity. So close, indeed, was the outward resemblance between Eclecticism and the Divine system of which it was the deadly enemy, that St. Austin remarks, in more than one passage, that the difference between the two professions lay only in the varied acceptation of a few words and propositions[4]. This peculiar character of the Eclectic philosophy must be carefully noticed, for it exculpates the Catholic Fathers from being really implicated in proceedings, of which at first they did not discern the drift; while it explains that apparent connexion which, at the distance of centuries, exists between them and the real originator of it.

The essential mark of Neologism is the denial of the exclusive divine mission and peculiar inspiration of the Scripture Prophets; accompanied the while with a profession of general respect for them as benefactors of mankind, as really instruments in God's hand, and as in some sense the organs of His revelations; nay, in a fuller measure such, than other religious and moral teachers. In its most specious

[4] Mosheim, Diss. de Turb. per recent. Plat. Eccl. § 12.

form, it holds whatever is good and true in the various religions in the world, to have actually come from God: in its most degraded, it accounts them all equally to be the result of mere human benevolence and skill. In all its shapes, it differs from the orthodox belief, primarily, in denying the miracles of Scripture to have taken place, in the peculiar way therein represented, as distinctive marks of God's presence accrediting the teaching of those who wrought them; next, as a consequence, in denying this teaching, as preserved in Scripture, to be in such sense the sole record of religious truth, that all who hear it are bound to profess themselves disciples of it. Its apparent connexion with Christianity lies (as St. Austin remarks) in the ambiguous use of certain terms, such as *divine*, *revelation*, *inspiration*, and the like; which may with equal ease be made to refer either to ordinary and merely providential, or to miraculous appointments in the counsels of Almighty Wisdom. And these words would be even more ambiguous than at the present day, in an age, when Christians were ready to grant, that the heathen were in some sense under a supernatural Dispensation, as was explained in the foregoing section.

The rationalism of the Eclectics, though equally opposed with the modern to the doctrine of the peculiar divinity of the Scripture revelations, was circumstantially different from it. The Neologists of the present day deny that the miracles took place in the manner related in the sacred record; the Eclectics denied their cogency as an evidence of the extraordinary presence of God. Instead of viewing them as events of very rare occurrence, and permitted for important objects in the course of God's providence, they considered them to be common to every age and country, beyond the knowledge rather than the power of ordinary men, attainable by submitting to the discipline of certain mysterious rules, and the immediate work of beings far inferior to the Supreme Governor of the world. It followed that, a display of miraculous agency having no connexion with the truth of the religious system which it accompanied, at least not more than any gift merely human was connected with it, such as learning or talent, the inquirer was at once thrown upon the examination of the doctrines for the evidence of the divinity of Christianity; and there being no place left for a claim on his allegiance to it as a whole, and for what is strictly termed faith, he admitted or rejected as he chose, compared and combined it with whatever was valuable elsewhere, and was at liberty to propose to himself that philosopher for a presiding authority, whom the Christians did but condescend to praise for his approximation towards some of the truths which Revelation had unfolded. The chapel of Alexander Severus was a fit emblem of that system, which placed on a level Abraham, Orpheus, Pythagoras, and the Sacred Name by which Christians are called. The zeal, the brotherly love, the beneficence, and the wise discipline of the Church, are applauded, and held up for imitation in the letters of the Emperor Julian; who at another time calls the Almighty Guardian of the Israelites a "great God[5]," while in common with his sect he professed to restore the Christian doctrine of the Trinity

[5] Gibbon, Hist. ch. xxiii.

to its ancient and pure Platonic basis. It followed as a natural consequence, that the claims of religion being no longer combined, defined, and embodied in a personal Mediator between God and man, its various precepts were dissipated back again and confused in the mass of human knowledge, as before Christ came; and in its stead a mere intellectual literature arose in the Eclectic School, and usurped the theological chair as an interpreter of sacred duties, and the instructor of the inquiring mind. "In the religion which he (Julian) had adopted," says Gibbon, "piety and learning were almost synonymous; and a crowd of poets, of rhetoricians, and of philosophers, hastened to the Imperial Court, to occupy the vacant places of the bishops, who had seduced the credulity of Constantius[6]." Who does not recognize in this old philosophy the chief features of that recent school of liberalism and false illumination, political and moral, which is now Satan's instrument in deluding the nations, but which is worse and more earthly than it, inasmuch as his former artifice, affecting a religious ceremonial, could not but leave so much of substantial truth mixed in the system as to impress its disciples with somewhat of a lofty and serious character, utterly foreign to the cold, scoffing spirit of modern rationalism?

The freedom of the Alexandrian Christians from the Eclectic error was shown above, when I was explaining the principles of their teaching; a passage of Clement being cited, which clearly distinguished between the ordinary and the miraculous appointments of Providence. An examination of the dates

[6] Ibid.

of the history will show that they could not do more than bear this indirect testimony against it by anticipation. Clement himself was prior to the rise of Eclecticism; Origen, prior to its public establishment as a sect. Ammonius opened his school at the end of the second century, and continued to preside in it at least till A.D. 243[7]; during which period, and probably for some years after his death, the real character of his doctrines was carefully hidden from the world. He committed nothing to writing, whether of his exoteric or esoteric philosophy, and when Origen, who was scarcely his junior, attended him in his first years, probably had not yet decidedly settled the form of his system. Plotinus, the first promulgator and chief luminary of Eclecticism, began his public lectures A.D. 244; and for some time held himself bound by the promise of secrecy made to his master. Moreover, he selected Rome as the seat of his labours, and there is even proof that Origen and he never met. In Alexandria, on the contrary, the infant philosophy languished; no teacher of note succeeded to Ammonius; and even had it been otherwise, Origen had left the city for ever, ten years previous to that philosopher's death. It is clear, then, that he had no means of detecting the secret infidelity of the Eclectics; and the proof of this is still stronger, if, as Brucker calculates[8], Plotinus did not divulge his master's secret till A.D. 255, since Origen died A.D. 253. Yet, even in this ignorance of the purpose of the Eclectics, we find Origen, in his letter to Gregory expressing

[7] Fabric. Biblioth. Græc. Harles. iv. 29.

[8] Brucker, ibid.

dissatisfaction at the actual effects which had resulted to the Church from that literature in which he himself was so eminently accomplished. "For my part," he says to Gregory, "taught by experience, I will own to you, that rare is the man, who, having accepted the precious things of Egypt, leaves the country, and uses them in decorating the worship of God. Most men who descend thither are brothers of Hadad (Jeroboam), inventing heretical theories with heathen dexterity, and establishing (so to say) calves of gold in Bethel, the house of God[9]." So much concerning Origen's ignorance of the Eclectic philosophy. As to his pupils, Gregory and Dionysius, the latter, who was Bishop of Alexandria, died A.D. 264; Gregory, on the other hand, pronounced his panegyrical oration upon Origen, in which his own attachment to heathen literature is avowed, as early as A.D. 239; and besides, he had no connexion whatever with Alexandria, having met with Origen at Cæsarea[1]. Moreover, just at this time there were heresies actually spreading in the Church of an opposite theological character, such as Paulianism; which withdrew their attention from the prospect or actual rise of a Platonic pseudo-theology; as will hereafter be shown.

Such, then, were the origin and principles of the Eclectic sect. It was an excrescence of the school of Alexandria, but not attributable to it, except as other heresies may be ascribed to other Churches, which give them birth indeed, but cast them out and condemn them when they become manifest. It went out from the

[9] Orig. Ep. ad Gregor. § 2.

[1] Tillemont, vol. iv. Chronolog.

Christians, but it was not of them :—whether it resembled the Arians, on the other hand, and what use its tenets were to them, are the next points to consider.

2.

The Arian school has already been attributed to Antioch as its birth-place, and its character determined to be what we may call Aristotelico-Judaic. Now, at very first sight, there are striking points of difference between it and the Eclectics. On its Aristotelic side, its disputatious temper was altogether uncongenial to the new Platonists. These philosophers were commonly distinguished by their melancholy temperament, which disposed them to mysticism, and often urged them to eccentricities bordering on insanity[2]. Far from cultivating the talents requisite for success in life, they placed the sublimer virtues in an abstraction from sense, and an indifference to ordinary duties. They believed that an intercourse with the intelligences of the spiritual world could only be effected by divesting themselves of their humanity ; and that the acquisition of miraculous gifts would compensate for their neglect of rules necessary for the well-being of common mortals. In pursuit of this hidden talent, Plotinus meditated a journey into India, after the pattern of Apollonius ; while bodily privations and magical rites were methods prescribed in their philosophy for rising in the scale of being. As might be expected from the professors of such a creed, the science of argumentation was disdained, as beneath the regard of those who were walking by an internal vision

[2] Brucker, supra.

of the truth, not by the calculations of a tedious and progressive reason; and was only employed in condescending regard for such as were unable to rise to their own level. When Iamblichus was foiled in argument by a dialectician, he observed that the syllogisms of his sect were not weapons which could be set before the many, being the energy of those inward virtues which are the peculiar ornament of the philosopher. Notions such as these, which have their measure of truth, if we substitute for the unreal and almost passive illumination of the mystics, that instinctive moral perception which the practice of virtue ensures, found no sympathy in the shrewd secular policy and the intriguing spirit of the Arians; nor again, in their sharp-witted unimaginative cleverness, their precise and technical disputations, their verbal distinctions, and their eager appeals to the judgment of the populace, which is ever destitute of refinement and delicacy, and has just enough acuteness of apprehension to be susceptible of sophistical reasonings.

On the other hand, viewing the school of Antioch on its judaical side, we are met by a different but not less remarkable contrast to the Eclectics. These philosophers had followed the Alexandrians in adopting the allegorical rule; both from its evident suitableness to their mystical turn of mind, and as a means of obliterating the scandals and reconciling the inconsistencies of the heathen mythology. Judaism, on the contrary, being carnal in its views, was essentially literal in its interpretations; and, in consequence, as hostile from its grossness, as the Sophists from their dryness, to the fanciful fastidiousness of the Eclectics. It had rejected the Messiah, because He did not fulfil its hopes of a temporal conqueror and king. It had clung to its obsolete ritual, as not discerning in it the anticipation of better promises and commands, then fulfilled in the Gospel. In the Christian Church, it was perpetuating the obstinacy of its unbelief in a disparagement of Christ's spiritual authority, a reliance on the externals of religious worship, and an indulgence in worldly and sensual pleasures. Moreover, it had adopted in its most odious form the doctrine of the Chiliasts or Millenarians, respecting the reign of the saints upon earth, a doctrine which Origen, and afterwards his pupil Dionysius, opposed on the basis of an allegorical interpretation of Scripture[3]. And in this controversy, Judaism was still in connexion, more or less, with the school of Antioch; which is celebrated in those times, in contrast to the Alexandrian, for its adherence to the theory of the literal sense[4].

It may be added, as drawing an additional distinction between the Arians and the Eclectics, that while the latter maintained the doctrine of Emanations, and of the eternity of matter, the hypothesis of the former required or implied the rejection of both tenets; so that the philosophy did not even furnish the argumentative foundation of the heresy, to which its theology outwardly bore a partial resemblance.

3.

But in seasons of difficulty men look about on all sides for support; and Eclecticism, which had no

[3] Mosh. de Rebus ante Const. Sæc. iii. c. 38.

[4] Conybeare, Bampt. Lect. iv. Orig. Opp. ed. Benedict. vol. ii. præf.

attractions for the Sophists of Antioch while their speculations were unknown to the world at large, became a seasonable refuge (as we learn from various authors[5]), in the hands of ingenious disputants, when pressed by the numbers and authority of the defenders of orthodoxy. First, there was an agreement between the Schools of Ammonius and of Paulus, in the cardinal point of an inveterate opposition to the Catholic doctrine of our Lord's Divinity. The judaizers admitted at most only His miraculous conception. The Eclectics, honouring Him as a teacher of wisdom, still, far from considering Him more than man, were active in preparing from the heathen sages rival specimens of holiness and power. Next, the two parties agreed in rejecting from their theology all mystery, in the ecclesiastical notion of the word. The Trinitarian hypothesis of the Eclectics was not perplexed by any portion of that difficulty of statement which, in the true doctrine, results from the very incomprehensibility of its subject. They declared their belief in a sublime tenet, which Plato had first propounded and the Christians corrupted; but their Three Divine Principles were in no sense one, and, while essentially distinct from each other, there was a successive subordination of nature in the second and the third[6]. In such speculations the judaizing Sophist found the very desideratum which he in vain demanded of the Church; a scripturally-worded creed, without its accompanying difficulty of conception.

[5] Vide Brucker, Hist. Phil. per. ii. part ii. i. 2. § 8. Baltus, Défense des Pères, ii. 19.

[6] ἀρχικαὶ ὑποστάσεις. Cudworth, Intell. Syst. i. 4 § 36.

Accordingly, to the doctrine thus put into his hands he might appeal by way of contrast, as fulfilling his just demands; nay, in proportion as he out-argued and unsettled the faith of his Catholic opponent, so did he open a way, as a matter of necessity and without formal effort, for the perverted creed of that philosophy which had so mischievously anticipated the labours and usurped the office of an ecclesiastical Synod.

And, further, it must be observed, that, when the Sophist had mastered the Eclectic theology, he had in fact a most powerful weapon to mislead or to embarrass his Catholic antagonist. The doctrine which Ammonius professed to discover in the Church, and to reclaim from the Christians, was employed by the Arian as if the testimony of the early Fathers to the truth of the heretical view which he was maintaining. What was but incaution, or rather unavoidable liberty, in the Ante-Nicene theology, was insisted on as apostolic truth. Clement and Origen, already subjected to a perverse interpretation, were witnesses provided by the Eclectics by anticipation against orthodoxy. This express appeal to the Alexandrian writers, seems, in matter of fact, to have been reserved for a late period of the controversy; but from the first an advantage would accrue to the Arians, by their agreement (as far as it went) with received language in the early Church. Perplexity and doubt were thus necessarily introduced into the minds of those who only heard the rumour of the discussion, and even of many who witnessed it, and who, but for this apparent primitive sanction, would have shrunk from the bold, irreverent inquiries and the idle subtleties which are the tokens of the genuine Arian temper. Nor was the allegorical principle of Eclecticism incompatible with the instruments of the Sophist. This also in the hands of a dexterous disputant, particularly in attack, would become more serviceable to the heretical than to the orthodox cause. For, inasmuch as the Arian controversialist professed to be asking for reasons why he should believe our Lord's divinity, an answer based on allegorisms did not silence him, while at the same time, it suggested to him the means of thereby evading those more argumentative proofs of the Catholic doctrine, which are built upon the explicit and literal testimonies of Scripture. It was notoriously the artifice of Arius, which has been since more boldly adopted by modern heretics, to explain away its clearest declarations by a forced figurative exposition. Here that peculiar subtlety in the use of language, in which his school excelled, supported and extended the application of the allegorical rule, recommended, as it was, to the unguarded believer, and forced upon the more wary, by its previous reception on the part of the most illustrious ornaments and truest champions of the Apostolic faith.

But after all there is no sufficient evidence in history that the Arians did make this use of Neo-Platonism[7],

[7] There seems to have been a much earlier coalition between the Platonic and Ebionitish doctrines, if the works attributed to the Roman Clement may be taken in evidence of it. Mosheim (de Turb. Eccl. § 34) says both the Recognitions and Clementines are infected with the latter, and the Clementines with the former doctrine. These works were written between A.D. 180 and A.D. 250: are they to be referred to the school of Theodotus and Artemon, which was humanitarian and Roman, expressly claimed the *Bishops* of Rome as countenancing its errors, and falsified the Scriptures at least? Plotinus came to Rome A.D. 244, and Philostratus com-

considered as a party. I believe they did not, and from the facts of the history should conclude Eusebius of Cæsarea alone to be favourable to that philosophy: but some persons may attach importance to the circumstance, that Syria was one of its chief seats from its very first appearance. The virtuous and amiable Alexander Severus openly professed its creed in his Syrian court, and in consequence of this profession, extended his favour to the Jewish nation. Zenobia, a Jewess in religion, succeeded Alexander in her taste for heathen literature, and attachment to the syncretistic philosophy. Her instructor in the Greek language, the celebrated Longinus, had been the pupil of Ammonius, and was the early master of Porphyry, the most bitter opponent of Christianity that issued from the Eclectic school. Afterwards, Amelius, the friend and successor of Plotinus, transferred the seat of the philosophy from Rome to Laodicea in Syria; which became remarkable for the number and fame of its Eclectics[8]. In the next century, Iamblicus and Libanius, the friend of Julian, both belonged to the Syrian branch of the sect. It is remarkable that, in the mean time, its Alexandrian branch declined in reputation on the death of Ammonius; probably, in consequence of the hostility it met with from the Church which had the misfortune to give it birth.

menced his life of Apollonius there as early as A.D. 217. This would account for the Platonism of the latter of the two compositions, and its absence from the earlier.

[8] Mosheim, Diss. de Turb. Eccl. § 11.

SECTION V.

SABELLIANISM.

ONE subject more must be discussed in illustration of the conduct of the Alexandrian school, and the circumstances under which the Arian heresy rose and extended itself. The Sabellianism which preceded it has often been considered the occasion of it;—viz. by a natural reaction from one error into its opposite; to separate the Father from the Son with the Arians, being the contrary heresy to that of confusing them together after the manner of the Sabellians. Here however, Sabellianism shall be considered neither as the proximate nor the remote cause, or even occasion, of Arianism; but first, as drawing off the attention of the Church from the prospective evil of the philosophical spirit; next, as suggesting such reasonings, and naturalizing such expressions and positions in the doctrinal statements of the orthodox, as seemed to countenance the opposite error; lastly, as providing a sort of justification of the Arians, when they first showed themselves;—that is, Sabellianism is here regarded as facilitating rather than originating the disturbances occasioned by the Arian heresy.

1.

The history of the heresy afterwards called Sabellian

is obscure. Its peculiar tenet is the denial of the distinction of Persons in the Divine Nature; or the doctrine of the *Monarchia*, as it is called by an assumption of exclusive orthodoxy, like that which has led to the term "Unitarianism" at the present day[1]. It was first maintained as a characteristic of party by a school established (as it appears) in Proconsular Asia, towards the end of the second century. This school, of which Noetus was the most noted master, is supposed to be an offshoot of the Gnostics; and doubtless it is historically connected with branches of that numerous family. Irenæus is said to have written against it; which either proves its antiquity, or seems to imply its origination in those previous Gnostic systems, against which his extant work is entirely directed[2]. It may be added, that Simon Magus, the founder of the Gnostics, certainly held a doctrine resembling that advocated by the Sabellians.

At the end of the second century, Praxeas, a presbyter of Ephesus, passed from the early school already mentioned to Rome. Meeting there with that determined resistance which honourably distinguishes the primitive Roman Church in its dealings with heresy, he retired into Africa, and there, as founding no sect, he was soon forgotten. However, the doubts and speculations which he had published, concerning the great doctrine in dispute, remained alive in that part of the world, though latent[3], till they burst into a

[1] Burton, Bampt. Lect. note 103. [The word Μοναρχία was adopted in opposition to the three ἀρχικαὶ ὑποστάσεις of the Eclectics; vide supra p. 112.]

[2] Dodwell in Iren. Diss. vi. 26.

[3] Tertull. in Prax. [It is not certain Praxeas was detected at Rome.]

flame about the middle of the third century, at the eventful era when the rudiments of Arianism were laid by the sophistical school at Antioch.

The author of this new disturbance was Sabellius, from whom the heresy has since taken its name. He was a bishop or presbyter in Pentapolis, a district of Cyrenaica, included within the territory afterwards called, and then virtually forming, the Alexandrian Patriarchate. Other bishops in his neighbourhood adopting his sentiments, his doctrine became so popular among a clergy already prepared for it, or hitherto unpractised in the necessity of a close adherence to the authorized formularies of faith, that in a short time (to use the words of Athanasius) "the Son of God was scarcely preached in the Churches." Dionysius of Alexandria, as primate, gave his judgment in writing; but being misunderstood by some orthodox but over-zealous brethren, he in turn was accused by them, before the Roman See, of advocating the opposite error, afterwards the Arian; and in consequence, instead of checking the heresy, found himself involved in a controversy in defence of his own opinions[4]. Nothing more is known concerning the Sabellians for above a hundred years; when it is inferred from the fact that the Council of Constantinople (A.D. 381) rejected their baptism, that they formed at that time a communion distinct from the Catholic Church.

Another school of heresy also denominated Sabellian, is obscurely discernible even earlier than the Ephesian, among the Montanists of Phrygia. The well-known doctrine of these fanatics, when adopted

[4] Vide Athan. de Sent. Dionys.

by minds less heated than its original propagators, evidently tended to a denial of the Personality of the Holy Spirit, Montanus himself probably was never capable of soberly reflecting on the meaning of his own words; but even in his lifetime, Æschines, one of his disciples, saw their real drift, and openly maintained the unreserved *monarchia* of the Divine Nature[5]. Hence it is usual for ancient writers to class the Sabellians and Montanists together, as if coinciding in their doctrinal views[6]. The success of Æschines in extending his heresy in Asia Minor was considerable, if we may judge from the condition of that country at a later period.—Gregory, the pupil of Origen, appears to have made a successful stand against it in Pontus. Certainly his writings were employed in the controversy after his death, and that with such effect, as completely to banish it from that country, though an attempt was made to revive it in the time of Basil (A.D. 375[7]).—In the patriarchate of Antioch we first hear of it at the beginning of the third century, Origen reclaiming from it Beryllus, Bishop of Bostra, in Arabia. In the next generation the martyr Lucian is said to have been a vigorous opponent of it; and he was at length betrayed to his heathen persecutors by a Sabellian presbyter of the Church of Antioch. At a considerably later date (A.D. 375) we hear of it in Mesopotamia[8].

At first sight it may seem an assumption to refer these various exhibitions of heterodoxy in Asia Minor,

[5] Tillemont, Mem. vol. ii. p. 204.

[6] Vales. ad Socr. i. 23 Soz. ii. 18.

[7] Basil. Epist. ccx. § 3.

[8] Epiphan. Hær. lxii. 1.

and the East, to some one school or system, merely on the ground of their distinguishing tenet being substantially the same. And certainly, in treating an obscure subject, on which the opinions of learned men differ, it must be owned that conjecture is the utmost that I am able to offer. The following statement will at once supply the grounds on which the above arrangement has been made, and explain the real nature of the doctrine itself in which the heresy consisted[9].

Let it be considered then, whether there were not two kinds of Sabellianism; the one taught by Praxeas, the other somewhat resembling, though less material than, the theology of the Gnostics :—the latter being a modification of the former, arising from the pressure of the controversy: for instance, parallel to the change which is said to have taken place in the doctrine of the Ebionites, and in that of the followers of Paulus of Samosata. Those who denied the distinction of Persons in the Divine Nature were met by the obvious inquiry, in what sense they believed God to be united to the human nature of Christ. The more orthodox, but the more assailable answer to this question, was to confess that God was, in such sense, one Person with Christ, as (on their Monarchistic principle) to be in no sense distinct from Him. This was the more orthodox answer, as preserving inviolate what is theologically called the doctrine of the hypostatic union,—the only safeguard against a gradual declension into the Ebionite, or modern Socinian heresy. But at the same time such an answer was repugnant to the plainest suggestions of scripturally-

[9] [Vid. Athan. Transl. vol. ii. p. 377.

enlightened reason, which leads us to be sure that, according to the obvious meaning of the inspired text, there is *some* real sense in which the Father is not the Son; that the Sender and the Sent cannot be in all respects the same; nor can the Son be said to make Himself inferior to the Father, and condescend to become man,—to come from God, and then again to return to Him,—if, after all, there is no distinction beyond that of words, between those Blessed and Adorable Agents in the scheme of our redemption. Besides, without venturing to intrude into things not as yet seen, it appeared evident to the primitive Church, that, in matter of fact, the Son of God, though equal in dignity of nature to the Father, and One with Him in essence, was described in Scripture as undertaking such offices of ministration and subjection, as are never ascribed, and therefore may not without blasphemy be ascribed, to the self-existent Father. Accordingly, the name of Patripassian was affixed to Praxeas, Noetus, and their followers, in memorial of the unscriptural tenet which was immediately involved in their denial of the distinction of Persons in the Godhead.

Such doubtless was the doctrine of Sabellius, if regard be paid to the express declarations of the Fathers. The discriminating Athanasius plainly affirms it, in his defence of Dionysius[1]. The Semi-Arian Creed called the Macrostich, published at Antioch, gives a like testimony[2]; distinguishing, moreover,

[1] De Sent. Dionys. § 5. 9, &c. [Orat. iii. 36. Origen. in Ep. ad. Tit. t. iv. p. 695: "Duos definimus, ne (ut vestra perversitas infert) Pater ipse credatur natus et passus." Tertull. adv. Prax. 13.]

[2] Athan de Synod. § 26.

between the Sabellian doctrine, and the doctrines of the Paulianists and Photinians, to which some modern critics have compared it. Cyprian and Austin, living in Africa, bear express witness to the existence of the Patripassian sect[3]. On the other hand, it cannot be denied, that authorities exist favourable to a view of the doctrine different from the above, and these accordingly may lead us, in agreement with certain theological writers[4], without interfering with the account of the heresy already given, to describe a modification of it which commonly succeeded to its primitive form.

The following apparently inconsistent testimonies, suggest both the history and the doctrine of this second form of Sabellianism. While the Montanists and Sabellians are classed together by some authors, there is separate evidence of the connexion of each of these with the Gnostics. Again, Ambrosius, the convert and friend of Origen was originally a Valentinian, or Marcionite, or Sabellian, according to different writers. Further, the doctrine of Sabellius is compared to that of Valentinus by Alexander of Alexandria, and (apparently) by a Roman Council (A.D. 324); and by St. Austin it is referred indifferently to Praxeas, or to Hermogenes, a Gnostic. On the other hand, one Leucius is described as a Gnostic and Montanist[5]. It would appear then, that it is so repugnant to the plain word of Scripture, and to the

[3] Cyprian. Epist. lxxiii. Tillemont, Mem. iv. 100.

[4] Beausobre, Hist. de Manich. iii. 6. § 7. Mosheim, de Reb. ant. Const. sæc. ii. § 68; sæc. iii. § 32. Lardner, Cred. part ii. ch. 41.

[5] Vide Tillemont, vol. ii. p. 204; iv. p. 100, &c. Waterland's Works, vol. i. p. 236, 237.

most elementary notions of doctrine thence derived, to suppose that Almighty God is in every sense one with the human nature of Christ, that a disputant, especially an innovator, cannot long maintain such a position. It removes the mystery of the Trinity, only by leaving the doctrine of the Incarnation in a form still more strange, than that which it unavoidably presents to the imagination. Pressed, accordingly, by the authority of Scripture, the Sabellian, instead of speaking of the substantial union of God with Christ, would probably begin to obscure his meaning in the decorum of a figurative language. He would speak of the presence rather than the existence of God in His chosen servant; and this presence, if allowed to declaim, he would represent as a certain power or emanation from the Centre of light and truth; if forced by his opponent into a definite statement, he would own to be but an inspiration, the same in kind, though superior in degree, with that which enlightened and guided the prophets. This is that second form of the Sabellian tenet, which some learned moderns have illustrated, though they must be considered to err in pronouncing it the only true one. That it should have resulted from the difficulties of the Patripassian creed, is natural and almost necessary; and viewed merely as a conjecture, the above account of its rise reconciles the discordant testimonies of ecclesiastical history. But we have almost certain evidence of the matter of fact in Tertullian's tract against Praxeas[6], in which the latter is apparently represented as holding successively, the two views of doctrine which have been here described. Parallel instances meet us in

[6] In Prax. §. 27.

the history of the Gnostics and Montanists. Simon Magus, for instance, seems to have adopted the Patripassian theory. But the Gnostic family which branched from him, modified it by means of their doctrine of emanations or æons, till in the theology of Valentinus, as in that of Cerinthus and Ebion, the incarnation of the Word, became scarcely more than the display of Divine Power with a figurative personality in the life and actions of a mere man. The Montanists, in like manner, from a virtual assumption of the Divinity of their founder, were led on, as the only way of extricating themselves from one blasphemy, into that other of denying the Personality of the Holy Spirit, and then of the Word. Whether the school of Noetus maintained its first position, we have no means of knowing ; but the change to the second, or semi-humanitarian, may be detected in the Sabellians, as in Praxeas before them. In the time of Dionysius of Alexandria, the majority was Patripassian ; but in the time of Alexander they advocated the Emanative, as it may be called, or in-dwelling theory[7].

2.

What there is further to be said on this subject shall be reserved for the next chapter. Here, however, it is necessary to examine, how, under these circumstances, the controversy with the Sabellians would affect the language of ecclesiastical theology. It will be readily seen, that the line of argument by which the two errors above specified are to be met, is nearly the same : viz. that of insisting upon the

[7] Theod. Hist. i. 4.

personality of the Word as distinct from the Father. For the Patripassian denied that the Word was in any real respect distinct from Him; the Emanatist, if he may so be called, denied that He was a Person, or more than an extraordinary manifestation of Divine Power. The Catholics, on the other hand, asserted His distinct personality; and necessarily appealed, in proof of this, to such texts as speak of His pre-existent relations towards the Father; in other words, His ministrative office in the revealed Economy of the Godhead. And thus, being obliged from the course of the controversy, to dwell on this truly scriptural tenet, and happening to do so without a protest against a denial, as if involved in it, of His equality with the Father in the One Indivisible Divine Nature (a protest, which nothing but the actual experience of that denial among them could render necessary or natural), they were sometimes forced by the circumstances of the case into an apparent anticipation of the heresy, which afterwards arose in the shape of Arianism.

This may be illustrated in the history of the two great pupils of Origen, who, being respectively opposed to the two varieties of Sabellianism above described, the Patripassian and the Emanative, incurred odium in a later age, as if they had been forerunners of Arius: Gregory of Neocæsarea, and Dionysius of Alexandria.

The controversy in which Dionysius was engaged with the Patripassians of Pentapolis has already been adverted to. Their tenet of the incarnation of the Father (that is, of the one God without distinction of Persons), a tenet most repugnant to every scripturally-informed mind, was refuted at once, by insisting on the essential character of the Son as representing and revealing the Father; by arguing, that on the very face of Scripture, the Christ who is there set before us, (whatever might be the mystery of His nature,) is certainly delineated as one absolute and real Person, complete in Himself, sent by the Father, doing His will, and mediating between Him and man; and that, this being the case, His Person could not be the same with that of the Father, who sent Him, by any process of reasoning, which would not also prove any two individual men to have one literal personality; that is, if there be any analogy at all between the ordinary sense of the word "person" and that in which the idea is applied in Scripture to the Father and the Son: for instance, by what artifice of interpretation can the beginning of St. John's Gospel, or the second chapter of St. Paul's Epistle to the Philippians be made to harmonize with the notion, that the one God, simply became and is man, in every sense in which He can still be spoken of as God?

Writing zealously and freely on this side of the Catholic doctrine, Dionysius laid himself open to the animadversion of timid and narrow-minded men, who were unwilling to receive the truth in that depth and fulness in which Scripture reveals it, and who thought that orthodoxy consisted in being at all times careful to comprehend in one phrase or formula the whole of what is believed on any article of faith. The Roman Church, even then celebrated for its vigilant, perhaps its over earnest exactness, in matters of doctrine and discipline, was made the arbiter of the controversy. A council was held under the presidency of Dionysius its Bishop (about A.D. 260), in which the Alexandrian prelate was accused by the Pentapolitans of asserting that the Son of God is made and created, distinct in nature from the incommunicable essence of the Father, "as the vine is distinct from the vine-dresser," and in consequence, not eternal. The illustration imputed to Dionysius in this accusation, being a reference to our Lord's words in the fifteenth chapter of St. John, is a sufficient explanation by itself of the real drift of his statement, even if his satisfactory answer were not extant, to set at rest all doubt concerning his orthodoxy. In that answer, addressed to his namesake of Rome, he observes first, that his letter to the Sabellians, being directed against a particular error, of course contained only so much of the entire Catholic doctrine as was necessary for the refutation of that error;—that his use of the words "Father and Son," in itself implied his belief in a oneness of nature between Them;—that in speaking of the Son as "made," he had no intention of distinguishing "made" from "begotten," but, including all kinds of origination under the term, he used it to discriminate between the Son and His underived self-originating Father;—lastly, that in matter of fact he did confess the Catholic doctrine in its most unqualified and literal sense, and in its fullest and most accurate exposition. In this letter he even recognizes the celebrated *Homoüsion (consubstantial)* which was afterwards adopted at Nicæa. However, in spite of these avowals, later writers, and even Basil himself, do not scruple to complain of Dionysius as having sown the first seeds of Arianism; Basil confessing the while that his error was accidental, occasioned by his vehement opposition to the Sabellian heresy.

Gregory of Neocæsarea, on the other hand, is so far more hardly circumstanced than Dionysius, first, inasmuch as the charge against him was not made till after his death, and next, because he is strangely accused of a tendency to Sabellian as well as Arian errors. Without accounting for the former of these charges, which does not now concern us, I offer to the reader the following explanation of the latter calumny. Sabellianism, in its second or emanative form, had considerable success in the East before and at the date of Gregory. In the generation before him, Hermogenes, who professed it, had been refuted by Theophilus and Tertullian, as well as by Gregory's master, Origen, who had also reclaimed from a similar error Ambrosius and Beryllus[8]. Gregory succeeded him in the controversy with such vigour, that his writings were sufficient to extinguish the heresy, when it reappeared in Pontus at a later period. He was, moreover, the principal bishop in the first Council held against Paulus of Samosata, whose heresy was derived from the emanative school. The Synodal Letter addressed by the assembled bishops to the heresiarch, whether we ascribe it to this first Council, with some critics, or with others to the second, or even with Basnage reject it as spurious, at least illustrates the line of argument which it was natural to direct against the heresy, and shows how easily it might be corrupted into an Arian meaning. To the notion that the Son was but inhabited by a divine power or presence impersonal, and therefore had no real existence before He came in the flesh, it was a sufficient answer to appeal to the

[8] Euseb. Hist. iv. 24. Theod. Hær. i. 19. Tertull. in Hermog. Huet. Origen, lib. i.

great works ascribed to Him in the beginning of all things, and especially to those angelic manifestations by which God revealed Himself to the elder Church, and which were universally admitted to be representations of the Living and Personal Word. The Synodal Letter accordingly professes a belief in the Son, as the Image and Power of God, which was before the worlds, in absolute existence, the living and intelligent Cause of creation; and cites some of the most striking texts descriptive of His ministrative office under the Jewish law, such as His appearance to Abraham and Jacob, and to Moses in the burning bush[9]. Such is the statement, in opposition to Paulus of Samosata, put forth by Gregory and his associate bishops at Antioch; and, the circumstances of the controversy being overlooked, it is obvious how easily it may be brought to favour the hypothesis, that the Son is in all respects distinct from the Father, and by nature as well as in revealed office inferior to Him.

Lastly, it so happened, that in the course of the third century, the word *Homoüsion* became more or less connected with the Gnostic, Manichæan, and Sabellian theologies. Hence early writers, who had but opposed these heresies, seemed in a subsequent age to have opposed what had been by that time received as the characteristic of orthodoxy; as, on the other hand, the Catholics, on their adopting it in that later age, were accused of what in an earlier time would have been the Sabellian error, or again of the introduction of corporeal notions into their creed. But of this more hereafter.

[9] Routh, Reliq. Sacr. vol. ii. p. 463

Here a close may be put to our inquiry into the circumstances under which Arianism appeared in the early Church. The utmost that has been proposed has been to classify and arrange phenomena which present themselves on the surface of the history; and this, with a view of preparing the reader for the direct discussion of the doctrine which Arianism denied, and for the proceedings on the part of the Church which that denial occasioned. Especially has it been my object in this introduction, following the steps of our great divines, to rescue the Alexandrian Fathers from the calumnies which, with bad intentions either to them or to the orthodox cause, have been so freely and so fearlessly cast upon them. Whether Judaism or whether Platonism had more or less to do in preparing the way for the Arian heresy, are points of minor importance, compared with the vindication of those venerable men, the most learned, most eloquent, and most zealous of the Ante-Nicene Christians. With this view it has been shown above, that, though the heresy openly commenced, it but accidentally commenced in Alexandria; that no Alexandrian of name advocated it, and that, on its appearance, it was forthwith expelled from the Alexandrian Church, together with its author[1];—next, that, even granting Platonism originated it, of which there is no proof, still there are no grounds for implicating the Alexandrian Fathers in its formation; that while the old Platonism, which they did favour, had no part in the origination of the Arian doctrine, the new Platonism or Eclecticism which may be conceived to have arianized, received no countenance from them; that

[1] [Vid. Athan. Apol. adv. Arian. 52, and Hist. Arian. 78 fin.]

Eclecticism must abstractedly be referred to their schools, it arose out of them in no more exact sense than error ever springs from truth; that, instead of being welcomed by them, the sight of it, as soon as it was detected, led them rather to condemn their own older and innocent philosophy; and that, in Alexandria, there was no Eclectic successor to Ammonius (who concealed his infidelity to the last), till after the commencement of the Arian troubles;—further, that granting (what is undeniable) that the Alexandrian Fathers sometimes use phrases which are similar to those afterwards adopted by the heretics, these were accidents, not the characteristics of their creed, and were employed from a studied verbal imitation of the Jewish and philosophical systems;—of the philosophical, in order to conceal their own depth of meaning, and to conciliate the heathen, a duty to which their peculiar functions in the Christian world especially bound them, and of the Jewish, from an affectionate reverence for the early traces, in the Old Testament, of God's long-meditated scheme of mercy to mankind; —or again, that where they seem to arianize, it is from incompleteness rather than from unsoundness in their confessions, occasioned by the necessity of opposing a contrary error then infecting the Church; that five Fathers, who have more especially incurred the charge of philosophizing in their creed, belong to the schools of Rome and Antioch, as well as of Alexandria, and that the most unguarded speculator in the Alexandrian, Origen, is the very writer first to detect for us, and to denounce the Arian tenet, at least sixty years before it openly presented itself to the world.

On the other hand, if, dismissing this side of the

question, we ask whence the heresy actually arose, we find that contemporary authors ascribe it partially to Judaism and Eclecticism, and more expressly to the influence of the Sophists; that Alexander, to whose lot it fell first to withstand it, refers us at once to Antioch as its original seat, to Judaism as its ultimate source, and to the subtleties of disputation as the instrument of its exhibition: that Arius and his principal supporters were pupils of the school of Antioch; and lastly, that in this school at the date fixed by Alexander, the above-mentioned elements of the heresy are discovered in alliance, almost in union, Paulus of Samosata, the judaizing Sophist, being the favourite of a court which patronized Eclecticism, when it was neglected at Alexandria.

It is evident that deeper and more interesting questions remain, than any which have here been examined. The real secret causes of the heresy; its connexion with the character of the age, with the opinions then afloat, viewed as active moral influences, not as parts of a system; its position in the general course of God's providential dealings with His Church, and in the prophecies of the New Testament; and its relation towards the subsequently developed corruptions of Christianity; these are subjects towards which some opening may have been incidentally made for inquirers, but which are too large to be imagined in the design of a work such as the present.

CHAPTER II.

THE TEACHING OF THE ANTE-NICENE CHURCH IN ITS RELATION TO THE ARIAN HERESY.

SECTION I.

ON THE PRINCIPLE OF THE FORMATION AND IMPOSITION OF CREEDS.

IT has appeared in the foregoing Chapter, that the temper of the Ante-Nicene Church was opposed to the imposition of doctrinal tests upon her members; and on the other hand, that such a measure became necessary in proportion as the cogency of Apostolic Tradition was weakened by lapse of time. This is a subject which will bear some further remarks; and will lead to an investigation of the principle upon which the formation and imposition of creeds rests. After this, I shall delineate the Catholic doctrine itself, as held in the first ages of Christianity; and then, the Arian substitution for it.

I.

I have already observed, that the knowledge of the Christian mysteries was, in those times, accounted as a privilege, to be eagerly coveted. It was not likely, then, that reception of them would be accounted a test; which implies a concession on the part of the recipient, not an advantage. The idea of disbelieving, or criticizing the great doctrines of the faith, from the nature of the case, would scarcely occur to the primitive Christians. These doctrines were the subject of an Apostolical Tradition; they were the very truths which had been lately revealed to mankind. They had been committed to the Church's keeping, and were dispensed by her to those who sought them, as a favour. They were facts, not opinions. To come to the Church was all one with expressing a readiness to receive her teaching; to hesitate to believe, after coming for the sake of believing, would be an inconsistency too rare to require a special provision against the chance of it[1]. It was sufficient to meet the evil as it arose: the power of excommunication and deposition was in the hands of the ecclesiastical authorities, and, as in the case of Paulus, was used impartially. Yet, in the matter of fact, such instances of contumacy were comparatively rare; and the Ante-Nicene heresies were in many instances the innovations of those who had never been in the Church, or who had already been expelled from it.

We have some difficulty in putting ourselves into the situation of Christians in those times, from the circumstance that the Holy Scriptures are now our sole means of satisfying ourselves on points of doctrine. Thus, every one who comes to the Church considers himself entitled to judge and decide individually upon its creed. But in that primitive age, the

[1] [Hoc penitus absurdum est, ut discipulus, ad magistrum vadens, ante sit artifex quam doceatur, &c. Hieron. adv. Lucif. 12.]

Apostolical Tradition, that is, the Creed, was practically the chief source of instruction, especially considering the obscurities of Scripture ; and being withdrawn from public view, it could not be subjected to the degradation of a comparison, on the part of inquirers and half-Christians, with those written documents which are vouchsafed to us from the same inspired authorities. As for the baptized and incorporate members of the Church, they of course had the privilege of comparing the written and the oral tradition, and might exercise it as profitably as in comparing and harmonizing Scripture with itself. But before baptism, the systematic knowledge was withheld ; and without it, Scripture, instead of being the source of instruction on the doctrines of the Trinity and Incarnation, was scarcely more than a sealed book, needing an interpretation, amply and powerfully as it served the purpose of proving those doctrines, when they were once disclosed. And so much on the reluctance of the primitive Fathers to publish creeds, on the ground that the knowledge of Christian doctrines was a privilege reserved for those who were baptized, and in no sense a subject of hesitation and dispute.—It may be added, that the very love of power, which in every age will sway the bulk of those who are exposed to the temptation of it, and ecclesiastics in the number, would indispose them to innovate upon a principle which made themselves the especial guardians of revealed truth[2].

Their backwardness proceeded also from a profound reverence for the sacred mysteries of which they were the dispensers. Here they present us with the true

[2] Vide Hawkins on Unauthoritative Tradition.

exhibition of that pious sensitiveness which the heathen had conceived, but could not justly execute. The latter had their mysteries, but their rude attempts were superseded by the divine discipline of the Gospel, which here acted in the office which is peculiarly its own, rectifying, combining, and completing the inventions of uninstructed nature. If the early Church regarded the very knowledge of the truth as a fearful privilege, much more did it regard that truth itself as glorious and awful; and scarcely conversing about it to her children, shrank from the impiety of subjecting it to the hard gaze of the multitude[3]. We still pray, in the Confirmation service, for those who are introduced into the full privileges of the Christian covenant, that they may be "filled with the spirit of God's holy fear;" but the meaning and practical results of deep-seated religious reverence were far better understood in the primitive times than now, when the infidelity of the world has corrupted the Church. Now, we allow ourselves publicly to canvass the most solemn truths in a careless or fiercely argumentative way; truths, which it is as useless as it is unseemly to discuss in public, as being attainable only by the sober and watchful, by slow degrees, with

[3] Sozomen gives this reason for not inserting the Nicene Creed in his history: "I formerly deemed it necessary to transcribe the confession of faith drawn up by the unanimous consent of this Council [the Nicene], in order that posterity might possess a public record of the truth; but subsequently I was persuaded to the contrary by some godly and learned friends, who represented that such matters ought to be kept secret, as being only requisite to be known by disciples and their instructors (μύσταις καὶ μυσταγωγοῖς), and it is possible that the volume will fall into the hands of the unlearned (τῶν ἀμυήτων)." Hist. i. 20. Bohn's translation.

dependence on the Giver of wisdom, and with strict obedience to the light which has already been granted. Then, they would scarcely express in writing, what is now not only preached to the mixed crowds who frequent our churches, but circulated in print among all ranks and classes of the unclean and the profane, and pressed upon all who choose to purchase it. Nay, so perplexed is the present state of things, that the Church is obliged to change her course of acting, after the spirit of the alteration made at Nicæa, and unwillingly to take part in the theological discussions of the day, as a man crushes venomous creatures of necessity, powerful to do it, but loathing the employment. This is the apology which the author of the present work, as far as it is worth while to introduce himself, offers to all sober-minded and zealous Christians, for venturing to exhibit publicly the great evangelical doctrines, not indeed in the medium of controversy or proof (which would be a still more humiliating office), but in an historical and explanatory form. And he earnestly trusts, that, while doing so, he may be betrayed into no familiarity or extravagance of expression, cautiously lowering the Truth, and (as it were), wrapping it in reverent language, and so depositing it in its due resting-place, which is the Christian's heart: guiltless of those unutterable profanations with which a scrutinizing infidelity wounds and lacerates it. Here, again, is strikingly instanced the unfitness of books, compared with private communication, for the purposes of religious instruction; levelling, as they do, the distinctions of mind and temper by the formality of the written character, and conveying each kind of knowledge the less perfectly, in proportion as it is of a moral nature, and requires to be treated with delicacy and discrimination.

2.

As to the primitive Fathers, with their reverential feelings towards the Supreme Being, great must have been their indignation first, and then their perplexity, when apostates disclosed and corrupted the sacred truth, or when the heretical or philosophical sects made guesses approximating to it. Though the heretics also had their mysteries, yet, it is remarkable, that as regards the high doctrines of the Gospel, they in great measure dropped that restraint and reserve by which the Catholics partly signified, and partly secured a reverence for them. Tertullian sharply exposes the want of a grave and orderly discipline among them in his day. "It is uncertain," he says, who among them is catechumen, who believer. They meet alike, they hear alike, they pray alike; nay, though the heathen should drop in, they will cast holy things to dogs, and their pearls, false jewels as they are, to swine. This overthrow of order they call simplicity, and our attention to it they call meretricious embellishment. They communicate with all men promiscuously; it being nothing to them in what they differ from them, provided they join with them for the destruction of the truth. They are all high-minded; all make pretence of knowledge. Their catechumens are perfect in the faith before they are fully taught. Even their women are singularly forward; venturing, that is, to teach, to argue, to exorcise, to undertake cures, nay, perhaps to baptise[4]."

[4] Tertull. de Præscr. hæret. § 41.

The heretical spirit is ever one and the same in its various forms: this description of the Gnostics was exactly paralleled, in all those points for which we have introduced it here, in the history of Arianism; historically distinct as is the latter system from Gnosticism. Arius began by throwing out his questions as a subject of debate for public consideration; and at once formed crowds of controversialists from those classes who were the least qualified or deserving to take part in the discussion. Alexander, his diocesan, accuses him of siding with the Jews and heathen against the Church; and certainly we learn from the historians, that the heathen philosophers were from the first warmly interested in the dispute, so that some of them attended the Nicene Council, for the chance of ascertaining the orthodox doctrine. Alexander also charges him with employing women in his disturbance of the Church, apparently referring at the same time to the Apostle's prediction of them. He speaks especially of the younger females as zealous in his cause, and as traversing Alexandria in their eagerness to promote it;—a fact confirmed by Epiphanius, who speaks (if he may be credited) of as many as seven hundred from the religious societies of that city at once taking part with the heresiarch[5]. But Arius carried his agitation lower still. It is on no other authority than that of the historian Philostorgius, his own partisan, that we are assured of his composing and setting to music, songs on the subject of his doctrine for the use of the rudest classes of society, with a view of familiarizing them to it. Other of his compositions, of a higher literary excellence,

[5] Soc. i. 6. Theod. Hist. i. iv. Soz. i. 18. Epiph. hær. lxix. 3.

were used at table as a religious accompaniment to the ordinary meal; one of which, in part preserved by Athanasius, enters upon the most sacred portions of the theological question[6]. The success of these exertions in drawing public attention to his doctrine is recorded by Eusebius of Cæsarea, who, though no friend of the heresiarch himself, is unsuspicious evidence as being one of his party. "From a little spark a great fire was kindled. The quarrel began in the Alexandrian Church, then it spread through the whole of Egypt, Lybia, and the farther Thebais; then it ravaged the other provinces and cities, till the war of words enlisted not only the prelates of the churches, but the people too. At length the exposure was so extraordinary, that even in the heathen theatres, the divine doctrine became the subject of the vilest ridicule[7]." Such was Arianism at its commencement; and if it was so indecent in the hands of its originator, who, in spite of his courting the multitude, was distinguished by a certain reserve and loftiness in his personal deportment, much more flagrant was its impiety under the direction of his less refined successors. Valens, the favourite bishop of Constantius, exposed the solemnities of the Eucharist in a judicial examination to which Jews and heathen were admitted; Eudoxius, the Arianizer of the Gothic nations, when installed in the patriarchal throne of Constantinople, uttered as his first words a profane jest, which was received with loud laughter in the newly-consecrated Church of St. Sophia; and Aetius, the founder of the Anomœans, was the grossest and most

[6] Philost. ii. 2. Athan. in Arian. i. 5; de Syn. 15.

[7] Euseb. Vit. Const. ii. 61. Vid. Greg. Naz. Orat. i. 142; [ii. 81, 82.]

despicable of buffoons[8]. Later still, we find the same description of the heretical party in a discourse of the kind and amiable Gregory of Nazianzus. With a reference to the Arian troubles he says, "Now is priest an empty name; contempt is poured upon the rulers, as Scripture says. . . . All fear is banished from our souls, shamelessness has taken its place. Knowledge is now at the will of him who chooses it, and all the deep mysteries of the Spirit. We are all pious, because we condemn the impiety of others. We use the infidels as our arbiters, and cast what is holy to dogs, and pearls before swine, publishing divine truths to profane ears and minds; and, wretches as we are, we carefully fulfil the wishes of our enemies, while, without blushing, we 'pollute ourselves in our inventions[9].'"

Enough has now been said, by way of describing the condition of the Catholic Church, defenceless from the very sacredness and refinement of its discipline, when the attack of Arianism was made upon it; insulting its silence, provoking it to argue, unsettling and seducing its members[1], and in consequence requring its authoritative judgment on the point in dispute. And in addition to the instruments of evil

[8] Athan. Apol. contr. Arian. 31. Socr. ii. 43. Cave, Hist. Literar. vol. i. [Eustathius speaks of the παράδοξοι τῆς 'Αρείου θυμέλης μεσόχοροι. Phot. Bibl. p. 759. 30.]

[9] Greg. Naz. Orat, i. 135; [ii. 79.]

[1] ["Is it not enough to distract a man, on mere hearing, though unable to controvert, and to make him stop his ears, from astonishment at the novelty of what he hears said, which even to mention is to blaspheme?" Ath. Orat. i. 35. Hence, as if feeling the matter to be beyond argument, Athanasius could but call the innovators "Ariomaniacs," from the fierceness of their "ipse dixit." Vid. Athan. Transl. vol. ii. p. 377.]

which were internally directed against it, the Eclectics had by this time extended their creed among the learned, with far greater decorum than the Arians, but still so as practically to interpret the Scriptures in the place of the Church, and to state dogmatically the conclusions for which the Arian controvertists were but indirectly preparing the mind by their objections and sophisms.

3.

Under these circumstances, it was the duty of the rulers of the Church, at whatever sacrifice of their feelings, to discuss the subject in controversy fully and unreservedly, and to state their decision openly. The only alternative was an unmanly non-interference, and an arbitrary or treacherous prohibition of the discussion. To enjoin silence on perplexed inquirers, is not to silence their thoughts ; and in the case of serious minds, it is but natural to turn to the spiritual ruler for advice and relief, and to feel disappointment at the timidity, or irritation at the harshness, of those who refuse to lead a lawful inquiry which they cannot stifle[2]. Such a course, then, is most unwise as well as cruel, inasmuch as it throws the question in dispute upon other arbitrators ; or rather, it is more commonly insincere, the traitorous act of those who care little for the question in dispute, and are content that opinions should secretly prevail which they profess to condemn. The Nicene Fathers might despair of reclaiming the Arian party, but they were bound to

[2] [κίνδυνος γὰρ προδοσίας, ἐν τῷ μὴ προχείρως ἀποδιδόναι τὰς περὶ θεοῦ ἀποκρίσεις τοῖς ἀγαπῶσι τὸν κύριον. Basil, Ep. 7. Vide Hil. de Trin. xii. 20.

erect a witness for the truth, which might be a guide and a warning to all Catholics, against the lying spirit which was abroad in the Church. These remarks apply to a censure which is sometimes passed on them, as if it was their duty to have shut up the question in the words of Scripture; for the words of Scripture were the very subject in controversy, and to have prohibited the controversy, would, in fact, have been but to insult the perplexed, and to extend real encouragement to insidious opponents of the truth.—But it may be expedient here to explain more fully the principle of the obligation which led to their interposition.

Let it be observed then, that as regards the doctrine of the Trinity, the mere text of Scripture is not calculated either to satisfy the intellect or to ascertain the temper of those who profess to accept it as a rule of faith.

1. Before the mind has been roused to reflection and inquisitiveness about its own acts and impressions, it acquiesces, if religiously trained, in that practical devotion to the Blessed Trinity, and implicit acknowledgment of the divinity of Son and Spirit, which holy Scripture at once teaches and exemplifies. This is the faith of uneducated men, which is not the less philosophically correct, nor less acceptable to God, because it does not happen to be conceived in those precise statements which presuppose the action of the mind on its own sentiments and notions. Moral feelings do not directly contemplate and realize to themselves the objects which excite them. A heathen in obeying his conscience, implicitly worships Him of whom he has never distinctly heard. Again, a child

feels not the less affectionate reverence towards his parents, because he cannot discriminate in words, nay, or in idea, between them and others. As, however, his reason opens, he might ask himself concerning the ground of his own emotions and conduct towards them; and might find that these are the correlatives of their peculiar tenderness towards him, long and intimate knowledge of him, and unhesitating assumption of authority over him; all which he continually experiences. And further, he might trace these characteristics of their influence on him to the essential relation itself, which involves his own original debt to them for the gift of life and reason, the inestimable blessing of an indestructible, never-ending existence. And now his intellect contemplates the object of those affections, which acted truly from the first, and are not purer or stronger merely for this accession of knowledge. This will tend to illustrate the sacred subject to which we are directing our attention.

As the mind is cultivated and expanded, it cannot refrain from the attempt to analyze the vision which influences the heart, and the Object in which that vision centres; nor does it stop till it has, in some sort, succeeded in expressing in words, what has all along been a principle both of its affections and of its obedience. But here the parallel ceases; the Object of religious veneration being unseen, and dissimilar from all that is seen, reason can but represent it in the medium of those ideas which the experience of life affords (as we see in the Scripture account, as far as it is addressed to the intellect); and unless these ideas, however inadequate, be correctly applied to it, they re-act upon the affections, and deprave the religious principle. This is exemplified in the case of the heathen, who, trying to make their instinctive notion of the Deity an object of reflection, pictured to their minds false images, which eventually gave them a pattern and a sanction for sinning. Thus the systematic doctrine of the Trinity may be considered as the shadow, projected for the contemplation of the intellect, of the Object of scripturally-informed piety: a representation, economical; necessarily imperfect, as being exhibited in a foreign medium, and therefore involving apparent inconsistencies or mysteries; given to the Church by tradition contemporaneously with those apostolic writings, which are addressed more directly to the heart; kept in the background in the infancy of Christianity, when faith and obedience were vigorous, and brought forward at a time when, reason being disproportionately developed, and aiming at sovereignty in the province of religion, its presence became necessary to expel an usurping idol from the house of God.

If this account of the connexion between the theological system and the Scripture implication of it be substantially correct, it will be seen how ineffectual all attempts ever will be to secure the doctrine by mere general language. It may be readily granted that the intellectual representation should ever be subordinate to the cultivation of the religious affections. And after all, it must be owned, so reluctant is a well-constituted mind to reflect on its own motive principles, that the correct intellectual image, from its hardness of outline, may startle and offend those who have all along been acting upon it. Doubtless there are portions of the ecclesiastical doctrine, presently to be exhibited, which may at first sight seem a refinement, merely because the object and bearings of them are not understood without reflection and experience. But what is left to the Church but to speak out, in order to exclude error? Much as we may wish it, we cannot restrain the rovings of the intellect, or silence its clamorous demand for a formal statement concerning the Object of our worship. If, for instance, Scripture bids us adore God, and adore His Son, our reason at once asks, whether it does not follow that there are two Gods; and a system of doctrine becomes unavoidable; being framed, let it be observed, not with a view of explaining, but of arranging the inspired notices concerning the Supreme Being, of providing, not a consistent, but a connected statement. There the inquisitiveness of a pious mind rests, viz., when it has pursued the subject into the mystery which is its limit. But this is not all. The intellectual expression of theological truth not only excludes heresy, but directly assists the acts of religious worship and obedience; fixing and stimulating the Christian spirit in the same way as the knowledge of the One God relieves and illuminates the perplexed conscience of the religious heathen.—And thus much on the importance of Creeds to tranquillize the mind; the text of Scripture being addressed principally to the affections, and of a religious, not a philosophical character.

2. Nor, in the next place, is an assent to the text of Scripture sufficient for the purposes of Christian fellowship. As the sacred text was not intended to satisfy the intellect, neither was it given as a test of the religious temper which it forms, and of which it is

an expression. Doubtless no combination of words will ascertain an unity of sentiment in those who adopt them; but one form is more adapted for the purpose than another. Scripture being unsystematic, and the faith which it propounds being scattered through its documents, and understood only when they are viewed as a whole, the Creeds aim at concentrating its general spirit, so as to give security to the Church, as far as may be, that its members take that definite view of that faith which alone is the true one. But, if this be the case, how idle is it to suppose that to demand assent to a form of words which happens to be scriptural, is on that account sufficient to effect an unanimity in thought and action! If the Church would be vigorous and influential, it must be decided and plain-spoken in its doctrine, and must regard its faith rather as a character of mind than as a notion. To attempt comprehensions of opinion, amiable as the motive frequently is, is to mistake arrangements of words, which have no existence except on paper, for habits which are realities; and ingenious generalizations of discordant sentiments for that practical agreement which alone can lead to co-operation. We may indeed artificially classify light and darkness under one term or formula; but nature has her own fixed courses, and unites mankind by the sympathy of moral character, not by those forced resemblances which the imagination singles out at pleasure even in the most promiscuous collection of materials. However plausible may be the veil thus thrown over heterogeneous doctrines, the flimsy artifice is discomposed so soon as the principles beneath it are called upon to move and act. Nor are these attempted comprehensions innocent ; for, it being the interest of our enemies to weaken the Church, they have always gained a point, when they have put upon us words for things, and persuaded us to fraternize with those who, differing from us in essentials, nevertheless happen, in the excursive range of opinion, somewhere to intersect that path of faith, which centres in supreme and zealous devotion to the service of God.

Let it be granted, then, as indisputable, that there are no two opinions so contrary to each other, but some form of words may be found vague enough to comprehend them both. The Pantheist will admit that there is a God, and the Humanitarian that Christ is God, if they are suffered to say so without explanation. But if this be so, it becomes the duty, as well as the evident policy of the Church, to interrogate them, before admitting them to her fellowship. If the Church be the pillar and ground of the truth, and bound to contend for the preservation of the faith once delivered to it ; if we are answerable as ministers of Christ for the formation of one, and one only, character in the heart of man ; and if the Scriptures are given us, as a means indeed towards that end, but inadequate to the office of interpreting themselves, except to such as live under the same Divine Influence which inspired them, and which is expressly sent down upon us that we may interpret them,—then, it is evidently our duty piously and cautiously to collect the sense of Scripture, and solemnly to promulgate it in such a form as is best suited, as far as it goes, to exclude the pride and unbelief of the world. It will be admitted that, to deny to individual

Christians the use of terms not found in Scripture, as such, would be a superstition and an encroachment on their religious liberty; and in like manner, doubtless, to forbid the authorities of the Church to require an acceptance of such terms, when necessary, from its members, is to interfere with the discharge of their peculiar duties, as appointed of the Holy Ghost to be overseers of the Lord's flock. And, though the discharge of this office is the most momentous and fearful that can come upon mortal man, and never to be undertaken except by the collective illumination of the Heads of the Church, yet, when innovations arise, they must discharge it to the best of their ability; and whether they succed or fail, whether they have judged rightly or hastily of the necessity of their interposition, whether they devise their safeguard well or ill, draw the line of Church fellowship broadly or narrowly, countenance the profane reasoner, or cause the scrupulous to stumble,—to their Master they stand or fall, as in all other acts of duty, the obligation itself to protect the Faith remaining unquestionable.

This is an account of the abstract principle on which ecclesiastical confessions rest. In its practical adoption it has been softened in two important respects. First, the Creeds imposed have been compiled either from Apostolical traditions, or from primitive writings; so that in fact the Church has never been obliged literally to collect the sense of Scripture. Secondly, the test has been used, not as a condition of communion, but of authority. As learning is not necessary for a private Christian, so neither is the full knowledge of the theological system. The clergy, and others in station, must be questioned as to their doctrinal views : but for the mass of the laity, it is enough if they do not set up such counter-statements of their own, as imply that they have systematized, and that erroneously. In the Nicene Council, the test was but imposed on the Rulers of the Church. Lay communion was not denied to such as refused to take it, provided they introduced no novelties of their own ; the anathemas or excommunications being directed solely against the Arian innovators.

SECTION II.

THE SCRIPTURE DOCTRINE OF THE TRINITY.

I BEGIN by laying out the matter of evidence for the Catholic Doctrine, as it is found in Scripture; that is, assuming it to be there contained, let us trace out the form in which it has been communicated to us,—the disposition of the phenomena, which imply it, on the face of the Revelation. And here be it observed, in reference to what has already been admitted concerning the obscurity of the inspired documents, that it is nothing to the purpose whether or not we should have been able to draw the following view of the doctrine from them, had it never been suggested to us in the Creeds. For it has been (providentially) so suggested to all of us; and the question is not, what we should have done, had we never had external assistance, but, taking things as we find them, whether, the clue to the meaning of Scripture being given, (as it ever has been given,) we may not deduce the doctrine thence, by as argumentative a process as that which enables us to verify the received theory of gravitation, which perhaps we could never have discovered for ourselves, though possessed of the data from which the inventor drew his conclusions. Indeed, such a state of the case is analogous to that in which the evidence for Natural Religion is presented to us. It is very doubtful, whether the phenomena of the visible world would in themselves have brought us to a knowledge of the Creator; but the universal tradition of His existence has been from the beginning His own comment upon them, graciously preceding the study of the evidence. With this remark I address myself to an arduous undertaking.

First, let it be assumed as agreeable both to reason and revelation, that there are Attributes and Operations, or by whatever more suitable term we designate them, peculiar to the Deity; for instance, creative and preserving power, absolute prescience, moral sovereignty, and the like. These are ever included in our notion of the incommunicable nature of God; and, by a figure of speech, were there occasion for using it, might be called one with God, present, actively co-operating, and exerting their own distinguishing influence, in all His laws, providences, and acts. Thus, if He be eternal, or omnipresent, we consider His knowledge, goodness, and holiness, to be co-eternal and co-extensive with Him. Moreover, it would be an absurdity to form a comparison between these and God Himself; to regard them as numerically distinct from Him; to investigate the particular mode of their existence in the Divine Mind; or to treat them as parts of God, inasmuch as they are all included in the idea of the one Indivisible Godhead. And, lastly, subtle and unmeaning questions might be raised about some of these; for instance, God's power: whether, that is, it did or did not exist from eternity, on the ground, that bearing a relation to things created, it could not be said to have existence before the era of creation[1].

[1] Origen de Principiis, i. 2, § 10.

Next, it is to be remarked, that the Jewish Scriptures introduce to our notice certain peculiar Attributes or Manifestations (as they would seem) of the Deity, corresponding in some measure to those already mentioned as conveyed to us by Natural Religion, though of a more obscure character. Such is what is called "the Spirit of God;" a phrase which denotes sometimes the Divine energy, sometimes creative or preserving power, sometimes the assemblage of Divine gifts, moral and intellectual, vouchsafed to mankind; having in all cases a general connexion with the notion of the vivifying principle of nature. Such again, is "the Wisdom of God," as introduced into the book of Proverbs; and such is the "Name," the "Word," the "Glory," of God.

Further, these peculiar Manifestations (to give them a name) are sometimes in the same elder Scriptures singularly invested with the properties of personality; and, although the expressions of the sacred text may in some places be interpreted figuratively, yet there are passages so strangely worded, as at first sight to be inconsistent with themselves, and such as would be ascribed, in an uninspired work, to forgetfulness or inaccuracy in the writer;—as, for instance, when what is first called the Glory of God is subsequently spoken of as an intelligent Agent, often with the characteristics, or even the name of an Angel. On the other hand, it elsewhere occurs, that what is introduced as an Angel, is afterwards described as God Himself.

Now, when we pass on to the New Testament, we find these peculiar Manifestations of the Divine Essence concentrated and fixed in two, called the Word, and the Spirit. At the same time, the apparent Personality ascribed to Them in the Old Testament, is changed for a real Personality, so clearly and explicitly marked as to resist all critical experiments upon the language, all attempts at allegorical interpretation. Here too the Word is also called the Son of God, and appears to possess such strict personal attributes, as to be able voluntarily to descend from heaven, and assume our nature without ceasing to be identically what He was before; so as to speak of Himself, though a man, as one and the same with the Divine Word who existed in the beginning. The Personality of the Spirit in some true and sufficient sense is as accurately revealed; and that the Son is not the Spirit, is also evident from the fixed relations which are described as separating Them from each other in the Divine Essence.

Reviewing this process of revelation, Gregory Nazianzen, somewhat after the manner of the foregoing account, remarks that, as Almighty God has in the course of His dispensations changed the ritual of religion by successive abrogations, so He has changed its theology by continual additions till it has come to perfection. "Under the Old Dispensation," he proceeds, "the Father was openly revealed, and the Son but obscurely. When the New was given, the Son was manifested, but the Divinity of the Spirit intimated only. Now the Spirit dwells with us, affording us clearer evidence about Himself, . . . that by gradual additions, and flights, as David says, and by advancing and progressing from glory to glory, the radiance of the Trinity might shine out on those who are illuminated[2]."

[2] Greg. Naz. Orat. xxxvii. p. 608; [xxxi. 26.]

Now from this peculiar method in which the doctrine is unfolded to us in Scripture, we learn so much as this in our contemplation of it; viz. the absurdity, as well as the presumption, of inquiring minutely about the actual relations subsisting between God and His Son and Spirit, and drawing large inferences from what is told us of Them. Whether They are equal to Him or unequal, whether posterior to Him in existence or coeval, such inquiries (though often they must be answered when once started) are in their origin as superfluous as similar questions concerning the Almighty's relation to His own attributes (which still we answer as far as we can, when asked); for the Son and the Spirit are *one* with Him, the ideas of number and comparison being excluded. Yet this statement must be qualified from the evidence of Scripture, by two additional remarks. On the one hand, the Son and Spirit are represented to us in the Economy of Revelation, as ministering to God, and as, so far, personally subordinate to Him; and on the other hand, in spite of this personal inequality, yet, as being partakers of the fulness of the Father, they are equal to Him in nature, and in Their claims upon our faith and obedience, as is sufficiently proved by the form of baptism.

The mysteriousness of the doctrine evidently lies in our inability to conceive a sense of the word *person*, such, as to be more than a mere character, yet less than an individual intelligent being; our own notions, as gathered from our experience of human agents, leading us to consider *personality* as equivalent, in its very idea, to the unity and independence of the immaterial substance of which it is predicated.

SECTION III.

THE ECCLESIASTICAL DOCTRINE OF THE TRINITY.

THIS being the general Scripture view of the Holy Trinity, it follows to describe the Ecclesiastical Doctrine, chiefly in relation to our Lord, as contained in the writings of the Fathers, especially the Ante-Nicene[1].

Scripture is express in declaring both the divinity of Him who in due time became man for us, and also His personal distinction from God in His pre-existent state. This is sufficiently clear from the opening of St. John's Gospel, which states the mystery as distinctly as an ecclesiastical comment can propound it. On these two truths the whole doctrine turns, viz. that our Lord is one with, yet personally separate from God. Now there are two appellations given to Him in Scripture, enforcing respectively these two essentials of the true doctrine; appellations imperfect and open to misconception by themselves, but qualifying and completing each other. The title of the

[1] The examples cited are principally borrowed from the elaborate catalogues furnished by Petavius, Bishop Bull, and Suicer, in his Thesaurus and his Comment on the Nicene Creed.

Son marks His derivation and distinction from the Father, that of the *Word* (i.e. Reason) denotes His inseparable inherence in the Divine Unity; and while the former taken by itself, might lead the mind to conceive of Him as a second being, and the latter as no real being at all, both together witness to the mystery, that He is at once *from*, and yet *in*, the Immaterial, Incomprehensible God. Whether or not these titles contain the proof of this statement, (which, it is presumed, they actually do,) at least, they will enable us to classify our ideas: and we have authority for so using them. "The Son," says Athanasius, "is the Word and Wisdom of the Father: from which titles we infer His impassive and indivisible derivation from the Father, inasmuch as the word (or reason) of a man is no mere part of him, nor when exercised, goes forth from him by a passion; much less, therefore, is it so with the Word of God. On the other hand, the Father calls Him His Son, lest, from hearing only that He was the Word, we should consider Him such as the word of man, impersonal, whereas the title of Son, designates Him as a Word which exists, and a substantial Wisdom[2]."

Availing ourselves of this division, let us first dwell on the appellation of Son, and then on that of Word or Reason.

[2] Athan. de Syn. 41.

In the same way the Semi-Arian Basil (of Ancyra), speaking of such heretics as argued that the Son has no existence separate from the Father, because He is called the Word, says, "For this reason our predecessors, in order to signify that the Son has a reality, and is in being, and not a mere word which comes and goes, were obliged to call Him a substance. . . . For a word has no real existence, and cannot be a Son of God, else were there many sons." Epiph. Hær. lxxiii. 12.

1.

Nothing can be plainer to the attentive student of Scripture, than that our Lord is there called the Son of God, not only in respect of His human nature, but of His pre-existent state also. And if this be so, the very fact of the revelation of Him as such, implies that we are to gather something from it, and attach in consequence of it some ideas to our notion of Him, which otherwise we should not have attached; else would it not have been made. Taking then the word in its most vague sense, so as to admit as little risk as possible of forcing the analogy, we seem to gain the notion of derivation from God, and therefore, of the utter dissimilarity and distance existing between Him and all beings except God His Father, as if He partook of that unapproachable, incommunicable Divine Nature, which is increate and imperishable.

But Scripture does not leave us here: in order to fix us in this view, lest we should be perplexed with another notion of the analogy, derived from that adopted sonship, which is ascribed therein to created beings, it attaches a characteristic epithet to His Name, as descriptive of the peculiar relation of Him who bears it to the Father. It designates Him as the *Only-begotten* or the *own*[3] Son of God, terms evidently referring, where they occur, to His heavenly nature, and thus becoming the inspired comment on the more general title. It is true that the term *generation* is also applied to certain events in our Lord's mediatorial history: to His resurrection from the dead[4];

[3] [John i. 1. 14. 18; iii. 16; v. 18. Rom. viii. 32. Heb. i. 1—14.]
[4] Ps. ii. 7. Acts xiii. 33. Heb. v. 5. Rev. i. 5. Rom. i. 4.

and, according to the Fathers[5], to His original mission in the beginning of all things to create the world; and to His manifestation in the flesh. Still, granting this, the sense of the word "only-begotten" remains, defined by its context to relate to something higher than any event occurring in time, however great or beneficial to the human race.

Being taken then, as it needs must be taken, to designate His original nature, it witnesses most forcibly and impressively to that which is peculiar in it, viz. His origination from God, and such as to exclude all resemblance to any being but Him, whom nothing created resembles. Thus, without irreverently and idly speculating upon the generation in itself, but considering the doctrine as given us as a practical direction for our worship and obedience, we may accept it in token, that whatever the Father is, such is the Son. And there are some remarkable texts in Scripture corroborative of this view: for instance, that in the fifth chapter of St. John, "As the Father hath life in Himself, so hath He given to the Son to have life in Himself. . What things soever the Father doeth, these also doeth the Son likewise. For the Father loveth the Son, and showeth Him all things that Himself doeth. . As the Father raiseth up the dead and quickeneth them, even so the Son quickeneth whom He will . . that all men should honour the Son even as they honour the Father. He that honoureth not the Son, honoureth not the Father which hath sent Him."

This is the principle of interpretation acknowledged by the primitive Church. Its teachers warn us against

[5] Bull, Defens. Fid. Nic. iii. 9, § 12.

resting in the word "generation," they urge us on to seize and use its practical meaning. "Speculate not upon the divine generation *(gennesis)*," says Gregory Nazianzen, "for it is not safe . . . . let the doctrine be honoured silently; it is a great thing for thee to know the fact; the mode, we cannot admit that even Angels understand, much less thou[6]." Basil says, "Seek not what is undiscoverable, for you will not discover; . . if you will not comply, but are obstinate, I shall deride you, or rather I weep at your daring: . . . . believe what is written, seek not what is not written[7]." Athanasius and Chrysostom repel the profane inquiry argumentatively. "Such speculators," the former says, "might as well investigate, where God is, and how God is, and of what nature the Father is. But as such questions are irreligious, and argue ignorance of God, so is it also unlawful to venture such thoughts about the generation of the Son of God." And Chrysostom; "I know that He begat the Son: the manner how, I am ignorant of. I know that the Holy Spirit is from Him; how from Him, I do not understand. I eat food; but how this is converted into my flesh and blood, I know not. We know not these things, which we see every day when we eat, yet we meddle with inquiries concerning the substance of God[8]."

While they thus prohibited speculation, they boldly used the doctrine for the purposes for which it was given them in Scripture. Thus Justin Martyr speaks of Christ as the Son, "who alone is literally called by that name:" and arguing with the heathen, he says,

[6] Greg. Naz. Orat. xxxv. 29, 30 [xxix. 8].

[7] Petav. v. 6, § 2.

[8] Ibid.

"Jesus might well deserve from His wisdom to be called the Son of God, though He were only a man like others, for all writers speak of God as the 'Father of both men and gods.' But let it not be strange to you, if, besides this common generation, we consider Him, as the Word of God, to have been begotten of God in a special way[9]." Eusebius of Cæsarea, unsatisfactory as he is as an authority, has nevertheless well expressed the general Catholic view in his attack upon Marcellus. "He who describes the Son as a creature made out of nothing," he says, "does not observe that he is bestowing on Him only the name of Son, and denying Him to be really such; for He who has come out of nothing, cannot truly be the Son of God, more than other things which are made. But He who is truly the Son, born from God, as from a Father, He may reasonably be called the singularly beloved and only-begotten of the Father, and therefore He is Himself God[1]." This last inference, that what is born of God, is God, of course implicitly appeals to, and is supported by, the numerous texts which expressly call the Son God, and ascribe to Him the divine attributes[2].

[9] Bull, Defens. ii. 4, § 2. [The sentence runs on thus:—τοῖς τὸν Ἑρμῆ λόγον τὸν παρὰ θεοῦ ἀγγελτικὸν λέγουσιν. Apol. i. 22.]

[1] Euseb. de Eccles. Theol. i. 9, 10.

[2] The following are additional specimens from primitive theology. Clement calls the Son "the *perfect* Word, born of the *perfect* Father." Tertullian, after quoting the text, "All that the Father hath are Mine," adds, "If so, why should not the Father's titles be His? When then we read that God is Almighty, and the Highest, and the God of Hosts, and the King of Israel, and Jehovah, see to it whether the Son also be not signified by these passages, as being in His own right the Almighty God, inasmuch as He is the Word of the Almighty God." Bull, Defens. ii. 6, § 3. 7, § 4.

The reverential spirit in which the Fathers held the doctrine of the *gennesis*, led them to the use of other forms of expression, partly taken from Scripture, partly not, with a view of signifying the fact of the Son's full participation in the divinity of Him who is His Father, without dwelling on the mode of participation or origination, on which they dared not speculate[3]. Such were the images of the sun and its radiance, the fountain and the stream, the root and its shoots, a body and its exhalation, fire and the fire kindled from it ; all which were used as emblems of the sacred mystery in those points in which it was declared in Scripture, viz. the mystery of the Son's being from the Father and, as such, partaker in His Divine perfections. The first of these is found in the first chapter of the Epistle to the Hebrews, where our Lord is called, "the brightness of God's glory." These illustrations had a further use in their very variety, as reminding the Christian that he must not dwell on any one of them for its own sake. The following passage from Tertullian will show how they were applied in the inculcation of the sacred doctrine. "Even when a ray is shot forth from the sun, though it be but a part from the whole, yet the sun is in the ray, inasmuch as it is the ray of the sun ; nor is its substance separated, but drawn out. In like manner there is Spirit from Spirit, and God from God. As when a light is kindled from another, the original light remains entire and undiminished, though you borrow from it many like itself ; so That which proceeds from God, is called at once God, and the Son of God, and Both are One[4]."

[3] Vid Athan. ad Serap. i. 20.

[4] Bull, Defens. ii. 7, § 2.

So much is evidently deducible from what Scripture tells us concerning the generation of the Son; that there is, (so to express it,) a reiteration of the One Infinite Nature of God, a communicated divinity, in the Person of our Lord; an inference supported by the force of the word "only begotten," and verified by the freedom and fulness with which the Apostles ascribe to Christ the high incommunicable titles of eternal perfection and glory. There is one other notion conveyed to us in the doctrine, which must be evident as soon as stated, little as may be the practical usefulness of dwelling upon it. The very name of Son, and the very idea of derivation, imply a certain subordination of the Son to the Father, so far forth as we view Him as distinct from the Father, or in His personality: and frequent testimony is borne to the correctness of this inference in Scripture, as in the descriptions of the Divine Angel in the Old Testament, revived in the closing revelations of the New[5]; and in such passages as that above cited from St. John's Gospel[6]. This is a truth which every Christian feels, admits, and acts upon; but from piety he would not allow himself to reflect on what he does, did not the attack of heresies oblige him. The direct answer which a true religious loyalty leads him to make to any question about the subordination of the Son, is that such comparisons are irreverent, that the Son is *one* with the Father, and that unless he honours the Son in all the fulness of honour which he ascribes to the Father, he is disobeying His express command. It may serve as a very faint illustration of the offence given him, to consider the manner in which he would

[5] Rev. viii. 3. [6] John v. 19—30.

receive any question concerning the love which he feels respectively for two intimate friends, or for a brother and sister, or for his parents: though in such cases the impropriety of the inquiry, arises from the incommensurableness, not the coincidence, of the respective feelings. But false doctrine forces us to analyze our own notions, in order to exclude it. Arius argued that, since our Lord was a Son, therefore He was not God: and from that time we have been obliged to determine how much we grant and what we deny, lest, while praying without watching, we lose all. Accordingly, orthodox theology has since his time worn a different aspect; first, inasmuch as divines have measured what they said themselves; secondly, inasmuch as they have measured the Ante-Nicene language, which by its authors was spoken from the heart, by the necessities of controversies of a later date. And thus those early teachers have been made appear technical, when in fact they have only been reduced to system; just as in literature what is composed freely, is afterwards subjected to the rules of grammarians and critics. This must be taken as an apology for whatever there is that sounds harsh in the observations which I have now to make, and for the injustice which I may seem incidentally to do in the course of them to the ancient writers whose words are in question.

"The Catholic doctors," says Bishop Bull, "both before and after the Nicene Council, are unanimous in declaring that the Father is greater than the Son, even as to divinity [paternity?]; i.e. not in nature or any essential perfection, which is in the Father and not in the Son, but alone in what may be called authority, that is in point of origin, since the Son is from the Father, not the Father from the Son[7]." Justin, for instance, speaks of the Son as "having the second place after the unchangeable and everlasting God and Father of all." Origen says that "the Son is not more powerful than the Father, but subordinate (ὑποδεέστερον); according to His own words, 'The Father that sent Me, is greater than I.'" This text is cited in proof of the same doctrine by the Nicene, and Post-Nicene Fathers, Alexander, Athanasius, Basil, Gregory Nazianzen, Chrysostom, Cyril, and others, of whom we may content ourselves with the words of Basil: "'My Father is greater than I,' that is, so far forth as Father, since what else does 'Father' signify, than that He is cause and origin of Him who was begotten by Him?" and in another place,

[7] Bull, Defens. iv. 2, § 1. Or, again, to take the words of Petavius: [" Filius eandem numero cum Patre divinitatem habet, sed proprietate differt. Proinde Filietas ipsa Paternitat equodammodo minor est, vel Filius, qua Filius, Patre, ut Pater est, minor dicitur, quoniam origine est posterior, non autem ut Deus," ii. 2, § 15.] Cudworth, too, observes: "Petavius himself, expounding the Athanasian creed, writeth in this manner: 'The Father is in a right Catholic manner affirmed by most of the ancients, to be greater than the Son, and He is commonly said also, without reprehension, to be before Him in respect of original.' Whereupon he concludeth the true meaning of that Creed to be this, that no Person of the Trinity is greater or less than other in respect of the essence of the Godhead common to them all . . . . . but that notwithstanding there may be some inequality in them, as they are Hic Deus et Hæc Persona. Wherefore when Athanasius, and the other orthodox Fathers, writing against Arius, do so frequently assert the equality of all the Three Persons, this is to be understood in way of opposition to Arius only, who made the Son to be unequal to the Father, as ἑτεροούσιος . . . . . one being God, and the other a creature; they affirming on the contrary, that He was equal to the Father, as ὁμοούσιος . . . . that is, as God and not a creature." Cudw. Intell. Syst. 4, § 36.

"The Son is second in order to the Father, since He is from Him ; and in dignity, inasmuch as the Father is the origin and cause of His existence[8]."

Accordingly, the primitive writers, with an unsuspicious yet reverent explicitness, take for granted the ministrative character of the relation of both Son and Spirit towards the Father ; still of course speaking of Them as included in the Divine Unity, not as external to it. Thus Irenæus, clear and undeniable as is his orthodoxy, still declares, that the Father "is ministered to in all things by His own Offspring and Likeness, the Son and Holy Ghost, the Word and Wisdom, of whom all angels are servants and subjects[9]." In like manner, a ministry is commonly ascribed to the Son and Spirit, and a bidding and willing to the Father, by Justin, Irenæus, Clement, Origen, and Methodius[1], altogether in the spirit of the Post-Nicene authorities already cited: and without any risk of misleading the reader, as soon as the second and third Persons are understood to be internal to the Divine Mind, *connaturalia instrumenta*, concurrent (at the utmost) in no stronger sense, than when the human will is said to concur with the reason. Gregory Nazianzen lays down the same doctrine with an explanation, in the following sentence : "It is plain," he says, "that the things, of which the Father designs in Him the forms, these the Word executes ; not as a servant, nor unskilfully, but with full know-

[8] Justin, Apol. i. 13. 60. Bull, Defens. iv. 2, § 6, § 9. Petav. ii. 2, § 2, &c.

[9] Petav. i. 3, § 7.

[1] ὑπηρεσία, βούλησις, θέλημα, præceptio. Petav. ibid. et. seqq.

ledge and a master's power, and, to speak more suitably, as if He were the Father [2]."

Such is the Scriptural and Catholic sense of the word *Son;* on the other hand, it is easy to see what was the defect of this image, and the consequent danger in the use of it. First, there was an appearance of materiality, the more suspiciously to be viewed because there were heresies at the time which denied or neglected the spiritual nature of Almighty God. Next, too marked a distinction seemed to be drawn between the Father and Son, tending to give a separate individuality to each, and so to introduce a kind of ditheism; and here too heresy and philosophy had prepared the way for the introduction of the error. The Valentinians and Manichees are chargeable with both misconceptions. The Eclectics, with the latter; being Emanatists, they seem to have considered the Son to be both individually distinct from the Father, and of an inferior nature.—Against these errors we have the following among other protests.

Tertullian says, "We declare that two are revealed as God in Scripture, two as Lord; but we explain ourselves, lest offence should be taken. They are not called two, in respect of their both being God, or Lord, but in respect of their being Father and Son; and this moreover, not from any division of substance, but from mutual relation, since we pronounce the Son to be individual with and inseparable from the Father [3]." Origen also, commenting upon the word

[2] Bull, Defens. ii. 13, § 10. [Greg. Orat. xxx. 11. For the subordination of mediatorship, vid. Athan. Orat. iv. 6.]

[3] Bull, Defens. ii. 4, § 3. 7, § 5. Petav. i. 4, § 1.

"brightness [4]," in the first chapter of the Hebrews, says, "Holy Scripture endeavours to give to men a refined perception of its teaching, by introducing the illustration of breath [5]. It has selected this material image, in order to our understanding even in some degree, how Christ, who is Wisdom, issues, as though Breath, from the perfection of God Himself. . . . . In like manner from the analogy of material objects, He is called a pure and perfect Emanation of the Almighty glory [6]. Both these resemblances most clearly show the fellowship of nature between the Son and Father. For an emanation seems to be of one substance with that body of which it is the emanation or breath [7]." And to guard still more strongly against any misconception of the real drift of the illustration, he cautions his readers against "those absurd fictions which give the notion of certain literal extensions in the Divine Nature; as if they would distribute it into parts, and divide God the Father, if they could; whereas to entertain even the light suspicion of this, is not only an extreme impiety, but an utter folly also, nay not even intelli-

4 ἀπαύγασμα.

5 ἀτμίς. Wisd. vii. 25.

6 ἀπόρροια, ibid.

7 In like manner Justin, after saying that the Divine Power called the Word is born from the Father, adds, "but not by separation from Him (κατ' ἀποτομήν) as if the Father lost part of Himself, as corporeal substances are not the same before and after separation." [Tryph. 128.] "The Son of God," says Clement, "never relinquishes His place of watch, not parted or separated off, not passing from place to place, but always every where, illimitable, all intellect, all the light of the Father, all eye, all-seeing, all-hearing, all-knowing, searching the powers with His power." [Strom. vii. 2.]

gible at all, that an incorporeal nature should be capable of division[8]."

2.

To meet more fully this misconception to which the word *Son* gave rise, the ancient Fathers availed themselves of the other chief appellation given to our Lord in Scripture. The Logos or Sophia, the Word, Reason, or Wisdom of God, is only by St. John distinctly applied to Christ; but both before his time and by his contemporary Apostles it is used in that ambiguous sense, half literal, half evangelical, which, when it is once known to belong to our Lord, guides us to the right interpretation of the metaphor. For instance, when St. Paul declares that "the Word of God is alive and active, and keener than a two-edged sword, and so piercing as to separate soul and spirit, joints and nerves, and a judge of our thoughts and designs, and a witness of every creature," it is scarcely possible to decide whether the revealed law of God be spoken of, or the Eternal Son. On the whole it would appear that our Lord is called the Word or Wisdom of God in two respects; first, to denote His essential presence in the Father, in as full a sense as the attribute of wisdom is essential to Him; secondly, His mediatorship, as the Interpreter or Word between God and His creatures. No appellation, surely, could have been more appositely bestowed, in order to counteract the notions of materiality and of distinct individuality, and of beginning of existence, which the title of the Son was likely to introduce into the Catholic doctrine. Accordingly, after the words

[8] Bull, Defens. ii. 9, § 19.

lately cited, Origen uses it (or a metaphor like it) for this very purpose. Having mentioned the absurd idea, which had prevailed, of parts or extensions in the Divine Nature, he proceeds: "Rather, as will proceeds out of the mind, and neither tears the mind, nor is itself separated or divided from it, in some such manner must we conceive that the Father has begotten the Son, who is His Image." Elsewhere he says, "It were impious and perilous, merely because our intellect is weak, to deprive God, as far as our words go, of His only-begotten co-eternal Word, viz. the 'wisdom in which He rejoiced.' We might as well conceive that He was not for ever in joy[9]." Hence it was usual to declare that to deny the eternity of our Lord was all one as saying that Almighty God was once without intelligence[1]: for instance, Athenagoras says, that the Son is "the first-born of the Father; not as made, for God being Mind Eternal, had from the beginning reason in Himself, being eternally intellectual; but as issuing forth upon the chaotic mass as the Idea and Agent of Creation[2]." The same interpretation of the sacred figure is continued after the Nicene Council; thus Basil says, "If Christ be the Power of God, and the Wisdom, and these be increate and co-eternal with God, (for He never was without wisdom and power,) then, Christ is increate and co-eternal with God[3]."

But here again the metaphor was necessarily imper-

[9] Bull, Defens. iii. 3, § 1.

[1] ἄλογος.

[2] Bull, Defens. iii. 5, § 2, τὸν λόγον . . . λογικὸς . . . προελθόν . . . ἰδέα καὶ ἐνέργεια.

[3] Petav. vi. 9, § 2.

fect; and, if pursued, open to misconception. Its obvious tendency was to obliterate the notion of the Son's Personality, that is, to introduce Sabellianism. Something resembling this was the error of Paulus of Samosata and Marcellus: who, from the fleeting and momentary character of a word spoken, inferred that the Divine Word was but the temporary manifestation of God's glory in the man Christ. And it was to counteract this tendency, that is, to witness against it, that the Fathers speak of Him as the Word in an *hypostasis*[4], the permanent, real, and living Word.

3.

The above is a sketch of the primitive doctrine concerning our Lord's divine nature, as contained in the two chief appellations which are ascribed to Him in Scripture. The opposite ideas they convey may be further denoted respectively by the symbols "of God," and "in God[5];" as though He were so derived from the simple Unity of God as in no respect to be divided or extended from it, (to speak metaphorically,) but to inhere within that ineffable individuality. Of these two conditions[6] of the doctrine, however, the divinity of Christ, and the unity of God, the latter was much more earnestly insisted on in the early times. The divinity of our Lord was, on the whole, too plain a

[4] ἐνυπόστατος Λογός.

[5] ἐκ θεοῦ and ἐν θεῷ.

[6] [Son and Word, "*of God*," and "*in God*" however, imply each other. "If not Son, neither is He Word: if not Word, neither is He Son." Athan. Orat. iv. 24. "The Son's Being, because of the Father, is therefore in the Father." Athan. iii. 3. "Quia Verbum ideo Filius." August. in Psalm. vii. 14, § 5.]

truth to dispute; but in proportion as it was known to the heathen, it would seem to them to involve this consequence,—that, much as the Christians spoke against polytheism, still, after all, they did admit a polytheism of their own instead of the Pagan. Hence the anxiety of the Apologists, while they assail the heathen creed on this account, to defend their own against a similar charge. Thus Athenagoras, in the passage lately referred to, says; "Let no one ridicule the notion that God has a Son. For we have not such thoughts either about God the Father or about the Son as your poets, who, in their mythologies, make the Gods no better than men. But the Son of God is the Word of the Father [as Creator] both in idea and in active power[7] . . . . the Father and the Son being one. The Son being in the Father, and the Father in the Son, in the unity and power of the Spirit, the Son of God is the Mind and Word of the Father." Accordingly, the divinity of the Son being assumed, the early writers are earnest in protecting the doctrine of the Unity; protecting it both from the materialism of dividing the Godhead, and the paganism of separating the Son and Spirit from the Father. And to this purpose they made both the "of God," and the "in God," subservient, in a manner which shall now be shown.

First, the "in God." It is the clear declaration of Scripture, which we must receive without questioning, that the Son and Spirit are in the one God, and He in Them. There is that remarkable text in the first chapter of St. John which says that the Son is "in the

[7] ἰδέᾳ καὶ ἐνεργείᾳ, as at p. 170.

bosom of the Father." In another place it is said that "the Son is in the Father and the Father in the Son." (John xiv. 11.) And elsewhere the Spirit of God is compared to "the spirit of a man which is in him" (1 Cor. ii. 11). This is, in the language of theology, the doctrine of the *coinherence* [8]; which was used from the earliest times on the authority of Scripture, as a safeguard and witness of the Divine Unity. A passage from Athenagoras to this purpose has just been cited. Clement has the following doxology at the end of his Christian Instructor. "To the One Only Father and Son, Son and Father, Son our guide and teacher, with the Holy Spirit also, to the One in all things, in whom are all things, &c. . . . to Him is the glory, &c." And Gregory of Neocæsarea, if the words form part of his creed, "In the Trinity there is nothing created, nothing subservient, nothing of foreign nature, as if absent from it once, and afterwards added. The Son never failed the Father, nor the Spirit the Son, but the Trinity remains evermore unchangeable, unalterable." These authorities belong to the early Alexandrian School. The Ante-Nicene school of Rome is still more explicit. Dionysius of Rome says, "We must neither distribute into three divinities the awful and divine Unity, nor diminish the dignity and transcendant majesty of our Lord by the name of creature, but we must believe in God the Father Almighty, and in Christ Jesus His Son, and in the Holy Spirit; and believe that the Word is united with the God of the universe. For He says, I and the Father are One; and, I am in the

[8] περιχώρησις, or circumincessio.

Father, and the Father in Me. For thus the Divine Trinity and the holy preaching of the *monarchia* will be preserved[9]."

This doctrine of the *coinherence*, as protecting the Unity without intrenching on the perfections of the Son and Spirit, may even be called the characteristic of Catholic Trinitarianism as opposed to all counterfeits, whether philosophical, Arian, or Oriental. One Post-Nicene statement of it shall be added. "If any one truly receive the Son, says Basil, "he will find that He brings with him on one hand His Father, on the other the Holy Spirit. For neither can He from the Father be severed, who is of and ever in the Father; nor again from His own Spirit disunited, who in It operates all things. . . For we must not conceive separation or division in any way; as if either the Son could be supposed without the Father, or the Spirit disunited from the Son. But there is discovered between them some ineffable and incomprehensible, both communion and distinction[1]."

[9] Shortly before he had used the following still stronger expressions: *ἡνῶσθαι γὰρ ἀνάγκη τῷ Θεῷ τῶν ὅλων τὸν θεῖον Λόγον· ἐμφιλοχωρεῖν δὲ τῷ Θεῷ καὶ ἐνδιαιτᾶσθαι δεῖ τὸ Ἅγιον Πνεῦμα.* The Ante-Nicene African school is as express as the Roman. Tertullian says, "Connexus Patris in Filio, et Filii in Paracleto, tres efficit cohærentes, qui tres unum sint, non unus." Bull, Defens. ii. 6, § 4; 12, § 1. 11; iv. 4, 12, § 1. 11; iv. 4, § 10.

[1] Petav. iv. 16, § 9. The Semi-Arian creed, called *Macrostichos*, drawn up at Antioch A.D. 345, which is in parts unexceptionable in point of orthodoxy, contains the following striking exposition of the Catholic notion of the *coinherence*. "Though we affirm the Son to have a distinct existence and life as the Father has, yet we do not therefore separate Him from the Father, inventing place and distance between Their union after a corporeal manner. For we believe that they are united without medium or interval, and are inseparable." And then follow words to which our

Secondly, as the "in God" led the Fathers to the doctrine of the *coinherence*, so did the "of God" lead them to the doctrine of the *monarchia*[2]; still, with the one object of guarding against any resemblance to Polytheism in their creed. Even the heathen had shown a disposition, designedly or from a spontaneous feeling, to trace all their deities up to one Principle or *arche;* as is evident by their Theogonies[3]. Much more did it become that true religion, which prominently put forth the Unity of God, jealously to guard its language, lest it should seem to admit the existence of a variety of original Principles. It is said to have been the doctrine of the Marcionists and Manichees, that there were three unconnected independent Beings in the Divine Nature. Scripture and the Church avoid the appearance of tritheism, by tracing back, (if we may so say,) the infinite perfections of the Son and Spirit to Him whose Son and Spirit They are. They are, so to express it, but the new manifestation and repetition of the Father; there being no room for numeration or comparison between Them, nor any resting-place for the contemplating mind, till They are referred to Him in whom They centre. On the other hand, in naming the Father, we imply the Son and Spirit, whether They be named or not[4]. Without this key, the language of Scripture is per-

language is unequal: ὅλου μὲν τοῦ Πατρὸς ἐνεστερνισμένου τὸν Υἱόν· ὅλον δὲ τοῦ Υἱοῦ ἐξηρτημένου καὶ προσπεφυκότος τῷ Πατρὶ, καὶ μόνου τοῖς πατρώοις κόλποις ἀναπαυομένου διηνεκῶς. Bull, Defens. iv. 4, § 9.

[2] [Vid. Athan. Tr. vol. i. pp. 110—112.]

[3] Cudw. Intell. Syst. 4, § 13.

[4] Athan. ad Serap. i. 14.

plexed in the extreme[5]. Hence it is, that the Father is called "the only God," at a time when our Lord's name is also mentioned, John xvii. 3, 1 Tim. i. 16, 17, as if the Son was but the reiteration of His Person, who is the Self-Existent, and therefore not to be contrasted with Him in the way of number. The Creed, called the Apostles', follows this mode of stating the doctrine; the title of God standing in the opening against the Father's name, while the Son and Spirit are introduced as distinct forms or modes, (so to say,) of and in the One Eternal Being. The Nicene Creed, commonly so called, directed as it is against the impugners both of the Son's and of the Spirit's divinity, nevertheless observes the same rule even in a stricter form, beginning with a confession of the "*One* God." Whether or not this mode of speaking was designed in Scripture to guard the doctrine of the Unity from all verbal infringement (and there seems evidence that it was so, as in 1 Cor. viii. 5, 6,) it certainly was used for this purpose in the primitive Church. Thus Tertullian says, that it is a mistake "to suppose that the number and arrangement of the Trinity is a division of its Unity; inasmuch as the Unity drawing out the Trinity from itself, is not destroyed by it, but is subserved[6]." Novatian, in like manner, says, "God originating from God, so as to be the Second Person, yet not interfering with the Father's right to be called the one God. For, had

[5] Let 1 John v. 20 be taken as an example; or again, 1 Cor. xii. 4—6. John xiv. 16—18; xvi. 7—15.

[6] Again he says, that "the Trinity descending from the Father by closely knit and connected steps, both is consistent with the *monarchia* (Unity), and protects the *economia* (revealed dispensation)."

He not a birth, then indeed when compared with Him who had no birth, He would seem, from the appearance of equality in both, to make two who were without birth[7], and therefore two Gods[8]."

Accordingly it is impossible to worship One of the Divine Persons, without worshipping the Others also. In praying to the Father, we only arrive at His mysterious presence through His Son and Spirit; and in praying to the Son and Spirit, we are necessarily carried on beyond them to the source of Godhead from which They are derived. We see this in the very form of many of the received addresses to the Blessed Trinity; in which, without intended reference to the mediatorial scheme, the Son and Spirit seem, even in the view of the Divine Unity, to take a place in our thoughts between the Father and His creatures; as in the ordinary doxologies "to the Father through the Son and by the Spirit," or "to the Father and Son in the unity of the Holy Ghost."

This gives us an insight into the force of expressions, common with the primitive Fathers, but bearing, in

[7] [Or unoriginate; viz. on ἀγέννητος and ἄναρχος, in the next Section.]

[8] Petav. Præf. 5, I. iii.; § 8. Dionysius of Alexandria implies the same doctrine, when he declares; "We extend the indivisible Unity into the Trinity, and again we concentrate the indestructible Trinity into the Unity." And Hilary, to take a Post-Nicene authority, "We do not detract from the Father, His being the one God, when we say also that the Son is God. For He is God from God, one from one; therefore one God, because God is from Himself. On the other hand, the Son is not on that account the less God, because the Father is the one God. For the only-begotten Son of God is not without birth, so as to detract from the Father His being the one God, nor is He other than God, but because He is born of God." De Trin. i. Vide also Athan. de Sent. Dionys. 17. Bull, Defens. iv. 4, § 7.

the eyes of inconsiderate observers, a refined and curious character. They call the Son, "God of God, Light of Light," &c., much more frequently than simply God, in order to anticipate in the very form of words, the charge or the risk of ditheism. Hence, also, the illustrations of the sun and his rays, &c., were in such repute; viz. as containing, not only a description, but also a defence of the Catholic doctrine. Thus Hippolytus says, "When I say that the Son is distinct from the Father, I do not speak of two Gods; but, as it were, light of light, and the stream from the fountain, and a ray from the sun [9]." It was the same reason which led the Fathers to insist upon the doctrine of the divine generation.

[9] Bull, Defens. iv. 4, § 5.

SECTION IV.

VARIATIONS IN THE ANTE-NICENE THEOLOGICAL STATEMENTS.

THERE will, of course, be differences of opinion, in deciding how much of the ecclesiastical doctrine, as above described, was derived from direct Apostolical Tradition, and how much was the result of intuitive spiritual perception in scripturally informed and deeply religious minds. Yet it does not seem too much to affirm, that copious as it may be in theological terms, yet hardly one can be pointed out which is not found or strictly implied in the New Testament itself. And indeed so much perhaps will be granted by all who have claim to be considered Trinitarians; the objections, which some among them may be disposed to raise, lying rather against its alleged over-exactness in systematizing Scripture, than against the truths themselves which are contained in it. But it should be remembered, that it is we in after times who systematize the statements of the Fathers, which, as they occur in their works, are for the most part as natural and unpremeditated as those of the inspired volume itself. If the more exact terms and phrases of any writer be brought together, that is, of a writer who has fixed principles at all, of course they will appear technical and severe. We count the words of the Fathers, and measure their sentences; and so convert doxologies into creeds. That we do so, that the Church has done so more or less from the Nicene Council downwards, is the fault of those who have obliged us, of those who, "while men slept," have "sowed tares among the wheat."

This remark applies to the statements brought together in the last Section, from the early writers: which, even though generally subservient to certain important ends, as, for instance, the maintenance of the Unity of God, &c., are still on the whole written freely and devotionally. But now the discussion passes on to that more intentional systematizing on the part of the Ante-Nicene Fathers, which, unavoidable as it was, yet because it was in part conventional and individual, was ambiguous, and in consequence afforded at times an apparent countenance to the Arian heresy. It often becomes necessary to settle the phraseology of divinity, in points, where the chief problem is, to select the clearest words to express notions in which all agree; or to find the proposition which will best fit in with, and connect, a number of received doctrines. Thus the Calvinists dispute among themselves whether or not God *wills* the damnation of the non-elect; both parties agree in doctrine, they doubt how their own meaning may be best expressed[1]. However clearly we see, and firmly we grasp the truth, we have a natural fear of the appearance of inconsistency; nay, a becoming fear of mis-

[1] Vid. another instance infra, ch. v. § 2, in the controversy about the use of the word *hypostasis*.

leading others by our inaccuracy of language ; and especially when our words have been misinterpreted by opponents, are we anxious to guard against such an inconvenience in future. There are two characteristics of opinions subjected to this intellectual scrutiny: first, they are variously expressed during the process ; secondly, they are consigned to arbitrary formulas, at the end of it. Now, to exemplify this in certain Ante-Nicene statements of the great Catholic doctrine.

1.

The word ἀγεννητος, *ingenitus (unborn, ingenerate)*, was the philosophical term to denote that which had existed from eternity. It had accordingly been applied by Aristotle to the world or to matter, which was according to his system without beginning ; and by Plato to his ideas. Now since the Divine Word was according to Scripture *generate*, He could not be called *ingenerate* (or eternal), without a verbal contradiction. In process of time a distinction was made between ἀγένητος and ἀγέννητος, *(increate* and *ingenerate,)* according as the letter ν was or was not doubled, so that the Son might be said to be ἀγενήτως γεννητός *(increately generate)*. The argument which arose from this perplexity of language, is urged by Arius himself; who ridicules the ἀγεννητογενὲς, *ingenerately-generate*, which he conceives must be ascribed, according to the orthodox creed, to the Son of God[2]. Some years afterwards, the same was the palmary, or rather the essential argument of Eunomius, the champion of the Anomœans.

[2] Vid. infra, Section 5.

2.

The *ἄναρχον (unoriginate).* As is implied in the word *monarchia*, as already explained, the Father alone is the *arche*, or *origin*, and the Son and Spirit are not origins. The heresy of the Tritheists made it necessary to insist upon this. Hence the condemnation, in the (so-called) Apostolical Canons, of those who baptized "into the name of Three Unoriginate[3]." And Athanasius says, "We do not teach three Origins, as our illustration shows; for we do not speak of three Suns, but of the Sun and its radiance[4]." For the same reason the early writers spoke of the Father as the Fount of Divinity. At the same time, lest they should in word dishonour the Son, they ascribed to Him "an unoriginate generation" or "birth[5]." Thus Alexander, the first champion of orthodox truth against Arius, in his letter to his namesake of Byzantium: "We must reserve to the unbegotten (or unborn) Father His peculiar prerogative, confessing that no one is the cause of His existence, and to the Son we must pay the due honour, attributing to Him the unoriginate generation from the Father, and as we have said already, paying Him worship, so as ever to speak of Him piously and reverently, as 'pre-existent, ever-living,' and 'before the worlds[6].'" This distinction however, as might be expected, was but partially re-

[3] Bull, Defens. iv. 1, § 6.

[4] Cudw. Intell. Syst. 4, § 36 [p. 709, ed. Mosheim. But the Benedictine Ed. in Cyril, Catech. xi., says that Athanasius maintained the Son's ἄναρχον. Epiphanius, from 1 Cor. xi. 3, argues that the Father is the κεφαλή, not the ἀρχή, of the Son. Hær. 76, fin.]

[5] Suicer. Symb. Nicen. c. viii.

[6] Theod. Hist. i. 4, p. 18.

ceived among the Catholics. Contrasted with all created beings, the Son and Spirit are of necessity Unoriginate in the Unity of the Father. Clement, for instance, calls the Son, "the everlasting, unoriginate, origin and commencement of all things [7]." It was not till they became alive to the seeming ditheism of such phrases, which the Sabellian controversy was sure to charge upon them, that they learned the accurate discrimination observed by Alexander. On the other hand, when the Arian contest urged them in the contrary direction to Sabellius, then they returned more or less to the original language of Clement, though with a fuller explanation of their own meaning. Gregory Nyssen gives the following plain account of the variations of their practice: "Whereas the word *Origin* has many significations . . . sometimes we say that the appellation of the Unoriginate is not unsuitable to the Son. For when it is taken to mean derivation of substance from no cause, this indeed we ascribe to the Father alone. But according to the other senses of the word, since creation, time, the order of the world are referred to an origin, in respect of these we ascribe to the Only-begotten, superiority to any origin; so as to believe Him to be beyond creation, time, and mundane order, through whom were made all things. And thus we confess Him, who is not unoriginate in regard to His subsistence, in all other respects to be unoriginate, and, while the Father is unoriginate and unborn, the Son to be unoriginate in the sense explained, but not unborn [8]."

[7] *τὴν ἄχρονον, ἄναρχον, ἀρχήν τε καὶ ἀπαρχὴν τῶν πάντων.*

[8] Gregory Nazianzen says the same more concisely: ὁ Υἱός, ἐὰν ὡς

The word *cause* (αἴτιος) used in this passage, as a substitute for that use of *Origin* which peculiarly applies to the Father as the Fount of Divinity, is found as early as the time of Justin Martyr, who in his dialogue with Trypho, declares the Father is to the Son the αἴτιος, or cause of His being; and it was resumed by the Post-Nicene writers, when the Arian controversy was found to turn in no small degree on the exact application of such terms. Thus Gregory Nazianzen says, "There is One God, seeing that the Son and Spirit are referred to One Cause [9]."

3.

The Ante-Nicene history of the word homoüsion or *consubstantial*, which the Council of Nicæa adopted as its test, will introduce a more important discussion.

It is one characteristic of Revelation, that it clears up all doubts about the existence of God, as separate from, and independent of nature; and shows us that the course of the world depends not merely on a system, but on a Being, real, living, and individual. What we ourselves witness, evidences to us the operation of laws, physical and moral; but it leaves us unsatisfied, whether or not the principle of these be a mere nature or fate, whether the life of all things be a mere Anima Mundi, a spirit connatural with the body in

αἴτιον τὸν Πατέρα λαμβάνῃς, οὐκ ἄναρχος· ἀρχὴ γὰρ Υἱοῦ Πατὴρ, ὡς αἴτιος. Bull, Defens. iv. 2, § 8. 1; § 3. Petav. i. 4, § i. Suicer, ibid.

[9] However, here too we have a variation in the use of the word: αἴτιος being sometimes applied to the Son in the sense ἀρχή. The Latin word answering to αἴτιος is sometimes *causa*, more commonly *principium* or *auctor*. Bull, Defens. iv. 1, § 2; § 4. Petav. v. 5, § 10.

which it acts, or an Agent powerful to make or un make, to change or supersede, according to His will. It is here that Revelation supplies the deficiency of philosophical religion ; miracles are its emblem, as well as its credentials, forcing on the imagination the existence of an irresponsible self-dependent Being, as well as recommending a particular message to the reason. This great truth, conveyed in the very circumstances under which Revelation was made, is explicitly recognized in its doctrine. Among other modes of inculcating it, may be named the appellation under which Almighty God disclosed Himself to the Israelites; Jehovah (or, as the Septuagint translates it, *ὁ ὢν*) being an expressive appellation of Him, who is essentially separate from those variable and perishable beings or substances, which creation presents to our observation. Accordingly, the description of Him as *τὸ ὄν*, or in other words, the doctrine of the *οὐσία* of God, that is, of God viewed as Being and as the one Being, became familiar to the minds of the primitive Christians ; as embodying the spirit of the Scriptures, and indirectly witnessing against the characteristic error of pagan philosophy, which considered the Divine Mind, not as a reality, but as a mere abstract name, or generalized law of nature, or at best as a mere mode, principle, or an animating soul, not a Being external to creation, and possessed of individuality. Cyril of Alexandria defines the word *οὐσία*, *(usia, being, substance,)* to be "that which has existence in itself, independent of every thing else to constitute it[1] ;" that is, an individual. This sense

[1] *πρᾶγμα αὐθύπαρκτον, μὴ δεόμενον ἑτέρου πρὸς τὴν ἑαυτοῦ σύστασιν.* Suicer, Thesaur. verb. *οὐσία.*

of the word must be carefully borne in mind, since it was *not* that in which it is used by philosophers, who by it denoted the genus or species, or the "ens unum in multis,"—a sense which of course it could not bear when applied to the One Incommunicable God. The word, thus appropriated to the service of the God of Revelation, was from the earliest date used to express the reality and subsistence of the Son; and no word could be less metaphorical and more precise for this purpose, although the Platonists chose to refine, and from an affectation of reverence refused to speak of God except as *hyperusios*[2]. Justin Martyr, for instance, speaks of heretics, who considered that God put forth and withdrew His Logos when it pleased Him, as if He were an influence, not a Person[3], somewhat in the sense afterwards adopted by Paulus of Samosata and others. To meet this error, he speaks of Him as inseparable from the substance or being, *usia*, of the Father; that is, in order to exclude all such evasions of Scripture, as might represent the man Christ as inhabited by a divine glory, power, nature, and the like, evasions which in reality lead to the conclusion that He is not God at all.

For this purpose the word *homoüsion* or *consubstantial* was brought into use among Christian writers; viz. to express the real divinity of Christ, and that, as being derived from, and one with the Father's. Here again, as in the instance of its root, the word was adopted, from the necessity of the case, in a sense

[2] [Or ἐπέκεινα οὐσίας] Petav. [t. i. i. 6] t. ii. iv. 5, § 8. [Brucker, t. 2, p. 395. Plot. Enn. v. lib. i. We find ὑπερούσιος or ἐπέκεινα οὐσίας in Orig. c. Cels. vi. 64. Damasc. F. O. i. 4, 8, and 12.]

[3] Justin, Tryph. 128.

different from the ordinary philosophical use of it. *Homoüsion* properly means *of the same nature,* or under the same *general* nature, or species ; that is, it is applied to things, which are but similar to each other, and are considered as one by an abstraction of our minds ; or, it may mean of the same material. Thus Aristotle speaks of the stars being consubstantial with each other ; and Porphyry of the souls of brute animals being consubstantial to ours[4]. When, however, it was used in relation to the incommunicable Essence of God, there was obviously no abstraction possible in contemplating Him, who is above all comparison with His works. His nature is solitary, peculiar to Himself, and one ; so that whatever was accounted to be consubstantial or co-essential with Him, was necessarily included in His individuality, by all who would avoid recurring to the vagueness of philosophy, and were cautious to distinguish between the incommunicable Essence of Jehovah and all created intelligences. And hence the fitness of the term to denote without metaphor the relation which the Logos bore in the orthodox creed to His eternal Father. Its use is explained by Athanasius as follows. "Though," he says, "we cannot understand what is meant by the *usia*, being, or *substance* of God, yet we know as much as this, that God is, which is the way in which Scripture speaks of Him ; and after this pattern, when we wish to designate Him distinctly, we say God, Father, Lord. When then He says in Scripture, 'I am *ὁ ὢν*,' the Being, and 'I am Jehovah, God,' or uses the plain word 'God,' we understand by such statements nothing but His incompre-

[4] Bull, Defens. ii. 1, § 2, &c.

hensible *οὐσία* (being or substance), and that He, who is there spoken of, is. Let no one then think it strange, that the Son of God should be said to be *ἐκ τῆς οὐσίας* (from the being or substance) of God; rather, let him agree to the explanation of the Nicene fathers, who, for the words 'of God' substituted 'of the divine being or substance.' They considered the two phrases substantially the same, because, as I have said, the word 'God' denotes nothing but the *οὐσία αὐτοῦ τοῦ ὄντος*, the being of Him who is. On the other hand, if the Word be not in such sense 'of God,' as to be the true Son of the Father according to His nature, but be said to be 'of God,' merely as all creatures are such because they are His work, then indeed He is not 'from the being of the Father,' nor Son 'according to being or substance,' but so called from His virtue, as we may be, who receive the title from grace[5]."

The term *homoüsios* is first employed for this purpose by the author of the *Pæmander*, a Christian of the beginning of the second century. Next it occurs in several writers at the end of the second and the beginning of the third. In Tertullian, the equivalent phrase, "unius substantiæ," "*of one substance*," is applied to the Trinity. In Origen's comment on the Hebrews, the *homoüsion* of the Son is deduced from the figurative title *ἀπαύγασμα*, or *radiance*, there given to Him. In the same age, it was employed by various writers, bishops and historians, as we learn from the testimonies of Eusebius and Athanasius[6]. But at this era, the middle of the third century, a change took

[5] Athan. de Decr. Nic. 22.

[6] [Vide Ath. Tr. vol. ii. p. 438. Also Archelaus speaks of our Lord as "de substantiâ Dei." Routh, t. iv. p. 228.]

place in the use of it and other similar words, which is next to be explained.

The oriental doctrine of Emanations was at a very early period combined with the Christian theology. According to the system of Valentinus, a Gnostic heresiarch, who flourished in the early part of the second century, the Supreme Intelligence of the world gave existence to a line of Spirits or Eons, who were all more or less partakers of His nature, that is, of a nature *specifically* the same, and included in His glory (πλήρωμα), though individually separate from the true and Sovereign Deity. It is obvious, that such a teaching as this abandons the great revealed principle above insisted on, the incommunicable character and individuality of the Divine Essence. It considers all spiritual beings as like God, in the same sense that one man resembles or has the same nature as another: and accordingly it was at liberty to apply, and did actually apply, to the Creator and His creatures the word *homoüsion* or *consubstantial*, in the philosophical sense which the word originally bore. We have evidence in the work of Irenæus that the Valentinians did thus employ it. The Manichees followed, about a century later; they too were Emanatists, and spoke of the human soul as being *consubstantial* or *co-essential* with God, of one substance with God. Their principles evidently allowed of a kind of Trinitarianism; the Son and Spirit being considered Eons of a superior order to the rest, *consubstantial* with God because Eons, but one with God in no sense which was not true also of the soul of man. It is said, moreover, that they were materialists; and used the word *consubstantial* as it may be applied to different vessels or instruments, wrought out from some one mass of metal or wood. However, whether this was so or not, it is plain that anyhow the word in question would become unsuitable to express the Catholic doctrine, in proportion as the ears of Christians were familiarized to the terms employed in the Gnostic and Manichean theologies; nor is it wonderful that at length they gave up the use of it.

The history of the word *probole* or *offspring* is parallel to that of the *consubstantial*[7]. It properly means any thing which proceeds, or is sent forth from the substance of another, as the fruit of a tree, or the rays of the sun; in Latin it is translated by *prolatio*, *emissio*, or *editio*, an *offspring* or *issue*. Accordingly Justin employed it, or rather a cognate phrase[8], to designate what Cyril calls above the self-existence[9] of the Son, in opposition to the evasions which were necessary for the system of Paulus, Sabellius, and the rest. Tertullian does the same; but by that time, Valentinus had given the word a material signification. Hence Tertullian is obliged to apologize for using it, when writing against Praxeas, the forerunner of the Sabellians. "Can the Word of God," he asks, "be unsubstantial, who is called the Son, who is even named God? He is said to be in the form or image of God. Is not God a body [substance], Spirit though He be? .. Whatever then has been the substance of the Word,[1] that, I call a Person, and claim for it the name of Son, and being such, He comes next to the Father. Let no one suppose that I am bringing in the notion of

[7] Beausobre, Hist. Manich. iii. 7. § 6. [Vide Ath. Tr. vol. ii. p. 458.]

[8] προβληθὲν γέννημα. Justin. Tryph. 62.

[9] αὐτόγονος. [Vide Ath. Tr. art. υἱοπάτωρ, vol. ii. p. 475, ed. 1881.]

[1] [Ibid. p. 340, art. *Word*.]

any such *probole* (*offspring*) as Valentinus imagined, drawing out his Eons the one from the other. Why must I give up the word in a right sense, because heresy uses it in a wrong? besides, heresy borrowed it from us, and has turned truth into a lie. . . . . This is the difference between the uses of it. Valentinus separates his *probolæ* from their Father; they know Him not. But we hold that the Son alone knows the Father, reveals Him, performs His will, and is within Him. He is ever in the Father, as He has said; ever with God, as it is written; never separated from Him, for He and the Father are one. This is the true *probole*, the safeguard of unity, sent forth, not divided off[1]." Soon after Tertullian thus defended his use of the word *probole*, Origen in another part of the Church gave it up, or rather assailed it, in argument with Candidus, a Valentinian. "If the Son is a *probole* of the Father," he says, "who begets Him from Himself, like the birth of animals, then of necessity both offspring and original are of a bodily nature[2]." Here we see two writers, with exactly the same theological creed before them, taking opposite views as to the propriety of using a word which heresy had corrupted[3].

But to return to the word *consubstantial*: though Origen gave up the word *probole*, yet he used the word *consubstantial*, as has already been mentioned[4]. But shortly after his death, his pupils abandoned it at the

[1] Tertull. in Prax. 7, 8, abridged.

[2] [Periarch. iv. p. 190.]

[3] Vide an apposite note of Coustant. Epp. Pont. Rom. p. 496, on Damasus's Words: "nec prolativum, ut generationem ei demas."]

[4] [But he was not consistent. Vide Hieron. contr. Ruff. ii. 19. Also the dissertation in Jackson's preface to Novatian, p. xlviii, &c.]

celebrated Council held at Antioch (A.D. 264) against Paulus of Samosata. When they would have used it as a test, this heretic craftily objected to it on the very ground on which Origen had surrendered the *probole.* He urged that, if Father and Son were of one substance, *consubstantial,* there was some common substance in which they partook, and which consequently was distinct from and prior to the Divine Persons Themselves; a wretched sophism, which of course could not deceive Firmilian and Gregory, but which, being adapted to perplex weak minds, might decide them on withdrawing the word. It is remarkable too, that the Council was held about the time when Manes appeared on the borders of the Antiochene Patriarchate. The disputative school of Paulus pursued the advantage thus gained; and from that time used the charge of materialism as a weapon for attacking all sound expositions of Scripture truth. Having extorted from the Catholics the condemnation of a word long known in the Church, almost found in Scripture, and less figurative and material in its meaning than any which could be selected, and objectionable only in the mouths of heretics, they employed this concession as a ground of attacking expressions more directly metaphorical, taken from visible objects, and sanctioned by less weighty authority. In a letter which shall afterwards be cited, Arius charges the Catholics with teaching the errors of Valentinus and Manes; and in another of the original Arian documents, Eusebius of Nicomedia, maintains in like manner that their doctrine involves the materiality of the Divine Nature. Thus they were gradually silencing the Church by a process which legitimately led to

Pantheism, when the Alexandrians gave the alarm, and nobly stood forward in defence of the faith [5].

It is worth observing that, when the Asiatic Churches had given up the *consubstantial*, they, on the contrary, had preserved it. Not only Dionysius willingly accepts the challenge of his namesake of Rome, who reminded him of the value of the symbol; but Theognostus also, who presided at the Catechetical School at the end of the third century, recognizes it by implication in the following passage, which has been preserved by Athanasius. "The substance [6] of the Son," he says, "is not external to the Father, or created; but it is by natural derivation from that of the Father, as the radiance comes from light (Heb. i. 3). For the radiance is not the sun, . . . and yet not foreign to it; and in like manner there is an effluence (ἀπόῤῥοια, Wisd. vii. 25.) from the Father's substance, though it be indivisible from Him. For as the sun remains the same without infringement of its nature, though it pour forth its radiance, so the Father's substance is unchangeable, though the Son be its Image [7]."

4.

Some notice of the θελήσει γεννηθὲν, or voluntary generation, will suitably follow the discussion of the

[5] [Parallel to the above instances is Basil's objection to γέννημα, when used of the Son, which Athanasius and others apply to him. Vide Ath. Tr. vol. ii. p. 396.]

[6] [It may be questioned, however, whether the word *substance* in this passage is not equivalent to *hypostasis* or *subsistence*; vide Appendix, No. 4.]

[7] Athan. de Decr. Nic. 25.

consubstantial; though the subject does not closely concern theology. It has been already observed that the tendency of the heresies of the first age was towards materialism and fatalism. As it was the object of Revelation to destroy all theories which interfered with the belief of the Divine Omniscience and active Sovereignty, so the Church seconded this design by receiving and promulgating the doctrine of the "*He that is,*" or the Divine "*Being*" or "*Essence,*" as a symbol of His essential distinction from the perishable world in which He acts. But when the word *substance* or *essence* itself was taken by the Gnostics and Manichees in a material sense, the error was again introduced by the very term which was intended to witness against it. According to the Oriental Theory, the emanations from the Deity were eternal with Himself, and were considered as the result, not of His will and personal energy, but of the necessary laws to which His nature was subjected; a doctrine which was but fatalism in another shape. The Eclectics honourably distinguished themselves in withstanding this blasphemous, or rather atheistical tenet. Plotinus declares, that "God's substance and His will are the same; and if so, as He willed, so He is; so that it is not a more certain truth that, as is His substance or nature, so is His will and action, than, as His will and action, so is His substance." Origen had preceded them in their opposition to the same school. Speaking of the simplicity and perfection of the Divine Essence, he says, "God does not even participate in substance, rather He is partaken; by those, namely, who have the Spirit of God. And our Saviour does not share in holiness, but, being holiness itself, is shared by the holy." The meaning of this doctrine is clear;—to protest, in the manner of Athanasius, in a passage lately cited, against the notion that the substance of God is something distinct from God Himself, and not God viewed as self-existent, the one immaterial, intelligent, all-perfect Spirit; but the risk of it lay in its tendency to destroy the doctrine of His individual and real existence (which the Catholic use of *substance* symbolized), and to introduce in its stead the notion that a quality or mode of acting was the governing principle of nature; in other words, Pantheism. This is an error of which Origen of course cannot be accused; but it is in its measure chargeable on the Platonic Masters, and is countenanced even by their mode of speaking of the Supreme Being, as not substantial, but above the notion of substance[8]."

The controversy did not terminate in the subject of Theism, but was pursued by the heretical party into questions of Christian Theology. The Manichees considered the Son and Spirit as necessary emanations from the Father; erring, first, in their classing those Divine Persons with intelligences confessedly imperfect and subservient; next, in introducing a sort of materialism into their notion of the Deity. The Eclectics on the other hand, maintained, by a strong figure, that the Eternal Son originated from the Father at His own will; meaning thereby, that the everlasting mystery, which constitutes the relation between Father and Son, has no physical or material conditions, and is such as becomes Him who is alto-

[8] ὑπερούσιος. Cudw. Intell. Syst. iv. § 23. Petav. vi. 8, § 19, ibid t. i. ii, 6, § 9.

gether Mind, and bound by no laws, but those established by His own perfection as a first cause. Thus Iamblichus calls the Son self-begotten[9].

The discussion seems hardly to have entered farther into the Ante-Nicene Church, than is implied in the above notice of it: though some suppose that Justin and others referred the divine *gennesis* or *generation* to the will of God. However, it is easy to see that the ground was prepared for the introduction of a subtle and irreverent question, whenever the theologizing Sophists should choose to raise it. Accordingly, it was one of the first and principal interrogations put to the Catholics by their Arian opponents, whether the *generation* of the Son was voluntary or not on the part of the Father; their dilemma being, that Almighty God was subject to laws external to Himself, if it were not voluntary, and that, if on the other hand it was voluntary, the Son was in the number of things created. But of this more in the next Section.

3.

The Word as internal or external to the Father; *λόγος ἐνδιάθετος* and *προφορικός*[1]:—One theory there was, adopted by several of the early Fathers, which led them to speak of the Son's generation or birth as resulting from the Father's will, and yet did not interfere with His consubstantiality. Of the two titles ascribed in Scripture to our Lord, that of the "*Word*" expresses with peculiar force His co-eternity in the One Almighty Father. On the other hand, the title

[9] αὐτόγονος. [Vide Ath. Tr. vol. ii. p. 475.]

[1] [Vide Ath. Tr. vol. ii. pp. 340—342.]

"*Son*" has more distinct reference to His derivation and ministrative office. A distinction resembling this had already been applied by the Stoics to the Platonic Logos, which they represented under two aspects, the ἐνδιάθετος and προφορικός, that is, the internal Thought and Purpose of God, and its external Manifestation, as if in words spoken. The terms were received among Catholics; the "Endiathetic" standing for the Word, as hid from everlasting in the bosom of the Father, while the "Prophoric" was the Son sent forth into the world, in apparent separation from God, with His Father's name and attributes upon Him, and His Father's will to perform [2]. This contrast is acknowledged by Athanasius, Gregory Nyssen, Cyril, and other Post-Nicene writers; nor can it be confuted, being Scriptural in its doctrine, and merely expressed in philosophical language, found ready for the purpose. But further, this change of state in the Eternal Word, from repose to energetic manifestation, as it took place at the creation, was called by them a *gennesis*: and here too, no blame attaches to them, for the expression is used in Scripture in different senses, one of which appears to be the very signification which they put on it, the mission of the Word to make and govern all things. Such is the text in St. Paul, that He is "the image of the Invisible God, the First-born of every creature;" such is His title in St. John as "the Beginning of the Creation of God [3]." This *gennesis* or *generation* was called also the "going-

[2] Burton, Bampt. Lect., note 91. Petav. vi. 1—3.

[3] Col. i. 15. Rev. iii. 14. Vide also Gen. i. 3. Heb. xi. 3. Eccl. xxiv. 3—9.

forth," or "condescension," of the Son, which may Scripturally be ascribed to the will of the all-bountiful Father[4]. However, there were some early writers who seem to interpret the *gennesis* in this meaning exclusively, ascribing the title of "*Son*" to our Lord only after the date of His mission or economy, and considering that of the "*Word*" as His peculiar appellation during the previous eternity[5]. Nay, if we carry off their expressions hastily or perversely, as some theologians have done, we shall perhaps conclude that they conceived that God existed in One Person before the "*going-forth,*" and then, if it may be said, by a change in His nature began to exist in a Second Person; as if an attribute (the Internal Word, "*Endiathetic,*") had come into substantive being, as "*Prophoric.*" The Fathers, who have laid themselves open to this charge, are Athenagoras, Tatian, Theophilus, Hippolytus, and Novatian, as mentioned in the first Chapter.

Now that they did not mean what a superficial reader might lay to their charge, may be argued, first, from the parallel language of the Post-Nicenes, as mentioned above, whose orthodoxy no one questions. Next, from the extreme absurdity, not to speak of the impiety, of the doctrine imputed to them; as if, with a more than Gnostic extravagance, they conceived that any change or extension could take place in that Individual Essence, which is without parts or passions,

[4] προέλευσις, συγκατάβασις, Bull, Defens. iii. 9. [Other writers support him in this view, as Maranus, in Just. Tryph. 61, and in his work Divin. Jes. Christi, lib. iv. c. 6. Vide contr. Dissert. 3 and 4 in the Author's "Theological Tracts."]

[5] [Vide "Theological Tracts," iii.]

or that the divine *generation* could be an event in time, instead of being considered a mere expression of the eternal relation of the Father towards the Son[6]. Indeed, the very absurdity of the literal sense of the words, in whatever degree they so expressed themselves, was the mischief to be apprehended from them. The reader, trying a rhetorical description by too rigid a rule, would attempt to elicit sense by imputing a heresy, and would conclude that they meant by the External or *Prophoric* Word a created being, made in the beginning of all things as the visible emblem of the Internal or *Endiathetic*, and the instrument of God's purposes towards His creation. This is in fact the Arian doctrine, which doubtless availed itself in its defence of the declarations of incautious piety; or rather we have evidence of the fact, that it did so avail itself, in the letter of Arius to Alexander, and from the anathema of the Nicene Creed directed against such as said that "the Son was not before His *gennesis*."

Lastly, the orthodoxy of the five writers in question is ascertained by a careful examination of the passages, which give ground for the accusation. Two of these shall here be quoted without comment. Theophilus then says, "God having His own Word in His womb, begat Him together with His Wisdom" (that is, His Spirit), "uttering them prior to the universe." "He had this Word as the Minister of His works, and did all things through Him. . . . The prophets were not in existence when the world was made; but the

[6] ['οὔτε ἀρχὴν ἔχει ἡ ἀκατάληπτος αὐτοῦ γέννησις οὔτε τέλος, ἀνάρχως, ἀκαταπαύστως, &c. Damasc. F. O. p. 8. Vide Ath. Tr. vol. ii. pp. 350 and 108.]

Wisdom of God, which is in Him, and His Holy Word, who is ever present with Him[7]." Elsewhere he speaks of "the Word, eternally seated in the heart of God[8];" "for," he presently adds, "before anything was made, He possessed this Counseller, as being His mind and providence. And when He purposed to make all that He had deliberated on, He begat this Word as external to Him, being the First-born antecedent to the whole creation; not, however, Himself losing the Word" (that is, the Internal), "but begetting it, and yet everlastingly communing with it[9]."

In like manner Hippolytus in his answer to Noetus:—"God was alone, and there was no being coeval with Him, when He willed to create the world. . . . . Not that He was destitute of reason (the Logos), wisdom or counsel. They are all in Him, He was all. At the time and in the manner He willed, He manifested His Word [Logos], . . through whom He made all things. . . Moreover He placed over them His Word, whom He begat as His Counseller and Instrument; whom He had within Him, invisible to creation, till He manifested Him, uttering the Word, and begetting Light from Light. . . . And so Another stood by Him, not as if there were two Gods, but as though Light from Light, or a ray from the Sun[1]."

And thus closes our survey of Catholic Ante-Nicene theology.

[7] ἔχον . . ὁ θεὸς τὸν ἑαυτοῦ λόγον ἐνδιάθετον ἐν τοῖς ἰδίοις σπλάγχνοις, ἐγέννησεν αὐτὸν μετὰ τῆς ἑαυτοῦ σοφίας, ἐξερευξάμενος (Psalm xlv. 1), πρὸ τῶν ὅλων . . . ὁ ἀεὶ συμπαρὼν αὐτῷ.

[8] τὸν λόγον διαπαντὸς ἐνδιαθετον ἐν καρδίᾳ θεοῦ.

[9] ἐγέννησε προφορικόν.

[1] Vide Bull, Defens. iii. 7, 8.

SECTION V.

THE ARIAN HERESY

IT remains to give some account of the heretical doctrine, which was first promulgated within the Church by Arius. There have been attempts to attribute this heresy to Catholic writers previous to his time; yet its contemporaries are express in their testimony that he was the author of it, nor can anything be adduced from the Ante-Nicene theology to countenance such an imputation. Sozomen expressly says, that Arius was the first to introduce into the Church the formulæ of the "out of nothing," and the "once He was not," that is, the creation and the non-eternity of the Son of God. Alexander and Athanasius, who had the amplest means of information on the subject, confirm his testimony [1]. That the heresy existed before his time outside the Church, may be true,—though little is known on the subject; and that there had been certain speculators, such as Paulus of Samosata, who were simply humanitarians, is undoubtedly true; but they did not hold the formal doctrine of Arius, that an Angelic being had been exalted into a God. How-

[1] Soz. i. 15. Theod. His. i. 4. Athan. Decr. Nic. 27. de Sent. Dionys. 6.

ever, he and his supporters, though they do not venture to adduce in their favour the evidence of former Catholics, nevertheless speak in a general way of their having received their doctrines from others. Arius too himself appears to be only a partisan of the Eusebians, and they in turn are referable to Lucian of Antioch, who for some cause or other was at one time under excommunication. But here we lose sight of the heresy; except that Origen assails a doctrine, whose we know not[2], which bears a resemblance to it; nay, if we may trust Ruffinus, which was expressed in the very same heterodox formulæ, which Sozomen declares that Arius was the first to preach within the Church.

1.

Before detailing, however, the separate characteristics of his heresy, it may be right briefly to confront it with such previous doctrines, in and out of the Church, as may be considered to bear a resemblance to it.

The fundamental tenet of Arianism was, that the Son of God was a creature, not born of the Father, but, in the scientific language of the times, made "out of nothing[3]." It followed that He only possessed a super-angelic nature, being made at God's good pleasure before the worlds, before time, after the pattern of the attribute Logos or Wisdom, as existing in the Divine Mind, gifted with the illumination of it, and in consequence called after it the Word and the

[2] The ἦν ποτὲ ὅτε οὐκ ἦν; it might be Tertullian who was aimed at, especially as St. Dionysius of Rome denounces the doctrine also.]

[3] ἐξ ὀυκ ὄντων; hence the Arians were called Exucontii.

Wisdom, nay inheriting the title itself of God; and at length united to a human body, in the place of its soul, in the person of Jesus Christ.

1. This doctrine resembled that of the five philosophizing Fathers, as described in the foregoing Section, so far as this, that it identified the Son with the External or Prophoric Logos, spoke of the Divine Logos Itself as if a mere internal attribute, and yet affected to maintain a connexion between the Logos and the Son. Their doctrine differed from it, inasmuch as they believed, that He who was the Son had ever been in personal existence as the Logos in the Father's bosom, whereas Arianism dated His personal existence from the time of His manifestation.

2. It resembled the Eclectic theology, so far as to maintain that the Son was by nature separate from and inferior to the Father; and again, formed at the Father's will. It differed from Eclecticism, in considering the Son to have a beginning of existence, whereas the Platonists held Him, as they held the universe, to be an eternal Emanation, and the Father's will to be a concomitant, not an antecedent, of His *gennesis*.

3. It agreed with the teaching of Gnostics and Manichees, in maintaining the Son's essential inferiority to the Father: it vehemently opposed them in their material notions of the Deity.

4. It concurred with the disciples of Paulus, in considering the Intellectual and Ruling Principle in Christ, the Son of God, to be a mere creature, by nature subject to a moral probation, as other men, and exalted on the ground of His obedience, and gifted, moreover, with a heavenly wisdom, called the Logos,

which guided Him. The two heresies also agreed, as the last words imply, in holding the Logos to be an attribute or manifestation, not a Person [4]. Paulus considered it as if a voice or sound, which comes and goes ; so that God may be said to have *spoken* in Christ. Arius makes use of the same illustration: "Many words speaketh God," he says, "which of them is manifested in the flesh [5]?" He differs from Paulus, in holding the pre-existence of the spiritual intelligence in Christ, or the Son, whom he considers to be the first and only creation of the Father's Hand, superangelic, and the God of the Christian Economy.

5. Arianism agreed with the heresy of Sabellius, in teaching God to exist only in one Person, and His true Logos to be an attribute, manifested in the Son, who was a creature [6]. It differed from Sabellianism, as regards the sense in which the Logos was to be accounted as existing in Christ. The Sabellian, lately a Patripassian, at least insisted much upon the formal and abiding presence of the Logos in Him. The Arian, only partially admitting the influence of the Divine Logos on that superangelic nature, which was the Son, and which in Christ took the place of a soul, nevertheless gave it the name of Logos, and maintained accordingly that the incarnate Logos was not the true Wisdom and Word of God, which was one with Him, but a created semblance of it.

4 [When the Eternal Word, after the Nicene Council, was defined to have a personal subsistence, then the Samosatene doctrine would become identical with Nestorianism. Both heresies came from Antioch.]

5 Athan. Decret. Nicen. 16.

6 Athan. Sent. Dionys. 25.

6. Such is Arianism in its relations to the principal errors of its time; and of these it was most opposed to the Gnostic and Sabellian, which, as we shall see, it did not scruple to impute to its Catholic adversaries. Towards the Catholics, on the other hand, it stood thus: it was willing to ascribe to the Son all that is commonly attributed to Almighty God, His name, authority, and power; all but the incommunicable nature or being *(usia)*, that is, all but that which alone could give Him a right to these prerogatives of divinity in a real and literal sense. Now to turn to the arguments by which the heresy defended itself, or rather, attacked the Church.

2.

1. Arius commenced his heresy thus, as Socrates informs us :—"(1) If the Father gave birth to the Son, He who was born has an origin of existence; (2) therefore once the Son was not; (3) therefore He is created out of nothing[7]." It appears, then, that he inferred his

[7] Socr. i. 5. That is, the Son, as such, (1) had *ἀρχὴν ὑπάρξεως*, (2) *ἦν ὅτε οὐκ ἦν*, (3) *ἐξ οὐκ ὄντων ἔχει τὴν ὑπόστασιν*. The argument thus stated in the history, answers to the first three propositions anathematized at Nicæa, which are as follows, the figures prefixed marking the correspondence of each with Arius's theses, as set down by Socrates:—*τοὺς λέγοντας* (2) *ὅτι ἦν ποτε ὅτε οὐκ ἦν*, (1) *καὶ πρὶν γεννηθῆναι οὐκ ἦν*, (3) *καὶ ὅτι ἐξ οὐκ ὄντων ἐγένετο*, (4) *ἢ ἐξ ἑτέρας ὑποστάσεως ἢ οὐσίας εἶναι, ἢ κτιστὸν*, (5) *ἢ τρεπτὸν ἢ ἀλλοιωτὸν τὸν υἱὸν τοῦ θεοῦ, ἀναθεματίζει ἡ ἁγία καθολικὴ ἐκκλησία.* [The fourth of these propositions is the denial of the *ὁμοούσιον*.] The last, viz. the mutability of the Son, was probably not one of Arius's original propositions, but forced from him by his opponents as a necessary consequence of his doctrine. He retracts it in his letters to Eusebius and Alexander, who, on the other hand, bear testimony to his having avowed it.

doctrine from the very meaning of the word "*Son*," which is the designation of our Lord in Scripture; and so far he adopted a fair and unexceptionable mode of reasoning. Human relations, though the merest shadows of "heavenly things," yet would not of course be employed by Divine Wisdom without fitness, nor unless with the intention of instructing us. But what should be the exact instruction derived by us from the word "*Son*" is another question[8]. The Catholics (not to speak of their guidance from tradition in determining it) had taken "*Son*" in its most obvious meaning; as interpreted moreover by the title "*Only-begotten*," and as confirmed by the general tenor of Revelation. But the Arians selected as the sense of the figure, that part of the original import of the word, which, though undeniably included in it, when referred to us, is at best what logicians call a *property* deduced from the essence or nature, not an element of its essential idea, and which was especially out of place, when the word was used to express a truth about the Divine Being. That a *father* is prior to his *son*, is not suggested, though it is implied, by the force of the terms, as ordinarily used; and it is an inference altogether irrelevant, when the inquiry has reference to that Being, from our notion of whom time as well as space is necessarily excluded. It is fair, indeed, to object at the outset to the word "Father" being applied at all in its primary sense to the Supreme Being; but this was not the Arian ground, which was to argue from, not against, the

[8] "[Non recte faciunt, qui vim adhibent, ut sic se habeat exemplum, ut prototypum. Non enim esset jam exemplum, nisi haberet aliquid dissimile." Leont. Contr. Nest. i. p. 539, ed. Canis.]

metaphor employed. Nor was even this the extent of perverseness which their argument evidences. Let it be observed, that they admitted the primary sense of the word, *in order* to introduce a mere secondary sense, contending that, because our Lord was to be considered really as a Son, therefore in fact He was no Son at all. In the first proposition Arius assumes that He is really a Son, and argues as if He were; in the third he has arrived at the conclusion that He was created, that is, no Son at all, except in a secondary sense, as having received from the Father a sort of *adoption.* An attempt was made by the Arians to smooth over their inconsistency, by adducing passages of Scripture, in which the works of God are spoken of as births,—as in the instance from Job, "He giveth birth to the drops of dew." But this is obviously an entirely new mode of defending their theory of a divine adoption, and does not relieve their original fault; which consisted in their arguing from an assumed analogy, which the result of that argument destroyed. For, if He be the Son of God, no otherwise than man is, that is, by adoption, what becomes of the argument from the *anterior* and *posterior* in existence[9]? as if the notion of adoption, contained in it any necessary reference to the nature and circumstances of the two parties between whom it takes place.

2. Accordingly, the Arians were soon obliged to betake themselves to a more refined argument. They dropped the consideration of time, and withdrew the inference involving it, which they had drawn from the literal sense of the word "*Son.*" Instead of this, they

9 [That is, an adopted son is not necessarily younger, but might be older, than the person adopting him.]

maintained that the relation of Father and Son, as such, in whatever sense considered, could not but imply the notion of voluntary originator, and on the other hand, of a free gift conferred; and that the Son must be essentially inferior to Him, from whose will His existence resulted. Their argument was conveyed in the form of a dilemma:—"Whether the Father gave birth to the Son *volens* or *nolens?*" The Catholics wisely answered them by a counter inquiry, which was adapted to silence, without countenancing, the presumptuous disputant. Gregory of Nazianzus asked them, "Whether the Father is God, *volens* or *nolens?*" And Cyril of Alexandria, "Whether He is good, compassionate, merciful, and holy, with or against His choice? For, if He is so in consequence of choosing it, and choice ever precedes what is chosen, these attributes once did not exist in God." Athanasius gives substantially the same answer, solving, however, rather than confuting, the objection. "The Arians," he says, "direct their view to the *contradictory* of willing, instead of considering the more important and the *previous* question; for, as *unwillingness* is opposed to *willing*, so is *nature* prior to willing, and leads the way to it [1]."

3. Further:—the Arians attempted to draw their conclusion as to the dissimilarity of the Father and the Son, from the divine attribute of the "Ingenerate" (*unborn* or increate), which, as I have already said, was acknowledged on all hands to be the peculiar attribute

[1] Petav. ii. 5, § 9; vi. 8. 14. ["Generatio non potestatis est, sed naturæ." Ambros. Incarn. 79. Ἡ γέννησις φύσεως ἔργον, ἡ δὲ κτίσις θελήσεως. Damasc. F. O. i. 8. p. 133.]

of the Father, while it had been the philosophical as well as Valentinian appellation of the Supreme God. This was the chief resource of the Anomœans, who revived the pure Arian heresy, some years after the death of its first author. Their argument has been expressed in the following form:—that "it is the essence of the Father to be *ingenerate*, and of the Son to be *generate*; but *unborn* and *born* cannot be the same[2]." The shallowness, as well as the miserable trifling of such disputations on a serious subject, renders them unworthy of a refutation.

4. Moreover, they argued against the Catholic sense of the word "*Son*," from what they conceived to be its *materiality*; and, unwarrantably contrasting its primary with its figurative signification, as if both could not be preserved, they contended that, since the word must be figurative, therefore it could not retain its primary sense, but must be taken in the secondary sense of *adoption*.

5. Their reasonings (so to call them) had now conducted them thus far:—to maintain that our Lord was a creature, advanced, after creation, to be a Son of God. They did not shrink from the inference which these positions implied, viz. that He had been put on trial as other moral agents, and adopted on being found worthy; that His holiness was not essential, but acquired.

6. It was next incumbent on them to explain in what sense our Lord was the "*Only-begotten*," since they refused to understand that title in the Catholic sense of the *Homoüsion* or *consubstantial*. Accordingly,

[2] Beausobre, Hist. Manich. iii. 7, §

while pronouncing the divine birth to be a kind of creation, or an adoption, they attempted to hide the offensiveness of the heretical doctrine by the variety and dignity of the prerogatives, by which they distinguished the Son from other creatures. They declared that He was, strictly speaking, the only creature of God, as being alone made immediately by Him; and hence He was called *Only-begotten*, as "born alone from Him alone[3]," whereas all others were made through Him, as the instrument of Divine Power; and that in consequence He was "a creature, *but not* as being *one* of the creatures, a birth or production, but not as being one of the produced[4];" that is, to express their sentiment with something of the same ambiguity, "He was not a creature like other creatures." Another ambiguity of language followed. The idea of time depending on that of creation, they were able to grant that He, who was employed in forming all things, therefore brought time itself into being, and was "before all time;" not granting thereby that He was everlasting, but meaning that He was brought into existence "timelessly," independent of that succession of second causes (as they are called), that elementary system, seemingly self-sustained and self-renovating, to the laws of which creation itself may be considered as subjected.

7. Nor, lastly, had they any difficulty either in allowing or in explaining away the other attributes of divinity ascribed to Christ in Scripture. They might

[3] Pearson on the Creed, vol. ii. p. 148. Suicer. Thes. verb. μονογενής.

[4] κτίσμα, ἀλλ' οὐχ ὡς ἓν τῶν κτισμάτων· γέννημα, ἀλλ' οὐχ ὡς ἓν τῶν γεγεννημένων.

safely confess Him to be perfect God, one with God, the object of worship, the author of good; still with the reserve, that sacred appellations belonged to Him only in the same general sense in which they are sometimes accidentally bestowed on the faithful servants of God, and without interfering with the prerogatives of the One, Eternal, Self-existing Cause of all things [5].

3.

This account of the Arian theology may be suitably illustrated by some of the original documents of the controversy. Here, then, shall follow two letters of Arius himself, an extract from his Thalia, a letter of Eusebius of Nicomedia, and parts of the encyclical Epistle of Alexander of Alexandria, in justification of his excommunication of Arius and his followers [6].

1. "To his most dear Lord, Eusebius, a man of God, faithful and orthodox, Arius, the man unjustly persecuted by the Pope Alexander for the all-conquering truth's sake, of which thou too art a champion, sends health in the Lord. As Ammonius, my father, was going to Nicomedia, it seemed becoming to address this through him; and withal to represent to that deep-seated affection which thou bearest towards the brethren for the sake of God and His

[5] It may be added that the chief texts, which the Arians adduced in controversy were, Prov. viii. 22. Matt. xix. 17; xx. 23. Mark xiii. 32. John v. 19; xiv. 28. 1 Cor. xv. 28. Col. i. 15; and others which refer to our Lord's mediatorial office (Petav. ii. 1, &c. Theod. Hist. i. 14). But it is obvious, that the strength of their cause did not lie in the text of Scripture.

[6] Theodor. Hist. i. 4—6. Socr. i. 6. Athan. in Arian. i. 5. Synod 15, 16. Epiphan. Hær. lxix. 6, 7. Hilar. Trin. iv. 12; vi. 5.

Christ, how fiercely the bishop assaults and drives us, leaving no means untried in his opposition. At length he has driven us out of the city, as men without God, for dissenting from his public declarations, that, 'As God is eternal, so is His Son: where the Father, there the Son; the Son co-exists in God without a beginning (or birth): ever generate, an ingenerately-generate; that neither in idea, nor by an instant of time, does God precede the Son; an eternal God, an eternal Son; the Son is from God Himself.' Since then, Eusebius, thy brother of Cæsarea, Theodotus, Paulinus, &c. . . . and all the Bishops of the East declare that God exists without origin before the Son, they are made anathema by Alexander's sentence; all but Philogonius, Hellanicus, and Macarius, heretical, ill-grounded men, who say, one that He is an utterance, another an offspring, another co-ingenerate. These blasphemies we cannot bear even to hear; no, not if the heretics should threaten us with ten thousand deaths. What, on the other hand, are our statements and opinions, our past and present teaching? that the Son is not ingenerate, nor in any way a part of the Ingenerate, nor made of any subject-matter[7]; but that, by the will and counsel of God, He subsisted before times and ages, perfect God, Only-begotten, unchangeable; and that before this generation, or

[7] The Greek of most of these scientific expressions has been given; of the rest it is as follows:—men without God, ἀθέους; without a beginning or birth, ἀγεννήτως; ever-generate, ἀειγενής; ingenerately-generate, ἀγεννητογενής; an utterance, ἐρυγή (Psalm xlv. 1); off-spring, προβολή; co-ingenerate, συναγεννητόν; of any subject-matter, ἐξ ὑποκειμένου τινός.

creation, or determination, or establishment[8], He was not, for He is not ingenerate. And we are persecuted for saying, The Son has an origin, but God is unoriginate; for this we are under persecution, and for saying that He is out of nothing, inasmuch as He is neither part of God, nor of any subject-matter. Therefore we are persecuted; the rest thou knowest. I pray that thou be strong in the Lord, remembering our afflictions, fellow-Lucianist, truly named Eusebius[9]."

2. The second letter is written in the name of himself and his partisans of the Alexandrian Church; who, finding themselves excommunicated, had withdrawn to Asia, where they had a field for propagating their opinions. It was composed under the direction of Eusebius of Nicomedia, and is far more temperate and cautious than the former.

"To Alexander, our blessed Pope and Bishop, the Priests and Deacons send health in the Lord. Our hereditary faith, which thou too, blessed Pope, hast taught us, is this:—We believe in One God, alone ingenerate, alone everlasting, alone unoriginate, alone truly God, alone immortal, alone wise, alone good, alone sovereign, alone judge of all, ordainer, and dispenser, unchangeable and unalterable, just and good, of the Law and the Prophets, and of the New Covenant. We believe that this God gave birth to the Only-begotten Son before age-long times, through whom He has made those ages themselves, and all things else; that He generated Him, not in semblance,

[8] These words are selected by Arius, as being found in Scripture; [Vide Heb. i. 5. Rom. i. 4. Prov. viii. 22, 23.]

[9] [i.e. the pious, or rather, the orthodox.]

but in truth, giving Him a real subsistence (or *hypostasis*), at His own will, so as to be unchangeable and unalterable, God's perfect creature, but not as other creatures, His production, but not as other productions; nor as Valentinus maintained, an offspring *(probole)*; nor again, as Manichæus, a consubstantial part; nor, as Sabellius, a Son-Father, which is to make two out of one; nor, as Hieracas, one torch from another, or a flame divided into two; nor, as if He were previously in being, and afterwards generated or created again to be a Son, a notion condemned by thyself, blessed Pope, in full Church and among the assembled Clergy; but, as we affirm, created at the will of God before times and before ages, and having life and being from the Father, who gave subsistence as to Him, so to His glorious perfections. For, when the Father gave to Him the inheritance of all things, He did not thereby deprive Himself of attributes, which are His ingenerately, who is the Source of all things.

"So there are Three Subsistences (or Persons); and, whereas God is the Cause of all things, and therefore unoriginate simply by Himself, the Son on the other hand, born of the Father time-apart, and created and established before all periods, did not exist before He was born, but being born of the Father time-apart, was brought into substantive existence (subsistence), He alone by the Father alone. For He is not eternal, or co-eternal, or co-ingenerate with the Father; nor hath an existence together with the Father, as if there were two ingenerate Origins; but God is before all things, as being a Monad, and the Origin of all;—and therefore before the Son also, as indeed we have learned from thee in thy public preaching. Inasmuch then as it is from God that He hath His being, and His glorious perfections, and His life, and His charge of all things, for this reason God is His Origin, as being His God and before Him. As to such phrases as 'from Him,' and 'from the womb,' and 'issued forth from the Father, and am come,' if they be understood, as they are by some, to denote a part of the consubstantial, and a *probole* (offspring), then the Father will be of a compound nature, and divisible, and changeable, and corporeal; and thus, as far as their words go, the incorporeal God will be subjected to the properties of matter. I pray for thy health in the Lord, blessed Pope[1]."

3. About the same time Arius wrote his Thalia, or song for banquets and merry-makings, from which the following is extracted. He begins thus:—"According to the faith of God's elect, who know God, holy children, sound in their creed, gifted with the Holy Spirit of God, I have received these things from the partakers of wisdom, accomplished, taught of God, and altogether wise. Along their track I have pursued my course with like opinions,—I, the famous among men, the much-suffering for God's glory; and, taught of God, I have gained wisdom and knowledge." After this exordium, he proceeds to declare, "that God made the Son the origin (or beginning) of

[1] Before age-long periods, *πρὸ χρόνων αἰωνίων;* giving Him a real subsistence, *ὑποστήσαντα*; Son-Father, *υἱοπατόρα* [Vide Ath. Tr. p. 97, k and p. 514, o; also Didym. de Trin. iii. 18]; gave subsistence, as to Him, so to His glorious perfections, *τὰς δόξας συνυποστήσαντος αὐτῷ;* Three Subsistences, *τρεῖς ὑποστάσεις*; born time-apart, *ἀχρόνως γεννηθείς;* of a compound nature, *σύνθετος*. The texts to which Arius refers are Ps. cx. 3, and John xvi. 28.

creation, being Himself unoriginate, and adopted Him to be His Son; who, on the other hand, has no property of divinity in His own *Hypostasis*, not being equal, nor consubstantial with Him; that God is invisible, not only to the creatures created through the Son, but to the Son Himself; that there is a Trinity, but not with an equal glory, the *Hypostases* being incommunicable with each other, One infinitely more glorious than the other; that the Father is foreign in substance to the Son, as existing unoriginate; that by God's will the Son became Wisdom, Power, the Spirit, the Truth, the Word, the Glory, and the Image of God; that the Father, as being Almighty, is able to give existence to a being equal to the Son, though not superior to Him; that, from the time that He was made, being a mighty God, He has hymned the praises of His Superior; that He cannot investigate His Father's nature, it being plain that the originated cannot comprehend the unoriginate; nay, that He does not know His own[2]."

4. On the receipt of the letter from Arius, which was the first document here exhibited, Eusebius of Nicomedia addressed a letter to Paulinus of Tyre, of which the following is an extract:—"We have neither heard of two Ingenerates, nor of One divided into two, subjected to any material affection; but of One Ingenerate, and one generated by Him really; not from His substance, not partaking of the nature of the Ingenerate at all, but made altogether other than He in

[2] Incommunicable, ἀνεπίμικτοι, (this is in opposition to the περιχώρησις, or co-inherence); foreign in substance ξένος κατ' οὐσίαν; investigate, ἐξιχνιάσαι.

nature and in power, though made after the perfect likeness of the character and excellence of His Maker. . . . But, if He were of Him in the sense of 'from Him,' as if a part of Him, or from the effluence of His substance[3], He would not be spoken of (in Scripture) as created or established . . . for what exists as being from the Ingenerate ceases to be created or established, as being from its origin ingenerate. But, if His being called generate suggests the idea that He is made out of the Father's substance, and has from Him a sameness of nature, we know that not of Him alone does Scripture use the word 'generate,' but also of things altogether unlike the Father in nature. For it says of men, 'I have begotten sons and exalted them, and they have set Me at nought;' and, 'Thou hast left the God who begat thee;' and in other instances, as 'Who has given birth to the drops of dew?' . . . Nothing is of His substance; but all things are made at His will."

5. Alexander, in his public accusation of Arius and his party to Alexander of Constantinople, writes thus:—"They say that once the Son of God was not, and that He, who before had no existence, was at length made, made such, when He was made, as any other man is by nature. Numbering the Son of God among created things, they are but consistent in adding that He is of an alterable nature, capable of virtue and vice. . . . When it is urged on them that the Saviour differs from others, called sons of God, by the unchangeableness of His nature, stripping off all reverence, they answer, that God,

[3] Generated, γεγονός; effluence of His substance, ἐξ ἀπορροίας τῆς οὐσίας; being from the Ingenerate, ἐκ τοῦ ἀγεννήτου ὑπάρχον.

foreknowing and foreseeing His obedience, chose Him out of all creatures; chose Him, I say, not as possessing aught by nature and prerogative above the others (since, as they say, there is no Son of God by nature), nor bearing any peculiar relation towards God; but, as being, as well as others, of an alterable nature, and preserved from falling by the pursuit and exercise of virtuous conduct; so that, if Paul or Peter had made such strenuous progress, they would have gained a sonship equal to His."

In another letter, which was addressed to the Churches, he says, "It is their doctrine, that 'God was not always a Father', that 'the Word of God has not always existed, but was made out of nothing; for the self-existing God made Him, who once was not, out of what once was not. . . . Neither is He like the Father in substance, nor is He the true and natural Logos of the Father, nor His true Wisdom, but one of His works and creatures; and He is catachrestically the Word and Wisdom, inasmuch as He Himself was made by the proper Logos of God, and by that Wisdom which is in God, by which God made all things, and Him in the number. Hence He is mutable and alterable by nature, as other rational beings; and He is foreign and external to God's substance, being excluded from it. He was made for our sakes, in order that God might create us by Him as by an instrument; and He would not have had subsistence, had not God willed our making.' Some one asked them, if the Word of God could change, as the devil changed? They scrupled not to answer, 'Certainly, He can[4].'"

[4] Like in substance, ὅμοιος κατ' οὐσίαν [This, as we shall see afterwards, in the Homœüsian, the symbol of the Eusebians or Semi-Arians],

4.

More than enough has now been said in explanation of a controversy, the very sound of which must be painful to any one who has a loving faith in the Divinity of the Son. Yet so it has been ordered, that He who was once lifted up to the gaze of the world, and hid not His face from contumely, has again been subjected to rude scrutiny and dishonour in the promulgation of His religion to the world. And His true followers have been themselves obliged in His defence to raise and fix their eyes boldly on Him, as if He were one of themselves, dismissing the natural reverence, which would keep them ever at His feet. The subject may be dismissed with the following remarks :—

1. First, it is obvious to notice the unscriptural character of the arguments on which the heresy was founded. It is true that the Arians did not neglect to support their case from such detached portions of the Inspired Volume as suited their purpose; but still it can never be said that they showed that earnest desire of sacred truth, and careful search into its documents, which alone mark the Christian inquirer. The question is not merely whether they confined themselves to the language of Scripture, but whether they began with the study of it. Doubtless, to forbid in controversy the use of all words but those which actually occur in Scripture, is a superstition, an encroachment on Scripture liberty, and an impediment to freedom

mutable and alterable, τρεπτὸς καὶ ἀλλοιωτός; excluded, ἀπεσχοινισμένος.

of thought; and especially unreasonable, considering that a traditional system of theology, consistent with, but independent of, Scripture, has existed in the Church from the Apostolic age. "Why art thou in that excessive slavery to the letter," says Gregory Nazianzen, "and employest a Judaical wisdom, dwelling upon syllables, while letting slip realities? Suppose, on thy saying twice five, or twice seven, I were to understand thence ten or fourteen; or, if I spoke of a man, when thou hadst named an animal rational and mortal, should I in that case appear to thee to trifle? How could I so appear, in merely expressing your own meaning[5]?" But, inasmuch as this liberty was an evangelical privilege, which might be allowed to the Arian disputants, on the other hand it was a dangerous privilege also, ever to be subjected to a profound respect for the sacred text, a cautious adherence to the whole of the doctrine therein contained, and a regard also for those received statements, which, though not given to us as inspired, probably are derived from inspired teachers. Now the most liberal admission which can be made in behalf of the Arians, is, to grant that they did not in controversy throw aside the authority of Scripture altogether; that is, proclaim themselves unbelievers; for it is evident that they took only just so much of it as would afford them a basis for erecting their system of heresy by an abstract logical process. The mere

[5] Petav. iv. 5, § 6. [Athanasius ever exalts the theological sense over the words, whether sacred or ecclesiastical, which are its vehicle, and this even to the apparent withholding of the symbol ὁμοούσιον. Vide Orat. ii. 3, and Ath. Tr. vol. i., notes pp. 163, 212, 214, 231, &c.]

words "Father and Son," "birth," "origin," &c., were all that they postulated of revealed authority for their argument; they professed to do all the rest for themselves. The meaning of these terms in their context, the illustration which they afford to each other, and, much more, the divine doctrine considered as one undivided message, variously exhibited and dispersed in the various parts of Scripture, were excluded from the consideration of controversialists, who thought that truth was gained by disputing instead of investigating.

2. Next, it will be observed that, throughout their discussions, they assumed as an axiom, that there could be no mystery in the Scripture doctrine respecting the nature of God. In this, indeed, they did but follow the example of the contemporary spurious theologies; though their abstract mode of reasoning from the mere force of one or two Scripture terms, necessarily forced them more than other heretics into the use and avowal of the principle. The Sabellian, to avoid mystery, denied the distinction of Persons in the Divine Nature. Paulus, and afterwards Apollinaris, for the same reason, denied the existence of two Intelligent Principles at once, the Word and the human soul, in the Person of Christ. The Arians adopted both errors. Yet what is a mystery in doctrine, but a difficulty or inconsistency in the intellectual expression of it? And what reason is there for supposing, that Revelation addresses itself to the intellect, except so far as intellect is necessary for conveying and fixing its truths on the heart? Why are we not content to take and use what is given us, without asking questions? The Catholics, on the other

hand, pursued the intellectual investigation of the doctrine, under the guidance of Scripture and Tradition, merely as far as some immediate necessity called for it; and cared little, though one mode of expression seemed inconsistent with another. Thus, they developed the notion of "*substance*" against the Pantheists, of the "*Hypostatic Word*" against the Sabellians, of the "*Internal Word*" to meet the imputation of Ditheism; still they did not use these formulæ for any thing beyond shadows of sacred truth, symbols witnessing against the speculations into which the unbridled intellect fell.

Accordingly, they were for a time inconsistent with each other in the minor particulars of their doctrinal statements, being far more bent on opposing error, than on forming a theology:—inconsistent, that is, before the experience of controversy and the voice of tradition had detached them from less accurate or advisable expressions, and made them correct, or at least compare and adjust their several declarations. Thus, some said that there was but one *hypostasis*, meaning *substance*, in God; others three *hypostases*, meaning *Subsistences* or Persons; and some spoke of one *usia*, meaning substance, while others spoke of more than one *usia*. Some allowed, some rejected, the terms *probole* and *homoüsion*, according as they were guided by the prevailing heresy of the day, and by their own judgment how best to meet it. Some spoke of the Son as existing from everlasting in the Divine Mind; others implied that the Logos was everlasting, and became the Son in time. Some asserted that He was unoriginate, others denied it. Some, when interrogated by heretics, taught that He was born of the Father at the Father's will; others, from His nature, not His will; others, neither with His willing nor not willing[6]. Some declared that God was in number Three; others, that He was numerically One; while to others it perhaps appeared more philosophical to exclude the idea of number altogether, in discussions about that Mysterious Nature, which is beyond comparison with itself, whether viewed as Three or One, and neither falls under nor involves any conceivable species[7].

In all these various statements, the object is clear and unexceptionable, being merely that of protesting and practically guarding against dangerous deductions from the Scripture doctrine; and the problem implied in all of them is, to determine how this end may best be effected. There are no signs of an intellectual curiosity in the tenor of these Catholic expositions, prying into things not seen as yet; nor of an ambition to account for the representations of the truth given us in the sacred writings. But such a temper is the very characteristic of the Arian disputants. They insisted on taking the terms of Scripture and of the Church for more than they signified, and expected their opponents to admit inferences altogether foreign to the theological sense in which they were really used. Hence, they sometimes accused the orthodox of heresy, sometimes of self-contradiction. The Fathers of the Church have come down to us loaded with the imputation of the strangest errors, merely because they united truths, which heresies only

[6] Justin, Tryph. 61. 100, &c. Petav. vi. 8. § 14, 15. 18.
[7] Petav. iv. 13.

shared among themselves; nor have writers been wanting in modern times, from malevolence or carelessness, to aggravate these charges. The mystery of their creed has been converted into an evidence of concurrent heresies. To believe in the actual Incarnation of the Eternal Wisdom, has been treated, not as orthodoxy, but as an Ariano-Sabellianism[8]. To believe that the Son of God was the Logos, was Sabellianism; to believe that the pre-existent Logos was the Son of God, was Valentinianism. Gregory of Neo-Cæsarea was called a Sabellian, because he spoke of one substance in the Divine Nature; he was called a forerunner of Arius, because he said that Christ was a creature. Origen, so frequently accused of Arianism, seemed to be a Sabellian, when he said that the Son was the Auto-aletheia, the Archetypal Truth. Athenagoras is charged with Sabellianism by the very writer (Petau), whose general theory it is that he was one of those Platonizing Fathers who anticipated Arius[9]. Alexander, who at the opening of the controversy, was accused by Arius of Sabellianizing, has in these latter times been detected by the flippant Jortin to be an advocate of Semi-Arianism[1], which was the peculiar enemy and assailant of Sabellianism in all its forms. The celebrated word, *homoüsion*, has not escaped a similar contrariety of charges. Arius himself ascribes it to the Manichees; the Semi-Arians at Ancyra anathematize it, as Sabellian. It is in the same spirit

[8] [" Eorum error veritati testimonium dicit, et in consona perfidorum sententia in unum recte fidei modulum concinunt." Vigil. Thaps. contr. Eut. ii. init.]

[9] Bull, Defens. iii. 5. § 4.

[1] Jortin, Eccles. Hist. vol. ii. pp. 179, 180.

that Arius, in his letter to Eusebius, scoffs at the "eternal birth," and the "ingenerate generation," as ascribed to the Son in the orthodox theology; as if the inconsistency, which the words involved, when taken in their full sense, were a sufficient refutation of the heavenly truth, of which they are, each in its place, the partial and relative expression.

The Catholics sustained these charges with a prudence, which has (humanly speaking) secured the success of their cause, though it has availed little to remove the calumnies heaped upon themselves. The great Dionysius, who has himself been defamed by the "accuser of the brethren," declares perspicuously the principle of the orthodox teaching. "The particular expressions which I have used," he says, in his defence, "cannot be taken separate from each other . . . . whereas my opponents have taken two bald words of mine, and sling them at me from a distance; not understanding, that, in the case of subjects, partially known, illustrations foreign to them in nature, nay, inconsistent with each other, aid the inquiry [2]."

However, the Catholics of course considered it a duty to remove, as far as they could, their own verbal inconsistencies, and to sanction one form of expression, as orthodox in each case, among the many which might be adopted. Hence distinctions were made between the *unborn* and *unmade*, *origin* and *cause*, as already noticed. But these, clear and intelligible as they were in themselves, and valuable, both as facilitating the argument and disabusing the perplexed inquirer, opened to the heretical party the opportunity

[2] Athan. de Sent. Dionys. 18.

of a new misrepresentation. Whenever the orthodox writers showed an anxiety to reconcile and discriminate their own expressions, the charge of Manicheism was urged against them ; as if to dwell upon, were to rest in the material images which were the signs of the unknown truths. Thus the phrase, "Light of Light," the orthodox and almost apostolic emblem of the derivation of the Son from the Father, as symbolizing Their inseparability, mutual relation, and the separate fulness and exact parallelism and unity of Their perfections, was interpreted by the gross conceptions of the Manichæan Hieracas[3].

3. When in answer to such objections the Catholics denied that they attached other than a figurative meaning to their words, their opponents suddenly turned round, and professed the figurative meaning of the terms to be that which they themselves advocated. This inconsistency in their mode of conducting the argument deserves notice. It has already been instanced in the original argument of Arius, who maintained, that, since the word *Son* in its literal sense included among other ideas that of a beginning of being, the Son of God had had a beginning or was

[3] The ἐκ Θεοῦ was treated thus : εἰ γὰρ ἐκ Θεοῦ ἐστὶ, καὶ ἐγέννησεν ἐξ αὐτοῦ ὁ Θεὸς, ὡς εἰπεῖν, ἐξ ἰδίας ὑποστάσεως φύσει ἢ ἐκ τῆς ἰδίας οὐσίας, οὐκοῦν ὠγκώθη, ἢ τομὴν ἐδέξατο ἢ ἐν τῷ γεννᾷν ἐπλατύνθη, ἢ συνεστάλη, ἤ τι τῶν κατὰ τὰ πάθη τὰ σωματικὰ ὑπέστη. Epiph. Hær. lxix. 15. Or, to take the objection made at Nicæa to the ὁμοούσιον by Eusebius and some others : ἐπεὶ γὰρ ἔφασαν ὁμοούσιον εἶναι, ὃ ἐκ τινὸς ἐστὶν, ἢ κατὰ μερισμὸν, ἢ κατὰ ῥεῦσιν, ἢ κατὰ προβολήν· κατὰ προβολὴν μὲν, ὡς ἐκ ῥιζῶν βλάστημα, κατὰ δὲ ῥεῦσιν, ὡς οἱ πατρικοὶ παῖδες, κατὰ μερισμὸν δὲ, ὡς βώλου χρυσίδες δύο ἢ τρεῖς· κατ' οὐδὲν δὲ τούτων ἔστιν ὁ Υἱὸς, διὰ τοῦτο οὐ συγκατατίθεσθαι τῇ πίστει ἔλεγον. Socr. i. 8.

created, and therefore was not really a Son of God at all. It was on account of such unscrupulous dexterity in the controversy, that Alexander and Athanasius give them the title of chameleons. "They are as variable and uncertain in their opinions," (says the latter,) "as chameleons in their colour. When refuted, they look confused, and when examined they are perplexed; however, at length they recover their assurance, and bring forward some evasion. Then, if this in turn is exposed, they do not rest till they have devised some new absurdity, and, as Scripture says, meditate vain things, so that they may secure the privilege of being profane[4]."

Let us, however, pursue the Arians on their new ground of allegory. It has been already observed, that they explain the word *Only-begotten* in the sense of *only-created;* and considered the oneness of the Father and Son to consist in an unity of character and will, such as exists between God and His Saints, not in nature.

Now, surely, the temper of mind, which had recourse to such a comparison between Christ and us, to defend a heresy, was still more odious, if possible, than the original impiety of the heresy itself. Thus, the honours graciously bestowed upon human nature, as well as the condescending self-abasement of our Lord, were made to subserve the cause of the blasphemer. It is a known peculiarity of the message of mercy, that it views the Church of Christ as if clothed with, or hidden within, the glory of Him who ransomed it; so that there is no name or title belonging to Him literally, which is not in a secondary sense

[4] Athan. de Decr. Nic. 1. Socr. i. 6. [Vide Ath. Tr. vol. ii. p. 71.]

applied to the reconciled penitent. As our Lord is the Priest and King of His redeemed, they, as members of Him, are accounted kings and priests also. They are said to be Christs, or the anointed, to partake of the Divine Nature, to be the well-beloved of God, His sons, one with Him, and heirs of glory; in order to express the fulness and the transcendent excellence of the blessings gained to the Saints by Christ. In all these forms of speech, no religious mind runs the risk of confusing its own privileges with the real prerogatives of Him who gave them; yet it is obviously difficult in argument to discriminate between the primary and secondary use of the words, and to elicit and exhibit the delicate reasons lying in the context of Scripture for conclusions, which the common sense of a Christian is impatient as well as shocked to hear disputed. Who would so trifle with words, to take a parallel case, as to argue that, because Christians are said by St. John to "know all things," that therefore God is not omniscient in a sense infinitely above man's highest intelligence?

It may be observed, moreover, that the Arians were inconsistent in their application of the allegorical rule, by which they attempted to interpret Scripture; and showed as great deficiency in their philosophical conceptions of God, as in their practical devotion to Him. They seem to have fancied that some of His acts were more comprehensible than others, and might accordingly be made the basis on which the rest might be interpreted. They referred the divine *gennesis* or *generation* to the notion of creation; but creation is in fact as mysterious as the divine *gennesis;* that is, we are as little able to understand our own words, when we speak of the world's being brought out of nothing at God's word, as when we confess that His Eternal Perfections are reiterated, without being doubled, in the person of His Son. "How is it," asks Athanasius, "that the impious men dare to speak flippantly on subjects too sacred to approach, mortals as they are, and incapable of explaining even God's works upon earth? Why do I say, His earthly works? Let them treat of themselves, if so be they can investigate their own nature; yet venturous and self-confident, they tremble not before the glory of God, which Angels are fain reverently to look into, though in nature and rank far more excellent than they[5]." Accordingly, he argues that nothing is gained by resolving one of the divine operations into another; that to make, when attributed to God, is essentially distinct from the same act when ascribed to man, as incomprehensible as to give birth or beget[6]; and consequently that it is our highest wisdom to take the truths of Scripture as we find them there, and use them for the purposes for which they are vouchsafed, without proceeding accurately to systematize them or to explain them away. Far from elucidating, we are evidently enfeebling the revealed doctrine, by substituting *only-created* for *only-begotten;* for if the words are synonymous, why should the latter be insisted on in Scripture? Accordingly, it is proper to make a distinction between the primary and the literal meaning of a term. All the terms which human language applies to the Supreme Being, may perhaps

[5] Athan. on Matt. xi. 22. § 6.

[6] Athan. de Decr. Nic. 11; vide also Greg. Naz. Orat. 35, p. 566. Euseb. Eccl. Theol. i. 12.

be more or less figurative; but their primary and secondary meaning may still remain as distinct, as when they are referred to earthly objects. We need not give up the primary meaning of the word *Son* as opposed to the secondary sense of adoption, because we forbear to use it in its literal and material sense.

4. This being the general character of the Arian reasonings, it is natural to inquire what was the object towards which they tended. Now it will be found, that this audacious and elaborate sophistry could not escape one of two conclusions:—the establishment either of a sort of ditheism, or, as the more practical alternative, of a mere humanitarianism as regards our Lord; either a heresy tending to paganism, or the virtual atheism of philosophy. If the professions of the Arians are to be believed, they confessed our Lord to be God, God in all respects [7], full and perfect, yet at the same time to be infinitely distant from the perfections of the One Eternal Cause. Here at once they are committed to a ditheism; but Athanasius drives them on to the extreme of polytheism. "If," he says, "the Son were an object of worship for His transcendent glory, then every subordinate being is bound to worship his superior [8]." But so repulsive is the notion of a secondary God both to reason, and much more to Christianity, that the real tendency of Arianism lay towards the sole remaining alternative, the humanitarian doctrine.—Its essential agreement with the heresy of Paulus has already been incidentally shown; it differed from it only when the pressure of controversy required it. Its history is the proof of

[7] πληρὴς Θεός.

[8] Cudw. Intell. Syst. 4. § 36. Petav. ii. 12. § 6.

this. It started with a boldness not inferior to that of Paulus ; but as soon as it was attacked, it suddenly coiled itself into a defensive posture, and plunged amid the thickets of verbal controversy. At first it had not scrupled to admit the peccable nature of the Son ; but it soon learned to disguise such consequences of its doctrine, and avowed that, in matter of fact, He was indefectible. Next it borrowed the language of Platonism, which, without committing it to any real renunciation of its former declarations, admitted of the dress of a high and almost enthusiastic piety. Then it professed an entire agreement with the Catholics, except as to the adoption of the single word *consubstantial*, which they urged upon it, and concerning which, it affected to entertain conscientious scruples. At this time it was ready to confess that our Lord was the true God, God of God, born time-apart, or before all time, and not a creature as other creatures, but peculiarly the Son of God, and His accurate Image. Afterwards, changing its ground, it protested, as we shall see, against non-scriptural expressions, of which itself had been the chief inventor ; and proposed an union of all opinions, on the comprehensive basis of a creed, in which the Son should be merely declared to be "*in all things like the Father*," or simply "*like Him*." This versatility of profession is an illustration of the character given of the Arians by Athanasius, some pages back, which is further exemplified in their conduct at the Council in which they were condemned ; but it is here adduced to show the danger to which the Church was exposed from a party who had no fixed tenet, except that of opposition to the true notion of Christ's divinity ; and whose teaching, accordingly, had no firm footing of internal consistency to rest upon, till it descended to the notion of His simple humanity, that is, to the doctrine of Artemas and Paulus, though they too, as well as Arius, had enveloped their impieties in such admissions and professions, as assimilated it more or less in appearance to the Faith of the Catholic Church.

The conduct of the Arians at Nicæa, as referred to, was as follows. "When the Bishops in Council assembled," says Athanasius, an eye-witness, "were desirous of ridding the Church of the impious expressions invented by Arius, '*the Son is out of nothing*,' '*is a creature*,' '*once was not*,' 'of an *alterable nature*,' and perpetuating those which we receive on the authority of Scripture, that the Son is the Only-begotten of God by nature, the Word, Power, the sole Wisdom of the Father, very God, as the Apostle John says, and as Paul, the Radiance of His glory, and the express Image of His Person; the Eusebians, influenced by their own heterodoxy, said one to another, 'Let us agree to this; for we too are of God, there being one God, *of whom* are all things.' . . . . . The Bishops, however, discerning their cunning, and the artifice adopted by their impiety, in order to express more clearly the '*of God*,' wrote down 'of God's *substance*,' creatures being said to be 'of God,' as not existing of themselves without cause, but having an origin of their production; but the Son being peculiarly of the substance of the Father. . . . Again, on the Bishops asking the few advocates of Arianism present, whether they allowed the Son to be, not a creature, but the sole Power, Wisdom, and Image, eternal and in all respects[9], of the Father, and very God, the followers of Eusebius were detected making signs to each other, to express that this also could be applied to ourselves. 'For we too,' they said, 'are called in Scripture the image and glory of God; we are said to live always . . . There are many powers; the locust is called in Scripture "a great power." Nay, that we are God's own sons, is proved expressly from the text, in which the Son calls us brethren. Nor does their assertion, that He is very (true) God, distress us; He is very God, because He was made such.' This was the unprincipled meaning of the Arians. But here too the Bishops, seeing through their deceit, brought together from Scripture, the radiance, source and stream, express Image of Person, 'In Thy Light we shall see light,' 'I and the Father are one,' and last of all, expressed themselves more clearly and concisely, in the phrase 'consubstantial with the Father;' for all that was beforesaid has this meaning. As to their complaint about non-scriptural phrases, they themselves are evidence of its futility. It was they who began with their impious expressions; for, after their 'Out of nothing,' and 'Once was not,' going beyond Scripture in order to be impious, now they make it a grievance, that, in condemning them, we go beyond Scripture, in order to be pious[1]." The last remark is important; even those traditional statements of the Catholic doctrine, which were more explicit than Scripture, had not as yet, when the controversy began, taken the shape of formulæ. It was the Arian defined propositions of the "*out of*

[9] ἀπαράλλακτον.

[1] Athan. Ep. ad Afros., 5, 6.

nothing," and the like, which called for the imposition of the "*consubstantial.*"

It has sometimes been said, that the Catholics anxiously searched for some offensive test, which might operate to the exclusion of the Arians. This is not correct, inasmuch as they have no need to search; the "*from God's substance*" having been openly denied by the Arians, five years before the Council, and no practical distinction between it and the *consubstantial* existing, till the era of Basil and his Semi-Arians. Yet, had it been necessary, doubtless it would have been their duty to seek for a test of this nature; nay, to urge upon the heretical teachers the plain consequences of their doctrine, and to drive them into the adoption of them. These consequences are certain of being elicited in the long-run; and it is but equitable to anticipate them in the persons of the heresiarchs, rather than to suffer them gradually to unfold and spread far and wide after their day, sapping the faith of their deluded and less guilty followers. Many a man would be deterred from outstepping the truth, could he see the end of his course from the beginning. The Arians felt this, and therefore resisted a detection, which would at once expose them to the condemnation of all serious men. In this lies the difference between the treatment due to an individual in heresy, and to one who is confident enough to publish the innovations which he has originated. The former claims from us the most affectionate sympathy, and the most considerate attention. The latter should meet with no mercy; he assumes the office of the Tempter, and, so far forth as his error goes, must be dealt with by the competent authority, as if he were embodied Evil. To spare him is a false and dangerous pity. It is to endanger the souls of thousands, and it is uncharitable towards himself.

CHAPTER III.

THE ECUMENICAL COUNCIL OF NICÆA IN THE REIGN OF CONSTANTINE.

SECTION I.

HISTORY OF THE NICENE COUNCIL.

THE authentic account of the proceedings of the Nicene Council is not extant[1]. It has in consequence been judged expedient to put together in the foregoing Chapter whatever was necessary for the explanation of the Catholic and Arian creeds, and the controversy concerning them, rather than to reserve any portion of the doctrinal discussion for the present, though in some respects the more appropriate place for its introduction. Here then the transactions at Nicæa shall be reviewed in their political or ecclesiastical aspect.

[1] Vide Ittigius, Hist. Conc. Nic. § 1. The rest of this volume is drawn up from the following authorities: Eusebius, Vit. Const. Socrates, Sozomen, and Theodoret, Hist. Eccles., the various historical tracts of Athanasius, Epiphanius Hær. lxix. lxxiii., and the Acta Conciliorum. Of moderns, especially Tillemont and Petavius; then, Maimbourg's History of Arianism, the Benedictine Life of Athanasius, Cave's Life of Athanasius and Literary History, Gibbon's Roman History and Mr. Bridges' Reign of Constantine.

I.

Arius first published his heresy about the year 319. With his turbulent conduct in 306 and a few years later we are not here concerned. After this date, in 313, he is said, on the death of Achillas, to have aspired to the primacy of the Egyptian Church; and, according to Philostorgius[2], the historian of his party, a writer of little credit, to have generously resigned his claims in favour of Alexander, who was elected. His ambitious character renders it not improbable that he was a candidate for the vacant dignity; but, if so, the difference of age between himself and Alexander, which must have been considerable, would at once account for the elevation of the latter, and be an evidence of the indecency of Arius in becoming a competitor at all. His first attack on the Catholic doctrine was conducted with an openness which, considering the general duplicity of his party, is the most honourable trait in his character. In a public meeting of the clergy of Alexandria, he accused his diocesan of Sabellianism; an insult which Alexander, from deference to the talents and learning of the objector, sustained with somewhat too little of the dignity befitting "the ruler of the people." The mischief which ensued from his misplaced meekness was considerable. Arius was one of the public preachers of Alexandria; and, as some suppose, Master of the Catechetical School. Others of the city Presbyters were stimulated by his example to similar irregularities. Colluthus, Carponas, and Sarmatas began to form each his own party in a Church which Meletius

[2] Philos. i. 3.

had already troubled; and Colluthus went so far as to promulgate an heretical doctrine, and to found a sect. Still hoping to settle these disorders without the exercise of his episcopal power, Alexander summoned a meeting of his clergy, in which Arius was allowed to state his doctrines freely, and to argue in their defence; and, whether from a desire not to overbear the discussion, or from distrust in his own power of accurately expressing the truth, and anxiety about the charge of heresy brought against himself, the Primate, though in no wise a man of feeble mind, is said to have refrained from committing himself on the controverted subject, "applauding," as Sozomen tells us, "sometimes the one party, sometimes the other[3]." At length the error of Arius appeared to be of so serious and confirmed a nature, that countenance of it would have been sinful. It began to spread beyond the Alexandrian Church; the indecision of Alexander excited the murmurs of the Catholics; till, called unwillingly to the discharge of a severe duty, he gave public evidence of his real indignation against the blasphemies which he had so long endured, by excommunicating Arius with his followers.

This proceeding, obligatory as it was on a Christian Bishop, and ratified by the concurrence of a provincial Council, and expedient even for the immediate interests of Christianity, had other Churches been equally honest in their allegiance to the true faith, had the effect of increasing the influence of Arius, by throwing him upon his fellow-Lucianists of the rival dioceses of the East, and giving notoriety to his name and tenets. In Egypt, indeed, he had already been sup-

[3] Soz. i. 14.

ported by the Meletian faction ; which, in spite of its profession of orthodoxy, continued in alliance with him, through jealousy of the Church, even after he had fallen into heresy. But the countenance of these schismatics was of small consideration, compared with the powerful aid frankly tendered him, on his excommunication, by the leading men in the great Catholic communities of Asia Minor and the East. Cæsarea was the first place to afford him a retreat fròm Alexandrian orthodoxy, where he received a cordial reception from the learned Eusebius, Metropolitan of Palestine ; while Athanasius, Bishop of Anazarbus in Cilicia, and others, did not hesitate, by letters on his behalf, to declare their concurrence with him in the full extent of his heresy. Eusebius even declared that Christ was not very or true God ; and his associate Athanasius asserted, that He was in the number of the hundred sheep of the parable, that is, one of the creatures of God.

Yet, in spite of the countenance of these and other eminent men, Arius found it difficult to maintain his ground against the general indignation which his heresy excited. He was resolutely opposed by Philogonius, Patriarch of Antioch, and Macarius of Jerusalem ; who promptly answered the call made upon them by Alexander, in his circulars addressed to the Syrian Churches. In the meanwhile Eusebius of Nicomedia, the early friend of Arius, and the ecclesiastical adviser of Constantia, the Emperor's sister, declared in his favour ; and offered him a refuge, which he readily accepted, from the growing unpopularity which attended him in Palestine. Supported by the patronage of so powerful a prelate, Arius was now scarcely to be considered in the position of a schismatic or an outcast. He assumed in consequence a more calm and respectful demeanour towards Alexander; imitated the courteous language of his friend; and in his Epistle, which was introduced into the foregoing Chapter, addresses his diocesan with studious humility, and defers or appeals to previous statements made by Alexander himself on the doctrine in dispute[4]. At this time also he seems to have corrected and completed his system. George, afterwards Bishop of Laodicea, taught him an evasion for the orthodox test "*of God,*" by a reference to 1 Cor. xi. 12. Asterius, a sophist of Cappadocia, advocated the secondary sense of the word Logos as applied to Christ, with a reference to such passages as Joel ii. 25; and, in order to explain away the force of the word "*Only-begotten,*" (μονογενὴς,) maintained, that to Christ alone out of all creatures it had been given, to be fashioned under the immediate presence and perilous weight of the Divine Hand. Now too, as it appears, the title of "True God" was ascribed to Him by the heretical party; the "*of an alterable nature*" was withdrawn; and an admission of His actual indefectibility substituted for it. The heresy being thus placed on a less exceptionable basis, the influence of Eusebius was exerted in Councils both in Bithynia and Palestine; in which Arius was acknowledged, and more urgent solicitations addressed to Alexander, with the view of effecting his re-admission into the Church.

[4] [Alexander's siding with Arius, was nothing more than his disclaiming the views of the Five Fathers, vide supr. pp. 202, 220; also Appendix, No. 2, γέννησις. As to the Arian evasions which follow, vide supr. pp. 193, 216, 223, 238, &c.]

This was the history of the controversy for the first four or five years of its existence; that is, till the era of the battle of Hadrianople (A.D. 323), by the issue of which Constantine, becoming master of the Roman world, was at liberty to turn his thoughts to the state of Christianity in the Eastern Provinces of the Empire. From this date it is connected with civil history; a result natural, and indeed necessary under the existing circumstances, though it was the occasion of subjecting Christianity to fresh persecutions, in place of those which its nominal triumph had terminated. When a heresy, condemned and excommunicated by one Church, was taken up by another, and independent Christian bodies thus stood in open opposition, nothing was left to those who desired peace, to say nothing of orthodoxy, but to bring the question under the notice of a General Council. But as a previous step, the leave of the civil power was plainly necessary for so public a display of that wide-spreading Association, of which the faith of the Gospel was the uniting and animating principle. Thus the Church could not meet together in one, without entering into a sort of negotiation with the powers that be; whose jealousy it is the duty of Christians, both as individuals and as a body, if possible, to dispel. On the other hand, the Roman Emperor, as a professed disciple of the truth, was of course bound to protect its interests, and to afford every facility for its establishment in purity and efficacy. It was under these circumstances that the Nicene Council was convoked.

2.

Now we must direct our view for a while to the

character and history of Constantine. It is an ungrateful task to discuss the private opinions and motives of an Emperor who was the first to profess himself the Protector of the Church, and to relieve it from the abject and suffering condition in which it had lain for three centuries. Constantine is our benefactor; inasmuch as we, who now live, may be considered to have received the gift of Christianity by means of the increased influence which he gave to the Church. And, were it not that in conferring his benefaction he burdened it with the bequest of an heresy, which outlived his age by many centuries, and still exists in its effects in the divisions of the East, nothing would here be said, from mere grateful recollection of him, by way of analyzing the state of mind in which he viewed the benefit which he has conveyed to us. But his conduct, as it discovers itself in the subsequent history, natural as it was in his case, still has somewhat of a warning in it, which must not be neglected in after times.

It is of course impossible accurately to describe the various feelings with which one in Constantine's peculiar situation was likely to regard Christianity; yet the joint effect of them all may be gathered from his actual conduct, and the state of the civilized world at the time. He found his empire distracted with civil and religious dissensions, which tended to the dissolution of society; at a time too, when the barbarians without were pressing upon it with a vigour, formidable in itself, but far more menacing in consequence of the decay of the ancient spirit of Rome. He perceived the powers of its old polytheism, from whatever cause, exhausted; and a newly-risen philosophy vainly endeavouring to resuscitate a mythology which had done its work, and now, like all things of earth, was fast returning to the dust from which it was taken. He heard the same philosophy inculcating the principles of that more exalted and refined religion, which a civilized age will always require; and he witnessed the same substantial teaching, as he would consider it, embodied in the precepts, and enforced by the energetic discipline, the union, and the example of the Christian Church. Here his thoughts would rest, as in a natural solution of the investigation to which the state of his empire gave rise; and, without knowing enough of the internal characters of Christianity to care to instruct himself in them, he would discern, on the face of it, a doctrine more real than that of philosophy, and a rule of life more severe and energetic even than that of the old Republic. The Gospel seemed to be the fit instrument of a civil reformation[5], being but a new form of the old wisdom, which had existed in the world at large from the beginning. Revering, nay, in one sense, honestly submitting to its faith, still he acknowledged it rather as a school than joined it as a polity; and by refraining from the sacrament of baptism till his last illness, he acted in the spirit of men of the world in every age, who dislike to pledge themselves to engagements which they still intend to fulfil, and to descend from the position of judges to that of disciples of the truth[6].

Concord is so eminently the perfection of the Christian temper, conduct, and discipline, and it had been so wonderfully exemplified in the previous history of

[5] Gibbon, Hist. ch. xx.

[6] Vide his speech, Euseb. Vit. Const. iv. 62.

the Church, that it was almost unavoidable in a heathen soldier and statesman to regard it as the sole precept of the Gospel. It required a far more refined moral perception, to detect and to approve the principle on which this internal peace is grounded in Scripture; to submit to the dictation of truth, as such, as a primary authority in matters of political and private conduct; to understand how belief in a certain creed was a condition of Divine favour, how the social union was intended to result from an unity of opinions, the love of man to spring from the love of God, and zeal to be prior in the succession of Christian graces to benevolence. It had been predicted by Him, who came to offer peace to the world, that, in matter of fact, that gift would be changed into the sword of discord; mankind being offended by the doctrine, more than they were won over by the amiableness, of Christianity. But He alone was able thus to discern through what a succession of difficulties Divine truth advances to its final victory; shallow minds anticipate the end apart from the course which leads to it. Especially they who receive scarcely more of His teaching than the instinct of civilization recognizes (and Constantine must, on the whole, be classed among such), view the religious dissensions of the Church as simply evil, and (as they would fain prove) contrary to His own precepts; whereas in fact they are but the history of truth in its first stage of trial, when it aims at being "pure," before it is "peaceable;" and are reprehensible only so far as baser passions mix themselves with that true loyalty towards God, which desires His glory in the first place, and only in the second place, the tranquillity and good order of society.

The Edict of Milan (A.D. 313) was among the first effects of Constantine's anxiety to restore fellowship of feeling to the members of his distracted empire. In it an absolute toleration was given by him and his colleague Licinius, to the Christians and all other persuasions, to follow the form of worship which each had adopted for himself; and it was granted with the professed view of consulting for the peace of their people.

A year did not elapse from the date of this Edict, when Constantine found it necessary to support it by severe repressive measures against the Donatists of Africa, though their offences were scarcely of a civil nature. Their schism had originated in the disappointed ambition of two presbyters; who fomented an opposition to Cæcilian, illegally elevated, as they pretended, to the episcopate of Carthage. Growing into a sect, they appealed to Constantine, who referred their cause to the arbitration of successive Councils. These pronounced in favour of Cæcilian; and, on Constantine's reviewing and confirming their sentence, the defeated party assailed him with intemperate complaints, accused Hosius, his adviser, of partiality in the decision, stirred up the magistrates against the Catholic Church, and endeavoured to deprive it of its places of worship. Constantine in consequence took possession of their churches, banished their seditious bishops, and put some of them to death. A love of truth is not irreconcilable either with an unlimited toleration, or an exclusive patronage of a selected religion; but to endure or discountenance error, according as it is, or is not, represented in an independent system and existing authority, to spare the pagans and to tyrannize over the schismatics, is the conduct of one who subjected religious principle to expediency, and aimed at peace, as a supreme good, by forcible measures where it was possible, otherwise by conciliation.

It must be observed, moreover, that subsequently to the celebrated vision of the Labarum (A.D. 312), he publicly invoked the Deity as one and the same in all forms of worship; and at a later period (A.D. 321), he promulgated simultaneous edicts for the observance of Sunday, and the due consultation of the aruspices[7]. On the other hand, as in the Edict of Milan, so in his Letters and Edicts connected with the Arian controversy, the same reference is made to external peace and good order, as the chief object towards which his thoughts were directed. The same desire of tranquillity led him to summon to the Nicene Council the Novatian Bishop Acesius, as well as the orthodox prelates. At a later period still when he extended a more open countenance to the Church as an institution, the same principle discovers itself in his conduct as actuated him in his measures against the Donatists. In proportion as he recognizes the Catholic body, he drops his toleration of the sectaries. He prohibited the conventicles of the Valentinians, Montanists, and other heretics; who, at his bidding, joined the Church in such numbers (many of them, says Eusebius, "through fear of the Imperial threat, with hypocritical minds[8]"), that at length both heresy and schism might be said to disappear from the face of society.

[7] Gibbon, Hist. ibid.

[8] Euseb. Vit. Const. iii. 66. [νῦν πεπλήρωται ἡ ἐκκλησία κεκρυμμένων αἱρετικῶν. Cyril. Catech. xv. 4.]

Now let us observe his conduct in the Arian controversy.

Doubtless it was a grievous disappointment to a generous and large-minded prince, to discover that the Church itself, from which he had looked for the consolidation of his empire, was convulsed by dissensions such as were unknown amid the heartless wranglings of Pagan philosophy. The disturbances caused by the Donatists, which his acquisition of Italy (A.D. 312) had opened upon his view, extended from the borders of the Alexandrian patriarchate to the ocean. The conquest of the East (A.D. 323) did but enlarge his prospect of the distractions of Christendom. The patriarchate just mentioned had lately been visited by a deplorable heresy, which having run its course through the chief parts of Egypt, Lybia, and Cyrenaica, had attacked Palestine and Syria, and spread thence into the dioceses of Asia Minor and the Lydian Proconsulate.

Constantine was informed of the growing schism at Nicomedia, and at once addressed a letter to Alexander and Arius jointly[9]; a reference to which will enable the reader to verify for himself the account above given of the nature of the Emperor's Christianity. He professes therein two motives as impelling him in his public conduct; first, the desire of effecting the reception, throughout his dominions, of some one definite and complete form of religious worship; next, that of settling and invigorating the civil institutions of the empire. Desirous of securing an unity of sentiment among all the believers in the Deity, he first directed his attention to the religious dissen-

[9] Euseb. Vit. Const. ii. 64—72.

sions of Africa, which he had hoped, with the aid of the Oriental Christians, to terminate. "But," he continues, "glorious and Divine Providence! how fatally were my ears, or rather my heart, wounded, by the report of a rising schism among you, far more acrimonious than the African dissensions. . . . On investigation, I find that the reason for this quarrel is insignificant and worthless. . . . As I understand it, you, Alexander, were asking the separate opinions of your clergy on some passage of your law, or rather were inquiring about some idle question, when you, Arius, inconsiderately committed yourself to statements which should either never have come into your mind, or have been at once repressed. On this a difference ensued, Christian intercourse was suspended, the sacred flock was divided into two, breaking the harmonious unity of the common body. . . . . Listen to the advice of me, your fellow-servant:—neither ask nor answer questions which are not upon any injunction of your law, but from the altercation of barren leisure; at best keep them to yourselves, and do not publish them. . . . Your contention is not about any capital commandment of your law; neither of you is introducing any novel scheme of divine worship; you are of one and the same way of thinking, so that it is in your power to unite in one communion. Even the philosophers can agree together, one and all, in one dogma, though differing in particulars. . . . Is it right for brothers to oppose brothers, for the sake of trifles? . . . Such conduct might be expected from the multitude, or from the recklessness of boyhood; but is little in keeping with your sacred profession, and with your personal wisdom." Such is the substance of his letter, which, written on an imperfect knowledge of the facts of the case, and with somewhat of the prejudices of Eclectic liberalism, was inapplicable, even where abstractedly true ; his fault lying in his supposing, that an individual like himself, who had not even received the grace of baptism, could discriminate between great and little questions in theology. He concludes with the following words, which show the amiableness and sincerity of a mind in a measure awakened from the darkness of heathenism, though they betray the affectation of the rhetorician : "Give me back my days of calm, my nights of security ; that I may experience henceforth the comfort of the clear light, and the cheerfulness of tranquillity. Otherwise, I shall sigh and be dissolved in tears. . . So great is my grief, that I put off my journey to the East on the news of your dissension. . . . Open for me that path towards you, which your contentions have closed up. Let me see you and all other cities in happiness ; that I may offer due thanksgivings to God above, for the unanimity and free intercourse which is seen among you."

This letter was conveyed to the Alexandrian Church by Hosius, who was appointed by the Emperor to mediate between the contending parties. A Council was called, in which some minor irregularities were arranged, but nothing settled on the main question in dispute. Hosius returned to his master to report an unsuccessful mission, and to advise, as the sole measure which remained to be adopted, the calling of a General Council, in which the Catholic doctrine might be formally declared, and a judgment promulgated as to the basis upon which communion with the Church was henceforth to be determined. Constantine assented; and, discovering that the ecclesiastical authorities were earnest in condemning the tenets of Arius, as being an audacious innovation on the received creed, he suddenly adopted a new line of conduct towards the heresy; and in a Letter which he addressed to Arius, professes himself a zealous advocate of Christian truth, ventures to expound it, and attacks Arius with a vehemence which can only be imputed to his impatience in finding that any individual had presumed to disturb the peace of the community. It is remarkable, as showing his utter ignorance of doctrines, which were never intended for discussion among the unbaptized heathen, or the secularized Christian, that, in spite of this bold avowal of the orthodox faith in detail, yet shortly after he explained to Eusebius one of the Nicene declarations in a sense which even Arius would scarcely have allowed, expressed as it is almost after the manner of Paulus [1].

3.

The first Ecumenical Council met at Nicæa in Bithynia, in the summer of A.D. 325. It was attended by about 300 Bishops, chiefly from the eastern provinces of the empire, besides a multitude of priests, deacons, and other functionaries of the Church. Hosius, one of the most eminent men of an age of saints, was president. The Fathers who took the principal share in its proceedings were Alexander of Alexandria, attended by his deacon Athanasius, then

[1] Theod. Hist. i. 12.

about 27 years of age, and soon afterwards his successor in the see; Eustathius, patriarch of Antioch, Macarius of Jerusalem, Cæcilian of Carthage, the object of the hostility of the Donatists, Leontius of Cæsarea in Cappadocia, and Marcellus of Ancyra, whose name was afterwards unhappily notorious in the Church. The number of Arian Bishops is variously stated at 13, 17, or 22; the most conspicuous of these being the well-known prelates of Nicomedia and Cæsarea, both of whom bore the name of Eusebius.

The discussions of the Council commenced in the middle of June, and were at first private. Arius was introduced and examined; and confessed his impieties with a plainness and vehemence far more respectable than the hypocrisy which was the characteristic of his party, and ultimately was adopted by himself. Then followed his disputation with Athanasius [2], who afterwards engaged the Arian

[2] ["It is difficult," say the Notes, Ath. Tr. vol. ii. p. 17, "to gain a clear idea of the character of Arius. Athanasius speaks as if his Thalia was but in keeping with his life, calling him 'the Sotadean Arius,' while Constantine, Alexander, and Epiphanius give us a contrary view of him, still differing one from the other. Constantine, indeed, is not consistent with himself; first he cries out to him (as if with Athanasius), 'Arius, Arius, at least let the society of Venus keep you back,' then 'Look, look all men . . how his veins and flesh are possessed with poison, and are in a ferment of severe pain; how his whole body is wasted, and is all withered and sad and pale and shaking, and all that is miserable and fearfully emaciated. How hateful to see, and how filthy is his mass of hair, how he is half dead all over, with failing eyes and bloodless countenance, and woe-begone; so that, all these things combining in him at once, frenzy, madness, and folly, from the continuance of the complaint, have made thee wild and savage. But, not having any sense of the bad plight he is in, he cries out, "I am transported with delight, and I leap and skip for joy, and I fly;" and again, with boyish impetuosity, "Be it so," he says, "we are lost."'" Harduin. Conc. t. i. p. 457. St. Alexan-

Eusebius of Nicomedia, Maris, and Theognis. The unfortunate Marcellus also distinguished himself in the defence of the Catholic doctrine.

Reference has been already made to Gibbon's representation [3], that the Fathers of the Council were in doubt for a time, how to discriminate between their own doctrine and the heresy; but the discussions of the foregoing Chapter contain sufficient evidence, that they had rather to reconcile themselves to the adoption of a formula which expedience suggested, and to the use of it as a test, than to discover a means of ejecting or subduing their opponents. In the very beginning of the controversy, Eusebius of Nicomedia had declared, that he would not admit the "*from the substance*" as an attribute of our Lord [4]. A letter containing a similar avowal was read in the Council, and made clear to its members the objects for which they had met; viz. to ascertain the character and tendency of the heresy; to raise a protest and defence against it; lastly, for that purpose, to

der speaks of Arius's melancholy temperament. Epiphanius's account of him is as follows: "From elation of mind this old man swerved from the truth. He was in stature very tall, downcast in visage, with manners like a wily serpent, captivating to every guileless heart by that same crafty bearing. For, ever habited in cloke and vest, he was pleasant of address, ever persuading souls and flattering," &c. Hær. 69, 3. Arius is here said to be tall; Athanasius, unless Julian's description of him is but declamation, was short, μηδὲ ἀνὴρ, ἀλλ' ἀνθρωπίσκος εὐτελὴς ("not even a man, but a common little fellow"). Ep. 51. However, Gregory Nazianzen, who had never seen him, speaks of him, as "high in prowess, and humble in spirit, mild, meek, full of sympathy, pleasant in speech, more pleasant in manners, *angelical* in *person*, more angelical in mind, serene in his rebukes, instructive in his praises," &c. Orat. 21. 8.]

3 [Supr. p. 234.]

4 Theod. Hist. i. 6. [Vide Ath. Tr. vol. ii. p. 438.]

overcome their own reluctance to the formal and unauthoritative adoption of a word, in explanation of the true doctrine, which was not found in Scripture, had actually been perverted in the previous century to an heretical meaning, and was in consequence forbidden by the Antiochene Council which condemned Paulus.

The Arian party, on the other hand, anxious to avoid a test, which they themselves had suggested, presented a Creed of their own, drawn up by Eusebius of Cæsarea. In it, though the expression "*of the substance*" or "*consubstantial*" was omitted, every term of honour and dignity, short of this, was bestowed therein upon the Son of God; who was designated as the Logos of God, God of God, Light of Light, Life of Life, the Only-begotten Son, the First-born of the whole creation, of the Father before all worlds, and the Instrument of creating them. The Three Persons were confessed to be in real *hypostasis* or *subsistence* (in opposition to Sabellianism), and to be truly Father, Son, and Holy Ghost. The Catholics saw very clearly, that concessions of this kind on the part of the Arians did not conceal the real question in dispute. Orthodox as were the terms employed by them, naturally and satisfactorily as they would have answered the purposes of a test, had the existing questions never been agitated, and consistent as they were with certain producible statements of the Ante-Nicene writers, they were irrelevant at a time when evasions had been found for them all, and triumphantly proclaimed. The plain question was, whether our Lord was God in as full a sense as the Father, though not to be viewed as separable from Him; or whether, as the sole alternative, He was a creature; that is, whether He was literally of, and in, the one Indivisible Essence which we adore as God, "consubstantial with God," or of a substance which had a beginning. The Arians said that He was a creature, the Catholics that He was very God; and all the subtleties of the most fertile ingenuity could not alter, and could but hide, this fundamental difference. A specimen of the Arian argumentation at the Council has already been given on the testimony of Athanasius; happily it was not successful. A form of creed was drawn up by Hosius, containing the discriminating terms of orthodoxy [5]; and anathemas were added against all who maintained the heretical formulæ, Arius and his immediate followers being mentioned by name. In order to prevent misapprehension of the sense in which the test was used, explanations accompanied it. Thus carefully defined, it was offered for subscription to the members of the Council; who in consequence bound themselves to excommunicate from their respective bodies all who actually obtruded upon the Church the unscriptural and novel positions of Arius. As to the laity, they were not required to subscribe any test as the condition of communion; though they were of course exposed to the operation of the anathema, in case they ventured on positive innovations on the rule of faith.

While the Council took this clear and temperate

[5] [Justice has not been done here to the ground of tradition, on which the Fathers specially took their stand. For example, "Whoever heard such doctrine?" says Athanasius; "whence, from whom did they gain it? Who thus expounded to them when they were at school?" Orat. i. § 8. "Is it not enough to distract a man, and to make him stop his ears?" § 35. Vide Ath. Tr. vol. ii. pp. 247—253, 311.]

view of its duties, Constantine acted a part altogether consistent with his own previous sentiments, and praiseworthy under the circumstances of his defective knowledge. He had followed the proceedings of the assembled prelates with interest, and had neglected no opportunity of impressing upon them the supreme importance of securing the peace of the Church. On the opening of the Council, he had set the example of conciliation, by burning publicly, without reading, certain charges which had been presented to him against some of its members; a noble act, as conveying a lesson to all present to repress every private feeling, and to deliberate for the well-being of the Church Catholic to the end of time. Such was his behaviour, while the question in controversy was still pending; but when the decision was once announced, his tone altered, and what had been a recommendation of caution, at once became an injunction to conform. Opposition to the sentence of the Church was considered as disobedience to the civil authority; the prospect of banishment was proposed as the alternative of subscription; and it was not long before seven of the thirteen dissentient Bishops submitted to the pressure of the occasion, and accepted the creed with its anathemas as articles of peace.

Indeed the position in which Eusebius of Nicomedia had placed their cause, rendered it difficult for them consistently to refuse subscription. The violence, with which Arius originally assailed the Catholics, had been succeeded by an affected earnestness for unity and concord, so soon as his favour at Court allowed him to dispense with the low popularity by which he first rose into notice. The insignificancy of the points in dispute which had lately been the very ground of complaint with him and his party against the particular Church which condemned him, became an argument for their yielding, when the other Churches of Christendom confirmed the sentence of the Alexandrian. It is said, that some of them substituted the "*homœüsion*" ("*like in substance*"), for the "*homoüsion*" ("*one in substance*") in the confessions which they presented to the Council; but it is unsafe to trust the Anomœan Philostorgius, on whose authority the report rests[6], in a charge against the Eusebian party, and perhaps after all he merely means, that they explained the latter by the former as an excuse for their own recantation. The six, who remained unpersuaded, had founded an objection, which the explanations set forth by the Council had gone to obviate, on the alleged materialism of the word which had been selected as the test. At length four of them gave way; and the other two, Eusebius of Nicomedia and another, withdrawing their opposition to the "*homoüsion*," only refused to sign the condemnation of Arius. These, however, were at length released from their difficulty, by the submission of the heresiarch himself; who was pardoned on the understanding, that he never returned to the Church, which had suffered so much from his intrigues. There is, however, some difficulty in this part of the history. Eusebius shortly afterwards suffered a temporary exile, on a detection of his former practices with Licinius to the injury of Constantine; and Arius, apparently involved in his ruin, was banished with his followers into Illyria.

[6] Philost. i. 9.

SECTION II.

CONSEQUENCES OF THE NICENE COUNCIL

FROM the time that the Eusebians consented to subscribe the Homoüsion in accordance with the wishes of a heathen prince, they became nothing better than a political party. They soon learned, indeed, to call themselves Homœüsians, or believers in the "like" substance *(homœüsion,)* as if they still held the peculiarities of a religious creed; but in truth it is an abuse of language to say that they had any definite belief at all. For this reason, the account of the Homœusian or Semi-Arian doctrine shall be postponed, till such time as we fall in with individuals whom we may believe to be serious in their professions, and to act under the influence of religious convictions however erroneous. Here the Eusebians must be described as a secular faction, which is the true character of them in the history in which they bear a part.

Strictly speaking, the Christian Church, as being a visible society, is necessarily a political power or party. It may be a party triumphant, or a party under persecution; but a party it always must be, prior in existence to the civil institutions with which it is surrounded, and from its latent divinity formidable and influential, even to the end of time. The grant of permanency was made in the beginning, not to the mere doctrine of the Gospel, but to the Association itself built upon the doctrine [1]; in prediction, not only of the indestructibility of Christianity, but of the medium also through which it was to be manifested to the world. Thus the Ecclesiastical Body is a divinely-appointed means, towards realizing the great evangelical blessings. Christians depart from their duty, or become in an offensive sense political, not when they act as members of one community, but when they do so for temporal ends or in an illegal manner; not when they assume the attitude of a party, but when they split into many. If the primitive believers did not interfere with the acts of the civil government, it was merely because they had no civil rights enabling them legally to do so. But where they have rights, the case is different [2]; and the existence of a secular spirit is to be ascertained, not by their using these, but their using them for ends short of the ends for which they were given. Doubtless in criticizing the mode of their exercising them in a particular case, differences of opinion may fairly exist; but the principle itself, the duty of using their civil rights in the service of religion, is clear; and since there is a popular misconception, that Christians, and especially the Clergy, as such, have no concern in temporal affairs, it is expedient to take every opportunity of formally denying the position, and demanding proof of it. In truth, the Church was framed for the express purpose of interfering, or (as irreligious men will say) meddling with the world. It is the plain

[1] Matt. xvi. 18.

[2] Acts xvi. 37—39.

duty of its members, not only to associate internally, but also to develope that internal union in an external warfare with the spirit of evil, whether in Kings' courts or among the mixed multitude; and, if they can do nothing else, at least they can suffer for the truth, and remind men of it, by inflicting on them the task of persecution.

I.

These principles being assumed, it is easy to enter into the relative positions of the Catholics and Arians at the era under consideration. As to the Arians, it is a matter of fact, that Arius and his friends commenced their career with the deliberate commission of disorderly and schismatical acts; and it is a clear inference from their subsequent proceedings, that they did so for private ends. For both reasons, then, they were a mere political faction, usurping the name of religion; and, as such, essentially anti-christian. The question here is not whether their doctrine was right or wrong; but, whether they did not make it a secondary object of their exertions, an instrument towards attaining ends which they valued above it. Now it will be found, that the party was prior to the creed. They grafted their heresy on the schism of the Meletians, who continued to support them after they had published it; and they readily abandoned it, when their secular interests required the sacrifice. At the Council of Nicæa, they began by maintaining an erroneous doctrine; they ended by concessions which implied the further heresy that points of faith are of no importance; and, if they were odious when they blasphemed the truth, they were still more odious when they confessed it. It was the very principle of Eclecticism to make light of differences in belief; while it was involved in the primary notion of a Revelation that these differences were of importance, and it was taught with plainness in the Gospel, that to join with those who denied the right faith was a sin.

This adoption, however, on the part of the Eusebians, of the dreams of Pagan philosophy, served in some sort as a recommendation of them to a prince who, both from education and from knowledge of the world, was especially tempted to consider all truth as a theory which was not realized in a present tangible form. Accordingly, when once they had rid themselves of the mortification caused by their forced subscription, they had the satisfaction of finding themselves the most powerful party in the Church, as being the representative and organ of the Emperor's sentiments. They then at once changed places with the Catholics; who sustained a double defeat, both in the continued power of those whom they had hoped to exclude from the Church, and again, in the invidiousness of their own unrelenting suspicion and dislike of men, who had seemed by subscription to satisfy all reasonable doubt respecting their orthodoxy.

The Arian party was fortunate, moreover, in its leaders; one the most dexterous politician, the other the most accomplished theologian of the age. Eusebius of Nicomedia was a Lucianist, the fellow-disciple of Arius. He was originally Bishop of Berytus, in Phœnicia; but, having gained the confidence of Constantia, sister to Constantine, and wife to Licinius, he was by her influence translated to Nicomedia, where the Eastern Court then resided. Here he secretly engaged in the cause of Licinius against his rival, and is even reported to have been indifferent to the security of the Christians during the persecution which followed; a charge which certainly derives some confirmation from Alexander's circular epistle, in which the Arians are accused of directing the violence of the civil power against the orthodox of Alexandria. On the ruin of Licinius, he was screened by Constantia from the resentment of the conqueror; and, being recommended by his polished manners and shrewd and persuasive talent, he soon contrived to gain an influence over the mind of Constantine himself. From the time that Arius had recourse to him on his flight from Palestine, he is to be accounted the real head of the heretical party; and his influence is quickly discernible in the change which ensued in its language and conduct. While a courteous tone was assumed towards the defenders of the orthodox doctrine, the subtleties of dialectics, in which the sect excelled, were used, not in attacking, but in deceiving its opponents, in making unbelief plausible, and obliterating the distinctive marks of the true creed. It must not be forgotten that it was from Nicomedia, the see of Eusebius, that Constantine wrote his epistle to Alexander and Arius.

In supporting Arianism in its new direction, the other Eusebius, Bishop of Cæsarea, was of singular service. This distinguished writer, to whom the Christian world has so great a debt at the present day, though not characterized by the unprincipled ambition of his namesake, is unhappily connected in history with the Arian party. He seems to have had the faults and the virtues of the mere man of letters: strongly excited neither to good nor to evil, and careless at once of the cause of truth and the prizes of secular greatness, in comparison of the comforts and decencies of literary ease. His first master was Dorotheus of Antioch[3]; afterwards he became a pupil of the School of Cæsarea, which seems to have been his birth-place, and where Origen had taught. Here he studied the works of that great master, and the other writers of the Alexandrian school. It does not appear when he first began to arianize. At Cæsarea he is celebrated as the friend of the Orthodox Pamphilus, afterwards martyred, whom he assisted in his defence of Origen, in answer to the charges of heterodoxy then in circulation against him. The first book of this work is still extant in the Latin translation of Ruffinus, and its statements of the Catholic doctrines are altogether explicit and accurate. In his own writings, numerous as they are, there is very little which fixes on Eusebius any charge, beyond that of an attachment to the Platonic phraseology. Had he not connected himself with the Arian party, it would have been unjust to have suspected him of heresy. But his acts are his confession. He openly sided with those whose blasphemies a true Christian would have abhorred; and he sanctioned and shared their deeds of violence and injustice perpetrated on the Catholics.

But it is a different reason which has led to the mention of Eusebius in this connection. The grave accusation under which he lies, is not that of arian-

[3] Danz. de Eus. Cæsar. 22.

izing, but of corrupting the simplicity of the Gospel with an Eclectic spirit. While he held out the ambiguous language of the schools as a refuge, and the Alexandrian imitation of it as an argument, against the pursuit of the orthodox, his conduct gave countenance to the secular maxim, that difference in creeds is a matter of inferior moment, and that, provided we confess as far as the very terms of Scripture, we may speculate as philosophers, and live as the world[4]. A more dangerous adviser Constantine could hardly have selected, than a man thus variously gifted, thus exalted in the Church, thus disposed towards the very errors against which he required especially to be guarded. The remark has been made that, throughout his Ecclesiastical History no instance occurs of his expressing abhorrence of the superstitions of paganism, and that his custom is either to praise, or not to blame, such heretical writers as fall under his notice[5].

Nor must the influence of the Court pass unnoticed, in recounting the means by which Arianism secured a hold over the mind of the Emperor. Constantia, his favourite sister, was the original patroness of Eusebius of Nicomedia; and thus a princess, whose name would otherwise be dignified by her misfortunes, is

[4] In this association of the Eusebian with the Eclectic temper, it must not be forgotten, that Julian the Apostate was the pupil of Eusebius of Nicomedia, his kinsman; that he took part with the Arians against the Catholics; and that, in one of his extant epistles, he speaks in praise of the writings of an Arian Bishop, George of Laodicea. Vide Weisman, sec. iv. 35. § 12.

[5] Kestner de Euseb. Auctor. prolegom. § 17. Yet it must be confessed, he is strongly opposed to γοήτεια in all its forms; i. e. as being unworthy a philosopher.

known to Christians of later times only as a principal instrument of the success of heresy. Wrought upon by a presbyter, a creature of the bishop's, who was in her confidence, she summoned Constantine to her bed-side in her last illness, begged him, as her parting request, to extend his favour to the Arians, and especially commended to his regard the presbyter himself, who had stimulated her to this experiment on the feelings of a brother. The hangers-on of the Imperial Court imitated her in her preference for the polite and smooth demeanour of the Eusebian prelates, which was advantageously contrasted to the stern simplicity of the Catholics. The eunuchs and slaves of the palace (strange to say) embraced the tenets of Arianism; and all the most light-minded and frivolous of mankind allowed themselves to pervert the solemn subject in controversy into matter for fashionable conversation or literary amusement.

The arts of flattery completed the triumph of the heretical party. So many are the temptations to which monarchs are exposed of forgetting that they are men, that it is obviously the duty of the Episcopal Order to remind them that there is a visible Power in the world, divinely founded and protected, superior to their own. But Eusebius places himself at the feet of a heathen; and forgetful of his own ordination-grace, allows the Emperor to style himself "the bishop of Paganism," and "the predestined Apostle of virtue to all men [6]." The shrine of the Church was thrown open to his inspection; and, contrary to the spirit of Christianity, its mysteries were officiously explained to one who was not yet even a candidate for baptism.

[6] Euseb. Vit. Const. iii. 58. iv. 24. Vide also, i. 4. 24.

The restoration and erection of Churches, which is the honourable distinction of his reign, assimilated him, in the minds of his courtiers, to the Divine Founder and Priest of the invisible temple; and the magnificence, which soothed the vanity of a monarch, seemed in its charitable uses almost a substitute for personal religion [7].

2.

While events thus gradually worked for the secular advancement of the heretical party, the Catholics were allotted gratifications and anxieties of a higher character. The proceedings of the Council had detected the paucity of the Arians among the Rulers of the Church; which had been the more clearly ascertained, inasmuch as no temporal interests had operated to gain for the orthodox cause that vast preponderance of advocates which it had actually obtained. Moreover, it had confirmed by the combined evidence of the universal Church, the argument from Scripture and local tradition, which each separate Christian community already possessed. And there was a satisfaction in having found a formula adequate to the preservation of the all-important article in controversy in all its purity. On the other hand, in spite of these immediate causes of congratulation, the fortunes of the Church were clouded in prospect, by the Emperor's adoption of its Creed as a formula of peace, not of belief, and by the ready subscription of the unprincipled faction, which had previously objected to it. This immediate failure, which not unfrequently attends beneficial measures in their commencement,

[7] Ibid. iv. 22, and alibi. Vide Gibbon, ch. xx.

issued, as has been said, in the temporary triumph of the Arians. The disease, which had called for the Council, instead of being expelled from the system, was thrown back upon the Church, and for a time afflicted it [8]; nor was it cast out, except by the persevering fasting and prayer, the labours and sufferings, of the oppressed believers. Meanwhile, the Catholic prelates could but retire from the Court party, and carefully watch its movements; and, in consequence, incurred the reproach and the penalty of being "troublers of Israel." This may be illustrated from the subsequent history of Arius himself, with which this Chapter shall close.

It is doubtful, whether or not Arius was persuaded to sign the symbol at the Nicene Council; but at least he professed to receive it about five years afterwards. At this time Eusebius of Nicomedia had been restored to the favour of Constantine; who, on the other hand, influenced by his sister, had become less zealous in his adherence to the orthodox side of the controversy. An attempt was made by the friends of Arius to effect his re-admission into the Church at Alexandria. The great Athanasius was at this time Primate of Egypt; and in his instance the question was tried, whether or not the Church would adopt the secular principles, to which the Arians were willing to subject it, and would abandon its faith, as the condition of present peace and prosperity. He was already known as the counsellor of Alexander in the previous controversy; yet, Eusebius did not at once give up the hope of gaining him over, a hope which was strengthened by his recent triumph over

[8] Theod. Hist. i. 6. fin.

the orthodox prelates of Antioch, Gaza, and Hadrianople, whom he had found means to deprive of their sees to make way for Arians. Failing in his attempt at conciliation, he pursued the policy which might have been anticipated, and accused the Bishop of Alexandria of a youthful rashness, and an obstinate contentious spirit, incompatible with the good understanding which ought to subsist among Christians. Arius was summoned to Court, presented an ambiguous confession, and was favourably received by Constantine. Thence he was despatched to Alexandria, and was quickly followed by an imperial injunction addressed to Athanasius, in order to secure the restoration of the heresiarch to the Church to which he had belonged. "On being informed of my pleasure," says Constantine, in the fragment of the Epistle preserved by Athanasius, "give free admission to all, who are desirous of entering into communion with the Church. For if I learn of your standing in the way of any who were seeking it, or interdicting them, I will send at once those who shall depose you instead, by my authority, and banish you from your see[9]." It was not to be supposed, that Athanasius would yield to an order, though from his sovereign, which was conceived in such ignorance of the principles of Church communion, and of the powers of its Rulers; and, on his explanation, the Emperor professed himself well satisfied, that he should use his own discretion in the matter. The intrigues of the Eusebians, which followed, shall elsewhere be related; they ended in effecting the banishment of Athanasius into Gaul, the restoration of Arius at a Council held

[9] Athan. Apol. contr. Arian 59.

at Jerusalem, his return to Alexandria, and, when the anger of the intractable populace against him broke out into a tumult, his recall to Constantinople to give further explanations respecting his real opinions.

There the last and memorable scene of his history took place, and furnishes a fresh illustration of the clearness and integrity, with which the Catholics maintained the true principles of Church union, against those who would have sacrificed truth to peace. The aged Alexander, bishop of the see, underwent a persecution of entreaties and threats, such as had already been employed against Athanasius. The Eusebians urged upon him, by way of warning, their fresh successes over the Bishops of Ancyra and Alexandria; and appointed a day, by which he was to admit Arius to communion, or to be ejected from his see. Constantine confirmed this alternative. At first, indeed, he had been struck with doubts respecting the sincerity of Arius; but, on the latter professing with an oath that his tenets were orthodox, and presenting a confession, in which the terms of Scripture were made the vehicle of his characteristic impieties, the Emperor dismissed his scruples, observing with an anxiety and seriousness which rise above his ordinary character, that Arius had well sworn if his words had no double meaning; otherwise, God would avenge. The miserable man did not hesitate to swear, that he professed the Creed of the Catholic Church without reservation, and that he had never said nor thought otherwise, than according to the statements which he now made.

For seven days previous to that appointed for his re-admission, the Church of Constantinople, Bishop and people, were given up to fasting and prayer. Alexander, after a vain endeavour to move the Emperor, had recourse to the most solemn and extraordinary form of anathema allowed in the Church[1]; and with tears besought its Divine Guardian, either to take himself out of the world, or to remove thence the instrument of those extended and increasing spiritual evils, with which Christendom was darkening. On the evening before the day of his proposed triumph, Arius passed through the streets of the city with his party, in an ostentatious manner; when the stroke of death suddenly overtook him, and he expired before his danger was discovered.

Under the circumstances, a thoughtful mind cannot but account this as one of those remarkable interpositions of power, by which Divine Providence urges on the consciences of men in the natural course of things, what their reason from the first acknowledges, that He is not indifferent to human conduct. To say that these do not fall within the ordinary course of His governance, is merely to say that they *are* judgments; which, in the common meaning of the word, stand for events extraordinary and unexpected. That such do take place under the Christian Dispensation, is sufficiently proved by the history of Ananias and Sapphira. It is remarkable too, that the similar occurrences, which happen at the present day, are generally connected with some unusual perjury or extreme blasphemy; and, though we may not infer the sin from the circumstance of the temporal infliction, yet, the commission of the sin being ascertained, we may well account, that its guilt is providentially

[1] Bingham, Antiq. xvi. 2. § 17.

impressed on the minds and enlarged in the estimation of the multitude, by the visible penalty by which it is followed. Nor do we in such cases necessarily pass any absolute sentence upon the person, who appears to be the object of Divine Visitation ; but merely upon the particular act which provoked it, and which has its fearful character of evil stamped upon it, independent of the punishment which draws our attention to it. The man of God, who prophesied against the altar in Bethel, is not to be regarded by the light of his last act, though a judgment followed it, but according to the general tenor of his life. Arius also must thus be viewed ; though, unhappily, his closing deed is but the seal of a prevaricating and presumptuous career.

Athanasius, who is one of the authorities from whom the foregoing account is taken, received it from Macarius, a presbyter of the Church of Constantinople, who was in that city at the time. He adds, "while the Church was rejoicing at the deliverance, Alexander administered the communion in pious and orthodox form, praying with all the brethren and glorifying God greatly ; not as if rejoicing over his death, (God forbid ! for to all men it is appointed once to die,) but because in this event there was displayed somewhat more than a human judgment. For the Lord Himself, judging between the threats of the Eusebians and the prayer of Alexander, has in this event given sentence against the heresy of the Arians ; showing it to be unworthy of ecclesiastical fellowship, and manifesting to all, that though it have the patronage of Emperor and of all men, yet that by the Church itself it is condemned [2]."

[2] Epist. ad Scrap. 4

CHAPTER IV.[1]

COUNCILS IN THE REIGN OF CONSTANTIUS.[2]

SECTION I.

THE EUSEBIANS.

THE death of Arius was productive of no important consequences in the history of his party. They had never deferred to him as their leader, and since the Nicene Council had even abandoned his creed. The theology of the Eclectics had opened to Eusebius of Cæsarea a language less obnoxious to the Catholics and to Constantine, than that into which he had been betrayed in Palestine; while his namesake, possessing the confidence of the Emperor, was enabled to wield weapons more decisive in the controversy than those which Arius had used. From that time Semi-Arianism was their profession, and calumny their weapon, for the deposition, by legal process, of their Catholic opponents. This is the character of their proceedings from A.D. 328 to A.D. 350; when circumstances led them to adopt a third creed, and enabled them to support it by open force.

[1] [In this Chapter a change in the structure of the sentences has been made here and there, with the view of relieving the intricacies of the narrative.]

[2] [Vid. Appendix, No. 6.]

I.

It may at first sight excite our surprise, that men who were so little careful to be consistent in their professions of faith, should be at the pains to find evasions for a test, which they might have subscribed as a matter of course, and then dismissed from their thoughts. But, not to mention the natural desire of continuing an opposition to which they had once committed themselves, and especially after a defeat, there is, moreover, that in religious mysteries which is ever distasteful to secular minds. The marvellous, which is sure to excite the impatience and resentment of the baffled reason, becomes insupportable when found in those solemn topics, which it would fain look upon, as necessary indeed for the uneducated, but irrelevant when addressed to those who are already skilled in the knowledge and the superficial decencies of virtue. The difficulties of science may be dismissed from the mind, and virtually forgotten; the precepts of morality, imperative as they are, may be received with the condescension, and applied with the modifications, of a self-applauding refinement. But what at once demands attention, yet refuses to satisfy curiosity, places itself above the human mind, imprints on it the thought of Him who is eternal, and enforces the necessity of obedience for its own sake. And thus it becomes to the proud and irreverent, what the consciousness of guilt is to the sinner; a spectre haunting the field, and disturbing the complacency, of their intellectual investigations. In this at least, throughout their changes, the Eusebians are consistent,—in their hatred of the Sacred Mystery.

It has sometimes been scornfully said, on the other hand, that the zeal of Christians, in the discussion of theological subjects, has increased with the mysteriousness of the doctrine in dispute. There is no reason why we should shrink from the avowal. Doubtless, a subject that is dear to us, does become more deeply fixed in our affections by its very peculiarities and incidental obscurities. We desire to revere what we already love; and we seek for the materials of reverence in such parts of it, as exceed our intelligence or imagination. It should therefore excite our devout gratitude, to reflect how the truth has been revealed to us in Scripture in the most practical manner; so as both to humble and to win over, while it consoles, those who really love it. Moreover, with reference to the particular mystery under consideration, since a belief in our Lord's Divinity is closely connected (how, it matters not) with deep religious feeling generally,—involving a sense both of our need and of the value of the blessings which He has procured for us, and an emancipation from the tyranny of the visible world,—it is not wonderful, that those, who would confine our knowledge of God to things seen, should dislike to hear of His true and only Image. If the unbeliever has attempted to account for the rise of the doctrine, by the alleged natural growth of a veneration for the Person and acts of the Redeemer, let it at least be allowed to Christians to reverse the process of argument, and to maintain rather, that a low estimation of the evangelical blessings leads to unworthy conceptions of the Author of them. In the case of laymen it will show itself in a sceptical neglect of the subject of religion altogether; while ecclesiastics, on whose minds religion is forced, are tempted either to an undue exaltation of their order, or to a creed dishonourable to their Lord. The Eusebians adopted the latter alternative, and so merged the supremacy of Divine Truth amid the multifarious religions and philosophies of the world.

Their skilfulness in reasoning and love of disputation afford us an additional explanation of their pertinacious opposition to the Nicene Creed. Though, in possessing the favour of the Imperial Court, they had already the substantial advantages of victory, they disdained success without a battle. They loved the excitement of suspense, and the triumph of victory. And this sophistical turn of mind accounts, not only for their incessant wranglings, but for their frequent changes of view, as regards the doctrine in dispute. It may be doubted whether men, so practised in the gymnastics of the Aristotelic school, could carefully develope and consistently maintain a definite view of doctrine ; especially in a case, where the difficulties of an unsound cause combined with their own habitual restlessness and levity to defeat the attempt. Accordingly, in their conduct of the argument, they seem to be aiming at nothing beyond "living from hand to mouth," as the saying is ; availing themselves of some or other expedient, which would suffice to carry them through existing difficulties ; admissions, whether to satisfy the timid conscience of Constantius, or to deceive the Western Church ; or statements so faintly precise and so decently ambiguous, as to embrace the greatest number of opinions possible, and to deprive religion, in consequence, of its austere and commanding aspect.

That I may not seem to be indulging in vague accusation, I here present the reader with a sketch of the lives of the chief of them; from which he will be able to decide, whether the above explanation of their conduct is unnecessary or gratuitous.

The most distinguished of the party, after Eusebius himself, for ability, learning, and unscrupulousness, was Acacius, the successor of the other Eusebius in the see of Cæsarea. He had been his pupil, and on his death inherited his library. Jerome ranks him among the most learned commentators on Scripture. The Arian historian, Philostorgius, praises his boldness, penetration, and perspicuity in unfolding his views: and Sozomen speaks of his talents and influence as equal to the execution of the most difficult designs [3]. He began at first with professing himself a Semi-Arian after the example of Eusebius, his master; next, he became the founder of the party, which will presently be described as the *Homœan* or *Scriptural;* thirdly, he joined himself to the Anomœans or pure Arians, so as even to be the intimate associate of the wretched Aetius; fourthly, at the command of Constantius, he deserted and excommunicated him; fifthly, in the reign of the Catholic Jovian, he signed the *Homoüsion* or symbol of Nicæa.

George, of Laodicæa, another of the leading members of the Eusebian party, was originally a presbyter of the Alexandrian Church, and deposed by Alexander for the assistance afforded by him to Arius at Nicomedia. At the end of the reign of Constantius, he professed for a while the sentiments of the Semi-Arians; whether seriously or not, we have not the

[3] Tillemont, Mem. des Ariens, vol. vi. c. 28.

means of deciding, although the character given of him by Athanasius, who is generally candid in his judgments, is unfavourable to his sincerity. Certainly he deserted the Semi-Arians in no long time, and died an Anomœan. He is also accused of open and habitual irregularities of life.

Leontius, the most crafty of his party, was promoted by the Arians to the see of Antioch[4]; and though a pupil of the school of Lucian, and consistently attached to the opinions of Arius throughout his life, he seems to have conducted himself in his high position with moderation and good temper. The Catholic party was at that time still strong in the city, particularly among the laity; the crimes of Stephen and Placillus, his immediate Arian predecessors, had brought discredit on the heretical cause; and the theological opinions of Constantius, who was attached to the Semi-Arian doctrine, rendered it dangerous to avow the plain blasphemies of the first founder of their creed. Accordingly, with the view of seducing the Catholics to his own communion, he was anxious to profess an agreement with the Church, even where he held an opposite opinion; and we are told that in the public doxology, which was practically the test of faith, not even the nearest to him in the congregation could hear from him more than the words "for ever and ever," with which it concludes. It was apparently with the same design, that he converted the almshouses of the city, destined for the reception of strangers, into seminaries for propagating the Christian faith; and published a panegyrical

[4] A strange and scandalous transaction in early life, gave him the appellation of ὁ ἀπόκοπος. Athan. ad Monach. 4.

account of St. Babylas, when his body was to be removed to Daphne, by way of consecrating a place which had been before devoted to sensual excesses. In the meanwhile, he gradually weakened the Church, by a systematic promotion of heretical, and a discountenance of the orthodox Clergy; one of his most scandalous acts being his ordination of Aetius, the founder of the Anomœans, who was afterwards promoted to the episcopacy in the reign of Julian.

Eudoxius, the successor of Leontius, in the see of Antioch, was his fellow-pupil in the school of Lucian. He is said to have been converted to Semi-Arianism by the writings of the Sophist Asterius; but he afterwards joined the Anomœans, and got possession of the patriarchate of Constantinople. It was there, at the dedication of the cathedral of St. Sophia, that he uttered the wanton impiety, which has characterized him with a distinctness, which supersedes all historical notice of his conduct, or discussion of his religious opinions. "When Eudoxius," says Socrates, "had taken his seat on the episcopal throne, his first words were these celebrated ones, 'the Father is ἀσεβὴς, irreligious; the Son εὐσεβὴς, religious.' When a noise and confusion ensued, he added, 'Be not distressed at what I say; for the Father is irreligious, as worshipping none; but the Son is religious towards the Father.' On this the tumult ceased, and in its place an intemperate laughter seized the congregation; and it remains as a good saying even to this time[5]."

[5] Socr. Hist. ii. 43. [Εὐσέβεα, ἀσέβεια, δυσσέβεια, and their derivatives, in the language of Athanasius or his age, means orthodoxy, heterodoxy, orthodox, &c. This circumstance gives its point to the jest. This sense is traceable to St. Paul's words, "Great is the mystery of

Valens, Bishop of Mursa, in Pannonia, shall close this list of Eusebian Prelates. He was one of the immediate disciples of Arius; and, from an early age, the champion of his heresy in the Latin Church. In the conduct of the controversy, he inherited more of the plain dealing as well as of the principles of his master, than his associates; he was an open advocate of the Anomœan doctrine, and by his personal influence with Constantius balanced the power of the Semi-Arian party, derived from the Emperor's private attachment to their doctrine. The favour of Constantius was gained by a fortunate artifice, at the time the latter was directing his arms against the tyrant Magnentius. "While the two armies were engaged in the plains of Mursa," says Gibbon, "and the fate of the two rivals depended on the chance of war, the son of Constantine passed the anxious moments in a church of the martyrs, under the walls of the city. His spiritual comforter Valens, the Arian Bishop of the diocese, employed the most artful precautions to obtain such early intelligence, as might secure either his favour or his escape. A secret chain of swift and trusty messengers informed him of the vicissitudes of the battle; and while the courtiers stood trembling around their affrighted master, Valens assured him that

godliness (εὐσεβείας)," orthodoxy. Vide Athan. Opp. passim. Thus Arius also ends his letter to Eusebius with "ἀληθῶς εὐσέβιε." And St. Basil, defending his own freedom from Arian error, says that St. Macrina, his grandmother, "moulded him from his infancy in the dogmas of religion (εὐσεβείας)," and that, when he grew up, and travelled, he ever chose those for his fathers and guides, whom he found walking according to "the rule of religion (εὐσεβείας) handed down." Ep. 204. 6. Vide also, Basil. Opp. t. 2, p. 599. Greg. Naz. Orat. ii. 80. Euseb. cont. Marc. i. 7. Joan. Antioch. apud Facund. i. 1. Sozomen, i. 20. as supr. note p. 140.]

the Gallic legions gave way; and insinuated, with some presence of mind, that the glorious event had been revealed to him by an Angel. The grateful Emperor ascribed his success to the merits and intercession of the Bishop of Mursa, whose faith had deserved the public and miraculous approbation of Heaven[6]."

Such were the leaders of the Eusebian or Court faction; and on the review of them, do we not seem to see in each a fresh exhibition of their great type and forerunner, Paulus, on one side or other of his character, though surpassing him in extravagance of conduct, as possessing a wider field, and more powerful incentives for ambitious and energetic exertion? We see the same accommodation of the Christian Creed to the humour of an earthly Sovereign, the same fertility of disputation in support of their version of it, the same reckless profanation of things sacred, the same patient dissemination of error for the services of the age after them; and, if they are free from the personal immoralities of their master, they balance this favourable trait of character by the cruel and hard-hearted temper, which discovers itself in their persecution of the Catholics.

2.

This persecution was conducted till the middle of the century according to the outward forms of ecclesiastical law. Charges of various kinds were preferred in Council against the orthodox prelates of the principal sees, with a profession at least of regularity, whatever unfairness there might be in the details of

Gibbon, Hist. ch. xxi.

the proceedings. By this means all the most powerful Churches of Eastern Christendom, by the commencement of the reign of Constantius (A.D. 337), had been brought under the influence of the Arians; Constantinople, Heraclea, Hadrianople, Ephesus, Ancyra, both Cæsareas, Antioch, Laodicæa, and Alexandria. Eustathius of Antioch, for instance, had incurred their hatred, by his strenuous resistance to the heresy in the seat of its first origin. After the example of his immediate predecessor Philogonius, he refused communion to Stephen, Leontius, Eudoxius, George, and others; and accused Eusebius of Cæsarea openly of having violated the faith of Nicæa. The heads of the party assembled in Council at Antioch; and, on charges of heresy and immorality, which they professed to be satisfactorily maintained, pronounced sentence of deposition against him. Constantine banished him to Philippi, together with a considerable number of the priests and deacons of his Church. So again, Marcellus of Ancyra, another of their inveterate opponents, was deposed, anathematized, and banished by them, with greater appearance of justice, on the ground of his leaning to the errors of Sabellius. But their most rancorous enmity and most persevering efforts were directed against the high-minded Patriarch of Alexandria; and, in illustration of their principles and conduct, the circumstances of his first persecution shall here be briefly related.

When Eusebius of Nicomedia failed to effect the restoration of Arius into the Alexandrian Church by persuasion, he had threatened to gain his end by harsher means. Calumnies were easily invented against the man who had withstood his purpose: and it so happened, that willing tools were found on the spot for conducting the attack. The Meletian sectaries have already been noticed, as being the original associates of Arius; who had troubled the Church by taking part in their schism, before he promulgated his peculiar heresy. They were called after Meletius, Bishop of Lycopolis in the Thebaid; who, being deposed for lapsing in the Dioclesian persecution, separated from the Catholics, and, propagating a spurious succession of clergy by his episcopal prerogative, formed a powerful body in the heart of the Egyptian Church. The Council of Nicæa, desirous of terminating the disorder in the most temperate manner, instead of deposing the Meletian bishops, had arranged, that they should retain a nominal rank in the sees, in which they had respectively placed themselves; while, by forbidding them to exercise their episcopal functions, it provided for the termination of the schism at their death. But, with the bad fortune which commonly attends conciliatory measures, unless accompanied by such a display of vigour as shows that concession is but condescension, the clemency was forgotten in the restriction, which irritated, without repressing them; and, being bent on the overthrow of the dominant Church, they made a sacrifice of their principles, which had hitherto been orthodox, and joined the Eusebians. By this intrigue, the latter gained an entrance into the Egyptian Church, as effectual as that which had already been opened to them, by means of their heresy itself, in Syria and Asia Minor [7].

[7] The Meletians, on the other hand, were not in the event equally advantaged by the coalition; for, after the success of their attack upon

Charges against Athanasius were produced and examined in Councils successively held at Cæsarea and Tyre (A.D. 333—335); the Meletians being the accusers, and the Eusebians the judges in the trial. At an earlier date, it had been attempted to convict him of political offences; but, on examination, Constantine became satisfied of his innocence. It had been represented, that, of his own authority, he had imposed and rigorously exacted a duty upon the Egyptian linen cloth; the pretended tribute being in fact nothing beyond the offerings, which pious persons had made to the Church, in the shape of vestments for the service of the sanctuary. It had moreover been alleged, that he had sent pecuniary aid to one Philumenus, who was in rebellion against the Emperor; as at a later period they accused him of a design of distressing Constantinople, by stopping the corn vessels of Alexandria, destined for the supply of the metropolis.

The charges brought against him before these Councils were both of a civil and of an ecclesiastical character; that he, or Macarius, one of his deacons, had broken a consecrated chalice, and the holy table itself, and had thrown the sacred books into the fire; next, that he had killed Arsenius, a Meletian bishop, whose hand, amputated and preserved for magical purposes, had been found in Athanasius's house. The latter of these strange accusations was refuted at the Council of Cæsarea by Arsenius himself, whom Athanasius had gained, and who, on the production of a

Athanasius, Constantine, true to his object of restoring tranquillity to the Church, while he banished Athanasius to Treves, banished also John, the leader of the Meletians, who had been forward in procuring his condemnation.

human hand at the trial, presented himself before the judges, thus destroying the circumstantial evidence by which it was to be identified as his. The former charge was refuted at Tyre by the testimony of the Egyptian bishops; who, after exposing the equivocating evidence of the accuser, went on to prove that at the place where their Metropolitan was said to have broken the chalice, there was neither church, nor altar, nor chalice, existing. These were the principal allegations brought against him; and their extraordinary absurdity, (certain as the charges are as matters of history, from evidence of various kinds,) can only be accounted for by supposing, that the Eusebians were even then too powerful and too bold, to care for much more than the bare forms of law, or to scruple at any evidence, which the unskilfulness of their Egyptian coadjutors might set before them. A charge of violence in his conduct towards certain Meletians was added to the above; and, as some say, a still more frivolous accusation of incontinence, but whether this was ever brought, is more than doubtful.

Cæsarea and Tyre were places too public even for the audacity of the Eusebians, when the facts of the case were so plainly in favour of the accused. It was now proposed that a commission of inquiry should be sent to the Mareotis, which was in the neighbourhood, and formed part of the diocese, of Alexandria, and was the scene of the alleged profanation of the sacred chalice. The leading members of this commission were Valens and Ursacius, Theognis, Maris, and two others, all Eusebians; they took with them the chief accuser of Athanasius as their guide and host, leaving Athanasius and Macarius at Tyre, and refusing admittance into the court of inquiry to such of the clergy of the Mareotis, as were desirous of defending their Bishop's interests in his absence. The issue of such proceedings may be anticipated. On the return of the commission to Tyre, Athanasius was formally condemned of rebellion, sedition, and a tyrannical use of his episcopal power, of murder, sacrilege, and magic; was deposed from the see of Alexandria, and prohibited from ever returning to that city. Constantine confirmed the sentence of the Council, and Athanasius was banished to Gaul.

3.

It has often been remarked that persecutions of Christians, as in St. Paul's case, "fall out rather unto the furtherance of the Gospel[8]." The dispersion of the disciples, after the martyrdom of St. Stephen, introduced the word of truth together with themselves among the Samaritans; and in the case before us, the exile of Athanasius led to his introduction to the younger Constantine, son of the great Emperor of that name, who warmly embraced his cause, and gave him the opportunity of rousing the zeal, and gaining the personal friendship of the Catholics of the West. Constans also, another son of Constantine, declared in his favour; and thus, on the death of their father, which took place two years after the Council of Tyre, one third alone of his power, in the person of the Semi-Arian Constantius, Emperor of the East, remained with that party, which, while Constantine lived, was able to wield the whole strength of the State against

[8] Phil. i. 12.

the orthodox Bishops. The support of the Roman See was a still more important advantage gained by Athanasius. Rome was the natural mediator between Alexandria and Antioch, and at that time possessed extensive influence among the Churches of the West. Accordingly, when Constantius re-commenced the persecution, to which his father had been persuaded, the exiles betook themselves to Rome; and about the year 340 or 341 we read of Bishops from Thrace, Syria, Phœnicia, and Palestine, collected there, besides a multitude of Presbyters, and among the former, Athanasius himself, Marcellus, Asclepas of Gaza, and Luke of Hadrianople. The first act of the Roman See in their favour was the holding a provincial Council, in which the charges against Athanasius and Marcellus were examined, and pronounced to be untenable. And its next act was to advocate the summoning of a Council of the whole Church with the same purpose, referring it to Athanasius to select a place of meeting, where his cause might be secure of a more impartial hearing, than it had met with at Cæsarea and Tyre.

The Eusebians, on the other hand, perceiving the danger which their interests would sustain, should a Council be held at any distance from their own peculiar territory, determined on anticipating the projected Council by one of their own, in which they might both confirm the sentence of deposition against Athanasius, and, if possible, contrive a confession of faith, to allay the suspicions which the Occidentals entertained of their orthodoxy[9]. This was the occa-

[9] ["After the Nicene Council, the Eusebians did not dare avow their heresy in Constantine's time, but merely attempted the banishment of

sion of the Council of the Dedication, as it is called, held by them at Antioch, in the year 341, and which is one of the most celebrated Councils of the century. It was usual to solemnize the consecration of places of worship, by an attendance of the principal prelates of the neighbouring districts; and the great Church of the Metropolis of Syria, called the Dominicum Aureum, which had just been built, afforded both the pretext and the name to their assembly. Between ninety and a hundred bishops came together on this occasion, all Arians or Arianizers, and agreed without difficulty upon the immediate object of the Council, the ratification of the Synods of Cæsarea and Tyre in condemnation of Athanasius.

So far their undertaking was in their own hands; but a more difficult task remained behind, viz., to gain the approval and consent of the Western Church, by an exposition of the articles of their faith. Not intending to bind themselves by the decision at Nicæa, they had to find some substitute for the *Homoüsion.* With this view four, or even five creeds, more or less resembling the Nicene in language, were successively adopted. The first was that ascribed to the martyr Lucian, though doubts are entertained concerning its genuineness. It is in itself almost unexceptionable; and, had there been no controversies on the subjects contained in it, would have been a satisfactory evidence of the orthodoxy of its promulgators. The Son is therein styled the exact Image of the substance, will, power, and glory of the

Athanasius, and the restoration of Arius. Their first Council was A.D. 341, four years after Constantine's death and Constantius's accession."—Ath. Tr. vol. i. pp. 92, 93.]

Father; and the Three Persons of the Holy Trinity are said to be three in substance, one in will[1]. An evasive condemnation was added of the Arian tenets; sufficient, as it might seem, to delude the Latins, who were unskilled in the subtleties of the question. For instance, it was denied that our Lord was born "in time," but in the heretical school, as was shown above, time was supposed to commence with the creation of the world; and it was denied that He was "in the number of the creatures," it being their doctrine, that He was the sole immediate work of God, and, as such, not like others, but separate from the whole creation, of which indeed He was the author. Next, for some or other reason, two new creeds were proposed, and partially adopted by the Council; the same in character of doctrine, but shorter. These three were all circulated, and more or less received in the neighbouring Churches; but, on consideration, none of them seemed adequate to the object in view, that of recommending the Eusebians to the distant Churches of the West. Accordingly, a fourth formulary was drawn up after a few months' delay, among others by Mark, Bishop of Arethusa, a Semi-Arian Bishop of religious character, afterwards to be mentioned; its composers were deputed to present it to Constans; and, this creed proving unsatisfactory, a fifth confession was drawn up with considerable care and ability; though it too failed to quiet the suspicions of the Latins. This last is called the Macrostich, from the number of its paragraphs, and did not make its appearance till three years after the former.

[1] Exact image, ἀπαράλλακτος εἰκών; substance, οὐσία; subsistence, or person, ὑπόστασις.

In truth, no such exposition of the Catholic faith could satisfy the Western Christians, while they were witnesses to the exile of its great champion on account of his fidelity to it. Here the Eusebians were wanting in their usual practical shrewdness. Words, however orthodox, could not weigh against so plain a fact. The Occidentals, however unskilled in the niceties of the Greek language, were able to ascertain the heresy of the Eusebians in their malevolence towards Athanasius. Nay, the anxious attempts of his enemies, to please them by means of a confession of faith, were a refutation of their pretences. For, inasmuch as the sense of the Catholic world, had already been recorded in the *Homoüsion*, why should they devise a new formulary, if after all they agreed with the Church? or, why should they themselves be so fertile in confessions, if they had all of them but one faith? It is brought against them by Athanasius, that in their creeds they date their exposition of the Catholic doctrine, as if it were something new, instead simply of its being declared, which was the sole design of the Nicene Fathers; while at other times, they affected to acknowledge the authority of former Councils, which nevertheless they were indirectly opposing[2]. Under these circumstances the Roman Church, as the representative of the Latins, only became more bent upon the convocation of a General Council in which the Nicene Creed might be ratified, and any innovation upon it reprobated; and the innocence of Athanasius, which it had already ascertained in its provincial Synod, might be formally proved, and proclaimed to the whole of Christendom. This object was at length

[2] Athan. de Syn. 3. 37.

accomplished. Constans, whom Athanasius had visited and gained, successfully exerted his influence with his brother Constantius, the Emperor of the East; and a Council of the whole Christian world was summoned at Sardica for the above purposes, the exculpation of Marcellus and others being included with that of Athanasius.

Sardica was chosen as the place of meeting, as lying on the confines of the two divisions of the Empire. It is on the borders of Mœsia, Thrace, and Illyricum, and at the foot of Mount Hæmus, which separates it from Philippopolis. There the heads of the Christian world assembled in the year 347, twenty-two years after the Nicene Council, in number above 380 bishops, of whom seventy-six were Arian. The President of the Council was the venerable Hosius; whose name was in itself a pledge, that the decision of Nicæa was simply to be preserved, and no fresh question raised on a subject already exhausted by controversy. But, almost before the opening of the Council, matters were brought to a crisis; a schism took place in its members; the Arians retreated to Philippopolis, and there excommunicated the leaders of the orthodox, Julius of Rome, Hosius, and Protogenes of Sardica, issued a sixth confession of faith, and confirmed the proceedings of the Antiochene Council against Athanasius and the other exiles.

This secession of the Arians arose in consequence of their finding, that Athanasius was allowed a seat in the Council; the discussions of which they refused to attend, while a Bishop took part in them, who had already been deposed by Synods of the East. The orthodox replied, that a later Council, held at Rome, had fully acquitted and restored him ; moreover, that to maintain his guilt was but to assume the principal point, which they were then assembled to debate ; and, though very consistent with their absenting themselves from the Council altogether, could not be permitted to those, who had by their coming recognized the object, for which it was called. Accordingly, without being moved by their retreat, the Council proceeded to the condemnation of some of the more notorious opponents among them of the Creed of Nicæa, examined the charges against Athanasius and the rest, reviewed the acts of the investigations at Tyre and the Mareotis, which the Eusebians had sent to Rome in their defence, and confirmed the decree of the Council of Rome, in favour of the accused. Constans enforced this decision on his brother by the arguments peculiar to a monarch ; and the timid Constantius, yielding to fear what he denied to justice, consented to restore to Alexandria a champion of the truth, who had been condemned on the wildest of charges, by the most hostile and unprincipled of judges.

The journey of Athanasius to Alexandria elicited the fullest and most satisfactory testimonies of the real orthodoxy of the Eastern Christians ; in spite of the existing cowardice or misapprehension, which surrendered them to the tyrannical rule of a few determined and energetic heretics. The Bishops of Palestine, one of the chief holds of the Arian spirit, welcomed, with the solemnity of a Council, a restoration, which, under the circumstances of the case, was almost a triumph over their own sovereign ; and so excited was the Catholic feeling even at Antioch, that

Constantius feared to grant to the Athanasians a single Church in that city, lest it should have been the ruin of the Arian cause.

One of the more important consequences of the Council of Sardica, was the public recantation of Valens, and his accomplice Ursacius, Bishop of Singidon, in Pannonia, two of the most inveterate enemies and calumniators of Athanasius. It was addressed to the Bishop of Rome, and was conceived in the following terms: "Whereas we are known heretofore to have preferred many grievous charges against Athanasius the Bishop, and, on being put on our defence by your excellency, have failed to make good our charges, we declare to your excellency, in the presence of all the presbyters, our brethren, that all which we have heretofore heard against the aforesaid, is false, and altogether foreign to his character; and therefore, that we heartily embrace the communion of the aforesaid Athanasius, especially considering your Holiness, according to your habitual clemency, has condescended to pardon our mistake. Further we declare, that, should the Orientals at any time, or Athanasius, from resentful feelings, be desirous to bring us to account, that we will not act in the matter without your sanction. As for the heretic Arius, and his partisans, who say that "*Once the Son was not*," that "*He is of created Substance*," and that "*He is not the Son of God before all time*," we anathematize them now, and once for all, according to our former statement which we presented at Milan. Witness our hand, that we condemn once for all the Arian heresy, as we have already said, and its advocates. Witness also the hand of Ursacius.—I, Ursacius the Bishop, have set my name to this statement[3]."

[3] Athan. Apol. cont. Arian. 58.

The Council of Milan, referred to in the conclusion of this letter, seems to have been held A.D. 347; two years after the Arian creed, called Macrostich, was sent into the West, and shortly after the declaration of Constans in favour of the restoration of the Athanasians.

SECTION II.

THE SEMI-ARIANS.

THE events recorded in the last Section were attended by important consequences in the history of Arianism. The Council of Sardica led to a separation between the Eastern and Western Churches; which seemed to be there represented respectively by the rival Synods of Sardica and Philippopolis, and which had before this time hidden their differences from each other, and communicated together from a fear of increasing the existing evil[1]. Not that really there was any discordance of doctrine between them. The historian, from whom this statement is taken, gives it at the same time as his own opinion, that the majority of the Asiatics were Homoüsians, though tyrannized over by the court influence, the sophistry, the importunity, and the daring, of the Eusebian party. This mere handful of divines, unscrupulously pressing forward into the highest ecclesiastical stations, set about them to change the condition of the Churches thus put into their power; and, as has been remarked in the case of Leontius of Antioch, filled the inferior offices with

[1] Soz. iii. 13.

their own creatures, and sowed the seeds of future discords and disorders, which they could not hope to have themselves the satisfaction of beholding. The orthodox majority of Bishops and divines, on the other hand, timorously or indolently, kept in the background; and allowed themselves to be represented at Sardica by men, whose tenets they knew to be unchristian, and professed to abominate. And in such circumstances, the blame of the open dissensions, which ensued between the Eastern and Western divisions of Christendom, was certain to be attributed to those who urged the summoning of the Council, not to those who neglected their duty by staying away. In qualification of this censure, however, the intriguing spirit of the Eusebians must be borne in mind; who might have means, of which we are not told, of keeping away their orthodox brethren from Sardica. Certainly the expense of the journey was considerable, whatever might be the imperial or the ecclesiastical allowances for it[2], and their absence

[2] [On the *cursus publicus*, vid. Gothofred. in Cod. Theod. viii. tit. 5. It was provided for the journeys of the Emperor, for persons whom he summoned, for magistrates, ambassadors, and for such private persons as the Emperor indulged in the use of it, which was gratis. The use was granted by Constantine to the Bishops who were summoned to Nicæa, as far as it went, in addition to other means of travelling. Euseb. V. Const. iii. 6. (though aliter Valesius in loc.) The *cursus publicus* brought the Bishops to the Council of Tyre. Ibid. iv. 43. In the conference between Liberius and Constantius (Theod. Hist. ii. 13), it is objected that the *cursus publicus* is not sufficient to convey Bishops to the Council, as Liberius proposes; he answers that the Churches are rich enough to convey their Bishops as far as the seas. Thus St. Hilary was compelled (datâ evectionis copiâ, Sulp. Sev. Hist. ii. 57) to attend at Seleucia, as Athanasius at Tyre. Julian complains of the abuse of the *cursus publicus*, perhaps with an allusion to these Councils of Constantius. Vide Cod. Theod. viii. tit. 5, l. 12; where Gothofred quotes Liban. Epitaph.

from their flocks, especially in an age fertile in Councils, was an evil. Still there is enough in the history of the times, to evidence a culpable negligence on the part of the orthodox of Asia.

However, this rupture between the East and West has here been noticed, not to censure the Asiatic Churches, but for the sake of its influence on the fortunes of Arianism. It had the effect of pushing forward the Semi-Arians, as they are called, into a party distinct from the Eusebian or Court party, among whom they had hitherto been concealed. This party, as its name implies, professed a doctrine approximating to the orthodox; and thus served as a means of deceiving the Western Churches, which were unskilled in the evasions, by which the Eusebians extricated themselves from even the most explicit confessions of the Catholic doctrine. Accordingly, the six heretical confessions hitherto recounted were all Semi-Arian in character, as being intended more or less to justify the heretical party in the eyes of the Latins. But when this object ceased to be feasible,

in Julian. (vol. i. p. 569, ed. Reiske). Vide the well-known passage of Ammianus, who speaks of the Councils as being the ruin of the *res vehicularia*, Hist. xxi. 16. The Eusebians at Philippopolis say the same, Hilar. Fragm. iii. 25. The Emperor provided board and perhaps lodging for the Bishops at Ariminum; which the Bishops of Aquitaine, Gaul, and Britain declined, except three British from poverty. Sulp. Hist. ii. 56. Hunmeric in Africa, after assembling 466 Bishops at Carthage, dismissed them without mode of conveyance, provision, or baggage. Victor. Utic. Hist. iii. init. In the Emperor's letter previous to the assembling of the sixth Ecumenical Council, A.D. 678 (Harduin. Conc. t. 3, p. 1043, fin.), he says he has given orders for the conveyance and maintenance of its members. Pope John VIII. reminds Ursus, Duke of Venice (A.D. 876), of the same duty of providing for the members of a Council, "secundum pios principes, qui in talibus munificè semper erant intenti." Colet. Concil. (Ven. 1730) t. xi. p. 14.]

by the event of the Sardican Council, the Semi-Arians ceased to be of service to the Eusebians, and a separation between the parties gradually took place.

I.

The Semi-Arians, whose history shall here be introduced, originated, as far as their doctrine is concerned, in the change of profession which the Nicene anathema was the occasion of imposing upon the Eusebians; and had for their founders Eusebius of Cæsarea, and the Sophist Asterius. But viewed as a party, they are of a later date [3]. The genuine Eusebians were never in earnest in the modified creeds, which they so ostentatiously put forward for the approbation of the West. However, while they clamoured in defence of the inconsistent doctrine contained in them, which, resembling the orthodox in word, might in fact subvert it, and at once confessed and denied our Lord, it so happened, that they actually recommended that doctrine to the judgment of some of their followers, and succeeded in creating a direct belief in an hypothesis, which in their own case was but the cloke for their own indifference to the truth. This at least seems the true explanation of an intricate subject in the history. There are always men of sensitive and subtle minds, the natural victims of the bold disputant; men, who, unable to take a broad and common-sense view of an important subject, try to satisfy their intellect and conscience by refined distinctions and perverse reservations. Men of this stamp were especially to be found among a people possessed of the language and

[3] [Vide Ath. Tr. vol. ii. pp. 282—286.]

acuteness of the Greeks. Accordingly, the Eusebians at length perceived, doubtless to their surprise and disgust, that a party had arisen from among themselves, with all the positiveness (as they would consider it), and nothing of the straightforward simplicity of the Catholic controversialists, more willing to dogmatize than to argue, and binding down their associates to the real import of the words, which they had themselves chosen as mere evasions of orthodoxy; and to their dismay they discovered, that in this party the new Emperor himself was to be numbered. Constantius, indeed, may be taken as a type of a genuine Semi-Arian; resisting, as he did, the orthodox doctrine from over-subtlety, timidity, pride, restlessness, or other weakness of mind, yet paradoxical enough to combat at the same time and condemn all, who ventured to teach anything short of that orthodoxy. Balanced on this imperceptible centre between truth and error, he alternately banished every party in the controversy, not even sparing his own; and had recourse in turn to every creed for relief, except that in which the truth was actually to be found.

The symbol of the Semi-Arians was the *Homœüsion*, "*like in substance*," which they substituted for the orthodox *Homoüsion*, "*one in substance*," or "*consubstantial*." Their objections to the latter formula took the following form. If the word *usia*, "*substance*," denoted the "first substance," or an individual being, then *Homoüsios* seemed to bear a Sabellian meaning, and to involve a denial of the separate personality of the Son [4]. On the other hand, if the word was understood as including two distinct Persons (or *Hypostases*),

[4] Epiph. Hær. lxxiii. 11. fin.

this was to use it, as it is used of created things ; as if by substance were meant some common nature, either divided in fact, or one merely by abstraction [5]. They were strengthened in this view by the decree of the Council, held at Antioch between the years 260 and 270, in condemnation of Paulus, in which the word *Homoüsion* was proscribed. They preferred, accordingly, to name the Son "*like in substance*[6]," or *Homœüsios*, with the Father, that is, of a substance like in all things, except in not being the Father's substance; maintaining at the same time, that, though the Son and Spirit were separate in substance from the Father, still they were so included in His glory that there was but one God.

Instead of admitting the evasion of the Arians, that the word *Son* had but a secondary sense, and that our Lord was in reality a creature, though "not like other creatures," they plainly declared that He was not a creature, but truly the Son, born of the substance *(usia)* of the Father, as if an Emanation from Him at His will ; yet they would not allow Him simply to be God, as the Father was ; but, asserting that there were various energies in the Divine Being, they considered creation to be one, and the *gennesis* or *generation* to be another, so that the Son, though distinct in substance from God, was at the same time essentially distinct from every created nature. Or they suggested that He was the offspring of the Person *(hypostasis)*, not of the *substance* or *usia* of the Father ; or, so to say, of the Divine Will, as if the force of the word "*Son*" consisted in this point. Further, instead of the "*once*

[5] Soz. iii. 18.

[6] ὅμοιος κατ' οὐσίαν.

He was not," they adopted the "*generated time-apart,*" for which even Arius had changed it. That is, as holding that the question of the beginning of the Son's existence was beyond our comprehension, they only asserted that there was such a beginning, but that it was before time and independent of it; as if it were possible to draw a distinction between the Catholic doctrine of the derivation or order of succession in the Holy Trinity (the "*unoriginately generated*") and this notion of a beginning simplified of the condition of time.

Such was the Semi-Arian Creed, really involving contradictions in terms, parallel to those of which the orthodox were accused;—that the Son was born before all times, yet not eternal; not a creature, yet not God; of His substance, yet not the same in substance; and His exact and perfect resemblance in all things, yet not a second Deity.

2.

Yet the men were better than their creed; and it is satisfactory to be able to detect amid the impiety and worldliness of the heretical party any elements of a purer spirit, which gradually exerted itself and worked out from the corrupt mass, in which it was embedded. Even thus viewed as distinct from their political associates, the Semi-Arians are a motley party at best; yet they may be considered as Saints and Martyrs, when compared with the Eusebians, and in fact some of them have actually been acknowledged as such by the Catholics of subsequent times. Their zeal in detecting the humanitarianism of Marcellus and Photinus, and their good service in withstanding the

Anomœans, who arrived at the same humanitarianism by a bolder course of thought, will presently be mentioned. On the whole they were men of correct and exemplary life, and earnest according to their views; and they even made pretensions to sanctity in their outward deportment, in which they differed from the true Eusebians, who, as far as the times allowed it, affected the manners and principles of the world. It may be added, that both Athanasius and Hilary, two of the most uncompromising supporters of the Catholic doctrine, speak favourably of them. Athanasius does not hesitate to call them brothers[7]; considering that, however necessary it was for the edification of the Church at large, that the Homoüsion should be enforced on the clergy, yet that the privileges of private Christian fellowship were not to be denied to those, who from one cause or other stumbled at the use of it[8]. It is remarkable, that the Semi-Arians, on the contrary, in their most celebrated Synod (at Ancyra, A.D. 358) anathematized the holders of the Homoüsion, as if crypto-Sabellians[9].

Basil, the successor of Marcellus, in the see of Ancyra, united in his person the most varied learning with the most blameless life, of all the Semi-Arians[1]. This praise of rectitude in conduct was shared with him by Eustathius of Sebaste, and Eleusius of Cyzicus. These three Bishops especially attracted the regard of Hilary, on his banishment to Phrygia by the intrigues of the Arians (A.D. 356). The zealous confessor feel-

[7] [However, he is severe upon Eustathius and Basil (ad Ep. Æg. 7.), as St. Basil is on the former, who had been his friend.]

[8] Athan. de Syn. 41.

[9] Epiph. supra.

[1] Theod. Hist. ii. 25.

ingly laments the condition, in which he found the Churches in those parts. "I do not speak of things strange to me:" he says, "I write not without knowledge; I have heard and seen in my own person the faults, not of laics merely, but of bishops. For, excepting Eleusius and a few with him, the ten provinces of Asia, in which I am, are for the most part truly ignorant of God [2]." His testimony in favour of the Semi-Arians of Asia Minor, must in fairness be considered as delivered with the same force of assertion, which marks his protest against all but them; and he elsewhere addresses Basil, Eustathius, and Eleusius, by the title of "Sanctissimi viri [3]."

Mark, Bishop of Arethusa, in Syria, has obtained from the Greek Church the honours of a Saint and Martyr. He indulged, indeed, a violence of spirit, which assimilates him to the pure Arians, who were the first among Christians to employ force in the cause of religion. But violence, which endures as freely as it assails, obtains our respect, if it is denied our praise. His exertions in the cause of Christianity were attended with considerable success. In the reign of Constantius, availing himself of his power as a Christian Bishop, he demolished a heathen temple, and built a church on its site. When Julian succeeded, it was Mark's turn to suffer. The Emperor had been saved by him, when a child, on the massacre of the other princes of his house; but on this occasion he considered that the claims at once of justice and of paganism outweighed the recollection of ancient

[2] Hilar. de Syn. 63.

[3] Ibid. 90. Vid. also the Life of St. Basil of Cæsarea, who was intimate for a time with Eustathius and others.

services. Mark was condemned to rebuild the temple, or to pay the price of it; and, on his flight from his bishoprick, many of his flock were arrested as his hostages. Upon this, he surrendered himself to his persecutors, who immediately subjected him to the most revolting, as well as the most cruel indignities. "They apprehended the aged prelate," says Gibbon, selecting some out of the number, "they inhumanly scourged him; they tore his beard; and his naked body, anointed with honey, was suspended, in a net, between heaven and earth, and exposed to the stings of insects and the rays of a Syrian sun[4]." The payment of one piece of gold towards the rebuilding of the temple, would have rescued him from these torments; but, resolute in his refusal to contribute to the service of idolatry, he allowed himself, with a generous insensibility, even to jest at his own sufferings[5], till he wore out the fury, or even, it is said, effected the conversion of his persecutors. Gregory Nazianzen, and Theodoret, besides celebrating his activity in making converts, make mention of his wisdom and piety, his cultivated understanding, his love of virtue, and the honourable consistency of his life[6].

Cyril of Jerusalem, and Eusebius of Samosata, are both Saints in the Roman Calendar, though connected in history with the Semi-Arian party. Eusebius was the friend of St. Basil, surnamed the Great; and Cyril is still known to us in his perspicuous and eloquent discourses addressed to the Catechumens.

Others might be named of a like respectability, though deficient, with those above-mentioned, either

[4] Gibbon, Hist. ch. xxiii. [5] Soz. v. 10.

[6] Tillem. Mem. vol. vii. p. 340.

in moral or in intellectual judgment. With these were mingled a few of a darker character. George of Laodicea, one of the genuine Eusebians, joined them for a time, and took a chief share together with Basil in the management of the Council of Ancyra. Macedonius, who was originally an Anomœan, passed through Semi-Arianism to the heresy of the Pneumatomachists, that is, the denial of the Divinity of the Holy Ghost, of which he is theologically the founder.

3.

The Semi-Arians, being such as above described, were at first both in faith and conduct an ornament and recommendation of the Eusebians. But, when once the latter stood at variance with the Latin Church by the event of the Sardican Council, they ceased to be of service to them as a blind, which was no longer available, or rather were an incumbrance to them, and formidable rivals in the favour of Constantius. The separation between the two parties was probably retarded for a while by the forced submission and recantation of the Eusebian Valens and Ursacius; but an event soon happened, which altogether released those two Bishops and the rest of the Eusebians from the embarrassments, in which the influence of the West and the timidity of Constantius had for the moment involved them. This was the assassination of the Catholic Constans which took place A.D. 350; in consequence of which (Constantine, the eldest of the brothers, being already dead) Constantius succeeded to the undivided empire. Thus the Eusebians had the whole of the West opened to their ambition[7];

[7] [The Eusebians, or political party, were renewed in the Acacians, immediately to be mentioned, Athanasius calling the latter the heirs of

and were bound by no impediment, except such as the ill-instructed Semi-Arianism of the Emperor might impose upon them. Their proceedings under these fortunate circumstances will come before us presently; here I will confine myself to the mention of the artifice, by which they succeeded in recommending themselves to Constantius, while they opposed and triumphed over the Semi-Arian Creed.

This artifice, which, obvious as it is, is curious, from the place which it holds in the history of Arianism, was that of affecting on principle to limit confessions of faith to Scripture terms; and was adopted by Acacius, Bishop of Cæsarea, in Palestine, the successor of the learned Eusebius, one of the very men, who had advocated the Semi-Arian non-scriptural formularies of the Dedication and of Philippopolis[8]. From the earliest date, the Arians had taken refuge from the difficulties of their own unscriptural dogmas in the letter of the sacred writers; but they had scarcely ventured on the inconsistency of objecting to the terms of theology, as such. But here Eusebius of Cæsarea anticipated the proceedings of his party; and, as he opened upon his contemporaries the evasion of Semi-Arianism, so did he also anticipate his pupil Acacius in the more specious artifice now under consideration. It is suggested in the apology which he put forth for signing the Nicene anathema of the Arian formulæ; which anathema he defends on the principle, that these formulæ were not conceived

the former, Hist. Arian. §§ 19 and 28; vid. also Ath. Tr. vol. ii. p. 28.) He ever distinguishes the Arians proper from the Eusebians (in his Ep. Enc. and Apol. Contr. Arian.), as afterwards the Anomœans were to be distinguished from the Acacians.]

[8] Athan. de Syn. 36—38.

in the language of Scripture[9]. Allusion is made to the same principle from time to time in the subsequent Arian Councils, as if even then the laxer Eusebians were struggling against the dogmatism of the Semi-Arians. Though the Creed of Lucian introduces the "usia," the three other Creeds of the Dedication omit it; and this hypothesis of differences of opinion in the heretical body at these Councils partly accounts for that hesitation and ambiguity in declaring their faith, which has been noticed in its place. Again, the Macrostich omits the "usia," professes generally that the Son is "*like in all things to the Father*," and enforces the propriety of keeping to the language of Scripture[1].

About the time which is at present more particularly before us, that is, after the death of Constans, this modification of Arianism becomes distinct, and collects around it the Eastern Eusebians, under the skilful management of Acacius. It is not easy to fix the date of his openly adopting it; the immediate cause of which was his quarrel with the Semi-Arian Cyril, which lies between A.D. 349—357. The distinguishing principle of his new doctrine was adherence to the Scripture phraseology, in opposition to the inconvenient precision of the Semi-Arians; its distinguishing tenet is the vague confession that the Son is generally "*like*," or at most "*in all things like*" the Father,—"*like*" as opposed to the "*one in substance*,"

[9] Vid. also Theod. Hist. ii. 3. [who tells us that the objection of "unscripturalness" had been suggested to Constantius by the Arian priest, the favourite of Constantia, to whom Constantine had entrusted his will. Eusebius, in his Letter about the Nicene Creed, does scarcely more than glance at this objection.]

[1] Vid. Athan. de Synod.

"*like in substance*," and "*unlike*[2],"—that is, the vague confession that the Son is *generally like*, or *altogether like*, the Father. Of these two expressions, the "*in all things like*" was allowed by the Semi-Arians, who included "*in substance*" under it; whereas the Acacians (for so they may now be called), or Homœans (as holding the *Homœon* or *like*), covertly intended to exclude the "*in substance*" by that very expression, mere similarity always implying difference, and "*substance*" being, as they would argue, necessarily excluded from the "*in all things*," if the "*like*" were intended to stand for any thing short of identity. It is plain then that, in the meaning of its authors, and in the practical effect of it, this new hypothesis was neither more nor less than the pure Arian, or, as it was afterwards called, Anomœan, though the phrase, in which it was conveyed, bore in its letter the reverse sense.

Such was the state of the heresy about the year 350; before reviewing its history, as carried on between the two rival parties into which its advocates, the Eusebians, were dividing, the Semi-Arian and Homœan, I shall turn to the sufferings of the Catholic Church at that period.

2 *ὅμοιον* or *κατὰ πάντα ὅμοιον* is the tenet of the Acacians or Homœans, as opposed to Catholic *ὁμοούσιον*, the Semi-Arian *ὁμοιούσιον*, and the *ἀνόμοιον* of the Eunomians or Aetians. [St. Cyril, however, adopts the *κατὰ πάντα ὅμοιον*, as does Damascene.]

SECTION III.

THE ATHANASIANS.

THE second Arian Persecution is spread over the space of about twelve years, being the interval between the death of Constans, and that of Constantius (A.D. 350—361). Various local violences, particularly at Alexandria and Constantinople, had occurred with the countenance of the Eusebians at an earlier date; but they were rather acts of revenge, than intended as means of bringing over the Catholics, and were conducted on no plan. The chief sees, too, had been seized, and their occupants banished. But now the alternative of subscription or suffering was generally introduced; and, though Arianism was more sanguinary in its later persecutions, it could not be more audacious and abandoned than it showed itself in this.

The artifice of the Homœon, of which Acacius had undertaken the management, was adapted to promote the success of his party, among the orthodox of the West, as well as to delude or embarrass the Oriental Semi-Arians, for whom it was particularly provided. The Latin Churches, who had not been exposed to those trials of heretical subtlety of which the Homoüsion was reluctantly made the remedy, had adhered with a noble simplicity to the decision of Nicæa; being satisfied (as it would seem), that, whether or not they had need of the test of orthodoxy at present, in it lay the security of the great doctrine in debate, whenever the need should come. At the same time, they were naturally jealous of the introduction of such terms into their theology, as chiefly served to remind them of the dissensions of foreigners ; and, as influenced by this feeling, even after their leaders had declared against the Eusebians at Sardica, they were exposed to the temptation of listening favourably to the artifice of the "*Homœon*" or "*like.*" To shut up the subject in Scripture terms, and to say that our Lord was *like* His Father, no explanation being added, seemed to be a peaceful doctrine, and certainly was in itself unexceptionable; and, of course would wear a still more favourable aspect, when contrasted with the threat of exile and poverty, by which its acceptance was enforced. On the other hand, the proposed measure veiled the grossness of that threat itself, and fixed the attention of the solicited Churches rather upon the argument, than upon the Imperial command. Minds that are proof against the mere menaces of power, are overcome by the artifices of an importunate casuistry. Those, who would rather have suffered death than have sanctioned the impieties of Arius, hardly saw how to defend themselves in refusing creeds, which were abstractedly true, though incomplete, and intolerable only because the badges of a prevaricating party. Thus Arianism gained its first footing in the West. And, when one concession was made, another was demanded ; or, at other times, the first concession was converted, not without speciousness, into a principle, as allowing change altogether in theological language, as if to depart from the Homoüsion were in fact to acquiesce in the open impieties of Arius and the Anomœans. This is the character of the history as more or less illustrated in this and the subsequent Section; the Catholics being harassed by sophistry and persecution, and the Semi-Arians first acquiescing in the Homœon, then retracting, and becoming more distinct upon the scene, as the Eusebians or Acacians ventured to speak of our Lord in less honourable terms.

But there was another subscription, required of the Catholics during the same period and from an earlier date, as painful, and to all but the most honest minds as embarrassing, as that to the creed of the Homœon; and that was the condemnation of Athanasius. The Eusebians were incited against him by resentment and jealousy; they perceived that the success of their schemes was impossible, while a Bishop was on the scene, so popular at home, so respected abroad, the bond of connexion between the orthodox of Europe and Asia, the organ of their sentiments, and the guide and vigorous agent of their counsels. Moreover, the circumstances of the times had attached an adventitious importance to his fortunes; as if the cause of the Homoüsion were providentially committed to his custody, and in his safety or overthrow, the triumph or loss of the truth were actually involved. And, in the eyes of the Emperor, the Catholic champion appeared as a rival of his own sovereignty; type, as he really was, and instrument of that Apostolic Order, which, whether or not united to the civil power, must, to the end of time, divide the rule with Cæsar as the minister of God. Considering then Athanasius too great for a subject, Constantius, as if for the peace of his empire, desired his destruction at any rate[1]. Whether he was unfortunate or culpable it mattered not; whether implicated in legal guilt, or forced by circumstances into his present position; still he was the fit victim of a sort of ecclesiastical ostracism, which, accordingly, he called upon the Church to inflict. He demanded it of the Church, for the very eminence of Athanasius rendered it unsafe, even for the Emperor, to approach him in any other way. The Patriarch of Alexandria could not be deposed, except after a series of successes over less powerful Catholics, and with the forced acquiescence or countenance of the principal Christian communities. And thus the history of the first few years of the persecution, presents to us the curious spectacle of a party warfare raging everywhere, except in the neighbourhood of the person who was the real object of it, and who was left for a time to continue the work of God at Alexandria, unmolested by the Councils, conferences, and usurpations, which perplexed the other capitals of Christendom.

As regards the majority of Bishops who were called upon to condemn him, there was, it would appear, little room for error of judgment, if they dealt honestly with their consciences. Yet, in the West, there were those, doubtless, who hardly knew enough of him to give him their confidence, or who had no means of forming a true opinion of the fresh charges to which he was subjected. Those, which were originally

[1] Gibbon, Hist. ch. xxi.

urged against him, have already been stated; the new allegations were as follows: that he had excited differences between Constantius and his brother; that he had corresponded with Magnentius, the usurper of the West; that he had dedicated, or used, a new Church in Alexandria without the Emperor's leave; and lastly, that he had not obeyed his mandate summoning him to Italy.—Now to review some of the prominent passages in the persecution:—

1.

Paul had succeeded Alexander in the See of Constantinople, A.D. 336. At the date before us (A.D. 350), he had already been thrice driven from his Church by the intrigues of the Arians; Pontus, Gaul, and Mesopotamia, being successively the places of his exile. He had now been two years restored, when he was called a fourth time, not merely to exile, but to martyrdom. By authority of the Emperor, he was conveyed from Constantinople to Cucusus in Cappadocia, a dreary town amid the deserts of the Taurus, afterwards the place of banishment of his successor St. Chrysostom. Here he was left for six days without food; when his conductors impatiently anticipated the termination of his sufferings by strangling him in prison. Macedonius, the Semi-Arian, took possession of the vacant see, and maintained his power by the most savage excesses. The confiscation of property, banishment, brandings, torture, and death, were the means of his accomplishing in the Church of Constantinople, a conformity with the tenets of heresy. The Novatians, as maintaining the Homoüsion, were included in the persecution. On their refusing to communicate with him, they were seized and scourged, and the sacred elements violently thrust into their mouths. Women and children were forcibly baptized; and, on the former resisting, they were subjected to cruelties too miserable to be described.

2.

The sufferings of the Church of Hadrianople occurred about the same time, or even earlier. Under the superintendence of a civil officer, who had already acted as the tool of the Eusebians in the Mareotis, several of the clergy were beheaded; Lucius, their Bishop, for the second time loaded with chains and sent into exile, where he died; and three other Bishops of the neighbourhood visited by an Imperial edict, which banished them, at the peril of their lives, from all parts of the Empire.

3.

Continuing their operations westward, the Arians next possessed themselves of the province of Sirmium in Pannonia, in which the dioceses of Valens and Ursacius were situated. These Bishops, on the death of Constans, had relapsed into the heresy of his brother, who was now master of the whole Roman world; and from that time they may be accounted as the leaders of the Eusebian party, especially in the West. The Church of Sirmium was opened to their assaults under the following circumstances. It had always been the policy of the Arians to maintain that the Homoüsion involved some or other heresy by necessary consequence. A Valentinian or a Manichean materialism was sometimes ascribed to the orthodox doctrine; and at another time, Sabellianism, which was especially hateful to the Semi-Arians. And it happened, most unhappily for the Church, that one of the most strenuous of her champions at Nicæa, had since fallen into a heresy of a Sabellian character; and had thus confirmed the prejudice against the true doctrine, by what might be taken to stand as an instance of its dangerous tendency. In the course of a work in refutation of the Sophist Asterius, one of the first professed Semi-Arians, Marcellus, Bishop of Ancyra, was led to simplify (as he conceived) the creed of the Church, by statements which savoured of Sabellianism; that is, he maintained the unity of the Son with the Father, at the expense of the doctrine of the personal distinction between the Two. He was answered, not only by Asterius himself, but by Eusebius of Cæsarea and Acacius; and, A.D. 335, he was deposed from his see by the Eusebians, in order to make way for the Semi-Arian Basil. In spite of the suspicions against him, the orthodox party defended him for a considerable time, and the Council of Sardica (A.D 347) acquitted him and restored him to his see; but at length, perhaps on account of the increasing definiteness of his heretical views, he was abandoned by his friends as hopeless, even by Athanasius, who quietly put him aside with the acquiescence of Marcellus himself. But the evil did not end there; his disciple Photinus, Bishop of Sirmium, increased the scandal, by advocating, and with greater boldness, an almost Unitarian doctrine. The Eusebians did not neglect the opportunity thus offered them, both to calumniate the Catholic teaching, and to seize on so considerable a see, which its present occupier had disgraced by his heresy. They held a Council at Sirmium (A.D. 351), to inquire into his opinions ; and at his request a formal disputation was held. Basil, the rival of Marcellus, was selected to be the antagonist of his pupil ; and having the easier position to defend, gained the victory in the judgment of impartial arbiters, who had been selected. The deposition of Photinus followed, and an Arian, Germinius, placed in his see. Also a new creed was promulgated of a structure between Homœusian and Homœan, being the first of three which are dated from Sirmium. Germinius some years afterwards adopted a Semi-Arianism bordering upon the Catholic doctrine, and that at a time when it may be hoped that secular views did not influence his change.

4.

The first open attack upon Athanasius and the independence of the West, was made two years later at Arles, at that time the residence of the Court. There the Emperor held a Council, with the intention of committing the Bishops of the West to an overt act against the Alexandrian prelate. It was attended by the deputies of Liberius, the new Bishop of Rome, whom the Eusebian party had already addressed, hoping to find him more tractable than his predecessor Julius. Liberius, however, had been decided in Athanasius's favour by the Letter of an Egyptian Council ; and, in order to evade the Emperor's overtures, he addressed to him a submissive message, petitioning him for a general and final Council at Aquileia, a measure which Constantius had already led the Catholics to expect. The Western Bishops at Arles, on their part, demanded that, as a previous step to the condemnation of Athanasius, the orthodox Creed should be acknowledged by the Council, and Arius anathematized. However, the Eusebians carried their point; Valens followed up with characteristic violence the imperiousness of Constantius; ill treatment was added, till the Fathers of the Council, worn out by sufferings, consented to depose and even excommunicate Athanasius. Upon this, an edict was published, denouncing punishment on all Bishops who refused to subscribe the decree thus obtained. Among the instances of cowardice, which were exhibited at Arles, none was more lamentable than that of Vincent of Capua, one of the deputies from Liberius to the Emperor. Vincent had on former occasions shown himself a zealous supporter of orthodoxy. He is supposed to be the presbyter of the same name who was one of the representatives of the Roman Bishop at Nicæa; he had acted with the orthodox at Sardica, and had afterwards been sent by Constans to Constantius, to effect the restoration of the Athanasians in A.D. 348. It was on this occasion, that he and his companion had been exposed to the malice of Stephen, the Arian Bishop of Antioch; who, anxious to destroy their influence, caused a woman of light character to be introduced into their chamber, with the intention of founding a calumny against them; and who, on the artifice being discovered, was deposed by order of Constantius. On the present occasion, Vincent was entirely in the confidence of Liberius; who, having entrusted him with his delicate commission from a sense of his vigour and experience, was deeply afflicted at his fall. It is satisfactory to know, that Vincent retrieved himself afterwards at Ariminum; where he boldly resisted the tyrannical attempt of the Eusebians, to force their creed on the Western Church.

5.

Times of trial bring forward men of zeal and boldness, who thus are enabled to transmit their names to posterity. Liberius, downcast at the disgrace of his representative, and liable himself to fluctuations of mind, was unexpectedly cheered by the arrival of the famous Lucifer, Bishop of Cagliari, in Sardinia, and Eusebius of Vercellæ. These, joined by a few others, proceeded as his deputies and advocates to the great Council of Milan, which was held by Constantius (A.D. 355), two years later than that in which Vincent fell. The Fathers collected there were in number above 300, almost all of the Western Church. Constantius was present, and Valens conducted the Arian manœuvres; and so secure of success were he and his party, that they did not scruple to insult the Council with the proposal of a pure Arian, or Anomœan, creed.

Whether this creed was generally subscribed, does not appear; but the condemnation of Athanasius was universally agreed upon, scarcely one or two of the whole number refusing to sign it. This is remarkable; inasmuch as, at first, the Occidentals demanded of the Eusebians an avowal of the orthodox faith, as the condition of entering upon the consideration of the charges against him. But herein is the strength of audacious men; who gain what is unjust, by asking what is extravagant. Sozomen attributes the concession of the Council to fear, surprise, and ignorance[2]. In truth, a collection of men, who were strangers to each other, and without organization or recognized leaders, without definite objects or policy, was open to every variety of influence, which the cleverness of the usurping faction might direct against them. The simplicity of honesty, the weakness of an amiable temper, the inexperience of a secluded life, and the slowness of the unpractised intellect, all combined with their alarm at the Emperor's manifested displeasure, to impel them to take part with his heresy. When some of them ventured to object the rule of the Church against his command, that they should condemn Athanasius, and communicate with the Arians, "My will must be its rule," he replied ; "so the Syrian Bishops have decided ; and so must yourselves, would you escape exile."

Several of the more noble-minded prelates of the principal Churches submitted to the alternative, and left their sees. Dionysius, Exarch of Milan, was banished to Cappadocia or Armenia, where he died before the end of the persecution; Auxentius being placed in his see, a bitter Arian, brought for the purpose from Cappadocia, and from his ignorance of Latin, singularly ill-fitted to preside over a Western province. Lucifer was sent off into Syria, and Eusebius of Vercellæ into Palestine. A fresh and more violent edict was published against Athanasius; orders were given to arrest him as an impious person, and to put the Arians in possession of his churches, and of the benefactions, which Constantine had left for ecclesiastical and charitable uses. All Bishops

[2] Soz. iv. 9.

were prohibited from communion with him, under pain of losing their sees; and the laity were to be compelled by the magistrates to join themselves to the heretical party. Hilary of Poictiers was the next victim of the persecution. He had taken part in a petition, presented to Constantius, in behalf of the exiled bishops. In consequence a Gallic Council was called, under the presidency of Saturninus, Bishop of Arles; and Hilary was banished into Phrygia.

6.

The history of Liberius, the occupier of the most powerful see in the West, possesses an interest, which deserves our careful attention. In 356, the year after the Council of Milan, the principal eunuch of the Imperial Court had been sent, to urge on him by threats and promises the condemnation of Athanasius; and, on his insisting on a fair trial for the accused, and a disavowal of Arianism on the part of his accusers, as preliminary conditions, had caused him to be forced away to Milan. There the same arguments were addressed to him in the more impressive words of the Emperor himself; who urged upon him "the notoriously wicked life of Athanasius, his vexatious opposition to the peace of the Church, his intrigues to effect a quarrel between the imperial brothers, and his frequent condemnation in the Councils of Eastern and Western Christendom;" and further exhorted him, as being by his pastoral office especially a man of peace, to be cautious of appearing the sole obstacle to the happy settlement of a question, which could not otherwise be arranged. Liberius replied by demanding of Constantius even more than his own deputies had proposed to the Milanese Council;—first, that there should be a general subscription to the Nicene faith throughout the Church; next, that the banished bishops should be restored to their sees; and lastly, should the trial of Athanasius be still thought advisable, that a Council should be held at Alexandria, where justice might be fairly dealt between him and his accusers. The conference between them ended in Liberius being allowed three days to choose between making the required subscription, and going into exile; at the end of which time he manfully departed for Berœa, in Thrace. Constantius and the empress, struck with the nobleness of his conduct, sent after him a thousand pieces of gold; but he refused a gift, which must have laid him under restraint towards heretical benefactors. Much more promptly did he reject the offer of assistance, which Eusebius, the eunuch before-mentioned, from whatever feeling, made him. "You have desolated the Churches of Christendom," he said to the powerful favourite, "and then you offer me alms as a convict. Go, first learn to be a Christian[3]."

There are men, in whose mouths sentiments, such as these, are becoming and admirable, as being the result of Christian magnanimity, and imposed upon them by their station in the Church. But the sequel of the history shows, that in the conduct of Liberius there was more of personal feeling and intemperate indignation, than of deep-seated fortitude of soul. His fall, which followed, scandalous as it is in itself, may yet be taken to illustrate the silent firmness of those others his fellow-sufferers, of whom we hear less,

[3] Soz. iv. 11. Theod. Hist. ii. 16.

because they bore themselves more consistently. Two years of exile, among the dreary solitudes of Thrace, broke his spirit; and the triumph of his deacon Felix, who had succeeded to his power, painfully forced upon his imagination his own listless condition, which brought him no work to perform, and no witness of his sufferings for the truth's sake. Demophilus, one of the foremost of the Eusebian party, was bishop of Berœa, the place of Liberius's banishment; and gave intelligence of his growing melancholy to his own associates. Wise in their generation, they had an instrument ready prepared for the tempter's office. Fortunatian, Bishop of Aquileia, who stood high in the opinion of Liberius for disinterestedness and courage, had conformed to the court-religion in the Arian Council of Milan; and he was now employed by the Eusebians, to gain over the wavering prelate. The arguments of Fortunatian and Demophilus shall be given in the words of Maimbourg. "They told him, that they could not conceive, how a man of his worth and spirit could so long obstinately resolve to be miserable upon a chimerical notion, which subsisted only in the imagination of people of weak or no understanding: that, indeed, if he suffered for the cause of God and the Church, of which God had given him the government, they should not only look upon his sufferings as glorious, but, being willing to partake of his glory, they should also become his companions in banishment themselves. But that this matter related neither to God nor religion; that it concerned merely a private person, named Athanasius, whose cause had nothing in common with that of the Church, whom the public voice had long since accused of numberless crimes, whom Councils had condemned, and who had been turned out of his see by the great Constantine, whose judgment alone was sufficient to justify all that the East and West had so often pronounced against him. That, even if he were not so guilty as men made him, yet it was necessary to sacrifice him to the peace of the Church, and to throw him into the sea to appease the storm, which he was the occasion of raising; but that, the greater part of the Bishops having condemned him, the defending him would be causing a schism, and that it was a very uncommon sight to see the Roman prelate abandon the care of the Church, and banish himself into Thrace, to become the martyr of one, whom both divine and human justice had so often declared guilty. That it was high time to undeceive himself, and to open his eyes at last; to see, whether it was not passion in Athanasius, which gave a false alarm, and opposed an imaginary heresy, to make the world believe that they had a mind to establish error[4]."

The arguments, diffusively but instructively reported in the above extract, were enforced by the threat of death as the consequence of obstinacy; while, on the other hand, a temptation of a peculiar nature presented itself to the exiled bishop in his very popularity with the Roman people, which was such, that Constantius had already been obliged to promise them his restoration. Moreover, as if to give a reality to the inducements by which he was assailed, a specific plan of mutual concession and concord had been projected, in which Liberius was required to take part. The

[4] Webster's translation is used: one or two irrelevant phrases, introduced by Maimbourg on the subject of Roman supremacy, being omitted.

Western Catholics were, as we have seen, on all occasions requiring evidence of the orthodoxy of the Eusebians, before they consented to take part with them against Athanasius. Constantius then, desirous of ingratiating himself with the people of Rome, and himself a Semi-Arian, and at that time alarmed at the increasing boldness of the Anomœans, or pure Arians, presently to be mentioned, perceived his opportunity for effecting a general acceptance of a Semi-Arian creed; and thus, while sacrificing the Anomœans, whom he feared, to the Catholics, and claiming from the Catholics in turn what were scarcely concessions, in the imperfect language of the West, for realizing that religious peace, which he held to be incompatible with the inflexible orthodoxy of Athanasius. Moreover, the heresies of Marcellus and Photinus were in favour of this scheme; for, by dwelling upon them, he withdrew the eyes of Catholics from the contrary errors of Semi-Arianism. A creed was compiled from three former confessions, that of the orthodox Council against Paulus (A.D. 264), that of the Dedication (A.D. 341), and one of the three published at Sirmium. Thus carefully composed, it was signed by all parties, by Liberius [5], by the Semi-Arians, and by the Eusebians; the Eusebians being compelled by the Emperor to submit for the time to the dogmatic formulæ, which they had gradually abandoned. Were it desirable to enlarge on this miserable apostasy, there are abundant materials in the letters, which Liberius wrote in renunciation of Athanasius, to his clergy, and to the Arian

[5] [Vide supr. pp. 131. 294. 323. There is much difference of opinion, however, among writers, which was the creed which Liberius signed: vide Appendix, No. 3.]

bishops. To Valens he protests, that nothing but his love of peace, greater than his desire of martyrdom itself, would have led him to the step which he had taken ; in another he declares, that he has but followed his conscience in God's sight[6]. To add to his misery, Constantius suffered him for a while to linger in exile, after he had given way. At length he was restored ; and at Ariminum in a measure retrieved his error, together with Vincent of Capua.

7.

The sufferings and trials of Hosius, which took place about the same time, are calculated to impress the mind with the most sorrowful feelings, and still more with a lively indignation against his inhuman persecutors. Shortly before the conference at Sirmium, at which Liberius gave his allegiance to the supremacy of Semi-Arianism, a creed had been drawn up in the same city by Valens and the other more daring members of the Eusebian body. It would seem, that at this date Constantius had not taken the alarm against the Anomœans, to the extent in which he felt it soon afterwards, on the news probably of their proceedings in the East. Accordingly, the creed in question is of a mixed character. Not venturing on the *Anomœon*, as at Milan, it nevertheless condemns the use of the *usia (substance)*, *Homoüsion*, and *Homœüsion*, on somewhat of the equivocal plan, of which Acacius, as I have said above, was the most conspicuous patron; and being such, it was presented for signature to the aged Bishop of Corduba. The cruelty which they

6 Hilar. Fragm. iv. and vi.

exercised to accomplish their purpose, was worthy of that singularly wicked faction which Eusebius had organized. Hosius was at this time 101 years old; and had passed a life, prolonged beyond the age of man, in services and sufferings in the cause of Christ. He had assisted in the celebrated Council of Elvira, in Spain (about the year 300), and had been distinguished as a confessor in the Maximinian persecution. He presided at the General Councils of Nicæa and Sardica, and was perhaps the only Bishop, besides Athanasius, who was known and reverenced at once in the East and West. When Constantius became possessed of the Western world, far from relaxing his zeal in a cause discountenanced at the Court, Hosius had exerted himself in his own diocese for the orthodox faith; and, when the persecution began, endeavoured by letter to rouse other bishops to a sense of the connexion between the acquittal of Athanasius, and the maintenance of divine truth. The Eusebians were irritated by his opposition; he was summoned to the Court at Milan, and, after a vain attempt to shake his constancy, dismissed back to his see. The importunities of Constantius being shortly after renewed, both in the way of threats and of promises, Hosius addressed him an admirable letter, which Athanasius has preserved. After declaring his willingness to repeat, should it be necessary, the good confession which he had made in the heathen persecution, he exhorts the Emperor to abandon his unscriptural creed, and to turn his ear from Arian advisers. He states his conviction, that the condemnation of Athanasius was urged merely for the establishment of the heresy; declares, that at Sardica his accusers had been challenged publicly to produce the proof of their allegations, and had failed, and that he himself had conversed with them in private, and could gain nothing satisfactory from them ; and he further reminds Constantius, that Valens and Ursacius had before now retracted the charges, which they once urged against him. "Change your course of action, I beseech you," continues the earnest Prelate ; "remember that you are a man. Fear the day of judgment ; keep your hands clean against it ; meddle not with Church matters ; far from advising us about them, rather seek instruction from us. God has put dominion into your hands ; to us He has entrusted the management of the Church ; and, as a traitor to you is a rebel to the God who ordained you, so be afraid on your part, lest, usurping ecclesiastical power, you become guilty of a great sin. It is written, 'Render unto Cæsar, Cæsar's, and what is God's, to God.' We may not bear rule ; you, O Emperor, may not burn incense. I write this from a care for your soul. As to your message, I remain in the same mind. I do not join the Arians. I anathematize them. I do not subscribe the condemnation of Athanasius[7]." Hosius did not address such language with impunity to a Court, which affected the majesty of oriental despotism. He was summoned to Sirmium, and thrown into prison. There he remained for a whole year. Tortures were added to force the old man from his resolution. He was scourged, and afterwards placed upon the rack. Mysterious it was, that so honoured a life should be preserved to an extremity of age, to become the sport and triumph of the Enemy of mankind. At length broken in spirit,

[7] Athan. Hist. Arian. ad Monach. 44.

the contemporary of Gregory and Dionysius[8] was induced to countenance the impieties of the generation, into which he had lived; not indeed signing the condemnation of Athanasius, for he spurned that baseness to the last, but yielding subscription to a formulary, which forbad the mention of the *Homoüsion*, and thus virtually condemned the creed of Nicæa, and countenanced the Arian proceedings. Hosius lived about two years after this tragical event: and, on his deathbed, he protested against the compulsion which had been used towards him, and, with his last breath, abjured the heresy which dishonoured his Divine Lord and Saviour.

8.

Meanwhile, the great Egyptian prelate, seated on his patriarchal throne, had calmly prosecuted the work, for which he was raised up, as if his name had not been mentioned in the Arian Councils, and the troubles, which agitated the Western Church, were not the prelude to the blow, which was to fall on himself. Untutored in concession to impiety, by the experience or the prospect of suffering, yet, sensitively alive to the difference between misbelief and misapprehension, while he punished he spared, and restored in the spirit of meekness, while he rebuked and rejected with power. On his return to Alexandria, seven years previous to the events last recorded, congratulations and professions of attachment poured in upon him from the provinces of the whole Roman world, near and distant. From Africa to Illyricum, and from

[8] Vide supr. p. 125.

England to Palestine, 400 episcopal letters solicited his communion or patronage; and apologies, and the officiousness of personal service were liberally tendered by those, who, through cowardice, dulness, or self-interest, had joined themselves to the heretical party. Nor did Athanasius fail to improve the season of prosperity, for the true moral strength and substantial holiness of the people committed to him. The sacred services were diligently attended; alms and benefactions supplied the wants of the friendless and infirm; and the young turned their thoughts to that generous consecration of themselves to God, recommended by St. Paul in times of trouble and persecution.

In truth the sufferings, which the Church of Alexandria had lately undergone from the hands of the Eusebians, were sufficient to indispose serious minds towards secular engagements, or vows of duty to a fellow-mortal; to quench those anticipations of quietness and peace, which the overthrow of paganism had at first excited; and to remind them, that the girdle of celibacy and the lamp of watchers best became those, on whom God's judgments might fall suddenly. Not more than ten years were gone by, since Gregory, appointed to the see of Athanasius by the Council of the Dedication[9], had been thrust upon them by the Imperial Governor, with the most frightful and revolting outrages. Philagrius, an apostate from the Christian faith, and Arsacius, an eunuch of the Court, introduced the Eusebian Bishop into his episcopal city. A Church besieged and spoiled, the massacre of the assembled worshippers, the clergy trodden under foot, the women subjected to the most infamous

[9] Vid. supra, p. 286.

profanations, these were the first benedictory greetings scattered by the Arian among his people. Next, bishops were robbed, beaten, imprisoned, banished; the sacred elements of the Eucharist were scornfully cast about by the heathen rabble, which seconded the usurping party; birds and fruits were offered in sacrifice on the holy table; hymns chanted in honour of the idols of paganism; and the Scriptures given to the flames.

Such had already been the trial of a much-enduring Church; and it might suddenly be renewed in spite of its present prosperity. The Council of Sardica, convoked principally to remedy these miserable disorders, had in its Synodal Letter warned the Alexandrian Catholics against relaxing in the brave testimony they were giving to the faith of the Gospel. "We exhort you, beloved brethren, before all things, that ye hold the right faith of the Catholic Church. Many and grievous have been your sufferings, and many are the insults and injuries inflicted on the Catholic Church, but 'he, who endureth unto the end, the same shall be saved.' Wherefore, should they essay further enormities against you, let affliction be your rejoicing. For such sufferings are a kind of martyrdom, and such confessions and tortures have their reward. Ye shall receive from God the combatant's prize. Wherefore struggle with all might for the sound faith, and for the exculpation of our brother Athanasius, your bishop. We on our part have not been silent about you, nor neglected to provide for your security; but have been mindful, and done all that Christian love requires of us, suffering with our suffering brethren, and accounting their trials as our own[1]."

[1] Athan. Apol. cont. Arian. 38.

The time was now at hand, which was anticipated by the prophetic solicitude of the Sardican Fathers. The same year in which Hosius was thrown into prison, the furies of heretical malice were let loose upon the Catholics of Alexandria. George of Cappadocia, a man of illiterate mind and savage manners, was selected by the Eusebians as their new substitute for Athanasius in the see of that city; and the charge of executing this extraordinary determination was committed to Syrianus, Duke of Egypt. The scenes which followed are but the repetition, with more aggravated horrors, of the atrocities perpetrated by the intruder Gregory. Syrianus entered Alexandria at night; and straightway proceeded with his soldiers to one of the churches, where the Alexandrians were engaged in the services of religion. We have the account of the irruption from Athanasius himself; who, being accused by the Arians of cowardice, on occasion of his subsequent flight, after defending his conduct from Scripture, describes the circumstances, under which he was driven from his Church. "It was now night," he says, "and some of our people were keeping vigil, as communion was in prospect; when the Duke Syrianus suddenly came upon us, with a force of above 5000 men, prepared for attack, with drawn swords, bows, darts, and clubs, . . . and surrounded the church with close parties of the soldiery, that none might escape from within. There seemed an impropriety in my deserting my congregation in such a riot, instead of hazarding the danger in their stead; so I placed myself in my bishop's chair, and bade the deacon read the Psalm (Ps. cxxxvi.), and the congregation alternate 'for His mercy endureth for ever,' and then all retire and go home. But the General bursting at length into the church, and his soldiers blocking up the chancel, with a view of arresting me, the clergy and some of my people present began in their turn clamorously to urge me to withdraw myself. However, I refused to do so, before one and all in the church were gone. Accordingly I stood up, and directed prayer to be said; and then I urged them all to depart first, for that it was better that I should run the risk, than any of them suffer. But by the time that most of them were gone out, and the rest were following, the Religious Brethren and some of the clergy, who were immediately about me, ran up the steps, and dragged me down. And so, be truth my witness, though the soldiers blockaded the chancel, and were in motion round about the church, the Lord leading, I made my way through them, and by His protection got away unperceived; glorifying God mightily, that I had been enabled to stand by my people, and even to send them out before me, and yet had escaped in safety from the hands of those who sought me[2]."

The formal protest of the Alexandrian Christians against this outrage, which is still extant, gives a stronger and fuller statement of the violences attending it. "While we were watching in prayer," they say, "suddenly about midnight, the most noble Duke Syrianus came upon us with a large force of legionaries, with arms, drawn swords, and other military weapons, and their helmets on. The prayers and sacred reading were proceeding, when they assaulted the doors, and, on these being laid open by the force of numbers,

[2] Athan. Apol. de Fug. 24.

he gave the word of command. Upon which, some began to let fly their arrows, and others to sound a charge; and there was a clashing of weapons, and swords glared against the lamplight. Presently, the sacred virgins were slaughtered, numbers trampled down one over another by the rush of the soldiers, and others killed by arrows. Some of the soldiers betook themselves to pillage, and began to strip the females, to whom the very touch of strangers was more terrible than death. Meanwhile, the Bishop sat on his throne, exhorting all to pray. . . . He was dragged down, and almost torn to pieces. He swooned away, and became as dead; we do not know how he got away from them, for they were bent upon killing him[3]."

The first purpose of Athanasius on his escape was at once to betake himself to Constantius; and he had begun his journey to him, when news of the fury, with which the persecution raged throughout the West, changed his intention. A price was set on his head, and every place was diligently searched in the attempt to find him. He retired into the wilderness of the Thebaid, then inhabited by the followers of Paul and Anthony, the first hermits. Driven at length thence by the activity of his persecutors, he went through a variety of strange adventures, which lasted for the space of six years, till the death of Constantius allowed him to return to Alexandria.

His suffragan bishops did not escape a persecution, which was directed, not against an individual, but against the Christian faith. Thirty of them were banished, ninety were deprived of their churches; and

[3] Athan. Hist. Arian. ad Monach. 81.

many of the inferior clergy suffered with them. Sickness and death were the ordinary result of such hardships as exile involved ; but direct violence in good measure superseded a lingering and uncertain vengeance. George, the representative of the Arians, led the way in a course of horrors, which he carried through all ranks and professions of the Catholic people ; and the Jews and heathen of Alexandria, sympathizing in his brutality, submitted themselves to his guidance, and enabled him to extend the range of his crimes in every direction. Houses were pillaged, churches were burned, or subjected to the most loathsome profanations, and cemeteries were ransacked. On the week after Whitsuntide, George himself surprised a congregation, which had refused to communicate with him. He brought out some of the consecrated virgins, and threatened them with death by burning, unless they forthwith turned Arians. On perceiving their constancy of purpose, he stripped them of their garments, and beat them so barbarously on the face, that for some time afterwards their features could not be distinguished. Of the men, forty were scourged ; some died of their wounds, the rest were banished. This is one out of many notorious facts, publicly declared at the time, and uncontradicted ; and which were not merely the unauthorized excesses of an uneducated Cappadocian, but recognized by the Arian body as their own acts, in a state paper from the Imperial Court, and perpetrated for the maintenance of the peace of the Church, and of a good understanding among all who agreed in the authority of the sacred Scriptures.

In the manifesto, issued for the benefit of the people

of Alexandria (A.D. 356), the infatuated Emperor applauds their conduct in turning from a cheat and impostor, and siding with those who were venerable men, and above all praise. "The majority of the citizens," he continues, "were blinded by the influence of one who rose from the abyss, darkly misleading those who seek the truth; who had at no time any fruitful exhortation to communicate, but abused the souls of his hearers with frivolous and superficial discussions. . . . That noble personage has not ventured to stand a trial, but has adjudged himself to banishment; whom it is the interest even of the barbarians to get rid of, lest by pouring out his griefs as in a play to the first comer, he persuade some of them to be profane. So we will wish him a fair journey. But for yourselves, only the select few are your equals, or rather, none are worthy of your honours; who are allotted excellence and sense, such as your actions proclaim, celebrated as they are almost in every place. . . . You have roused yourselves from the grovelling things of earth to those of heaven, the most reverend George undertaking to be your leader, a man of all others the most accomplished in such matters; under whose care you will enjoy in days to come honourable hope, and tranquillity at the present time. May all of you hang upon his words as upon a holy anchor, that any cutting and burning may be needless on our part against men of depraved souls, whom we seriously advise to abstain from paying respect to Athanasius, and to dismiss from their minds his troublesome garrulity; or such factious men will find themselves involved in extreme peril, which perhaps no skill will be able to avert from them. For it were absurd indeed, to drive about the pestilent Athanasius from country to country, aiming at his death, though he had ten lives, and not to put a stop to the extravagances of his flatterers and juggling attendants, such as it is a disgrace to name, and whose death has long been determined by the judges. Yet there is a hope of pardon, if they will desist from their former offences. As to their profligate leader Athanasius, he distracted the harmony of the state, and laid on the most holy men impious and sacrilegious hands[4]."

The ignorance and folly of this remarkable document are at first sight incredible; but to an observant mind the common experience of life brings sufficient proof, that there is nothing too audacious for party spirit to assert, nothing too gross for monarch or inflamed populace to receive.

[4] Athan. Apol. ad Constant. 30.

SECTION IV.

THE ANOMŒANS.

It remains to relate the circumstances of the open disunion and schism between the Semi-Arians and the Anomœans. In order to set this clearly before the reader, a brief recapitulation must first be made of the history of the heresy, which has been thrown into the shade in the last Section, by the narrative of the ecclesiastical events to which it gave occasion.

The Semi-Arian school was the offspring of the ingenious refinements, under which the Eusebians concealed impieties, which the temper of the faithful made it inexpedient for them to avow [1]. Its creed preceded the party; that is, those subtleties, which were too feeble to entangle the clear intellects of the school of Lucian, produced after a time their due effect upon the natural subjects of them, viz. men who, with more devotional feeling than the Arians, had less plain sense, and a like deficiency of humility. A Platonic fancifulness made them the victims of an Aristotelic subtlety; and in the philosophising Eusebius and the sophist Asterius, we recognize the appropriate inventors, though hardly the sincere disciples, of the new creed. For a time, the distinction between the Semi-Arians and the Eusebians did not

[1] [Plato made Semi-Arians, and Aristotle Arians.]

openly appear; the creeds put forth by the whole party being all, more or less, of a Semi-Arian cast, down to the Council of Sirmium inclusive (A.D. 351), in which Photinus was condemned. In the meanwhile the Eusebians, little pleased with the growing dogmatism of members of their own body, fell upon the expedient of confining their confessions to Scripture terms; which, when separated from their context, were of course inadequate to concentrate and ascertain the true doctrine. Hence the formula of the *Homœon;* which was introduced by Acacius with the express purpose of deceiving or baffling the Semi-Arian members of his party. This measure was the more necessary for Eusebian interests, inasmuch as a new variety of the heresy arose in the East at the same time, advocated by Aetius and Eunomius; who, by professing boldly the pure Arian tenet, alarmed Constantius, and threw him back upon Basil, and the other Semi-Arians. This new doctrine, called Anomœan, because it maintained that the *usia* or *substance* of the Son was unlike (*ἀνόμοιος*) the Divine *usia*, was actually adopted by one portion of the Eusebians, Valens and his rude Occidentals; whose language and temper, not admitting the refinements of Grecian genius, led them to rush from orthodoxy into the most hard and undisguised impiety. And thus the parties stand at the date now before us (A.D. 356—361); Constantius being alternately swayed by Basil, Acacius, and Valens, that is, by the Homœüsian, the Homœan, and the Anomœan,—the Semi-Arian, the Scripturalist, and the Arian pure; by his respect for Basil and the Semi-Arians, the talent of Acacius, and his personal attachment to Valens.

I.

Aetius, the founder of the Anomœans, is a remarkable instance of the struggles and success of a restless and aspiring mind under the pressure of difficulties. He was a native of Antioch; his father, who had an office under the governor of the province, dying when he was a child, he was made the servant or slave of a vine-dresser. He was first promoted to the trade of a goldsmith or travelling tinker, according to the conflicting testimony of his friends and enemies. Falling in with an itinerant practitioner in medicine, he acquired so much knowledge of the art, as to profess it himself; and, the further study of his new profession introducing him to the disputations of his more learned brethren, he manifested such acuteness and boldness in argument, that he was soon engaged, after the manner of the Sophists, as a paid advocate for such physicians as wished their own theories exhibited in the most advantageous form. The schools of Medicine were at that time infected with Arianism, and thus introduced him to the science of theology, as well as that of disputation; giving him a bias towards heresy, which was soon after confirmed by the tuition of Paulinus, Bishop of Tyre. At Tyre he so boldly conducted the principles of Arianism to their legitimate results, as to scandalize the Eusebian successor of Paulinus; who forced him to retire to Anazarbus, and to resume his former trade of a goldsmith. The energy of Aetius, however, could not be restrained by the obstacles which birth, education, and decency threw in his way. He made acquaintance with a teacher of grammar; and, readily acquiring a smattering of polite literature, he was soon enabled to criticise his master's expositions of sacred Scripture before his pupils. A quarrel, as might be expected, ensued; and Aetius was received into the house of the Bishop of Anazarbus, who had been one of the Arian prelates at Nicæa. This man was formerly mentioned as one of the rudest and most daring among the first assailants of our Lord's divinity[2]. It is probable, however, that, after signing the *Homoüsion*, he had surrendered himself to the characteristic duplicity and worldliness of the Eusebian party; for Aetius is said to have complained, that he was deficient in depth, and, in spite of his hospitality, looked out for another instructor. Such an one he found in the person of a priest of Tarsus, who had been from the first a consistent Arian; and with him he read the Epistles of St. Paul. Returning to Antioch, he became the pupil of Leontius, in the prophetical Scriptures; and, after a while, put himself under the instruction of an Aristotelic sophist of Alexandria. Thus accomplished, he was ordained deacon by Leontius (A.D. 350), who had been lately raised to the patriarchal See of Antioch. Thus the rise of the Anomœan sect coincides in point of time with the death of Constans, an event already noticed in the history of the Eusebians, as transferring the Empire of the West to Constantius, and, thereby furthering their division into the Homœan and Homœusian factions. Scarcely had Aetius been ordained, when the same notorious irregularities in his carriage, whatever they were, which had more than once led to his expulsion from the lay communion of the Arians, caused his deposition from the

[2] [Vide supra, p. 239.]

diaconate, by the very prelate who had promoted him to it. After this, little is known of him for several years; excepting a dispute, which he held with the Semi-Arian Basil, which marks his rising importance. During the interval, he ingratiated himself with Gallus, the brother of Julian; and was implicated in his political offences. Escaping, however, the anger of Constantius, by his comparative insignificance, he retired to Alexandria, and lived for some time in the train of George of Cappadocia, who allowed him to officiate as deacon. Such was at this time the character of the clergy, whom the Arians had introduced into the Syrian Churches, that this despicable adventurer, whose manners were as odious, as his life was eccentric, and his creed blasphemous, had sufficient influence to found a sect, which engaged the attention of the learned Semi-Arians at Ancyra (A.D. 358), and has employed the polemical powers of the orthodox Fathers, Basil and Gregory Nyssen.

Eunomius, his disciple, was the principal disputant in the controversy. With more learning than Aetius, he was enabled to complete and fortify the Anomœan system, inheriting from his master the two peculiarities of character which belong to his school; the first, a faculty of subtle disputation and hard mathematical reasoning, the second, a fierce, and in one sense an honest, disdain of compromise and dissimulation. These had been the two marks of Arianism at its first rise; and the first associates of Arius, who, after his submission to Constantine, had kept aloof from the Court party in disgust, now joyfully welcomed and joined the Anomœans. The new sect justified their anticipations of its boldness. The same impatience, with which Aetius had received the ambiguous explanations of the Eusebian Bishop of Anazarbus, was expressed by Eunomius for the Acacianism of Eudoxius of Antioch, who in vain endeavoured to tutor him into a less real and systematic profession of the Arian tenets. So far did his party carry their vehemence, as even to re-baptize their Christian converts, as though they had been heathen; and that, not in the case of Catholics only, but, to the great offence of the Eusebians, even of those, whom they converted from the other forms of Arianism[3]. Earnestness is always respectable; and, if it be allowable to speak with a sort of moral catachresis, the Anomœans merited on this account, as well as ensured, a success, which a false conciliation must not hope to obtain.

2.

The progress of events rapidly carried them forward upon the scene of ecclesiastical politics. Valens, who by this time had gained the lead of the Western Bishops, was seconded in his patronage of them by the eunuchs of the Court; of whom Eusebius, the Grand Chamberlain, had unlimited sway over the weak mind of the Emperor. The concessions, made

[3] Epiph. Hær. lxxvi. fin. Bingham, xi. 1. § 10. [Thus, bold as were the original Arians, the Anomœans were bolder and more consistent. Athanasius challenges the former, if they dare, to speak out. Basil says "Aetius was the first to teach openly that the Father's substance was unlike the Son's." Vide Ath. Tr. vol. ii. pp. 34, 287—292 However, Athanasius interprets Arius's Thalia to say that the Persons of the Holy Trinity are utterly unlike (ἀνόμοιοι) each other in substance and glory without limit." Orat. § 6. De Syn. § 15. Again, Arius held that the Divine Being was incomprehensible (Athan. de Syn. § 15), but the Anomœans denied it. Socr. iv. 7.]

by Liberius and Hosius to the Eusebian party, furnished an additional countenance to Arianism, being misrepresented as actual advances towards the heretical doctrine. The inartificial cast of the Western theology, which scarcely recognized any middle hypothesis between that of the Homoüsion and pure Arianism, strengthened the opinion that those, who had abandoned the one, must in fact have embraced the other. And, as if this were not enough, it appears that an Anomœan creed was circulated in the East, with the pretence that it was the very formula which Hosius and Liberius had subscribed. Under these circumstances, the Anomœans were soon strong enough to aid the Eusebians of the East in their contest with the Semi-Arians[4]. Events in the Churches of Antioch and Jerusalem favoured their enterprise. It happening that Acacius of Cæsarea and Cyril of Jerusalem were rivals for the primacy of Palestine, the reputed connexion of Cyril with the Semi-Arian party had the effect of throwing Acacius, though the author of the Homœon, on the side of its Anomœan assailants; accordingly, with the aid of the neighbouring Bishops, he succeeded in deposing Cyril, and sending him out of the country. At Antioch, the cautious Leontius, Arian Bishop, dying (A.D. 357), the eunuchs of the Court contrived to place Eudoxius in his see, a man of restless and intriguing temper, and opposed to the Semi-Arians. One of his first acts was to hold a Council, at which Acacius was present, as well as Aetius and Eunomius, the chiefs of the Anomœans. There the assembled Bishops did not venture beyond the language of the second creed of Sirmium, which Hosius

[4] Petav. tom. ii. i. 9, § 6. [Tillemont, t. 6. p. 429.]

had signed, and which kept clear of Anomœan doctrine; but they had no difficulty in addressing a letter of thanks and congratulations to the party of the Anomœan Valens, for having at Sirmium brought the troubles of the West to so satisfactory a termination.

The election, however, of Eudoxius, and this Council which followed it were not to pass unchallenged by the Semi-Arians. Mention has already been made of one George[5], a presbyter of Alexandria; who, being among the earliest supporters of Arius, was degraded by Alexander, but, being received by the Eusebians into the Church of Antioch, became at length Bishop of Laodicea. George was justly offended at the promotion of Eudoxius, without the consent of himself and Mark of Arethusa, the most considerable Bishops of Syria; and, at this juncture, took part against the combination of Homœans and Anomœans, at Antioch, who had just published their assent to the second creed of Sirmium. Falling in with some clergy whom Eudoxius had excommunicated, he sent letters by them to Macedonius, Basil of Ancyra, and other leaders of the Semi-Arians, intreating them to raise a protest against the proceedings of the Council of Antioch, and so to oblige Eudoxius to separate himself from Aetius and the Anomœans. This remonstrance produced its effect; and, under pretence of the dedication of a Church, a Council was immediately held by the Semi-Arian party at Ancyra (A.D. 358), in which the Anomœan heresy was condemned. The Synodal letter, which they published, professed to be grounded on the Semi-Arian creeds of the Dedication (A.D. 341), of Philippopolis (A.D. 347), and of Sirmium

[5] Vide supr. p. 240.

(A.D. 351), when Photinus was condemned and deposed. It is a valuable document, even as a defence of orthodoxy; its error consisting in its obstinate rejection of the Nicene *Homoüsion*, the sole practical bulwark of the Catholic faith against the misrepresentations of heresy,—against a sort of tritheism on the one hand, and a degraded conception of the Son and Spirit on the other.

The two parties thus at issue, appealed to Constantius at Sirmium. That weak Prince had lately sanctioned the almost Acacian creed of Valens, which Hosius had been compelled to subscribe, when the deputation from Antioch arrived at the Imperial Court; and he readily gave his assent to the new edition of it which Eudoxius had promulgated. Scarcely had he done so, when the Semi-Arians made their appearance from Ancyra, with Basil at their head; and succeeded so well in representing the dangerous character of the creed passed at Antioch, that, recalling the messenger who had been sent off to that city, he forthwith held the Conference, mentioned in the foregoing Section, in which he imposed a Semi-Arian creed on all parties, Eudoxius and Valens, the representatives of the Eusebians, being compelled, as well as the orthodox Liberius, to sign a formulary, which Basil compiled from the creeds against Paulus of Samosata, and Photinus (A.D. 264. 351), and the creed of Lucian, published by the Council of the Dedication (A.D. 341). Yet in spite of the learning, and personal respectability of the Semi-Arians, which at the moment exerted this strong influence over the mind of Constantius, the dexterity of the Eusebians in disputation and intrigue was ultimately successful.

Though seventy Bishops of their party were immediately banished, these were in a few months reinstated by the capricious Emperor, who from that time inclined first to the Acacian or Homœan, and then to the open Anomœan or pure Arian doctrine; and who before his death (A.D. 361) received baptism from the hands of Euzoius, one of the original associates of Arius, then recently placed in the see of Antioch.—The history of this change, with the Councils attending it, will bring us to the close of this chapter.

3.

The Semi-Arians, elated by their success with the Emperor, followed it up by obtaining his consent for an Ecumenical Council, in which the faith of the Christian Church should definitely be declared for good. A meeting of the whole of Christendom had not been attempted, except in the instance of the Council of Sardica, since the Nicene; and the Sardican itself had been convoked principally to decide upon the charges urged against Athanasius, and not to open the doctrinal question. Indeed it is evident, that none but the heterodox party, now dominant, could consistently debate an article of belief, which the united testimony of the Churches of the East and West had once for all settled at Nicæa. This, then, was the project of the Semi-Arians. They aimed at a renewal on an Ecumenical scale of the Council of the Dedication at Antioch in A.D. 341. The Eusebian party, however, had no intention of tamely submitting to defeat. Perceiving that it would be more for their own interest that the prelates of the East and West should not meet in the same place (two bodies being more manageable than one), they exerted themselves so strenuously with the assistance of the eunuchs of the palace, that at last it was determined, that, while the Orientals met at Seleucia in Isauria, the Occidental Council should be held at Ariminum, in Italy. Next, a previous Conference was held at Sirmium, in order to determine on the creed to be presented to the bipartite Council; and here again the Eusebians gained an advantage, though not at once to the extent of their wishes. Warned by the late indignation of Constantius against the Anomœan tenet, they did not attempt to rescue it from his displeasure; but they struggled for the adoption of the Acacian *Homœon*, which the Emperor had already both received and abandoned, and they actually effected the adoption of the "*like in all things according to the Scriptures*"—a phrase in which the Semi-Arians indeed included their "*like in substance*" or *Homœüsion*, but which did not necessarily refer to *substance* or *nature* at all. Under these circumstances the two Councils met in the autumn of A.D. 359, under the nominal superintendence of the Semi-Arians; but on the Eusebian side, the sharp-witted Acacius undertaking to deal with the disputatious Greeks, the overbearing and cruel Valens with the plainer Latins.

About 160 Bishops of the Eastern Church assembled at Seleucia[6], of whom not above forty were Eusebians. Far the greater number were professed Semi-Arians; the Egyptian prelates alone, of whom but twelve or thirteen were present, displaying themselves, as at the first, the bold and faithful adherents of the *Homoüsion*. It was soon evident that the forced reconciliation

[6] [Vide Ath. Tr. vol. i. p. 78, notes 8, 9.]

which Constantius had imposed on the two parties at Sirmium, was of no avail in their actual deliberations. On each side an alteration of the proposed formula was demanded. In spite of the sanction given by Basil and Mark to the "*like in all things*," the majority of their partisans would be contented with nothing short of the definite "*like in substance*," or *Homœüsion*, which left no opening (as they considered) to evasion; and in consequence proposed to return to Lucian's creed, adopted by the Council of the Dedication. Acacius, on the other hand, not satisfied with the advantage he had just gained in the preliminary meeting at Sirmium, where the mention of the *usia* or *substance* was dropped (although but lately imposed by Constantius on all parties, in the formulary which Liberius signed), proposed a creed in which the *Homoüsion* and *Homœüsion*, were condemned, the *Anomœon* anathematized, as the source of confusion and schism, and his own *Homœon* adopted (that is, "*like*," without the addition of "*in all things*"); and when he found himself unable to accomplish his purpose, not waiting for the formal sentence of deposition, which the Semi-Arians proceeded to pronounce upon himself and eight others, he set off to Constantinople, where the Emperor then was, hoping there, in the absence of Basil and his party, to gain what had been denied him in the preliminary meeting at Sirmium. It so happened, however, that his object had been effected even before his arrival; for, a similar quarrel having resulted from the meeting at Ariminum, and deputies from the rival parties having thence similarly been despatched to Constantius, a Conference had already taken place at a city called Nice or Nicæa, in the neighbourhood of Hadrianople, and an emendated creed adopted, in which, not only the safeguard of the "*in all things*" was omitted, and the *usia* condemned, but even the word *Hypostasis* (*Subsistence* or *Person*) also, on the ground of its being a refinement on Scripture. So much had been already gained by the influence of Valens, when the arrival of Acacius at Constantinople gave fresh activity to the Eusebian party.

Thereupon a Council was summoned in the Imperial city of the neighbouring Bishops, principally of those of Bithynia, and the Acacian formula of Ariminum confirmed. Constantius was easily persuaded to believe of Basil, what had before been asserted of Athanasius, that he was the impediment to the settlement of the question, and to the tranquillity of the Church. Various charges of a civil and ecclesiastical nature were alleged against him and other Semi-Arians, as formerly against Athanasius, with what degree of truth it is impossible at this day to determine; and a sentence of deposition was issued against them. Cyril of Jerusalem, Eleusius of Cyzicus, Eustathius of Sebaste, and Macedonius of Constantinople, were in the number of those who suffered with Basil; Macedonius being succeeded by Eudoxius, who, thus seated in the first see of the East, became subsequently the principal stay of Arianism under the Emperor Valens.

This triumph of the Eusebian party in the East, took place in the beginning of A.D. 360; by which time the Council of Ariminum in the West, had been brought to a conclusion. To it we must now turn our attention.

The Latin Council had commenced its deliberations, before the Orientals had assembled at Seleucia ; yet it did not bring them to a close till the end of the year. The struggle between the Eusebians and their opponents had been so much the more stubborn in the West, in proportion as the latter were more numerous there, and further removed from Arian doctrine, and Valens on the other hand more unscrupulous, and armed with fuller powers. Four hundred Bishops were collected at Ariminum, of whom but eighty were Arians ; and the civil officer, to whom Constantius had committed the superintendence of their proceedings, had orders not to let them stir out of the city, till they should agree upon a confession of faith. At the opening of the Council, Valens, Ursacius, Germinius, Auxentius, Caius, and Demophilus, the Imperial Commissioners, had presented to the assembly the formula of the "*like in all things*" agreed upon in the preliminary conference at Sirmium ; and demanded, that, putting aside all strange and mysterious terms of theology, it should be at once adopted by the assembled Fathers. They had received for answer, that the Latins determined to adhere to the formulary of Nicæa ; and that, as a first step in their present deliberations, it was necessary that all present should forthwith anathematize all heresies and innovations, beginning with that of Arius. The Commissioners had refused to do so, and had been promptly condemned and deposed, a deputation of ten being sent from the Council to Constantius, to acquaint him with the result of its deliberations. The issue of this mission to the Court, to which Valens opposed one from his own party, has been already related. Constantius, with a view of wearing out the Latin Fathers, pretended that the barbarian war required his immediate attention, and delayed the consideration of the question till the beginning of October, several months after the opening of the Council; and then, frightening the Catholic deputation into compliance, he effected at Nice the adoption of the Homœan creed (that is, the "*like*" without the "*in all things*") and sent it back to Ariminum.

The termination of the Council there assembled was disgraceful to its members, but more so to the Emperor himself. Distressed by their long confinement, impatient at their absence from their respective dioceses, and apprehensive of the approaching winter, they began to waver. At first, indeed, they refused to communicate with their own apostate deputies; but these, almost in self-defence, were active and successful in bringing over others to their new opinions. A threat was held out by Taurus, the Prætorian Prefect, who superintended the discussions, that fifteen of the most obstinate should be sent into banishment; and Valens was importunate in the use of such theological arguments and explanations, as were likely to effect his object. The Prefect conjured them with tears to abandon an unfruitful obstinacy, to reflect on the length of their past confinement, the discomfort of their situation, the rigours of the winter, and to consider, that there was but one possible termination of the difficulty, which lay with themselves, not with him. Valens, on the other hand, affirmed that the Eastern bishops at Seleucia had abandoned the *usia*; and he demanded of those who still stood their ground, what objection they could make to the Scriptural creed proposed to them, and whether, for the sake of a word, they would be the authors of a schism between Eastern and Western Christendom. He affirmed, that the danger apprehended by the Catholics was but chimerical; that he and his party condemned Arius and Arianism, as strongly as themselves, and were only desirous of avoiding a word, which confessedly is not in Scripture, and had in past time been productive of much scandal. Then, to put his sincerity to the proof, he began with a loud voice to anathematize the maintainers of the Arian blasphemies in succession; and he concluded by declaring, that he believed the Word to be God, begotten of God before all time, and not in the number of the creatures, and that whoever should say that He was a creature as other creatures, was anathema. The foregoing history of the heresy has sufficiently explained how the Arians evaded the force of these strong declarations; but the inexperienced Latins did not detect their insincerity. Satisfied, and glad to be released, they gave up the *Homoüsion*, and signed the formula of the *Homœon;* and scarcely had they separated, when Valens, as might be expected, boasted of his victory, arguing that the faith of Nicæa had been condemned by the very circumstance of his being allowed to confess, that the Son was "not a creature as other creatures," and so to imply, that, though not like *other* creatures, still He was created. Thus ended this celebrated Council; the result of which is well characterized in the lively statement of Jerome: "The whole world groaned in astonishment to find itself Arian [7]."

[7] ["Ingemuit totus orbis, et Arianum se esse miratus est."]

In the proceedings attendant on the Councils of Seleucia and Ariminum, the Eusebians had skilfully gained two important objects, by means of unimportant concessions on their part. They had sacrificed Aetius and his *Anomœon;* and effected in exchange the disgrace of the Semi-Arians as well as of the Catholics, and the establishment of the *Homœon,* the truly characteristic symbol of a party, who, as caring little for the sense of Scripture, found an excuse and an indulgence of their unconcern, in a pretended maintenance of the letter. As to the wretched mountebank just mentioned, whose profaneness was so abominable, as to obtain for him the title of the "Atheist," he was formally condemned in the Council at Constantinople (A.D. 360) already mentioned, in which the Semi-Arian Basil, Macedonius, and their associates had been deposed. During the discussions which attended it, Eleusius, one of the latter party, laid before the Emperor an Anomœan creed, which he ascribed to Eudoxius. The latter, when questioned, disowned it; and named Aetius as its author, who was immediately summoned. Introduced into the Imperial presence, he was unable to divine, in spite of his natural acuteness, whether the Emperor was pleased or displeased with the composition; and, hazarding an acknowledgement of it, he drew down on himself the full indignation of Constantius, who banished him into Cilicia, and obliged his patron Eudoxius to anathematize both the confession in question, and all the positions of the pure Arian heresy. Such was the fall of Aetius, at the time of the triumph of the Eusebians; but soon afterwards he was promoted to the episcopate (under what circumstances is unknown), and was favourably noticed, as a former friend of Gallus, by the Emperor Julian, who gave him a territory in the Island of Mitelene.

Eunomius, his disciple, escaped the jealousy of Constantius through the good offices of Eudoxius, and was advanced to the Bishoprick of Cyzicus ; but, being impatient of dissimulation, he soon fell into disgrace, and was banished. The death of the Emperor took place at the end of A.D. 361 ; his last acts evincing a further approximation to the unmitigated heresy of Arius. At a Council held at Antioch in the course of that year, he sanctioned the Anomœan doctrine in its most revolting form ; and shortly before his decease, received the sacrament of baptism, as has been stated above, from Euzoius, the personal friend and original associate of Arius himself[8].

[8] ["At this critical moment Constantius died, when the cause of truth was only not in the lowest state of degradation, because a party was in authority and vigour who could reduce it to a lower still ; the Latins committed to an Anti-Catholic creed, the Pope a renegade, Hosius fallen and dead, Athanasius wandering in the deserts, Arians in the sees of Christendom, and their doctrine growing in blasphemy, and their profession of it in boldness, every day. The Emperor had come to the throne when almost a boy, and at this time was but forty-four years old. In the ordinary course of things, he might have reigned till orthodoxy, humanly speaking, was extinct." Ath. Tr. vol. i. p. 121.]

CHAPTER V.

COUNCILS AFTER THE REIGN OF CONSTANTIUS.

SECTION I.

THE COUNCIL OF ALEXANDRIA IN THE REIGN OF JULIAN.

THE accession of Julian was followed by a general restoration of the banished Bishops; and all eyes throughout Christendom were at once turned towards Alexandria, as the Church, which, by its sufferings and its indomitable spirit, had claim to be the arbiter of doctrine, and the guarantee of peace to the Catholic world. Athanasius, as the story goes, was, on the death of his persecutor, suddenly found on his episcopal throne in one of the Churches of Alexandria[1]; a legend, happily expressive of the unwearied activity and almost ubiquity of that extraordinary man, who, while a price was set on his head, mingled unperceived in the proceedings at Seleucia and Ariminum[2], and directed the movements of his fellow-labourers by his

[1] Cave, Life of Athan. x. 9.

[2] [This is doubtful; vide Montfaucon, Athan., though Tillemont and Gibbon seem to admit it.]

writings, when he was debarred the exercise of his dexterity in debate, and his persuasive energy in private conversation. He was soon joined by his fellow-exile, Eusebius of Vercellæ; Lucifer, who had journeyed with the latter from the Upper Thebaid, on his return to the West, having gone forward to Antioch on business which will presently be explained. Meanwhile, no time was lost in holding a Council at Alexandria (A.D. 362) on the general state of the Church.

The object of Julian in recalling the banished Bishops, was the renewal of those dissensions, by means of toleration, which Constantius had endeavoured to terminate by force. He knew these prelates to be of various opinions, Semi-Arians, Macedonians, Anomœans, as well as orthodox; and, determining to be neuter himself, he waited with the satisfaction of an Eclectic for the event; being persuaded, that Christianity could not withstand the shock of parties, not less discordant, and far more zealous, than the sects of philosophy. It is even said that he "invited to his palace the leaders of the hostile sects, that he might enjoy the agreeable spectacle of their furious encounters[3]." But, in indulging such anticipations of overthrowing Christianity, he but displayed his own ignorance of the foundation on which it was built. It could scarcely be conceived, that an unbeliever, educated among heretics, would understand the vigour and indestructibility of the true Christian spirit; and Julian fell into the error, to which in all ages men of the world are exposed, of mistaking whatever shows itself on the surface of the

[3] Gibbon, ch. xxiii.

Apostolic Community, its prominences and irregularities, all that is extravagant, and all that is transitory, for the real moving principle and life of the system. It is trying times alone that manifest the saints of God; but they live notwithstanding, and support the Church in their generation, though they remain in their obscurity. In the days of Arianism, indeed, they were in their measure, revealed to the world; still to such as Julian, they were unavoidably unknown, both in respect to their numbers and their divine gifts. The thousand of silent believers, who worshipped in spirit and in truth, were obscured by the tens and twenties of the various heretical factions, whose clamorous addresses besieged the Imperial Court; and Athanasius would be portrayed to Julian's imagination after the picture of his own preceptor, the time-serving and unscrupulous Eusebius. The event of his experiment refuted the opinion which led to it. The impartial toleration of all religious persuasions, malicious as was its intent, did but contribute to the ascendancy of the right faith; that faith, which is the only true aliment of the human mind, which can be held as a principle as well as an opinion, and which influences the heart to suffer and to labour for its sake.

Of the subjects which engaged the notice of the Alexandrian Council, two only need here be mentioned; the treatment to be pursued towards the bishops, who had arianized in the reign of Constantius, and the settlement of the theological sense of the word *Hypostasis*. And here, of the former of these.

I.

Instances have already occurred, of the line of conduct pursued by Athanasius in ecclesiastical matters. Deliberate apostasy and systematic heresy were the objects of his implacable opposition ; but in his behaviour towards individuals, and in his judgment of the inconsistent, whether in conduct or creed, he evinces an admirable tenderness and forbearance. Not only did he reluctantly abandon his associate, the unfortunate Marcellus, on his sabellianizing, but he even makes favourable notice of the Semi-Arians, hostile to him both in word and deed, who rejected the orthodox test, and had confirmed against him personally at Philippopolis, the verdict of the commission at the Mareotis. When bishops of his own party, as Liberius of Rome, were induced to excommunicate him, far from resenting it, he speaks of them with a temper and candour, which, as displayed in the heat of controversy, evidences an enlarged prudence, to say nothing of Christian charity[4]. It is this union of opposite excellences, firmness with discrimination and discretion, which is the characteristic praise of Athanasius: as well as of several of his predecessors in the See of Alexandria. The hundred years, preceding his episcopate, had given scope to the enlightened zeal of Dionysius, and the patient resoluteness of Alexander. On the other hand, when we look around at the other more conspicuous champions of orthodoxy of his time, much as we must revere and bless their memory, yet as regards

[4] Athan. de Syn. 41. Apol. contr. Arian. 89. Hist. Arian. ad Monach. 41, 42.

this maturity and completeness of character, they are far inferior to Athanasius. The noble-minded Hilary was intemperate in his language, and assailed Constantius with an asperity unbecoming a dutiful subject. The fiery Bishop of Cagliari, exemplary as is his self-devotion, so openly showed his desire for martyrdom, as to lead the Emperor to exercise towards him a contemptuous forbearance. Eusebius of Vercellæ negotiated in the Councils, with a subtlety bordering on Arian insincerity. From these deficiencies of character Athanasius was exempt; and on the occasion which has given rise to these remarks, he had especial need of the combination of gifts, which has made his name immortal in the Church.

The question of the arianizing bishops was one of much difficulty. They were in possession of the Churches; and could not be deposed, if at all, without the risk of a permanent schism. It is evident, moreover, from the foregoing narrative, how many had been betrayed into an approval of the Arian opinions, without understanding or acting upon them. This was particularly the case in the West, where threats and ill-usage, had been more or less substituted for those fallacies, which the Latin language scarcely admitted. And even in the remote Greek Churches, there was much of that devout and unsuspecting simplicity, which was the easy sport of the supercilious sophistry of the Eusebians. This was the case with the father of Gregory Nazianzen; who, being persuaded to receive the Acacian confession of Constantinople (A.D. 359, 360), on the ground of its unmixed scripturalness, found himself suddenly deserted by a large portion of his flock, and was extricated from the charge of heresy, only by the dexterity of his learned son. Indeed, to many of the Arianizing bishops, may be applied the remarks, which Hilary makes upon the laity subjected to Arian teaching; that their own piety enabled them to interpret expressions religiously, which were originally invented as evasions of the orthodox doctrine[5].

And even in parts of the East, where a much clearer perception of the difference between truth and error existed, it must have been an extreme difficulty to such of the orthodox as lived among Arians, to determine, in what way best to accomplish duties, which were in opposition to each other. The same obligation of Christian unity, which was the apology for the laity who remained, as at Antioch, in communion with an Arian bishop, would lead to a similar recognition of his authority by clergy or bishops who were ecclesiastically subordinate to him. Thus Cyril of Jerusalem, who was in no sense either Anomœan or Eusebian, received consecration from the hands of his metropolitan Acacius; and St. Basil, surnamed the Great, the vigorous champion of orthodoxy against the Emperor Valens, attended the Council of Constantinople (A.D. 359, 360), as a deacon, in the train of his namesake Basil, the leader of the Semi-Arians.

On the other hand, it was scarcely safe to leave the deliberate heretic in possession of his spiritual power. Many bishops too were but the creatures of the times, raised up from the lowest of the people, and deficient in the elementary qualifications of learning and

[5] "Sanctiores sunt aures plebis," he says, "quàm corda sacerdotum." Bull, Defens. epilog. [Vide infr. Appendix, No 5.]

sobriety. Even those, who had but conceded to the violence of others, were the objects of a just suspicion; since, frankly as they now joined the Athanasians, they had already shown as much interest and reliance in the opposite party.

Swayed by these latter considerations, some of the assembled prelates advocated the adoption of harsh measures towards the Arianizers, considering that their deposition was due both to the injured dignity and to the safety of the Catholic Church. Athanasius, however, proposed a more temperate policy; and his influence was sufficient to triumph over the excitement of mind which commonly accompanies a deliverance from persecution. A decree was passed, that such bishops as had communicated with the Arians through weakness or surprise, should be recognized in their respective sees, on their signing the Nicene formulary; but that those, who had publicly defended the heresy, should only be admitted to lay-communion. No act could evince more clearly than this, that it was no party interest, but the ascendancy of the orthodox doctrine itself, which was the aim of the Athanasians. They allowed the power of the Church to remain in the hands of men indifferent to the interests of themselves, on their return to that faith, which they had denied through fear; and their ability to force on the Arianizers this condition, evidences what they might have done, had they chosen to make an appeal against the more culpable of them to the clergy and laity of their respective churches, and to create and send out bishops to supply their places. But they desired peace, as soon as the interests of truth were secured; and their magnanimous decision was forthwith adopted by

Councils held at Rome, in Spain, Gaul, and Achaia. The state of Asia was less satisfactory. As to Antioch, its fortunes will immediately engage our attention. Phrygia and the Proconsulate were in the hands of the Semi-Arians and Macedonians ; Thrace and Bithynia, controlled by the Imperial Metropolis, were the stronghold of the Eusebian or Court faction.

2.

The history of the Church of Antioch affords an illustration of the general disorders of the East at this period, and of the intention of the sanative measure passed at Alexandria respecting them. Eustathius, its Bishop, one of the principal Nicene champions, had been an early victim of Eusebian malice, being deposed on calumnious charges, A.D. 331. A series of Arian prelates succeeded ; some of whom, Stephen, Leontius, and Eudoxius, have been commemorated in the foregoing pages[6]. The Catholics of Antioch had disagreed among themselves, how to act under these circumstances. Some, both clergy and laity, refusing the communion of heretical teachers, had holden together for the time, as a distinct body, till the cause of truth should regain its natural supremacy ; while others had admitted the usurping succession, which the Imperial will forced upon the Church. When Athanasius passed through Antioch on his return from his second exile (A.D. 348), he had acknowledged the seceders, from a respect for their orthodoxy, and for the rights of clergy and laity in the election of a bishop. Yet it cannot be denied, that men of zeal and boldness were found among those who remained

[6] Vide supra, p. 280.

in the heretical communion. Two laymen, Flavian and Diodorus, protested with spirit against the heterodoxy of the crafty Leontius, and kept alive an orthodox party in the midst of the Eusebians.

On the translation of Eudoxius to Constantinople, the year before the death of Constantius, an accident occurred, which, skilfully improved, might have healed the incipient schism among the Trinitarians. Scarcely had Meletius, the new Bishop of the Eusebian party, taken possession of his see, when he conformed to the Catholic faith. History describes him as gifted with remarkable sweetness and benevolence of disposition. Men thus characterized are often deficient in sensibility, in their practical judgment of heresy; which they abhor indeed in the abstract, yet countenance in the case of their friends, from a false charitableness; which leads them, not merely to hope the best, but to overlook the guilt of opposing the truth, where the fact is undeniable. Meletius had been brought up in the communion of the Eusebians; a misfortune, in which nearly all the Oriental Christians of his day were involved. Being considered as one of their party, he had been promoted by them to the see of Sebaste, in Armenia; but, taking offence at the conduct of his flock, he had retired to Berœa, in Syria. During the residence of the Court at Antioch, A.D. 361, the election of the new prelate of that see came on; and the choice of both Arians and Arianizing orthodox fell on Meletius. Acacius was the chief mover in this business. He had lately[7] succeeded in establishing the principle of liberalism at Constantinople, where a condemnation had been passed on the use of words

[7] Vide supra, pp. 347, 350.

not found in Scripture, in confessions of faith; and he could scarcely have selected a more suitable instrument, as it appeared, of extending its influence, than a prelate, who united purity of life and amiableness of temper, to a seeming indifference to the distinctions between doctrinal truth and error.

On the new Patriarch's arrival at Antioch, he was escorted by the court bishops, and his own clergy and laity, to the cathedral. Desirous of solemnizing the occasion, the Emperor himself had condescended to give the text, on which the assembled prelates were to comment. It was the celebrated passage from the Proverbs, in which Origen has piously detected, and the Arians perversely stifled, the great article of our faith; "the Lord hath created [possessed] Me in the beginning of His ways, before His works of old." George of Laodicea, who, on the departure of Eudoxius from Antioch, had left the Semi-Arians and rejoined the Eusebians, opened the discussion with a dogmatic explanation of the words. Acacius followed with that ambiguity of language, which was the characteristic of his school. At length the new Patriarch arose, and to the surprise of the assembly, with a subdued manner, and in measured words, avoiding indeed the Nicene *Homoüsion*, but accurately fixing the meaning of his expressions, confessed the true Catholic tenet, so long exiled from the throne and altars of Antioch. A scene followed, such as might be expected from the excitable temper of the Orientals. The congregation received his discourse with shouts of joy; while the Arian archdeacon of the church running up, placed his hand before his mouth to prevent his speaking; on which Meletius thrust out his hand in sight of the people, and raising first three fingers, and then one, symbolized the great truth which he was unable to utter[8]. The consequences of this bold confession might be expected. Meletius was banished, and a fresh Bishop appointed, Euzoius, the friend of Arius. But an important advantage resulted to the orthodox cause by this occurrence ; Catholics and heretics were no longer united in one communion, the latter being thrown into the position of schismatics, who had rejected their own bishop. Such was the state of things, when the death of Constantius occasioned the return of Meletius, and the convocation of the Council of Alexandria, in which his case was considered.

The course to be pursued in this matter by the general Church was evident. There were now in Antioch, besides the heretical party, two communions professing orthodoxy, of which what may be called the Protestant body was without a head, Eustathius having died some years before. It was the obvious duty of the Council, to recommend the Eustathians to recognize Meletius, and to join in his communion, whatever original intrusion there might be in the episcopal succession from which he received his Orders, and whatever might have been his own previous errors of doctrine. The general principle of restoration, which they had made the rule of their conduct towards the Arianizers, led them to this. Accordingly, a commission was appointed to proceed to Antioch, and to exert their endeavours to bring the dissension to a happy termination.

Their charitable intentions, however, had been already frustrated by the unfortunate interference of

[8] Soz. iv. 28.

Lucifer. This Latin Bishop, strenuous in contending for the faith, had little of the knowledge of human nature, or of the dexterity in negotiation, necessary for the management of so delicate a point as that which he had taken upon himself to settle. He had gone straight to Antioch, when Eusebius of Vercellæ proceeded to Alexandria ; and, on the Alexandrian commission arriving at the former city, the mischief was done, and the mediation ineffectual. Indulging, instead of overcoming, the natural reluctance of the Eustathians to submit to Meletius, Lucifer had been induced, with the assistance of two others, to consecrate a separate head for their communion, and by so doing re-animate a dissension, which had run its course and was dying of itself. The result of this indiscretion was the rise of an additional, instead of the termination of the existing schism. Eusebius, who was at the head of the commission, retired from Antioch in disgust. Lucifer, offended at becoming the object of censure, separated first from Eusebius, and at length from all who acknowledged the conforming Arianizers. He founded a sect, which was called after his name, and lasted about fifty years.

As to the schism at Antioch, it was not terminated till the time of Chrysostom about the end of the century. Athanasius and the Egyptian Churches continued in communion with the Eustathians. Much as they had desired and exerted themselves for a reconciliation between the parties, they could not but recognize, while it existed, that body which had all along suffered and laboured with themselves. And certainly the intercourse, which Meletius held with the unprincipled Acacius, in the Antiochene

Council the following year, and his refusal to communicate with Athanasius, were not adapted to make them repent their determination[9]. The Occidentals and the Churches of Cyprus followed their example. The Eastern Christians, on the contrary, having for the most part themselves arianized, took part with the Meletians. At length St. Chrysostom successfully exerted his influence with the Egyptian and Western Catholics in behalf of Flavian, the successor of Meletius ; a prelate, it must be admitted, not blameless in the ecclesiastical quarrel, though he had acted a bold part with Diodorus, afterwards Bishop of Tarsus, in resisting the insidious attempts of Leontius to secularize the Church.

3.

The Council of Alexandria was also concerned in determining a doctrinal question ; and here too it exercised a virtual mediation between the rival parties in the Antiochene Church.

The word *Person* which we venture to use in speaking of those three distinct and real modes in which it has pleased Almighty God to reveal to us His being, is in its philosophical sense too wide for our meaning. Its essential signification, as applied to ourselves, is that of an individual intelligent agent, answering to the Greek *hypostasis*, or *reality*. On the other hand, if we restrict it to its etymological sense of *persona* or *prosopon*, that is *character*, it evidently means less than the Scripture doctrine, which we wish to define by

[9] Vit. S. Basil, p. cix, ed. Benedict. [Basil at length succeeded in reconciling Meletius to Athanasius. Vitt. Benedictt. S. Athanasii, p. lxxxvii, and S. Basilii, p. cix.]

means of it, as denoting merely certain outward manifestations of the Supreme Being relatively to ourselves, which are of an accidental and variable nature. The statements of Revelation then lie between these antagonistic senses in which the doctrine of the Holy Trinity may be erroneously conceived, between Tritheism, and what is popularly called Unitarianism.

In the choice of difficulties, then, between words which say too much and too little, the Latins, looking at the popular and practical side of the doctrine, selected the term which properly belonged to the external and defective notion of the Son and Spirit, and called Them Personæ, or Characters; with no intention, however, of infringing on the doctrine of their completeness and reality, as distinct from the Father, but aiming at the whole truth, as nearly as their language would permit. The Greeks, on the other hand, with their instinctive anxiety for philosophical accuracy of expression, secured the notion of Their existence in Themselves, by calling them Hypostases or Realities; for which they considered, with some reason, that they had the sanction of the Apostle in his Epistle to the Hebrews. Moreover, they were led to insist upon this internal view of the doctrine, by the prevalence of Sabellianism in the East in the third century; a heresy, which professed to resolve the distinction of the Three Persons, into a mere distinction of character. Hence the prominence given to the Three Hypostases or Realities, in the creeds of the Semi-Arians (for instance, Lucian's and Basil's, A.D. 341—358), who were the especial antagonists of Sabellius, Marcellus, Photinus, and kindred heretics. It was this praiseworthy jealousy of Sabellianism, which led the Greeks to lay stress upon the doctrine of the *Hypostatic Word*[1] (the Word in real existence), lest the bare use of the terms, Word, Voice, Power, Wisdom, and Radiance, in designating our Lord, should lead to a forgetfulness of His Personality. At the same time, the word *usia (substance)* was adopted by them, to express the simple individuality of the Divine Nature, to which the Greeks, as scrupulously as the Latins, referred the separate Personalities of the Son and Spirit.

Thus the two great divisions of Christendom rested satisfied each with its own theology, agreeing in doctrine, though differing in the expression of it. But, when the course of the detestable controversy, which Arius had raised, introduced the Latins to the phraseology of the Greeks, accustomed to the word Persona, they were startled at the doctrine of the three Hypostases; a term which they could not translate except by the word *substance*, and therefore considered synonymous with the Greek *usia*, and which, in matter of fact, had led to Arianism on the one hand, and Tritheism on the other. And the Orientals, on their part, were suspicious of the Latin maintenance of the One Hypostasis, and Three Personæ; as if such a formula tended to Sabellianism[2].

This is but a general account of the difference between the Eastern and Western theology; for it is difficult to ascertain, when the language of the Greeks first became fixed and consistent. Some eminent critics have considered, that *usia* was not discriminated from *hypostasis*, till the Council which has given rise to

[1] [λόγος ἐνυπόστατος. Vide supr. p. 171.]

[2] [For the meaning of *Usia* and *Hypostasis*, vide Appendix, No. 4.]

these remarks. Others maintain, that the distinction between them is recognized in the "substance *or* hypostasis[3]" of the Nicene Anathema; and these certainly have the authority of St. Basil on their side[4]. Without attempting an opinion on a point, obscure in itself, and not of chief importance in the controversy, the existing difference between the Greeks and Latins, at the times of the Alexandrian Council, shall be here stated.

At this date, the formula of the Three Hypostases seems, as a matter of fact, to have been more or less a characteristic of the Arians. At the same time, it was held by the orthodox of Asia, who had communicated with them; that is, interpreted by them, of course, in the orthodox sense which it now bears. This will account for St. Basil's explanation of the Nicene Anathema; it being natural in an Asiatic Christian, who seems (unavoidably) to have arianized[5] for the first thirty years of his life, to imagine (whether rightly or not) that he perceived in it the distinction between *Usia* and *Hypostasis*, which he himself had been accustomed to recognize. Again, in the schism at Antioch, which has been above narrated, the party of Meletius, which had so long arianized, maintained the Three Hypostases, in opposition to the Eustathians, who, as a body, agreed with the Latins, and had in consequence been accused by the Arians of Sabellianism. Moreover, this connexion of the Oriental orthodox with the Semi-Arians, partly

[3] ἐξ οὐσίας ἢ ὑποστάσεως.

[4] Vid. Petav. Theol. Dogm. tom. ii. lib. iv. Bull, Defens. Fid. Nic. ii. 9, § 11.

[5] i. e. Semi-Arianized.

accounts for some apparent tritheisms of the former; a heresy into which the latter certainly did fall[6].

Athanasius, on the other hand, without caring to be uniform in his use of terms, about which the orthodox differed, favours the Latin usage, speaking of the Supreme Being as one Hypostasis, i. e. substance. And in this he differed from the previous writers of his own Church; who, not having experience of the Latin theology, nor of the perversions of Arianism, adopt, not only the word *hypostasis* but (what is stronger) the words "*nature*" and "*substance*," to denote the separate Personalities of the Son and Spirit.

As to the Latins, it is said that, when Hosius came to Alexandria before the Nicene Council, he was desirous that some explanation should be made about the *Hypostasis;* though nothing was settled in consequence. But, soon after the Council of Sardica, an addition was made to its confession, which in Theodoret runs as follows: "Whereas the heretics maintain that the *Hypostases* of Father, Son, and Holy Ghost, are distinct and separate, we declare that according to the Catholic faith there is but one *Hypostasis* (which they call *Usia)* of the Three; and the *Hypostasis* of the Son is the same as the Father's[7]."

Such was the state of the controversy, if it may so

[6] Petav. i. fin. iv. 13, § 3. The illustration of three men, as being under the same nature (which is the ground of the accusation which some writers have brought against Gregory Nyssen and others, vid. Cudw. iv. 36. p. 597. 601, &c. Petav. iv. 7. and 10. Gibbon, ch. xxi.), was but an illustration of a particular point in the doctrine, and directed against the ἑτερουσιότης of the Arians. It is no evidence of tritheism. Vid. Petav. tom. i. iv. 13, § 6—16; and tom. i. ii. 4.

[7] Theod. Hist. ii. 8.

be called, at the time of the Alexandrian Council; the Church of Antioch being, as it were, the stage, upon which the two parties in dispute were represented, the Meletians siding with the orthodox of the East, and the Eustathians with those of the West. The Council, however, instead of taking part with either, determined, in accordance with the writings of Athanasius himself, that, since the question merely related to the usage of words, it was expedient to allow Christians to understand the "*hypostasis*" in one or other sense indifferently. The document which conveys its decision, informs us of the grounds of it. "If any propose to make additions to the Creed of Nicæa, (says the Synodal letter,) stop such persons and rather persuade them to pursue peace; for we ascribe such conduct to nothing short of a love of controversy. Offence having been given by a declaration on the part of certain persons, that there are Three *Hypostases*, and it having been urged that this language is not scriptural, and for that reason suspicious, we desired that the inquiry might not be pushed beyond the Nicene Confession. At the same time, because of this spirit of controversy, we questioned them, whether they spoke, as the Arians, of Hypostases foreign and dissimilar to each other, and diverse in substance, each independent and separate in itself, as in the case of individual creatures, or the offspring of man, or, as different substances, gold, silver, or brass; or, again, as other heretics hold, of Three Origins, and Three Gods. In answer, they solemnly assured us, that they neither said nor had imagined any such thing. On our inquiring, 'In what sense then do you say this, or why do you use such expressions at all?' they answered, 'Because we believe in the Holy Trinity, not as a Trinity in name only, but in truth and reality[8]. We acknowledge the Father truly and in real subsistence, and the Son truly in substance, and subsistent, and the Holy Ghost subsisting and existing[9].' They said too, that they had not spoken of Three Gods, or Three Origins, nor would tolerate that statement or notion; but acknowledged a Holy Trinity indeed, but only One Godhead, and One Origin, and the Son consubstantial with the Father, as the Council declared, and the Holy Spirit, not a creature, nor foreign, but proper to and indivisible from, the substance of the Son and the Father.

"Satisfied with this explanation of the expressions in question, and the reasons for their use, we next examined the other party, who were accused by the above-mentioned as holding but One Hypostasis, whether their teaching coincided with that of the Sabellians, in destroying the substance of the Son and the subsistence of the Holy Spirit. They were as earnest as the others could be, in denying both the statement and thought of such a doctrine; 'but we use *Hypostasis*' *(subsistence)*, they said, 'considering it means the same as *Usia (substance)*, and we hold that there is but one, because the Son is from the *Usia (substance)* of the Father, and because of the identity of Their nature; for we believe, as in One Godhead, so in One Divine Nature, and not that the Father's is one, and that the Son's is foreign, and the Holy Ghost's also.' It appeared then, that both those, who

[8] ὑφεστῶσαν.

[9] Υἱὸν ἀληθῶς ἐνούσιον ὄντα καὶ ὑφεστῶτα, καὶ Πνεῦμα Ἅγιον ὑφεστὸς καὶ ὑπάρχον.

were accused of holding three *Hypostases*, agreed with the other party, and those, who spoke of one Substance, professed the doctrine of the former in the sense of their interpretation; by both was Arius anathematized as an enemy of Christ, Sabellius and Paulus of Samosata as impious, Valentinus and Basilides as strangers to the truth, Manichæus, as an originator of evil doctrines. And, after these explanations, all, by God's grace, unanimously agree, that such expressions were not so desirable or accurate as the Nicene Creed, the words of which they promised for the future to acquiesce in and to use[1]."

Plain as was this statement, and natural as the decision resulting from it, yet it could scarcely be expected to find acceptance in a city, where recent events had increased dissensions of long standing. In providing the injured and zealous Eustathians with an ecclesiastical head, Lucifer had, under existing circumstances, administered a stimulant to the throbbings and festerings of the baser passions of human nature—passions, which it requires the strong exertion of Christian magnanimity and charity to overcome. The Meletians, on the other hand, recognized as they were by the Oriental Church as a legitimate branch of itself, were in the position of an establishment, and so exposed to the temptation of disdaining those whom the surrounding Churches considered as schismatics. How far each party was in fault, we are not able to determine; but blame lay somewhere, for the controversy about the *Hypostasis*, verbal as it was, became the watchword of the quarrel between the two parties, and only ended, when the Eustathians were finally absorbed by the larger and more powerful body.

[1] Athan. Tom. ad Antioch, 5 and 6.

SECTION II.

THE ECUMENICAL COUNCIL OF CONSTANTINOPLE IN THE REIGN OF THEODOSIUS.

THE second Ecumenical Council was held at Constantinople, A.D. 381—383. It is celebrated in the history of theology for its condemnation of the Macedonians, who, separating the Holy Spirit from the unity of the Father and Son, implied or inferred that He was a creature. A brief account of it is here added in its ecclesiastical aspect; the doctrine itself, to which it formally bore witness, having been incidentally discussed in the second Chapter of this Volume.

Eight years before the date of this Council, Athanasius had been taken to his rest. After a life of contest, prolonged, in spite of the hardships he encountered, beyond the age of seventy years, he fell asleep in peaceable possession of the Churches, for which he had suffered. The Council of Alexandria was scarcely concluded, when he was denounced by Julian, and saved his life by flight or concealment. Returning on Jovian's accession, he was, for a fifth and last time, forced to retreat before the ministers of his Arian successor Valens; and for four months lay hid in his father's sepulchre. On a representation being made to the new Emperor, even with the consent of the

Arians themselves, he was finally restored; and so it happened, through the good Providence of God, that the fury of persecution, heavily as it threatened in his last years, yet was suspended till his death, when it at once burst forth upon the Church with renewed vigour. Thus he was permitted to muse over his past trials, and his prospects for the future; to collect his mind to meet his God, gathering himself up with Jacob on his bed of age, and yielding up the ghost peaceably among his children. Yet, amid the decay of nature, and the visions of coming dissolution, the attention of Athanasius was in no wise turned from the active duties of his station. The vigour of his obedience to those duties remained unabated; one of his last acts being the excommunication of one of the Dukes of Lybia, for irregularity of life.

At length, when the great Confessor was removed, the Church sustained a loss, from which it never recovered. His resolute resistance of heresy had been but one portion of his services; a more excellent praise is due to him, for his charitable skill in binding together his brethren in unity. The Church of Alexandria was the natural mediator between the East and West; and Athanasius had well improved the advantages thus committed to him. His judicious interposition in the troubles at Antioch has lately been described; and the dissensions between his own Church and Constantinople, which ensued upon his death, may be taken to show how much the combination of the Catholics depended on his silent authority. Theological subtleties were for ever starting into existence among the Greek Christians; and the Arian controversy had corrupted their spirit, where it had failed to impair their orthodoxy. Disputation was the rule of belief, and ambition of conduct, in the Eusebian school ; and these evil introductions out-lived its day. Patronized by the secular power, the great Churches of Christendom conceived a jealousy of each other, and gradually fortified themselves in their own resources. As Athanasius drew towards his end, the task of mediation became more difficult. In spite of his desire to keep aloof from party, circumstances threw him against his will into one of the two divisions, which were beginning to discover themselves in the Christian world. Even before his time, traces appear of a rivalry between the Asiatic and Egyptian Churches. The events of his own day, developing their differences of character, at the same time connected the Egyptians with the Latins. The mistakes of his own friends obliged him to side with a seeming faction in the body of the Antiochene Church ; and, in the schism which followed, he found himself in opposition to the Catholic communities of Asia Minor and the East. Still, though the course of events tended to ultimate disruptions in the Catholic Church, his personal influence remained unimpaired to the last, and enabled him to interpose with good effect in the affairs of the East. This is well illustrated by a letter addressed to him shortly before his death, by St. Basil, who belonged to the contrary party, and had then recently been elevated to the exarchate of Cæsarea. It shall be here inserted, and may serve as a sort of valediction in parting with one, who, after the Apostles, has been a principal instrument, by which the sacred truths of Christianity have been conveyed and secured to the world.

"To Athanasius, Bishop of Alexandria. The more the sicknesses of the Church increase, so much the more earnestly do we all turn towards thy Perfection, persuaded that for thee to lead us is our sole remaining comfort in our difficulties. By the power of thy prayers, by the wisdom of thy counsels, thou art able to carry us through this fearful storm; as all are sure, who have heard or made trial of that perfection ever so little. Wherefore cease not both to pray for our souls, and to stir us up by thy letters; didst thou know the profit of these to us, thou wouldst never let pass an opportunity of writing to us. For me, were it vouchsafed to me, by the co-operation of thy prayers, once to see thee, and to profit by the gift lodged in thee, and to add to the history of my life a meeting with so great and apostolical a soul, surely I should consider myself to have received from the loving mercy of God a compensation for all the ills, with which my life has ever been afflicted[1]."

I.

The trials of the Church, spoken of by Basil in this letter, were the beginnings of the persecution directed against it by the Emperor Valens. This prince, who succeeded Jovian in the East, had been baptized by Eudoxius; who, from the time he became possessed of the See of Constantinople, was the chief, and soon became the sole, though a powerful, support of the Eusebian faction. He is said to have bound Valens by oath, at the time of his baptism, that he would establish Arianism as the state religion of the East; and thus to have prolonged its ascendancy for an

[1] Basil. Ep. 80.

additional sixteen years after the death of Constantius (A.D. 361—378). At the beginning of this period, the heretical party had been weakened by the secession of the Semi-Arians, who had not merely left it, but had joined the Catholics. This part of the history affords a striking illustration, not only of the gradual influence of truth over error, but of the remarkable manner in which Divine Providence makes use of error itself as a preparation for truth; that is, employing the lighter forms of it in sweeping away those of a more offensive nature. Thus Semi-Arianism became the bulwark and forerunner of the orthodoxy which it opposed. From A.D. 357, the date of the second and virtually Homœan formulary of Sirmium[2], it had protested against the impiety of the genuine Arians. In the successive Councils of Ancyra and Seleucia, in the two following years, it had condemned and deposed them; and had established the scarcely objectionable creed of Lucian. On its own subsequent disgrace at Court, it had concentrated itself on the Asiatic side of the Hellespont; while the high character of its leading bishops for gravity and strictness of life, and its influence over the monastic institutions, gave it a formidable popularity among the lower classes on the opposite coast of Thrace.

Six years after the Council of Seleucia (A.D. 365), in the reign of Valens, the Semi-Arians held a Council at Lampsacus, in which they condemned the Homœan formulary of Ariminum, confirmed the creed of the Dedication (A.D. 341), and, after citing the Eudoxians to answer the accusations brought against them, proceeded to ratify that deposition of them, which had

[2] [Vide supra, pp. 322, 323.]

already been pronounced at Seleucia. At this time they seem to have entertained hopes of gaining the Emperor; but, on finding the influence of Eudoxius paramount at Court, their horror or jealousy of his party led them to a bolder step. They resolved on putting themselves under the protection of Valentinian, the orthodox Emperor of the West; and, finding it necessary for this purpose to stand well with the Latin Church, they at length overcame their repugnance to the *Homoüsion*, and subscribed a formula, of which (at least till the Council of Constantinople, A.D. 360) they had been among the most eager and obstinate opposers. Fifty-nine Semi-Arian Bishops gave in their assent to orthodoxy on this memorable occasion, which took place A.D. 366. Their deputies were received into communion by Liberius, who had recovered himself at Ariminum, and who wrote letters in favour of these new converts to the Churches of the East. On their return, they presented themselves before an orthodox Council then sitting at Tyana, exhibited the commendatory letters which they had received from Italy, Gaul, Africa, and Sicily, as well as Rome, and were joyfully acknowledged by the assembled Fathers as members of the Catholic body. A final Council was appointed at Tarsus; whither it was hoped all the Churches of the East would send representatives, in order to complete the reconciliation between the two parties. But enough had been done, as it would seem, in the external course of events, to unite the scattered portions of the Church; and, when that end was on the point of accomplishment, the usual law of Divine Providence intervened, and left the sequel of the union as a task and a trial for Christians individually. The project of the Council failed ; thirty-four Semi-Arian bishops suddenly opposed themselves to the purpose of their brethren, and protested against the *Homoüsion.* The Emperor, on the other hand, recently baptized by Eudoxius, interfered ; forbade the proposed Council, and proceeded to issue an edict, in which all bishops were deposed from their Sees who had been banished under Constantius, and restored by Julian. It was at this time, that the fifth exile of Athanasius took place, which was lately mentioned. A more cruel persecution followed in A.D. 371, and lasted for several years. The death of Valens, A.D. 378, was followed by the final downfall of Arianism in the Eastern Church.

As to Semi-Arianism, it disappears from ecclesiastical history at the date of the proposed Council of Tarsus (A.D. 367) ; from which time the portion of the party, which remained non-conformist, is more properly designated Macedonian, or Pneumatomachist, from the chief article of their heresy.

2.

During the reign of Valens, much had been done in furtherance of evangelical truth, in the still remaining territory of Arianism, by the proceedings of the Semi-Arians ; but at the same period symptoms of returning orthodoxy, even in its purest form, had appeared in Constantinople itself. On the death of Eudoxius (A.D. 370), the Catholics elected an orthodox successor, by name Evagrius. He was instantly banished by the Emperor's command ; and the population of Constantinople seconded the act of Valens, by the most unprovoked excesses towards the Catholics. Eighty of their clergy, who were in consequence deputed to lay their grievances before the Emperor, lost their lives, under circumstances of extreme treachery and barbarity. Faith, which was able to stand its ground in such a season of persecution, was naturally prompted to more strenuous acts, when prosperous times succeeded. On the death of Valens, the Catholics of Constantinople looked beyond their own community for assistance, in combating the dominant heresy. Evagrius, whom they had elected to the See, seems to have died in exile; and they invited to his place the celebrated Gregory Nazianzen, a man of diversified accomplishments, distinguished for his eloquence, and still more for his orthodoxy, his integrity, and the innocence, amiableness, and refinement of his character.

Gregory was a native of Cappadocia, and an intimate friend of the great Basil, with whom he had studied at Athens. On Basil's elevation to the exarchate of Cæsarea, Gregory had been placed by him in the bishoprick of Sasime; but, the appointment being contested by Anthimus, who claimed the primacy of the lower Cappadocia, he retired to Nazianzus, his father's diocese, where he took on himself those duties, to which the elder Gregory had become unequal. After the death of the latter, he remained for several years without pastoral employment, till the call of the Catholics brought him to Constantinople. His election was approved by Meletius, patriarch of Antioch; and by Peter, the successor of Athanasius, who by letter recognized his accession to the metropolitan see.

On his first arrival there, he had no more suitable place of worship than his own lodgings, where he preached the Catholic doctrine to the dwindled communion over which he presided. But the result which Constantius had anticipated, when he denied to Athanasius a Church in Antioch, soon showed itself at Constantinople. His congregation increased ; the house, in which they assembled, was converted into a church by the pious liberality of its owner, with the name of Anastasia, in hope of that resurrection which now awaited the long-buried truths of the Gospel. The contempt, with which the Arians had first regarded him, was succeeded by a persecution on the part of the populace. An attempt was made to stone him ; his church was attacked, and he himself brought before a magistrate, under pretence of having caused the riot. Violence so unjust did but increase the influence, which a disdainful toleration had allowed him to establish ; and the accession of the orthodox Theodosius secured it.

On his arrival at Constantinople, the new Emperor resolved on executing in his capital the determination, which he had already prescribed by edict to the Eastern Empire. The Arian Bishops were required to subscribe the Nicene formulary, or to quit their sees. Demophilus, the Eusebian successor of Eudoxius, who has already been introduced to our notice as an accomplice in the seduction of Liberius, was first presented with this alternative ; and, with an honesty of which his party affords few instances, he refused at once to assent to opinions, which he had all through his life been opposing, and retired from the city. Many bishops, however, of the Arian party conformed ;

and the Church was unhappily inundated by the very evil, which in the reign of Constantine the Athanasians had strenuously and successfully withstood.

The unfortunate policy, which led to this measure, might seem at first sight to be sanctioned by the decree of the Alexandrian Council, which made subscription the test of orthodoxy; but, on a closer inspection, the cases will be found to be altogether dissimilar. When Athanasius acted upon that principle, in the reign of Julian, there was no secular object to be gained by conformity; or rather, the malevolence of the Emperor was peculiarly directed against those, whether orthodox or Semi-Arians, who evinced any earnestness about Christian truth. Even then, the recognition was not extended to those who had taken an active part on the side of heresy. On the other hand, the example of Athanasius himself, and of Alexander of Constantinople, in the reign of Constantine, sufficiently marked their judgment in the matter; both of them having resisted the attempt of the Court to force Arius upon the Church, even though he professed his assent to the *Homoüsion*.

Whether or not it was in Gregory's power to hinder the recognition of the Arianizers, or whether his firmness was not equal to his humility and zeal, the consequences of the measure are visible in the conduct of the General Council, which followed it. He himself may be considered as the victim of it; and he has left us in poetry and in oratory his testimony to the deterioration of religious principle, which the chronic vicissitudes of controversy had brought about in the Eastern Church.

The following passage, from one of his orations,

illustrates both the state of the times, and his own beautiful character, though unequal to struggle against them. "Who is there," he says, "but will find, on measuring himself by St. Paul's rules for the conduct of Bishops and Priests,—that they should be sober, chaste, not fond of wine, not strikers, apt to teach, unblamable in all things, unassailable by the wicked,—that he falls far short of its perfection? . . . . I am alarmed to think of our Lord's censure of the Pharisees, and his reproof of the Scribes; disgraceful indeed would it be, should we, who are bid be so far above them in virtue, in order to enter the kingdom of heaven, appear even worse than they. . . These thoughts haunt me night and day; they consume my bones, and feed on my flesh; they keep me from boldness, or from walking with erect countenance. They so humble me and cramp my mind, and place a chain on my tongue, that I cannot think of a Ruler's office, nor of correcting and guiding others, which is a talent above me; but only, how I myself may flee from the wrath to come, and scrape myself some little from the poison of my sin. First, I must be cleansed, and then cleanse others; learn wisdom, and then impart it; draw near to God, and then bring others to Him; be sanctified, and then sanctify. 'When will you ever get to the end of this?' say the all-hasty and unsafe, who are quick to build up and to pull down. 'When will you place your light on a candlestick? Where is your talent?' So say friends of mine, who have more zeal for me than religious seriousness. Ah, my brave men, why ask my season for acting, and my plan? Surely the last day of payment is soon enough, old age in its extreme term. Grey hairs have prudence, and youth is untaught. Best be slow and sure, not quick and thoughtless; a kingdom for a day, not a tyranny for a life; a little gold, not a weight of lead. It was the shallow earth shot forth the early blade. Truly there is cause of fear, lest I be bound hand and foot, and cast without the marriage-chamber, as an audacious intruder without fitting garment among the assembled guests. And yet I was called thither from my youth (to confess a matter which few know), and on God was I thrown from the womb; made over to Him by my mother's promise, confirmed in His service by dangers afterwards. Yea, and my own wish grew up beside her purpose, and my reason ran along with it; and all I had to give, wealth, name, health, literature, I brought and offered them to Him, who called and saved me; my sole enjoyment of them being to despise them, and to have something which I could resign for Christ. To undertake the direction and government of souls is above me, who have not yet well learnt to be guided, nor to be sanctified as far as is fitting. Much more is this so in a time like the present, when it is a great thing to flee away to some place of shelter, while others are whirled to and fro, and so to escape the storm and darkness of the evil one; for this is a time when the members of the Christian body war with each other, and whatever there was left of love is come to nought. Moabites and Ammonites, who were forbidden even to enter the Church of Christ, now tread our holiest places. We have opened to all, not gates of righteousness, but of mutual reviling and injury. We think those the best of men, not who keep from every idle word through fear of God, but such as have openly or covertly slandered their neighbour most. And we mark the sins of others, not to lament, but to blame them; not to cure, but to second the blow; and to make the wounds of others an excuse for our own. Men are judged good and bad, not by their course of life, but by their enmities and friendships. We praise to-day, we call names to-morrow. All things are readily pardoned to impiety. So magnanimously are we forgiving in wicked ways[3]!"

The first disturbance in the reviving Church of Constantinople had arisen from the ambition of Maximus, a Cynic philosopher, who aimed at supplanting Gregory in his see. He was a friend and countryman of Peter, the new Patriarch of Alexandria; and had suffered banishment in the Oasis, on the persecution which followed the death of Athanasius. His reputation was considerable among learned men of the day, as is shown by the letters addressed to him by Basil. Gregory fell in with him at Constantinople; and pleased at the apparent strictness and manliness of his conduct, he received him into his house, baptized him, and at length admitted him into inferior orders. The return made by Maximus to his benefactor, was to conduct an intrigue with one of his principal Presbyters; to gain over Peter of Alexandria, who had already recognized Gregory; to obtain from him the presence of three of his bishops; and, entering the metropolitan church during the night, to instal himself, with their aid, in the episcopal throne. A tumult ensued, and he was obliged to leave the city; but, far from being daunted at the immediate failure of his plot, he laid his case before a Council of the West, his

[3] Greg. Orat. i. 119—137. [ii. 69—73. 77—80. abridged.

plea consisting on the one hand, in the allegation that Gregory, as being Bishop of another Church, held the See contrary to the Canons, and on the other hand, in the recognition which he had obtained from the Patriarch of Alexandria. The Council, deceived by his representations, approved of his consecration; but Theodosius, to whom he next addressed himself, saw through his artifices, and banished him.

Fresh mortifications awaited the eloquent preacher, to whom the Church of Constantinople owed its resurrection. While the Arians censured his retiring habits, and his abstinence from the innocent pleasures of life, his own flock began to complain of his neglecting to use his influence at Court for their advantage. Overwhelmed with the disquietudes, to which these occurrences gave birth, Gregory resolved to bid adieu to a post which required a less sensitive or a more vigorous mind than his own. In a farewell oration, he recounted his labours and sufferings during the time he had been among them, commemorated his successes, and exhorted them to persevere in the truth, which they had learned from him. His congregation were affected by this address; and, a reaction of feeling taking place, they passionately entreated him to abandon a resolve, which would involve the ruin of orthodoxy in Constantinople, and they declared that they would not quit the church till he acceded to their importunities. At their entreaties, he consented to suspend the execution of his purpose for a while; that is, until the Eastern prelates who were expected at the General Council, which had by that time been convoked, should appoint a Bishop in his room.

The circumstances attending the arrival of Theodosius at Constantinople, connected as they were with the establishment of the true religion, still were calculated to inflict an additional wound on his feelings, and to increase his indisposition to continue in his post, endeared though it was to him by its first associations. The inhabitants of an opulent and luxurious metropolis, familiarized to Arianism by its forty years' ascendancy among them, and disgusted at the apparent severity of the orthodox school, prepared to resist the installation of Gregory in the cathedral of St. Sophia. A strong military force was appointed to escort him thither; and the Emperor gave countenance to the proceedings by his own presence. Allowing himself to be put in possession of the church, Gregory was nevertheless firm to his purpose of not seating himself upon the Archiepiscopal throne; and when the light-minded multitude clamorously required it, he was unequal to the task of addressing them, and deputed one of his Presbyters to speak in his stead.

Nor were the manners of the Court more congenial to his well-regulated mind, than the lawless spirit of the people. Offended at the disorders which he witnessed there, he shunned the condescending advances of the Emperor; and was with difficulty withdrawn from the duties of his station, the solitude of his own thoughts, and the activity of pious ministrations, prayer and fasting, the punishment of offenders and the visitation of the sick. Careless of personal splendour, he allowed the revenues of his see to be expended in supporting its dignity, by inferior ecclesiastics, who were in his confidence; and, while he defended the principle, on which Arianism had been dispossessed of its power, he exerted himself with earnestness to protect the heretics from all intemperate execution of the Imperial decree.

Nor was the elevated refinement of Gregory better adapted to sway the minds of the corrupt hierarchy which Arianism had engendered, than to rule the Court and the people. "If I must speak the truth," he says in one of his letters, "I feel disposed to shun every conference of Bishops; because I never saw Synod brought to a happy issue, nor remedying, but rather increasing, existing evils. For ever is there rivalry and ambition, and these have the mastery of reason;—do not think me extravagant for saying so; —and a mediator is more likely to be attacked himself, than to succeed in his pacification. Accordingly, I have fallen back upon myself, and consider quiet the only security of life[4]."

3.

Such was the state of things, under which the second Œcumenical Council, as it has since been considered, was convoked. It met in May, A.D. 381; being designed to put an end, as far as might be, to those very disorders, which unhappily found their principal exercise in the assemblies which were to remove them. The Western Church enjoyed at this time an almost perfect peace, and sent no deputies to Constantinople. But in the Oriental provinces, besides the distractions caused by the various heretical offshoots of Arianism, its indirect effects existed in the dissensions of the Catholics themselves; in the schism at Antioch; in the claims of Maximus to the see of

[4] Greg. Naz. Ep. 55. [Ep. 130.]

Constantinople; and in recent disturbances at Alexandria, where the loss of Athanasius was already painfully visible. Added to these, was the ambiguous position of the Macedonians; who resisted the orthodox doctrine, yet were only by implication heretical, or at least some of them far less than others. Thirty-six of their Bishops attended the Council, principally from the neighbourhood of the Hellespont; of the orthodox there were 150, Meletius, of Antioch, being the president. Other eminent prelates present were Gregory Nyssen, brother of St. Basil, who had died some years before; Amphilochius of Iconium, Diodorus of Tarsus, Cyril of Jerusalem, and Gelasius of Cæsarea, in Palestine.

The Council had scarcely accomplished its first act, the establishment of Gregory in the see of Constantinople, to the exclusion of Maximus, when Meletius, the President, died; an unhappy event, as not only removing a check from its more turbulent members, but in itself supplying the materials of immediate discord. An arrangement had been effected between the two orthodox communions at Antioch, by which it was provided, that the survivor of the rival Bishops should be acknowledged by the opposite party, and a termination thus put to the schism. This was in accordance with the principle acted upon by the Alexandrian Council, on the separation of the Meletians from the Arians. At that time the Eustathian party was called on to concede, by acknowledging Meletius; and now, on the death of Meletius, it became the duty of the Meletians in turn to submit to Paulinus, whom Lucifer had consecrated as Bishop of the Eustathians. Schism, however, admits not of these simple remedies. The self-will of a Latin Bishop had defeated the plan of conciliation in the former instance; and now the pride and jealousy of the Orientals revolted from communion with a prelate of Latin creation. The attempt of Gregory, who had succeeded to the presidency of the Council, to calm their angry feelings, and to persuade them to deal fairly with the Eustathians, as well as to restore peace to the Church, only directed their violence against himself. It was in vain that his own connection with the Meletian party evidenced the moderation and candour of his advice; in vain that the age of Paulinus gave assurance, that the nominal triumph of the Latins could be of no long continuance. Flavian, who, together with others, had solemnly sworn, that he would not accept the bishoprick in case of the death of Meletius, permitted himself to be elevated to the vacant see; and Gregory, driven from the Council, took refuge from its clamours in a remote part of Constantinople.

About this time the arrival of the Egyptian bishops increased the dissension. By some inexplicable omission they had not been summoned to the Council; and they came, inflamed with resentment against the Orientals. They had throughout taken the side of Paulinus, and now their earnestness in his favour was increased by their jealousy of his opponents. Another cause of offence was given to them, in the recognition of Gregory before their arrival; nor did his siding with them in behalf of Paulinus, avail to avert from him the consequences of their indignation. Maximus was their countryman, and the deposition of Gregory was necessary to appease their insulted patriotism. Accordingly, the former charge was revived of the illegality of his promotion. A Canon of the Nicene Council prohibited the translation of bishops, priests, or deacons, from Church to Church; and, while it was calumniously pretended, that Gregory had held in succession three bishopricks, Sasime, Nazianzus, and Constantinople, it could not be denied, that, at least, he had passed from Nazianzus, the place of his original ordination, to the Imperial city. Urged by this fresh attack, Gregory once more resolved to retire from an eminence, which he had from the first been reluctant to occupy, except for the sake of the remembrances, with which it was connected. The Emperor with difficulty accepted his resignation; but at length allowed him to depart from Constantinople, Nectarius being placed on the patriarchal throne in his stead.

In the mean while, a Council had been held at Aquileia of the bishops of the north of Italy, with a view of inquiring into the faith of two Bishops of Dacia, accused of Arianism. During its session, news was brought of the determination of the Constantinopolitan Fathers to appoint a successor to Meletius; and, surprised both by the unexpected continuation of the schism, and by the slight put on themselves, they petitioned Theodosius to permit a general Council to be convoked at Alexandria, which the delegates of the Latin Church might attend. Some dissatisfaction, moreover, was felt for a time at the appointment of Nectarius, in the place of Maximus, whom they had originally recognized. They changed their petition shortly after, and expressed a wish that a Council should be held at Rome.

These letters from the West were submitted to the Council of Constantinople, at its second, or, (as some say,) third sitting, A.D. 382 or 383, at which Nectarius presided. An answer was returned to the Latins, declining to repair to Rome, on the ground of the inconvenience, which would arise from the absence of the Eastern bishops from their dioceses; the Creed and other doctrinal statements of the Council were sent them, and the promotion of Nectarius and Flavian was maintained to be agreeable to the Nicene Canons, which determined, that the Bishops of a province had the right of consecrating such of their brethren, as were chosen by the people and clergy, without the interposition of foreign Churches; an exhortation to follow peace was added, and to prefer the edification of the whole body of Christians, to personal attachments and the interests of individuals.

Thus ended the second General Council. As to the addition made by it to the Nicene Creed, it is conceived in the temperate spirit, which might be expected from those men, who took the more active share in its doctrinal discussions. The ambitious and tumultuous part of the assembly seems to have been weary of the controversy, and to have left its settlement to the more experienced and serious-minded of their body. The Creed of Constantinople is said to be the composition of Gregory Nyssen[5].

From the date of this Council, Arianism was formed into a sect exterior to the Catholic Church; and,

[5] Whether or not the Macedonians explicitly denied the divinity of the Holy Spirit, is uncertain; but they viewed Him as essentially separate

taking refuge among the Barbarian Invaders of the Empire, is merged among those external enemies of Christianity, whose history cannot be regarded as strictly ecclesiastical. Such is the general course of religious error; which rises within the sacred precincts, but in vain endeavours to take root in a soil uncongenial to it. The domination of heresy, however prolonged, is but one stage in its existence; it ever hastens to an end, and that end is the triumph of the Truth. "I myself have seen the ungodly in great power," says the Psalmist, "and flourishing like a green bay tree; I went by, and lo, he was gone; I sought him, but his place could nowhere be found." And so of the present perils, with which our branch of the Church is beset, as they bear a marked resemblance to those of the fourth century, so are the lessons, which we gain from that ancient time, especially cheering and edifying to Christians of the present day. Then as now, there was the prospect, and partly the presence in the Church, of an Heretical Power enthralling it, exerting a varied influence and a usurped claim in the appointment of her functionaries, and interfering with the management of her internal affairs. Now as then, "whosoever shall fall upon this stone shall be broken, but on whomsoever it shall fall,

from, and external to, the One Indivisible Godhead. Accordingly, the Creed (which is that since incorporated into the public services of the Church), without declaring more than the occasion required, closes all speculations concerning the incomprehensible subject, by simply confessing his *unity with* the Father and Son. It declares, moreover, that He is the *Lord* (κύριος) or Sovereign Spirit, because the heretics considered Him to be but a minister of God; and the supreme *Giver* of life, because they considered Him a mere instrument, by whom we received the gift. The last clause of the second paragraph in the Creed, is directed against the heresy of Marcellus of Ancyra.

it will grind him to powder." Meanwhile, we may take comfort in reflecting, that, though the present tyranny has more of insult, it has hitherto had less of scandal, than attended the ascendancy of Arianism ; we may rejoice in the piety, prudence, and varied graces of our Spiritual Rulers ; and may rest in the confidence, that, should the hand of Satan press us sore, our Athanasius and Basil will be given us in their destined season, to break the bonds of the Oppressor, and let the captives go free.

The original Creed of Nicæa, as contained in Socr. Hist. i. 8.

Πιστεύομεν εἰς ἕνα θεὸν, πατέρα παντοκράτορα, πάντων ὁρατῶν τε καὶ ἀοράτων ποιητήν.

Καὶ εἰς ἕνα κύριον ἰησοῦν χριστὸν, τὸν υἱὸν τοῦ θεοῦ· γεννηθέντα ἐκ τοῦ πατρὸς μονογενῆ· τοῦτ' ἔστιν ἐκ τῆς οὐσίας τοῦ πατρὸς, θεὸν ἐκ θεοῦ, καὶ φῶς ἐκ φωτὸς, θεὸν ἀληθινὸν ἐκ θεοῦ ἀληθινοῦ· γεννηθέντα οὐ ποιηθέντα, ὁμοούσιον τῷ πατρί· δι' οὗ τὰ πάντα ἐγένετο, τά τε ἐν τῷ οὐρανῷ καὶ τὰ ἐν τῇ γῇ. Δι' ἡμᾶς τοὺς ἀνθρώπους καὶ διὰ τὴν ἡμετέραν σωτηρίαν κατελθόντα, καὶ σαρκωθέντα, καὶ ἐνανθρωπήσαντα· παθόντα, καὶ ἀναστάντα τῇ τρίτῃ ἡμέρᾳ, ἀνελθόντα εἰς τοὺς οὐρανοὺς, ἐρχόμενον κρῖναι ζῶντας καὶ νεκρούς.

Καὶ εἰς τὸ ἅγιον πνεῦμα.

Τοὺς δὲ λέγοντας, ὅτι ἦν ποτὲ ὅτε οὐκ ἦν· καὶ πρὶν γεννηθῆναι οὐκ ἦν· καὶ ὅτι ἐξ οὐκ ὄντων ἐγένετο· ἢ ἐξ ἑτέρας ὑποστάσεως ἢ οὐσίας φάσκοντας εἶναι· ἢ κτιστὸν, ἢ τρεπτὸν, ἢ ἀλλοιωτὸν τὸν υἱὸν τοῦ θεοῦ· ἀναθεματίζει ἡ ἁγία καθολικὴ καὶ ἀποστολικὴ ἐκκλησία.

CHRONOLOGICAL TABLE.

PERSONS AND EVENTS INTRODUCED INTO THE FOREGOING HISTORY.

(*The dates are, for the most part, according to* TILLEMONT.)

	A.D.
Philo Judæus, pp. 62, 101	40
St. Mark in Egypt, p. 41	49
Cerinthus and Ebion, heretics, pp. 20, 21.	90
Nazarenes, heretics, p. 21.,	137
Valentine, heretic, p. 55	140
Marcion, heretic, p. 55.	144
Justin, p. 68, martyred.	167
Theophilus, Bishop of Antioch, p. 95	168
Tatian, heretic, pp. 52, 95.	169
Montanus, heresiarch, p. 16	171
Athenagoras, pp. 42, 95, writes his Apology	177
Pantænus, Missionary to the Indians, pp. 42, 102.	189
Demetrius, Bishop of Alexandria, p. 42	189
Clement of Alexandria, Master of the Catechetical School, pp. 48—87	189
Theodotus and Artemon, heretics, pp. 22, 35, 114.	193
Severus, Emperor, p. 10	193
Victor, Bishop of Rome, pp. 13, 21, 35	197
Quarto-decimans of Asia Minor, p. 15.	197
Praxeas, heretic, p. 117	201

	A.D.
Irenæus, Bishop of Lyons, p. 54, martyred	202
Origen, aged 18, Master of the Catechetical School, p. 42	203
Tertullian, pp. 138, 188, falls away into Montanism .	204
Philostratus writes the Life of Apollonius Tyanæus, p. 109	217
Noetus, heretic, pp. 117, 124.	220
Origen converts Gregory Thaumaturgus, p. 66 . . .	231
Ammonius the Eclectic, p. 102	232
Gregory Thaumaturgus delivers his panegyric on Origen, p. 108	239
Plotinus at Rome, pp. 107, 115.	244
Babylas, Bishop of Antioch martyred, p. 3	250
Novatian, heresiarch, p. 16	250
Hippolytus, p. 200 ; martyr	252
Death of Origen, aged 69, p. 107	253
Sabellius, heresiarch, p. 118	255
Dionysius, Bishop of Rome, animadverts on Dionysius of Alexandria, p. 126.	260
Paulus of Samosata, heretic, pp. 3, 27, 171, 186, 203.	260
Council against Paulus, pp. 27, 128 ; with Creed, pp. 129, 192, 322, 343	264
Death of Dionysius of Alexandria, p. 108.	264
Paulus deposed, p. 3	272
Quarto-decimans of the Proconsulate come to an end, p. 14	276
Theonas, Bishop of Alexandria, p. 66	282
Hosius, Bishop of Corduba, pp. 249, 254, 289, 323 .	295
Meletian Schism in Egypt, pp. 239, 281-2	306
Donatist Schism in Africa, p. 245	306
Constantine's vision of the Labarum, p. 246. . . .	312
Lucian, martyred, p. 8	312
Edict of Milan, p. 245. . . . . , ...	313
Eusebius, Bishop of Nicomedia, p. 260	319

	A.D.
Arius, heresiarch, pp. 205, 237	319
Alexander excommunicates and writes against Arius, pp. 217, 238	320
Battle of Hadrianople, pp. 241, 247	323
Constantine writes to Athanasius and Arius, p. 247 .	324
Ecumenical Council of Nicæa, p. 250.	325
Audius, the Quarto-deciman in Mesopotamia, p. 15 .	325
Athanasius, Bishop of Alexandria, p. 266.	326
Arius recalled from exile, p. 266.	330
Eustathius, Bishop of Antioch, deposed by the Arians, pp. 280, 360	331
Eusebian Council of Cæsarea, p. 282	333
And of Tyre, *ibid.* Marcellus, Bishop of Ancyra, deposed, pp. 280, 313	335
Athanasius banished to Treves, p. 284.	335
Death of Arius, p. 269	336
Death of Constantine, who is succeeded in the East by Constantius, p. 280	337
Death of Eusebius of Cæsarea, who is succeeded by Acacius, p. 275.	340
Assemblage of exiled Bishops at Rome, Council at Rome, p. 285	340
Eusebian Council of the Dedication at Antioch, p. 285. Semi-Arian Creed of Lucian, pp. 286, 322, 343, .	341
Semi-Arian Creed of Antioch, called the Macrostich, p. 287	345
Great Council of Sardica, pp. 289, 313	347
Eusebian Council, p. 289, and Semi-Arian Creed, p. 342, of Philippopolis.	347
Council of Milan, p. 292	347
Athanasius returns from exile, pp. 290, 360	348
Formal recantation of Valens and Ursacius, p. 291 ,	349
Death of Constans, p. 303.	350
Paulus of Constantinople martyred, p. 311	350

Event	A.D.
Battle of Mursa, p. 278	351
Eusebian Council, pp. 314, 336, with Semi-Arian Creed of Sirmium, against Photinus, pp, 314, 322, 343	351
Eusebian Council of Arles, pp. 314, 315	353
Eusebian Council of Milan, p. 316	355
Hilary exiled in Phrygia, p. 300	356
Liberius tempted, p. 318	356
Syrianus and George in Alexandria, p. 329	356
Aetius and Eunomius, Anomœans, p. 337	357
Eusebian or Acacian Conferences and Creeds of Sirmium; fall of Liberius and Hosius, pp. 323—326, 341	358
Acacian Council of Antioch, p. 341	358
Semi-Arian Council of Ancyra, pp. 300, 342	358
Acacian Councils of Seleucia (p. 345) and Ariminum, p. 348	359
Eudoxius at Constantinople, p. 361	360
Acacian Council at Constantinople, pp. 347, 351, 358	360
Meletius, Bishop of Antioch, p. 361. Death of Constantius, pp. 344, 352	361
Julian restores the exiled Bishops, p. 353	362
Council of Alexandria, p. 355	362
Schism of Antioch, p. 364	362
Semi-Arian Council of Lampsacus, p. 377	365
Fifty-nine Semi-Arian Bishops accept the *Homoüsion*, p. 378	366
Apollinaris, heresiarch, p. 221	369
Basil, Exarch of Cæsarea, p. 375	370
Death of Eudoxius, p. 379	370
Eighty Catholic Clergy burned at sea, 380	370
Persecution of Catholics, p. 380	371
Athanasius excommunicates one of the dukes of Lybia p. 374	371

	A.D.
Death of Athanasius, 374	373
Death of Valens, p. 380	378
Theodosius, Emperor, p. 381.	379
Gregory Nazianzen at Constantinople, *ibid*	379
Ecumenical Council of Constantinople, pp. 373, &c. .	381
Sabbatius, Quarto-deciman, p. 17	395

APPENDIX.

NOTE I.

THE SYRIAN SCHOOL OF THEOLOGY.

(*Vide Supra*, p. 8.)

MUCH has been written at home, and more has come to us from abroad, on the subject of the early Syrian theology, since this Volume was published. At that time, it was at Oxford considered a paradox to look to Antioch for the origin of a heresy which takes its name from an Alexandrian ecclesiastic, and which Mosheim had ruled to be one out of many instances of the introduction of Neo-Platonic ideas into the Christian Church. The Divinity Professor of the day, a learned and kind man, Dr. Burton, in talking with me on the subject, did but qualify his surprise at the view which I had taken, by saying to me, " Of course you have a right to your own opinion." Since that time, it has become clear, from the works of Neander and others, that Arianism was but one out of various errors, traceable to one and the same mode of theologizing, and that mode, as well as the errors it originated, the characteristics of the Syrian school.

I have thought it would throw light on the somewhat meagre account of it at the beginning of this Volume, if I here added a passage on the same subject, as contained in one of my subsequent works[1].

The Churches of Syria and Asia Minor were the most intellectual portion of early Christendom. Alexandria was

[1] " Essay on the Development of Christian Doctrine," pp. 281, 323.

but one metropolis in a large region, and contained the philosophy of the whole Patriarchate; but Syria abounded in wealthy and luxurious cities, the creation of the Seleucidæ, where the arts and the schools of Greece had full opportunities of cultivation. For a time too,—for the first two hundred years, as some think,—Alexandria was the only See as well as the only School of Egypt; while Syria was divided into small dioceses, each of which had at first an authority of its own, and which, even after the growth of the Patriarchal power, received their respective bishops, not from the See of Antioch, but from their own metropolitan. In Syria too the schools were private, a circumstance which would tend both to diversity in religious opinion, and incaution in the expression of it; but the sole catechetical school of Egypt was the organ of the Church, and its Bishop could banish Origen for speculations which developed and ripened with impunity in Syria.

But the immediate source of that fertility in heresy, which is the unhappy distinction of the Syrian Church, was its celebrated Exegetical School. The history of that school is summed up in the broad characteristic fact, on the one hand that it devoted itself to the literal and critical interpretation of Scripture, and on the other that it gave rise first to the Arian and then to the Nestorian heresy. In all ages of the Church, her teachers have shown a disinclination to confine themselves to the mere literal interpretation of Scripture. Her most subtle and powerful method of proof, whether in ancient or modern times, is the mystical sense, which is so frequently used in doctrinal controversy as on many occasions to supersede any other. In the early centuries we find this method of interpretation to be the very ground for receiving as revealed the doctrine of the Holy Trinity. Whether we betake ourselves to the Ante-Nicene writers or the Nicene, certain texts will meet us, which do not obviously refer to that doctrine, yet are put forward as palmary proofs of it.

On the other hand, if evidence be wanted of the connexion of heterodoxy and biblical criticism in that age, it is found in the fact that, not long after their contemporaneous appearance in Syria, they are found combined in the person of Theodore of Heraclea, so called from the place both of his birth and his bishoprick, an able commentator and an active enemy of St. Athanasius, though a Thracian unconnected except by sympathy with the Patriarchate of Antioch. The case had been the same in a still earlier age;—the Jews clung to the literal sense of the Old Testament and rejected the Gospel; the Christian Apologists proved its divinity by means of the allegorical. The formal connexion of this mode of interpretation with Christian theology is noticed by Porphyry, who speaks of Origen and others as borrowing it from heathen philosophy, both in explanation of the Old Testament and in defence of their own doctrine. It may almost be laid down as an historical fact that the mystical interpretation and orthodoxy will stand or fall together.

This is clearly seen, as regards the primitive theology, by a recent writer, in the course of a Dissertation upon St. Ephrem. After observing that Theodore of Heraclea, Eusebius, and Diodorus gave a systematic opposition to the mystical interpretation, which had a sort of sanction from Antiquity and the orthodox Church, he proceeds; "Ephrem is not as sober in his interpretations, nor could he be, since he was a zealous disciple of the orthodox faith. For all those who are most eminent in such sobriety were as far as possible removed from the faith of the Councils. . . . . On the other hand, all who retained the faith of the Church never entirely dispensed with the spiritual sense of the Scriptures. For the Councils watched over the orthodox faith; nor was it safe in those ages, as we learn especially from the instance of Theodore of Mopsuestia, to desert the spiritual for an exclusive cultivation of the literal method. Moreover, the allegorical interpretation, even when the literal sense was not injured, was also preserved; because in those times, when both heretics and Jews in controversy were stubborn in their objections to Christian doctrine, maintaining that the Messiah was yet to come, or denying the abrogation of the Sabbath and ceremonial law, or ridiculing the Christian doctrine of the Trinity, and especially that of Christ's Divine Nature, under such circumstances ecclesiastical writers found it to their purpose, in answer to such exceptions, violently to refer every part of Scripture by allegory to Christ and His Church[2]."

The School of Antioch appears to have risen in the middle of the third century; but there is no evidence to determine whether it was a local institution, or, as is more probable, a discipline or method characteristic of the Syrian Church. Dorotheus is one of its earliest teachers; he is known as a Hebrew scholar, as well as a commentator on the sacred text, and he was the master of Eusebius of Cæsarea. Lucian, the friend of the notorious Paul of Samosata, and for three successive Episcopates after him a seceder from the Church, though afterwards a martyr in it, was the editor of a new edition of the Septuagint, and master of the chief original teachers of Arianism. Eusebius of Cæsarea, Asterius called the Sophist, and Eusebius of Emesa, Arians of the Nicene period, and Diodorus, a zealous opponent of Arianism, but the Master of Theodore of Mopsuestia, have all a place in the Exegetical School. St. Chrysostom and Theodoret, both Syrians, and the former the pupil of Diodorus, adopted the literal interpretation, though preserved from its abuse. But the principal doctor of the School was the master of Nestorius, that Theodore, who has just been mentioned, and who with his writings, and with the writings of Theodoret against St. Cyril, and the letter written by Ibas of Edessa to Maris, was condemned by the fifth Œcumenical Council. Ibas translated into Syriac, and Maris into Persian, the

[2] Lengerke, de Ephr. S. pp. 78—80.

books of Theodore and Diodorus[3]; and in so doing they became the immediate instruments of the formation of the great Nestorian school and Church in farther Asia.

As many as ten thousand tracts of Theodore are said in this way to have been introduced to the knowledge of the Christians of Mesopotamia, Adiabene, Babylonia, and the neighbouring countries. He was called by those Churches absolutely "the Interpreter," and it eventually became the very profession of the Nestorian communion to follow him as such. "The doctrine of all our Eastern Churches," says the Council under the patriarch Marabas, "is founded on the Creed of Nicæa; but in the exposition of the Scriptures we follow St. Theodore." "We must by all means remain firm to the commentaries of the great Commentator," says the Council under Sabarjesus; "whoso shall in any manner oppose them, or think otherwise, be he anathema[4]." No one since the beginning of Christianity, except Origen and St. Augustine, has had such great influence on his brethren as Theodore[5].

The original Syrian school had possessed very marked characteristics, which it did not lose when it passed into a new country and into strange tongues. Its comments on Scripture seem to have been clear, natural, methodical, apposite, and logically exact. "In all Western Aramæa," says Lengerke, that is, in Syria, "there was but one mode of treating whether exegetics or doctrine, the practical[6]." Thus Eusebius of Cæsarea, whether as a disputant or a commentator, is confessedly a writer of sense and judgment, and he belongs historically to the Syrian school, though he does not go so far as to exclude the mystical interpretation or to deny the verbal inspiration of Scripture. Again, we see in

[3] Asseman. t. 3, p. 30, p. lxviii., &c.

[4] Assem. t. 3, p. 84, Note 3.

[5] Wegnern, Proleg. in Theod. Opp. p. ix.

[6] De Ephræm Syr. p. 61.

St. Chrysostom a direct, straightforward treatment of the sacred text, and a pointed application of it to things and persons; and Theodoret abounds in modes of thinking and reasoning which without any great impropriety may be called English. Again, St. Cyril of Jerusalem, though he does not abstain from allegory, shows the character of his school by the great stress he lays upon the study of Scripture, and, I may add, by the peculiar clearness and neatness of his style, which will be appreciated by a modern reader.

It would have been well, had the genius of the Syrian theology been ever in the safe keeping of men such as St. Cyril, St. Chrysostom, and Theodoret; but in Theodore of Mopsuestia, nay in Diodorus before him, it developed into those errors, of which Paul of Samosata had been the omen on its rise. As its attention was chiefly directed to the examination of the Scriptures, in its interpretation of the Scriptures was its heretical temper discovered; and though allegory can be made an instrument of evading Scripture doctrine, criticism may more readily be turned to the destruction of doctrine and Scripture together. Bent on ascertaining the literal sense, Theodore was naturally led to the Hebrew text instead of the Septuagint, and thence to Jewish commentators. Jewish commentators naturally suggested events and objects short of evangelical as the fulfilment of the prophetical announcements, and when it was possible, an ethical sense instead of a prophetical. The eighth chapter of Proverbs ceased to bear a Christian meaning, because, as Theodore maintained, the writer of the book had received the gift, not of prophecy, but of wisdom. The Canticles must be interpreted literally; and then it was but an easy, or rather a necessary step, to exclude the book from the Canon. The book of Job too professed to be historical; yet what was it really but a Gentile drama? He also gave up the books of Chronicles and Ezra, and, strange to say, the Epistle of St. James, though it was contained in the Peschito Version of his Church. He denied that Psalms xxii. and lxix. applied to our Lord; rather he limited the Messianic passages of the whole book to four; of which the eighth Psalm was one, and the forty-fifth another. The rest he explained of Hezekiah and Zerubbabel, without denying that they might be accommodated to an evangelical sense[7]. He explained St. Thomas's words, "My Lord and my God," as a joyful exclamation; and our Lord's, "Receive ye the Holy Ghost," as an anticipation of the day of Pentecost. As might be expected, he denied the verbal inspiration of Scripture. Also, he held that the deluge did not cover the earth; and, as others before him, he was heterodox on the doctrine of original sin, and denied the eternity of punishment.

Maintaining that the real sense of Scripture was, not the scope of a Divine Intelligence, but the intention of the mere human organ of inspiration, Theodore was led to hold, not only that that sense was but one in each text, but that it was continuous and single in a context; that what was the subject of the composition in one verse, must be the subject in the next, and that if a Psalm was historical or prophetical in its commencement, it was the one or the other to its termination. Even that fulness of meaning, refinement of thought, subtle versatility of feeling, and delicate reserve or reverent suggestiveness, which poets exemplify, seem to have been excluded from his idea of a sacred composition. Accordingly, if a Psalm contained passages which could not be applied to our Lord, it followed that that Psalm did not properly apply to Him at all, except by accommodation. Such at least is the doctrine of Cosmas, a writer of Theodore's school, who on this ground passes over the twenty-second, sixty-ninth, and other Psalms, and limits the Messianic to the second, the eighth, the forty-fifth, and the hundred and tenth. "David," he says, "did not make common to the servants what belongs to the Lord[8] Christ, but what was proper to the

[7] Lengerke, de Ephræm Syr. pp. 73—75.

[8] δεσπότου, vide La Croze, Thesaur. Ep. t. 3, § 145.

Lord he spoke of the Lord, and what was proper to the servants, of servants[9]." Accordingly the twenty-second could not properly belong to Christ, because in the beginning it spoke of the "*verba delictorum meorum.*" A remarkable consequence would follow from this doctrine, that as Christ was divided from His Saints, so the Saints were divided from Christ; and an opening was made for a denial of the doctrine of their *cultus*, though this denial in the event has not been developed among the Nestorians. But a more serious consequence is latently contained in it, and nothing else than the Nestorian heresy, viz. that our Lord's manhood is not so intimately included in His Divine Personality that His brethren according to the flesh may be associated with the Image of the One Christ. Here St. Chrysostom pointedly contradicts the doctrine of Theodore, though his fellow-pupil and friend[1]; as does St. Ephræm, though a Syrian also[2]; and St. Basil[3].

One other characteristic of the Syrian school, viewed as independent of Nestorius, should be added:—As it tended to the separation of the Divine Person of Christ from His manhood, so did it tend to explain away His Divine Presence in the Sacramental elements. Ernesti seems to consider that school, in modern language, Sacramentarian: and certainly some of the most cogent passages brought by moderns against the Catholic doctrine of the Eucharist are taken from writers who are connected with that school; as the author, said to be St. Chrysostom, of the Epistle to Cæsarius, Theodoret in his Eranistes, and Facundus. Some countenance too is given to the same view of the Eucharist, at least in some parts of his works, by Origen, whose language concerning the Incarnation also leans to what was

[9] Montf. Coll. Nov. t. 2, p. 227.
[1] Rosenmuller, Hist. Interpr. t. 3, p. 278.
[2] Lengerke, de Ephr. Syr. pp. 165—167.
[4] Ernest. de Proph. Mess. p. 462.

afterwards Nestorianism. To these may be added Eusebius[4], who, far removed, as he was, from that heresy, was a disciple of the Syrian school. The language of the later Nestorian writers seems to have been of the same character[5]. Such then on the whole is the character of that theology of Theodore, which passed from Cilicia and Antioch to Edessa first, and then to Nisibis.

Edessa, the metropolis of Mesopotamia, had remained an Oriental city till the third century, when it was made a Roman colony by Caracalla[6]. Its position on the confines of two empires gave it great ecclesiastical importance, as the channel by which the theology of Rome and Greece was conveyed to a family of Christians, dwelling in contempt and persecution amid a still heathen world. It was the seat of various schools; apparently of a Greek school, where the classics were studied as well as theology, where Eusebius of Emesa[7] had originally been trained, and where perhaps Protogenes taught[8]. There were Syrian schools attended by heathen and Christian youths in common. The cultivation of the native language had been an especial object of its masters since the time of Vespasian, so that the pure and refined dialect went by the name of the Edessene[9]. At Edessa too St. Ephræm formed his own Syrian school, which lasted long after him; and there too was the celebrated Persian Christian school, over which Maris presided, who has been already mentioned as the translator of Theodore into Persian[1]. Even in the time of the predecessor of Ibas in the See (before A.D. 435) the Nestorianism of this Persian School was so notorious that Rabbula the Bishop had ex-

[4] Eccl. Theol. iij. 12.

[5] Professor Lee's Serm. Oct. 1838, pp. 144—152.

[6] Noris. Opp. t. 2, p. 112.

[7] Augusti. Euseb. Em. Opp.

[8] Asseman. p. cmxxv.

[9] Hoffman, Gram. Syr. Proleg. § 4.

[1] The educated Persians were also acquainted with Syriac.—Assem. t. i. p. 351, Note.

pelled its masters and scholars[2]; and they, taking refuge in the country with which they were connected, had introduced the heresy to the Churches subject to the Persian King.

Something ought to be said of these Churches; though little is known except what is revealed by the fact, in itself of no slight value, that they had sustained two persecutions at the hands of the heathen government in the fourth and fifth centuries. One testimony is extant as early as the end of the second century, to the effect that in Parthia, Media, Persia, and Bactria there were Christians who "were not overcome by evil laws and customs[3]." In the early part of the fourth century, a Bishop of Persia attended the Nicene Council, and about the same time Christianity is said to have pervaded nearly the whole of Assyria[4]. Monachism had been introduced there before the middle of the fourth century, and shortly after commenced that fearful persecution in which sixteen thousand Christians are said to have suffered. It lasted thirty years, and is said to have recommenced at the end of the century. The second persecution lasted for at least another thirty years of the next, at the very time when the Nestorian troubles were in progress in the Empire. Trials such as these show the populousness as well as the faith of the Churches in those parts; and the number of the Sees, for the names of twenty-seven Bishops are preserved who suffered in the former persecution. One of them was apprehended together with sixteen priests, nine deacons, besides monks and nuns of his diocese; another with twenty-eight companions, ecclesiastics or regulars; another with one hundred ecclesiastics of different orders; another with one hundred and twenty-eight; another with his chorepiscopus and two hundred and fifty of his clergy. Such was the Church, consecrated by the blood of so many

[2] Asseman. p. lxx.

[3] Euseb. Præp. vi. 10.

[4] Tillemont, Mem. t. 7, p. 77.

martyrs, which immediately after its glorious confession fell a prey to the theology of Theodore; and which through a succession of ages discovered the energy, when it had lost the purity of saints.

The members of the Persian school, who had been driven out of Edessa by Rabbula, found a wide field open for their exertions under the pagan government with which they had taken refuge. The Persian monarchs, who had often prohibited by edict[5] the intercommunion of the Church under their sway with the countries towards the west, readily extended their protection to exiles, who professed the means of destroying its Catholicity. Barsumas, the most energetic of them, was placed in the metropolitan See of Nisibis, where also the fugitive school was settled under the presidency of another of their party; while Maris was promoted to the See of Ardaschir. The primacy of the Church had from an early period belonged to the See of Seleucia in Babylonia. Catholicus was the title appropriated to its occupant, as well as to the Persian Primate, as being deputies of the Patriarch of Antioch, and was derived apparently from the Imperial dignity so called, denoting their function as Procurators-general, or officers-in-chief for the regions in which they were placed. Acacius, another of the Edessene party, was put into this principal See, and suffered, if he did not further, the innovations of Barsumas. The mode by which the latter effected his purposes has been left on record by an enemy. "Barsumas accused Barbuæus, the Catholicus, before King Pherozes, whispering, 'These men hold the faith of the Romans, and are their spies. Give me power against them to arrest them.[6]'" It is said that in this way he obtained the death of Barbuæus, whom Acacius succeeded. When a minority resisted[7] the process of schism, a persecution followed. The death of seven thousand seven

[5] Gibbon, ch. 47.

[6] Asseman. p. lxxviii.

[7] Gibbon, ibid.

hundred Catholics is said by Monophysite authorities to have been the price of the severance of the Chaldaic Churches from Christendom [8]. Their loss was compensated in the eyes of the government by the multitude of Nestorian fugitives, who flocked into Persia from the Empire, numbers of them industrious artisans, who sought a country where their own religion was in the ascendant.

The foundation of that religion lay, as we have already seen, in the literal interpretation of Scripture, of which Theodore was the principal teacher. The doctrine, in which it formerly consisted, is known by the name of Nestorius: it lay in the ascription of a human as well as a Divine Personality to our Lord; and it showed itself in denying the title of "Mother of God" or θεοτόκος, to St. Mary. As to our Lord's Personality, it is to be observed that the question of language came in, which always serves to perplex a subject and make a controversy seem a matter of words. The native Syrians made a distinction between the word "Person," and "Prosopon," which stands for it in Greek; they allowed that there was one Prosopon or Parsopa, as they called it, and they held that there were two Persons. It is asked what they meant by *parsopa:* the answer seems to be, that they took the word merely in the sense of *character* or *aspect*, a sense familiar to the Greek *prosopon*, and quite irrelevant as a guarantee of their orthodoxy. It follows moreover that, since the *aspect* of a thing is its impression upon the beholder, the personality to which they ascribed unity must have lain in our Lord's manhood, and not in His Divine Nature. But it is hardly worth while pursuing the heresy to its limits. Next, as to the phrase "Mother of God," they rejected it as unscriptural; they maintained that St. Mary was Mother of the humanity of Christ, not of the Word, and they fortified themselves by the Nicene Creed, in which no such title is ascribed to her.

[8] Asseman. t. 2, p. 403, t. 3, p. 393.

Whatever might be the obscurity or the plausibility of their original dogma, there is nothing obscure or attractive in the developments, whether of doctrine or of practice, in which it issued. The first act of the exiles of Edessa, on their obtaining power in the Chaldean communion, was to abolish the celibacy of the clergy, or, in Gibbon's forcible words, to allow "the public and reiterated nuptials of the priests, the bishops, and even the patriarch himself." Barsumas, the great instrument of the change of religion, was the first to set an example of the new usage, and is even said by a Nestorian writer to have married a nun . He passed a Canon at Councils, held at Seleucia and elsewhere, that Bishops and priests might marry, and might renew their wives as often as they lost them. The Catholic who followed Acacius went so far as to extend the benefit of the Canon to Monks, that is, to destroy the Monastic order; and his two successors availed themselves of this liberty, and are recorded to have been fathers. A restriction, however, was afterwards placed upon the Catholic, and upon the Episcopal order.

Such were the circumstances, and such the principles, under which the See of Seleucia became the Rome of the East. In the course of time the Catholic took on himself the loftier and independent title of Patriarch of Babylon; and though Seleucia was changed for Ctesiphon and for Bagdad[1], still the name of Babylon was preserved from first to last as a formal or ideal Metropolis. In the time of the Caliphs, it was at the head of as many as twenty-five Archbishops; its Communion extended from China to Jerusalem; and its numbers, with those of the Monophysites, are said to have surpassed those of the Greek and Latin Churches together.

[9] Asseman. t. 3, p. 67.

[1] Gibbon, ibid.

NOTE II.

THE DOCTRINE OF THE DIVINE GENNESIS ACCORDING TO THE EARLY FATHERS.

(*Vide supra*, p. 240.)

ALREADY in the Notes on Athanasius (Athan. Tr. pp. 272—280), and in Dissert. Theolog. iii. I have explained my difficulty in following Bull and others in the interpretation they assign to certain statements made in the first age of the Church concerning the Divine Sonship. Those statements, taken in their letter, are to the effect that our Lord was the Word of God before He was the Son; that, though, as the Word, He was from eternity, His *gennesis* is in essential connexion both with the design and the fact of creation; that He was born indeed of the Father apart from all time, but still with a definite relation to that beginning of time when the creation took place, and though born, and not created, nevertheless born definitely in order to create.

Before the Nicene Council, of the various Schools of the Church, the Alexandrian alone, is distinctly clear of this doctrine; and even after the Council it is found in the West, in Upper Italy, Rome, and Africa; France, as represented by Hilary[1] and Phœbadius, having no part in it. Nay, at Nicæa when it lay in the way of the Council to condemn it, it was not distinctly condemned, though to pass it over was in fact to give it some countenance. Bull indeed considers it was even recognized indirectly by the assembled Fathers, in their anathematizing those who contradicted its distinctive formula, "He was before He was born;" in this (as I have

[1] Vide however Hilar. in Matt. xxxi. 3; but he corrects himself, de Trin. xii.

said in the Notes on Athanasius), I cannot agree with him, but at least it is unaccountable that the Fathers should not have guarded their anathema from Bull's easy misinterpretation of it, if the opinion which it seems to countenance was as much reprobated then, as it rightly is now.

The opinion which I have been describing is, as far as words go, definitely held by Justin, Tatian, Theophilus, Methodius, in the East; by Hippolytus, Tertullian, Novatian, Lactantius, Zeno, and Victorinus, in the West; and that with so plain an identity of view in these various writers, and with such exact characteristics, that we cannot explain it away into carelessness of writing, personal idiosyncracy, or the influence of some particular school; but are forced to consider it as the common property of them all, so that we may interpret one writer by the other, and illustrate or supply from the rest what is obscure or deficient in each.

For instance: Justin says, "He was begotten, when God at the beginning through Him created and adorned all things" (Ap. ii. 6). "Not a perfect Son, without the flesh, though a perfect Word," says Hippolytus, "being the Only-begotten, . . . whom God called 'Son,' because He was to become such" (contr. Noet. 15). . . "There was a time when the Son was not," says Tertullian (adv. Herm. 3); "He proceeds unto a birth," says Zeno, "who was, before He was born" (Tract. ii. 3).

There can be no doubt what the literal sense is of words such as these, and that in consequence they require some accommodation in order to reconcile them with the received Catholic teaching *de Deo* and *de SS. Trinitate.* It is the object of Bull, as of others after him, to effect this reconciliation. He thinks it a plain duty both to the authors in question and to the Church, at whatever cost, to reconcile their statements in all respects with the orthodox belief; but unless he had felt it a duty, I do not think he would have ventured upon it. He would have taken them in their literal sense, had he found them in the writing of some Puritan or Quaker. If so, his defence of them is but a confirmation of a foregone conclusion; he starts with the assumption that the words of the early writers cannot mean what they naturally mean; and, though this bias is worthy of all respect, still the fact that it exists is a call on us to examine closely arguments which without it would not have been used. And what I have said of Bull applies of course to others, such as Maran and the Ballerini, who have followed in his track.

Bull then maintains that the terms "generation," "birth," and the like, which occur in the passages of the authors in question, must be taken figuratively, or *impropriè*, to mean merely our Lord's going forth to create, and the great manifestation of the Sonship made in and to the universe at its creation; and on these grounds:—1. The terms used cannot be taken literally, from the fact that in those very passages, or at least in other passages of the same authors, His co-eternity with the Father is expressly affirmed. 2. And they must be taken figuratively, first, because in those passages they actually stand in connexion with mention of His forthcoming or mission to create; and next, because unsuspected authors, such as Athanasius, distinctly connect His creative *office* with His title of "First-born," which belongs to His *nature*.

Now I do not think these arguments will stand; as to the negative argument, it is true that the Fathers, who speak of the *gennesis* as having a relation to time and to creation, do in the same passages or elsewhere speak of the eternity of the Word. Doubtless; but no one says that these Fathers deny His eternity, as the Word, but His eternity as the Son. Bull ought to bring passages in which they declare the Son and His *gennesis* to be eternal.

As to the positive argument, if they recognized, as he thinks, any *gennesis* besides that which had a relation to creation, and which he maintains to be only figuratively a *gennesis*, viz. an eternal *gennesis* from the substance of the Father, why do they not say so? do they ever compare and contrast the two births with each other? do they ever recognize them as two, one real and eternal, the other just before time; the one proper, the other metaphorical? We know they held a *gennesis* in order to creation, or with a relation to time; what reason have we for holding that they held any other? and what reason for saying that the *gennesis* which they connect with creation was not in their minds a real *gennesis*, that is, such a *gennesis* as we all now hold, all but, as they expressly state, its not being from eternity?

In other words, what reason have we for saying that the term *gennesis* is figurative in their use of it? It is true indeed that both the Son's *gennesis* and also His forthcoming, mission, or manifestation are sometimes mentioned together by these writers in the same sentence; but that does not prove they are not in their minds separate Divine acts; for His creation of the world is mentioned in such passages too, and as His creation of the world is not His mission, therefore His mission need not be His *gennesis;* and again, as His creating is (in their teaching) concurrent with His mission, so His mission may (in their teaching) be concurrent with His *gennesis.*

Nor are such expositions of the title "First-born of creation," as Athanasius has so beautifully given us, to the purpose of Bull. Bull takes it to show that *gennesis* may be considered to be a mission or forthcoming; whereas Athanasius does not mean by the "First-born" any *gennesis* of our Lord from the Father at all, but he simply means His coming to the creature, that is, His exalting the creature into a Divine sonship by a union with His own Sonship. The Son applies His own Sonship to the creation, and makes Himself, who is the real Son, the first and the representative of a family of adopted sons. The term expresses a relation, not towards God, but towards the creature. This Athanasius says expressly: "It is nowhere written [of the Son] in the Scriptures, 'the First-born *of God*,' nor 'the creature *of God*,' but it is 'Only-begotten,' and 'Son,' and 'Word,' and 'Wisdom,' that have relation to the Father. The same cannot be both Only-begotten and First-born, except in different relations, —Only-begotten because of His *gennesis*, First-born because of His condescension." Thus Athanasius expressly denies that, because our Lord is First-born at and to the creation, therefore He can be said to be begotten at the creation; "Only-begotten" is internal to the Divine Essence; "First-born" external to It: the one is a word of nature, the other, of office. If then the authors, whom Bull is defending, had wished to express a figurative *gennesis*, they would always have used the word "First-born," never "Only-begotten:" and never have associated the generation from the Father with the coming forth to create. It is true they sometimes associate the Word's creative office with the term "First-born;" but they also associate it with "Only-begotten."

There seems no reason then why the words of Theophilus, Hippolytus, and the rest should not be taken in their obvious sense; and so far I agree with Petavius against Bull, Fabricius, Maran, the Ballerini, and Routh. But, this being granted, still I am not disposed to follow Petavius in his severe criticism upon those Fathers, and for the following reasons:—

1. They considered the "Theos Logos" to be really distinct from God, (that is, the Father,) not a mere attribute, quality, or power, as the Sabellians did, and do.

2. They considered Him to be distinct from God *from everlasting*.

3. Since, as Dionysius says, "He who speaks is father of his words," they considered the Logos always to be of the *nature* of a Son. Hence Zeno says He was from everlasting

"Filii non sine *affectu*," and Hippolytus, τέλειος λόγος, ὢν μονογενής.

4. They considered, to use the Scripture term, that He was "*in utero Patris*" before His actual *gennesis*. Victorinus applies the word "fœtus" to Him; "Non enim fœtus non est ante partum; sed in occulto est; generatio est manifestatio" (apud Galland, v. 8, p. 146, col. 2). Zeno says that He "prodivit *ex ore Dei* ut rerum naturam fingeret," "*cordis* ejus nobilis inquilinus," and was embraced by the Father "profundo suæ sacræ *mentis arcano* sine revelamine."

5. Hippolytus even considered that the perfection of His Sonship was not attained till His incarnation, τέλειος λόγος υἱὸς ἀτελής; but even he recognized the identity of the Son with the Logos.

6. Further, this change of the Logos into the Son was internal to the Divine Mind, Tertull. adv. Prax. 8. contr. Hermog. 18, and therefore was unlike the *probole* of the Gnostics.

7. Such an opinion was not only not inconsistent with the *Homoüsion*, but implied it. It took for granted that the Son was from the substance of the Father, and consubstantial with Him; though it implied a very defective view of the immutability and simplicity of the Divine Essence.

8. Accordingly, though I cannot allow that it was actually protected at the Council by the anathema on those who said that our Lord "was not before He was born," at least it was passed over on an occasion when the Arian error had to be definitively reprobated.

This may be said in its favour: but then, on the other hand,—

1. It seriously compromised, as I have said, the simplicity and immutability of the Divine Essence.

2. It could be resolved, with very little alteration, into Semi-Arianism on the one hand, or into Sabellianism on the other.

3. On this account it had all along been resisted with definiteness and earnestness by the Fathers of the Alexandrian School, by whom finally it was eradicated. Origen urges the doctrine of the ἀειγεννές; "Perfect Son from Perfect Father," says Gregory Thaumaturgus in his creed; "The Father being everlasting the Son is everlasting," says Dionysius; "The Father," says Alexander, "is ever Father of the ever-present Son," and Athanasius reprobates the λόγος ἐν τῷ θεῷ ἀτελὴς, γεννηθεὶς τέλειος (Orat. iv. 11). Hence Gregory Nazianzen in like manner condemns the ἀτελῆ πρότερον, εἶτα τέλειον ὥσπερ νόμος ἡμέτερος γενέσεως (Orat. xx. 9, fin.). And at length it was classed, and duly, among the heresies. "Alia (hæresis)," says Augustine, "sempiternè natum non intelligens Filium, putat illam nativitatem sumpsisse à tempore initium; et tamen volens coæternum Patri Filium confiteri, apud illum fuisse, antequàm de illo nasceretur, existimat; hoc est, semper eum fuisse, veruntamen semper eum Filium non fuisse, sed ex quo de illo natus est, Filium esse cœpisse" (Hær. 50).

However, this subject should be treated at greater length than I can allow it here.

NOTE III[1].

THE CONFESSIONS AT SIRMIUM.

(*Vide supra, p.* 314.)

I. A.D. 351. *Confession against Photinus.* (*First Sirmian Council*).

THIS Confession was published at a Council of Eastern Bishops (Coustant. in Hil. p. 1174, Note 1), and was drawn up by the whole body, Hil. de Syn. 37 (according to Sirmond. Diatr. I. Sirm. p. 366, Petavius de Trin. I. 9. § 8. Animadv. in Epiph. p. 318 init., and Coustant. in Hil. l. c.); or by Basil of Ancyra (as Valesius conjectures in Soz. iv. 22, and Larroquanus, de Liberio, p. 147); or by Mark of Arethusa, Socr. ii. 30, but Socrates, it is considered, confuses together the dates of the different Confessions, and this ascription is part of his mistake (vide Vales. in loc., Coustant. in Hil. de Syn. l. c., Petav. Animad. in Epiph. l.c.). It was written in Greek.

Till Petavius, Socrates was generally followed in ascribing all three Sirmian Confessions to this one Council, though at the same time he was generally considered mistaken as to the year. E. g. Baronius places them all in 357. Sirmond defended Baronius against Petavius (though in Facund. x. 6, Note c, he agrees with Petavius); and, assigning the third Confession to 359, adopted the improbable conjecture of two Councils, the one Catholic and the other Arian, held at Sirmium at the same time, putting forth respectively the first and second Creeds, somewhat after the manner of the contemporary rival Councils of Sardica. Pagi. Natalis

[1] From the Oxford Translation of Athanasius, p. 160.

Alexander, Valesius, de Marca, Tillemont, S. Basnage, Montfaucon, Coustant, Larroquanus agree with Petavius in placing the Council, at which Photinus was deposed and the Confession published, in A.D. 351. Mansi dates it at 358.

Gothofred considers that there were two or three successive Councils at Sirmium, between A.D. 357 and 359 (in Philostorg. Index, pp. 74, 75; Dissert. pp. 200. 211—214). Petavius, and Tillemont, speak of three Councils or Conferences held in A.D. 351. 357, and 359. Mansi, of three in 358, 359; Zaccaria (Dissert. 8) makes in all five, 349 (in which Photinus was condemned), 351; 357 (in which Hosius lapsed); 357 (following Valesius and Pagi); and 359. Mamachi makes three, 351. 357. 359; Basnage four, 351. 357, 358, 359.

This was the Confession which Pope Liberius signed, according to Baronius, Natalis Alexander, and Coustant in Hil. Note n. pp. 1335—1337, and as Tillemont thinks probable. Zaccaria says it is the general opinion, in which he is willing to concur (p. 18).

It would appear (Ath. Tr. p. 114, b.) that Photinus was condemned at Antioch in the Macrostich, A.D. 345; at Sardica, 347; at Milan, 348; and at his own See, Sirmium, 351, if not there, in 349 also;—however, as this is an intricate point on which there is considerable difference of opinion among critics, it may be advisable to state here the dates of his condemnation as they are determined by various writers.

Petavius (de Photino Hæretico, 1) enumerates in all five condemnations:—1. at Constantinople, A.D. 336, when Marcellus was deposed. 2. At Sardica, A.D. 347. 3. At Milan, A.D. 347. 4. At Sirmium, A.D. 349. 5. At Sirmium, when he was deposed, A.D. 351. Of these the 4th and 5th were first brought to light by Petavius, who omits mention of the Macrostich in 345.

Petavius is followed by Natalis Alexander, Montfaucon (vit. Athan.), and Tillemont; and by De Marca (Diss. de temp. Syn. Sirm.) and S. Basnage (Annales), and Valesius (in Theod. Hist. ii. 16. p. 23; Socr. ii. 20), as regards the Council of Milan, except that Valesius places it with Sirmond in 346; but for the Council of Sirmium in 349, they substitute a Council of Rome of the same date, while De Marca considers Photinus condemned again in the Eusebian Council of Milan in 355. De la Roque, on the other hand (Larroquan. Dissert. de Photino Hær.), considers that Photinus was condemned, 1. in the Macrostich, 344 [345]. 2. At Sardica, 347. 3. At Milan, 348. 4. At Sirmium, 350. 5. At Sirmium, 351. Zaccaria, besides 345 and 347; at Milan, 347; at Sirmium, 349; at Sirmium again, 351, when he was deposed.

Petavius seems to stand alone in assigning to the Council of Constantinople, 336, his first condemnation.

2. A.D. 357. *The Blasphemy of Potamius and Hosius (Second Sirmian).*

Hilary calls it by the above title, de Syn. 11; vide also Soz. iv. 12, p. 554. He seems also to mean it by the blasphemia Ursacii et Valentis, contr. Const. 26.

This Confession was the first overt act of disunion between Arians and Semi-Arians.

Sirmond, De Marca, and Valesius (in Socr. ii. 30), after Phœbadius, think it put forth by a Council; rather, at a Conference of a few leading Arians about Constantius, who seems to have been present; e. g. Ursacius, Valens, and Germinius. Soz. iv. 12. Vide also Hil. Fragm. vi. 7.

It was written in Latin, Socr. ii. 30. Potamius wrote very barbarous Latin, judging from the Tract ascribed to him in Dacher. Spicileg. t. 3. p. 299, unless it be a translation from the Greek, vide also Galland. Bibl. t. v. p. 96. Petavius thinks the Creed not written, but merely subscribed by Potamius (de Trin. i. 9. § 8); and Coustant (in Hil. p. 1155, Note f) that it was written by Ursacius, Valens, and Potamius. It is remarkable that the Greek in Athanasius is clearer than the original.

This at first sight is the Creed which Liberius signed, because S. Hilary speaks of the latter as "perfidia Ariana," Fragm. 6. Blondel (Prim. dans l'Eglise, p. 484), Larroquanus, &c., are of this opinion. And the Roman Breviary, Ed. Ven. 1482, and Ed. Par. 1543, in the Service for S. Eusebius of Rome, August. 14, says that "Pope Liberius consented to the Arian misbelief," Launnoi, Ep. v. 9. c. 13. Auxilius says the same, Ibid. vi. 14. Animadv. 5. n. 18. Petavius grants that it must be this, *if* any of the three Sirmian (Animadv. in Epiph. p. 316), but we shall see his own opinion presently. Zaccaria says that Hosius signed it, but not Liberius (Diss. 8. p. 20, Diss. 7). Zaccaria seems also to consider that there was another Council or Conference at Sirmium this same year, and it was at this Conference that Liberius subscribed "formulæ, quæ contra Photinum Sirmii edita fuerat, primæ scilicet Sirmiensi, in unum cum Antiochensi (against Paul of Samosata, also the creed of the Dedication) libellum conjectæ." *Vide infra.* He says he subscribed it "iterum," the first time being in Berrhœa.

3. A.D. 357. *The foregoing interpolated.*

A creed was sent into the East in Hosius's name, Epiph. Hær. 73. 14. Soz. iv. 15, p. 558, of an Anomœan character, which the "blasphemia" was not. And St. Hilary may allude to this when he speaks of the "deliramenta Osii, et *incrementa* Ursacii et Valentis," contr. Const. 23. An

Anomœan Council of Antioch under Eudoxius of this date, makes acknowledgments to Ursacius, Valens, and Germinius, Soz. iv. 12 fin. as being agents in the Arianizing of the West.

Petavius and Tillemont consider this Confession to be the "blasphemia" interpolated. Petavius throws out a further conjecture, which seems gratuitous, that the whole of the latter part of the Creed is a later addition, and that Liberius only signed the former part. Animadv. in Epiph. p. 316.

4. A.D. 358. *The Ancyrene Anathemas.*

The Semi-Arian party had met in Council at Ancyra in the early spring of 358 to protest against the "blasphemia," and that with some kind of correspondence with the Gallic Bishops who had just condemned it, Phœbadius of Agen writing a Tract against it, which is still extant. They had drawn up and signed, besides a Synodal Letter, eighteen anathemas, the last against the "Consubstantial." These, except the last, or the last six, they submitted at the end of May to the Emperor who was again at Sirmium. Basil, Eustathius, Eleusius, and another formed the deputation; and their influence persuaded Constantius to accept the Anathemas, and even to oblige the party of Valens, at whose "blasphemia" they were levelled, to recant and subscribe them.

5. A.D. 358. *Semi-Arian Digest of Three Confessions.*

The Semi-Arian Bishops, pursuing their advantage, composed a Creed out of three, that of the Dedication, the first Sirmian, and the Creed of Antioch against Paul, 264—270, in which the "Consubstantial" is said to have been omitted or forbidden, Soz. iv. 15. This Confession was imposed by Imperial authority on the Arian party, who signed it. So did Liberius, Soz. ibid. Hil. Fragm. vi. 6, 7; and Petavius considers that this is the subscription by which he lapsed, de Trin. i. 9. § 5, Animadv. in Epiph. p. 316, and so Zaccaria, as above, and S. Basnage, in Ann. 358. 13.

It is a point of controversy whether or not the Arians at this time suppressed the "blasphemia." Socrates and Sozomen say that they made an attempt to recall the copies they had issued, and even obtained an edict from the Emperor for this purpose, but without avail. Socr. ii. 30 fin. Soz. iv. 6, p. 543.

Athanasius, on the other hand, de Syn. 29, relates this in substance of the third Confession of Sirmium, not of the "blasphemia" or second.

Tillemont follows Socrates and Sozomen, considering that Basil's influence with the Emperor enabled him now to insist on a retraction of the "blasphemia." And he argues that Germinius in 366, being suspected of orthodoxy, and obliged to make profession of heresy, was referred by his party to the formulary of Ariminum, no notice being taken of the "blasphemia," which looks as if it were suppressed; whereas Germinius himself appeals to the third Sirmian, which is a proof that it was not suppressed. Hil. Fragm. 15. Coustant, in Hil. contr. Const. 26, though he does not adopt the opinion himself, observes, that the charge brought against Basil, Soz. iv. 132, Hil. l. c., by the Acacians, of persuading the Africans against the second Sirmian is an evidence of a great effort on his part, at a time when he had the Court with him, to suppress it. We have just seen Basil uniting with the Gallic Bishops against it.

6. A.D. 359. *The Confession with a date (Third Sirmian).*

The Semi-Arians, with the hope of striking a further blow

at their opponents by a judgment against the Anomœans, Soz. iv. 16 init., seem to have suggested a general Council, which ultimately became the Councils of Seleucia and Ariminum. If this was their measure, they were singularly out-manœuvred by the party of Acacius and Valens, as may be seen in Athanasius's *de Synodis.* A preparatory Conference was held at Sirmium at the end of May in this year, in which the Creed was determined which should be laid before the great Councils then assembling. Basil and Mark were the chief Semi-Arians present, and in the event became committed to an almost Arian Confession. Soz. iv. 16, p. 562. It was finally settled on the Eve of Pentecost, and the dispute lasted till morning. Epiph. Hær. 73, 22. Mark at length was chosen to draw it up, Soz. iv. 22, p. 573, yet Valens so managed that Basil could not sign it without an explanation. It was written in Latin, Socr. ii. 30, Soz. iv. 17, p. 563. Coustant, however, in Hil. p. 1152, note i., seems to consider this dispute and Mark's confession to belong to the same date (May 22,) in the foregoing year; but p. 1363, note b, he seems to change his opinion.

Petavius, who, Animadv. in Epiph. p. 318, follows Socrates in considering that the second Sirmian is the Confession which the Arians tried to suppress, nevertheless, de Trin. i. 9, § 8, yields to the testimony of Athanasius in behalf of the third, attributing the measure to their dissatisfaction with the phrase "Like in all things," which Constantius had inserted, and with Basil's explanation on subscribing it, and to the hopes of publishing a bolder creed which their increasing influence with Constantius inspired. He does not think it impossible, however, that an attempt was made to suppress both. Coustant, again, in Hil. p. 1363, note b, asks *when* it could be that the Eusebians attempted to suppress the second Confession; and conjectures that the ridicule which followed their dating of the third and their wish to get rid of the "Like in all things," were the causes of their anxiety about it. He observes too with considerable speciousness that Acacius's Second formulary at Seleucia (Athan. de Syn. 29), and the Confession of Nice (Ibid. 30), resemble second editions of the third Sirmian. Valesius, in Socr. ii. 30, and Montfaucon, in Athan. Syn. § 29, take the same side.

Pagi in Ann. 357. n. 13, supposes that the third Sirmian was the Creed signed by Liberius. Yet Coustant in Hil. p. 1335, note n, speaking of Liberius's "perfidia Ariana," as St. Hilary calls it, says, "Solus Valesius existimat tertiam [confessionem] hic memorari:" whereas Valesius, making four, not to say five, Sirmian Creeds, understands Liberius to have signed, not the third, but an intermediate one, between the second and third, as Petavius does, in Soz. iv. 15 and 16. Moreover, Pagi fixes the date as A.D. 358 ibid.

This Creed, thus drawn up by a Semi-Arian, with an Acacian or Arian Appendix, then a Semi-Arian insertion, and after all a Semi-Arian protest on subscription, was proposed at Seleucia by Acacius, Soz. iv. 22, and at Ariminum by Valens, Socr. ii. 37, p. 132.

7. A.D. 359. *Nicene Edition of the Third Sirmian.*

The third Sirmian was rejected both at Seleucia and Ariminum; but the Eusebians, dissolving the Council of Seleucia, kept the Fathers at Ariminum together through the summer and autumn. Meanwhile at Nice in Thrace they confirmed the third Sirmian, Socr. ii. 37, p. 141, Theod. Hist. ii. 16, with the additional proscription of the word *hypostasis;* apparently lest the Latins should by means of it evade the condemnation of the "consubstantial." This Creed, thus altered, was ultimately accepted at Ariminum; and was confirmed in January 360 at Constantinople; Socr. ii. 41, p. 163. Soz. iv. 24 init.

Liberius retrieved his fault on this occasion ; for, whatever was the confession he had signed, he now refused his assent to the Ariminian, and, if Socrates is to be trusted, was banished in consequence, Socr. ii. 37, p. 140.

NOTE IV.[1]

THE TERMS *usia* AND *hypostasis*, AS USED IN THE EARLY CHURCH.

(*Vide supra, p.* 186.)

1. EVEN before we take into account the effect which would naturally be produced on the first Christians by the novelty and mysteriousness of doctrines which depend for their reception simply upon Revelation, we have reason to anticipate that there would be difficulties and mistakes in expressing them, when they first came to be set forth by unauthoritative writers. Even in secular sciences, inaccuracy of thought and language is but gradually corrected; that is, in proportion as their subject-matter is thoroughly scrutinized and mastered by the co-operation of many independent intellects, successively engaged upon it. Thus, for instance, the word *Person* requires the rejection of various popular senses, and a careful definition, before it can serve for philosophical uses. We sometimes use it for an *individual* as contrasted with a class or multitude, as when we speak of having "personal objections" to another; sometimes for the *body*, in contrast to the soul, as when we speak of "beauty of person." We sometimes use it in the abstract, as when we speak of another as "insignificant in person;" sometimes in the concrete, as when we call him "an insignificant person." How divergent in meaning are the derivatives, *personable*, *personalities*, *personify*, *personation*, *personage*, *parsonage!* This variety arises partly from our own carelessness, partly from the necessary developments of

[1] From the *Atlantis*, July, 1858.

language, partly from the exuberance of human thought, partly from the defects of our vernacular tongue.

Language then requires to be refashioned even for sciences which are based on the senses and the reason; but much more will this be the case, when we are concerned with subject-matters, of which, in our present state, we cannot possibly form any complete or consistent conception, such as the Catholic doctrines of the Trinity and Incarnation. Since they are from the nature of the case above our intellectual reach, and were unknown till the preaching of Christianity, they required on their first promulgation new words, or words used in new senses, for their due enunciation; and, since these were not definitely supplied by Scripture or by tradition, nor, for centuries, by ecclesiastical authority, variety in the use, and confusion in the apprehension of them, were unavoidable in the interval. This conclusion is necessary, admitting the premisses, antecedently to particular instances in proof.

Moreover, there is a presumption equally strong, that the variety and confusion that I have anticipated, would in matter of fact issue here or there in actual heterodoxy, as often as the language of theologians was misunderstood by hearers or readers, and deductions were made from it which the teacher did not intend. Thus, for instance, the word *Person*, used in the doctrine of the Holy Trinity, would on first hearing suggest Tritheism to one who made the word synonymous with *individual;* and Unitarianism to another, who accepted it in the classical sense of a *mask* or *character.*

Even to this day our theological language is wanting in accuracy: thus, we sometimes speak of the controversies concerning the *Person* of Christ, when we mean to include in them those also which belong to the two *natures* which are predicated of Him.

Indeed, the difficulties of forming a theological phraseology for the whole of Christendom were obviously so great, that we need not wonder at the reluctance which the first age of Catholic divines showed in attempting it, even apart from the obstacles caused by the distraction and isolation of the churches in times of persecution. Not only had the words to be adjusted and explained which were peculiar to different schools or traditional in different places, but there was the formidable necessity of creating a common measure between two, or rather three languages,—Latin, Greek, and Syriac. The intellect had to be satisfied, error had to be successfully excluded, parties the most contrary to each other, and the most obstinate, had to be convinced. The very confidence which would be felt by Christians in general that Apostolic truth would never fail,—and that they held it in each locality themselves and the *orbis terrarum* with them, in spite of all verbal contrarieties,—would indispose them to define it, till definition became an imperative duty.

2. I think this plain from the nature of the case; and history confirms me in the instance of the celebrated word *homoüsion*, which, as one of the first and most necessary steps, so again was apparently one of the most discouraging, in the attempt to give a scientific expression to doctrine. This formula, as Athanasius, Hilary, and Basil affirm, had been disowned, as savouring of heterodoxy, by the great Council of Antioch in A.D. 264—269; yet, in spite of this disavowal on the part of Bishops of the highest authority, it was imposed on all the faithful to the end of time in the Ecumenical Council of Nicæa, A.D. 325, as the one and only safeguard, as it really is, of orthodox teaching. The misapprehensions and protests which, after such antecedents, its adoption occasioned for many years, may be easily imagined. Though above three hundred Bishops had accepted it at Nicæa, the great body of the Episcopate in the next generation considered it inexpedient; and Athanasius himself, whose imperishable name is bound up with it, showed himself most

cautious in putting it forward, though he knew it had the sanction of a General Council. Moreover, the word does not occur in the *Catecheses* of St. Cyril of Jerusalem, A.D. 347, nor in the recantation made before Pope Julius by Ursacius and Valens, A.D. 349, nor in the cross-questionings to which St. Ambrose subjected Palladius and Secundianus, A.D. 381. At Seleucia, A.D. 359, as many as 100 Eastern Bishops, besides the Arian party, were found to abandon it, while at Ariminum in the same year the celebrated scene took place of 400 Bishops of the West being worried and tricked into a momentary act of the same character. They had not yet got it deeply fixed into their minds, as a sort of first principle, that to abandon the formula was to betray the faith.

3. This disinclination on the part of Catholics to dogmatic definitions was not confined to the instance of the *homoüsion.* In the use of the word *hypostasis,* a variation was even allowed by the authority of a Council [A.D. 362]; and the circumstances under which it was allowed, and the possibility of allowing it, without compromising Catholic truth, shall here be considered.

As to the use of the word. At least in the West, and in St. Athanasius's day, it was usual to speak of one *hypostasis,* as of one *usia,* of the Divine Nature. Thus the so-called Sardican Creed, A.D. 347, speaks of "one *hypostasis,* which the heretics call *usia.*" Theod. Hist. ii. 8; the Roman Council under Damasus, A.D. 371, says that the Three Persons are of the same *hypostasis* and *usia;* and the Nicene Anathema condemns those who say that the Son "came from other *hypostasis* or *usia.*" Epiphanius too speaks of "one *hypostasis,*" *Hær.* 74, 4, *Ancor.* 6 (and though he has the *hypostases, Hær.* 62, 3, 72, 1, yet he is shy of the plural, and prefers "the *hypostatic* Father, the *hypostatic* Son," &c., *ibid.* 3 and 4, *Ancor.* 6; and τρία, as *Hær.* 74, 4, where he says "three *hypostatic* of the same *hypostasis;*"

vide also "in *hypostasis* of perfection," *Hær.* 74, 12, *Ancor.* 7 *et alibi);* and Cyril of Jerusalem of the "uniform *hypostasis*" of God, *Catech.* vi. 7, vide also xvi. 12 and xvii. 9 (though the word may be construed one out of three in *Cat.* xi. 3); and Gregory Nazianzen, *Orat.* xxviii, 9, where he is speaking as a Natural, not as a Christian theologian.

In the preceding century Gregory Thaumaturgus had laid it down that the Father and the Son were in *hypostasis* one, and the Council of Antioch, A.D. 264—269, calls the Son in *usia* and *hypostasis* God, the Son of God. Routh, *Reliq.* t. 2, p. 466. Accordingly Athanasius expressly tells us, "*Hypostasis* is *usia*, and means nothing else but *αὐτὸ τὸ ὄν*," *ad Afros*, 4. Jerome says that "Tota sæcularium litterarum schola nihil aliud *hypostasin* nisi *usiam* novit," *Epist.* xv. 4; Basil, the Semi-Arian, that "the Fathers have called *hypostasis usia*," Epiph. *Hær*, 73, 12, fin. And Socrates says that at least it was frequently used for *usia*, when it had entered into the philosophical schools. *Hist.* iii. 7.

On the other hand the Alexandrians, Origen *(in Joan.* ii. 6 *et alibi)*, Ammonius *(ap. Caten. in Joan.* x. 30, if genuine), Dionysius *(ap.* Basil *de Sp. S.* n. 72), and Alexander *(ap.* Theod. *Hist.* i. 4), speak of more *hypostases* than one in the Divine Nature, that is, of Three; and apparently without the support of the divines of any other school, unless Eusebius, who is half an Alexandrian, be an exception. Going down beyond the middle of the fourth century, we find the Alexandrian Didymus committing himself to a bold and strong enunciation of the Three *hypostases*, (e.g. de Trin. I. 18, &c.), which is almost without a parallel in patristical literature.

It was under these circumstances that the Council of Alexandria in A.D. 362, to which I have already referred, a Council in which Athanasius and Eusebius of Vercellæ were the chief actors, determined to leave the sense and use of the word open, so that, according to the custom of their own church or school, Catholics might freely speak of three *hypostases* or of one.

Thus we are brought to the practice of Athanasius himself. It is remarkable that he should so far innovate on the custom of his own Church, as to use the word in each of these two applications of it. In his *In illud Omnia* he speaks of "the three perfect *Hypostases.*" On the other hand, he makes *usia* and *hypostasis* synonymous in *Orat.* iii. 65, 66, *Orat.* iv. 1 and 33 fin.

There is something more remarkable still in this innovation. Alexander, his immediate predecessor and master, published, A.D. 320—324, two formal letters against Arius, one addressed to his namesake of Constantinople, the other encyclical. It is scarcely possible to doubt that the latter was written by Athanasius; it is so unlike the former in style and diction, so like the writings of Athanasius. Now it is observable that in the former the word *hypostasis* occurs in its Alexandrian sense at least five times; in the latter, which I attribute to Athanasius, it is dropped, and *usia* is introduced, which is absent from the former. That is, Athanasius has, on this supposition, when writing in his Bishop's name a formal document, pointedly innovated on his Bishop's theological language, and that the received language of his own Church. I am not supposing he did this without Alexander's sanction. Indeed the character of the Arian polemic would naturally lead Alexander, as well as Athanasius, to be suspicious of their own formula of the "Three *Hypostases,*" which Arianism was using against them; and the latter would be confirmed in this feeling by his subsequent familiarity with Latin theology, and the usage of the Holy See, which, under Pope Damasus, as we have seen, A.D. 371, spoke of one *hypostasis*, and in the previous century, A.D. 260, protested by anticipation in the person of Pope Dionysius against the use, which might be made in the hands of enemies, of the formula of the Three *Hypostases.* Still it is undeniable that Athanasius does at least once speak of Three, though his practice is to dispense with the word and to use others instead of it.

4. Now then we come to the explanation of this difference of usage in the application of the word. It is difficult to believe that so accurate a thinker as Athanasius really used an important term in two distinct, nay contrasted senses; and I cannot but question the fact, so commonly taken for granted, that the divines of the beginning of the fourth century had appropriated any word whatever definitely to express either the idea of *Person* as contrasted with that of *Essence*, or of *Essence* as contrasted with *Person.* I altogether doubt whether we are correct in saying that they meant by *hypostasis*, in one country *Person*, in another *Essence.* I think such propositions should be carefully proved, instead of being taken for granted, as at present is the case. Meanwhile, I have an hypothesis of my own. I think they used the word both in East and West in one and the same substantial sense; with some accidental variation or latitude indeed, but that of so slight a character, as would admit of Athanasius, or any one else, speaking of one *hypostasis* or three, without any violence to that sense which remained on the whole one and the same. What this sense is I proceed to explain :—

The school-men are known to have insisted with great earnestness on the numerical unity of the Divine Being; each of the three Divine Persons being one and the same God, unicus, singularis, et totus Deus. In this, however, they did but follow the recorded doctrine of the Western theologians of the fifth century, as I suppose will be allowed by critics generally. So forcible is St. Austin upon the strict unity of God, that he even thinks it necessary to caution his readers lest they should suppose that he could allow them to speak of

One Person as well as of Three in the Divine nature *de Trin.*, vii. 11. Again, in the (so-called) Athanasian Creed, the same elementary truth is emphatically insisted on. The neuter *unum* of former divines is changed into the masculine, in enunciating the mystery. "Non tres æterni, sed unus æternus." I suppose this means, that each Divine Person is to be received as the one God as entirely and absolutely as He would be held to be, if we had never heard of the other Two, and that He is not in any respect less than the one and only God, because They are each that same one God also; or in other words, that, as each human individual being has one personality, the Divine Being has three.

Returning then to Athanasius, I consider that this same mystery is implied in his twofold application of the word *hypostasis*. The polytheism and pantheism of the heathen world imagined,—not the God whom natural reason can discover, conceive, and worship, one individual, living, and personal,—but a *divinitas*, which was either a quality, whether energy or life, or an extended substance, or something else equally inadequate to the real idea which the word conveys. Such a divinity could not properly be called an *hypostasis* or said to be *in hypostasi* (except indeed as brute matter may be called, as in one sense it can be called, an *hypostasis*), and therefore it was, that that word had some fitness, especially after the Apostle's adoption of it, *Hebr.* i. 3 to denote the Christian's God. And this may account for the remark of Socrates, that it was a new word, strange to the schools of ancient philosophy, which had seldom professed pure theism or natural theology. "The teachers of philosophy among the Greeks," he says, "have defined *usia* in many ways: but of *hypostasis*, they have made no mention at all. Irenæus, the grammarian, affirms that the word is barbarous." —*Hist.* iii. 7. The better then was it fitted to express that highest object of thought, of which the "barbarians" of Palestine had been the special witnesses. When the divine *hypostasis* was confessed, the word expressed or suggested the attributes of individuality, self-subsistence, self-action, and personality, such as go to form the idea of the Divine Being to the natural theologian ; and, since the difference between the theist and the Catholic divine in their idea of His nature is simply this, that, in opposition to the Pantheist, who cannot understand how the Infinite can be Personal at all, the one ascribes to him one personality, and the other three, it will be easily seen how a word, thus characterized and circumstanced, would admit of being used with but a slight modification of its sense, of the Trinity as well as of the Unity.

Let us take, by way of illustration, the word *monad*, which when applied to intellectual beings, includes the idea of personality. Dionysius of Alexandria, for instance, speaks of the *monad* and the *triad:* now, would it be very harsh, if, as he has spoken of "three *hypostases*" in monad so he had instead spoken of "the three monads," that is, in the sense of "thrice hypostatic *monad*," as if the intrinsic force of the word *monas* would preclude the possibility of his use of the plural *monad*s being mistaken to imply that he held more *monads* than one? To take an analogous case, it would be about the same improper use of plural for singular, if we said that a martyr by his one act gained three victories instead of a triple victory, over his three spiritual foes. And indeed, though Athanasius does not directly speak of three monads, yet he implies the possibility of such phraseology by teaching that, though the Father and the Son are two, the *monas* of the Deity (θεότης) is indivisible, and that the Deity is at once Father and Son.

This, then, is what I conceive that he means by sometimes speaking of one, somtimes of three *hypostases.* The word *hypostasis* stands neither for *Person* nor for *Essence* exclusively ; but it means the one Personal God of natural theology, the notion of whom the Catholic corrects and completes as often as he views him as a Trinity; of which correction Nazianzen's language (*Orat.* xxviii. 9) contrasted with his usual formula (*vid. Orat.* xx. 6) of the Three *Hypostases*, is an illustration. The specification of three *hypostases* does not substantially alter the sense of the word itself, but is a sort of *catachresis* by which this Catholic doctrine is forcibly brought out) as it would be by the phrase "three monads"), viz. that each of the Divine Persons is simply the Unus et Singularis Deus. If it be objected, that by the same mode of reasoning, Athanasius might have said *catachrestically* not only three *monads* or three *hypostases*, but three Gods, I deny it, and for this reason, because *hypostasis* is not equivalent to the simple idea of God, but is rather a definition of Him, and that in some special elementary points, as essence, personality, &c., and because such a mere improper use or varying application of the term *hypostasis* would not tend to compromise a truth, which never must even in forms of speech be trifled with, the absolute numerical unity of the Supreme Being. Though a Catholic could not say that there are three Gods, he could say, that the *definition* of God applies to *unus* and *tres*. Perhaps it is for this reason that Epiphanius speaks of the "*hypostatic* Three," "co-*hypostatic*," "of the same *hypostasis*," *Hær.* 74, 4 (*vid.* Jerome, *Ep.* 15, 3), in the spirit in which St. Thomas, I think, interprets the "non tres æterni, sed unus æternus," to turn on the contrast of adjective and substantive.

Petavius makes a remark which is apposite to my present purpose. "Nomen Dei," he says, *de Trin.* iii. 9. § 10, "cùm sit ex eorum genere quæ concreta dicuntur, formam significat, non abstractam ab individuis proprietatibus, sed in iis subsistentem. Est enim Deus substantia aliqua divinitatem habens. Sicut homo non humanam naturam separatam, sed in aliquo individuo subsistentem exponit, ita tamen ut individuum ac personam, non certam ac determinatam, sed confuse infiniteque representet, hoc est, *naturam in aliquo*, ut diximus, *consistentem* . . . sic nomen Dei propriè ac directe divinitatem naturamque divinam indicat, *assignificat autem eundem, ut in quâpiam personâ subsistentem, nullam de tribus expresse designans, sed confuse et universe.*" Here this great author seems to say, that even the word "Deus" may stand, not barely for the Divine Being, but besides "in quâpiam personâ subsistentem," without denoting *which* Person; and in like manner I would understand *hypostasis* to mean the *monas* with a like indeterminate notion of personality, (without which attribute the idea of God cannot be,) and thus, according as one *hypostasis* is spoken of, or three, the word may be roughly translated, in the one case "personal substance," or "being with personality," in the other "substantial person," or "person which is in being." In all cases it will be equivalent to the Deity, to the *monad*, to the divine *usia*, &c., though with that peculiarity of meaning which I have insisted on.

5. Since, as has been said above, *hypostasis* is a word more peculiarly Christian than *usia*, I have judged it best to speak of it first, that the meaning of it, as it has now been ascertained on inquiry, may serve as a key for explaining other parallel terms. *Usia* is one of these the most in use, certainly in the works of Athanasius; and we have his authority as well as St. Jerome's for stating that it was once simply synonymous with *hypostasis*. Moreover, in *Orat.* iii. 65, he uses the two words as equivalent to each other. If this be so, what has been said above in explanation of the sense he put on the word *hypostasis*, will apply to *usia* also. This conclusion is corroborated by the proper meaning of the word *usia* itself which answers to the English word "being." Now, when we speak of the Divine Being, we mean to speak of Him, as what he is, ὁ ὢν, including generally His attributes and characteristics, and among them, at least obscurely, His personality. By the "*Divine Being*" we do not commonly mean a mere *anima mundi*, or first principle of life or system

of laws. *Usia* then, thus considered, agrees very nearly in sense, from its very etymology, with *hypostasis.* Further, this was the sense in which Aristotle used it, viz. for what is "individuum," and "numero unum;" and it must not be forgotten that the Neo-platonists, who exerted so great an influence on the Alexandrian Church, professed the Aristotelic logic. And so St. Cyril himself, the successor of Athanasius (Suicer, *Thes. in voce, οὐσία.*)

This is the word, and not *hypostasis*, which Athanasius commonly uses in controversy with the Arians, to express the divinity of the Word. He speaks of the *usia* of the Son as being united to the Father, and His *usia* being the offspring of the Father's *usia.* In these and other passages *usia,* I conceive, is substantially equivalent to *hypostasis,* as I have explained it, viz. expressing the divine μονὰς with an obscure intimation of personality inclusively; and here I think I am able to quote the words of Father Passaglia, as agreeing (so far) in what I have said. "Quum *hypostasis,*" he says, *de Trinitate*, p. 1302, "esse nequeat sine substantiâ, nihil vetabat quominus trium hypostasum defensores *hypostasim* interdum pro substantiâ sumerent, præsertim ubi *hypostasis* opponitur rei non subsistenti ac efficientiæ." I should wish to complete the admission by adding, "Since an intellectual *usia* naturally implies an *hypostasis*, there was nothing to hinder *usia* being used, when *hypostasis* had to be expressed."

6. After what I have said of *usia* and *hypostasis*, it will not surprise the reader if I consider that φύσις (nature) also, in the Alexandrian theology, was equally capable of being applied to the Divine Being viewed as One, or viewed as Three or each of the Three separately. Thus Athanasius says, One is the Divine Nature, *(contr. Apoll.* ii. 13 *fin. de Incarn. V.* fin.) Alexander, on the other hand, calls the Father and Son the "two *hypostatic* natures," and speaks of the "only begotten nature," (Theod. Hist. i. 4,) and Clement of "the Son's nature" as "most intimately near the sole Almighty,"

(Strom. vii. 2,) and Cyril of a "generating nature" and a "generated" (Thes. xi. p. 85) and, in words celebrated in theological history, of "the Word's One Nature incarnate."

7. Εἶδος is a word of a similar character. As it is found in *John* v. 37, it may be indifferently interpreted of essence or of person; the Vulgate translates it "neque *speciem* ejus vidistis." In Athan. *Orat.* iii. 3, it is synonymous with *deity* or *usia;* as *ibid.* 6 also; and apparently in *ibid.* 16, where the Son is said to have the *species* of the Father. And so in *de Syn.* 52. Athanasius says that there is only one "species deitatis." Yet, as taken from *Gen.* xxxii. 31, it is considered to denote the Son; *e.g.* Athan. *Orat.* i. 20, where it is used as synonymous with Image, εἰκών. In like manner the Son is called "the very species deitatis." *Ep. Æg.* 17. But again in Athan. *Orat.* iii. 6, it is first said that the *species* of the Father and Son are one and the same, then that the Son is the *species* of the Father's (deity), and then that the Son is the *species* of the Father.

The outcome of this investigation is this:—that we need not by an officious piety arbitrarily force the language of separate Fathers into a sense which it cannot bear; nor by an unjust and narrow criticism accuse them of error; nor impose upon an early age a distinction of terms belonging to a later. The words *usia* and *hypostasis* were, naturally and intelligibly, for three or four centuries, practically synonymous, and were used indiscriminately for two ideas, which were afterwards respectively denoted by the one and the other.

NOTE V.[1]

THE ORTHODOXY OF THE BODY OF THE FAITHFUL DURING THE SUPREMACY OF ARIANISM.

(*Vide supra*, p. 358.)

THE episcopate, whose action was so prompt and concordant at Nicæa on the rise of Arianism, did not, as a class or order of men, play a good part in the troubles consequent upon the Council; and the laity did. The Catholic people, in the length and breadth of Christendom, were the obstinate champions of Catholic truth, and the bishops were not. Of course there were great and illustrious exceptions; first, Athanasius, Hilary, the Latin Eusebius, and Phœbadius; and after them, Basil, the two Gregories, and Ambrose; there are others, too, who suffered, if they did nothing else, as Eustathius, Paulus, Paulinus, and Dionysius; and the Egyptian bishops, whose weight was small in the Church in proportion to the great power of their Patriarch. And, on the other hand, as I shall say presently, there were exceptions to the Christian heroism of the laity, especially in some of the great towns. And again, in speaking of the laity, I speak inclusively of their parish-priests (so to call them), at least in many places; but on the whole, taking a wide view of the history, we are obliged to say that the governing body of the Church came short, and the governed were pre-eminent in faith, zeal, courage, and constancy.

This is a very remarkable fact: but there is a moral in it. Perhaps it was permitted, in order to impress upon the Church at that very time passing out of her state of persecution to

[1] From the *Rambler*, July, 1859.

her long temporal ascendancy, the great evangelical lesson, that, not the wise and powerful, but the obscure, the unlearned, and the weak constitute her real strength. It was mainly by the faithful people that Paganism was overthrown; it was by the faithful people, under the lead of Athanasius and the Egyptian bishops, and in some places supported by their Bishops or priests, that the worst of heresies was withstood and stamped out of the sacred territory.

The contrast stands as follows:—

I.

1. A.D. 325. The great Council of Nicæa of 318 Bishops, chiefly from the eastern provinces of Christendom, under the presidency of Hosius of Cordova. It was convoked against Arianism, which it once for all anathematized; and it inserted the formula of the "Consubstantial" into the Creed, with the view of establishing the fundamental dogma which Arianism impugned. It is the first Œcumenical Council, and recognized at the time its own authority as the voice of the infallible Church. It is so received by the *orbis terrarum* at this day.

2. A.D. 326. St. Athanasius, the great champion of the Homoüsion, was elected Bishop of Alexandria.

3. A.D. 334, 335. The Synods of Cæsarea and Tyre (sixty Bishops) against Athanasius, who was therein accused and formally condemned of rebellion, sedition, and ecclesiastical tyranny; of murder, sacrilege, and magic; deposed from his See, forbidden to set foot in Alexandria for life, and banished to Gaul. Also, they received Arius into communion.

4. A.D. 341. Council of Rome of fifty Bishops, attended by the exiles from Thrace, Syria, &c., by Athanasius, &c., in which Athanasius was pronounced innocent.

5. A.D. 341. Great Council of the Dedication at Antioch, attended by ninety or a hundred Bishops. The council ratified the proceedings of the Councils of Cæsarea and Tyre,

and placed an Arian in the See of Athanasius. Then it proceeded to pass a dogmatic decree in reversal of the formula of the "Consubstantial." Four or five creeds, instead of the Nicene, were successively adopted by the assembled Fathers.

Three of these were circulated in the neighbourhood; but as they wished to send one to Rome, they directed a fourth to be drawn up. This, too, apparently failed.

6. A.D. 345. Council of the creed called Macrostich. This Creed suppressed, as did the third, the word "substance." The eastern Bishops sent this to the Bishops of France, who rejected it.

7. A.D. 347. The great Council of Sardica, attended by more than 300 Bishops. Before it commenced, a division between its members broke out on the question whether or not Athanasius should have a seat in it. In consequence, seventy-six retired to Philippopolis, on the Thracian side of Mount Hæmus, and there excommunicated the Pope and the Sardican Fathers. These seceders published a sixth confession of faith. The Synod of Sardica, including Bishops from Italy, Gaul, Africa, Egypt, Cyprus, and Palestine, confirmed the act of the Roman Council, and restored Athanasius and the other exiles to their Sees. The Synod of Philippopolis, on the contrary, sent letters to the civil magistrates of those cities, forbidding them to admit the exiles into them. The Imperial power took part with the Sardican Fathers, and Athanasius went back to Alexandria.

8. A.D. 351. The Bishops of the East met at Sirmium. The semi-Arian Bishops began to detach themselves from the Arians, and to form a separate party. Under pretence of putting down a kind of Sabellianism, they drew up a new creed, into which they introduced the language of some of the ante-Nicene writers on the subject of our Lord's divinity, and dropped the word "substance."

9. A.D. 353. The Council of Arles. The Pope sent to it

several Bishops as legates. The Fathers of the Council, including the Pope's legate, Vincent, subscribed the condemnation of Athanasius. Paulinus, Bishop of Treves, was nearly the only one who stood up for the Nicene faith and for Athanasius. He was accordingly banished into Phrygia, where he died.

10. A.D. 355. The Council of Milan, of more than 300 Bishops of the West. Nearly all of them subscribed the condemnation of Athanasius; whether they generally subscribed the heretical creed, which was brought forward, does not appear. The Pope's four legates remained firm, and St. Dionysius of Milan, who died an exile in Asia Minor. An Arian was put into his See. Saturninus, the Bishop of Arles, proceeded to hold a Council at Beziers; and its Fathers banished St. Hilary to Phrygia.

11. A.D. 357-9. The Arians and Semi-Arians successively drew up fresh creeds at Sirmium.

12. A.D. 357-8. Hosius' fall. "Constantius used such violence towards the old man, and confined him so straitly, that at last, broken by suffering, he was brought, though hardly, to hold communion with Valens and Ursacius [the Arian leaders], though he would not subscribe against Athanasius." Athan. *Arian. Hist.* 45.

13. A.D. 357-8. And Liberius. "The tragedy was not ended in the lapse of Hosius, but in the evil which befell Liberius, the Roman Pontiff, it became far more dreadful and mournful, considering that he was Bishop of so great a city, and of the whole Catholic Church, and that he had so bravely resisted Constantius two years previously. There is nothing, whether in the historians and holy fathers, or in his own letters, to prevent our coming to the conclusion, that Liberius communicated with the Arians, and confirmed the sentence passed by them against Athanasius; but he is not at all on that account to be called a heretic." Baron. Ann. 357, 38-45. Athanasius says: "Liberius, after he had been

in banishment for two years, gave way, and from fear of threatened death was induced to subscribe. *Arian. Hist.* § 41. St. Jerome says: "Liberius, tædio victus exilii, et in hæreticam pravitatem subscribens, Romam quasi victor intraverat." *Chron.* ed. Val. p. 797.

14. A.D. 359. The great Councils of Seleucia and Ariminum, being one bi-partite Council, representing the East and West respectively. At Seleucia there were 150 Bishops, of which only the twelve or thirteen from Egypt were champions of the Nicene "Consubstantial." At Ariminum there were as many as 400 Bishops, who, worn out by the artifice of long delay on the part of the Arians, abandoned the "Consubstantial," and subscribed the ambiguous formula which the heretics had substituted for it.

15. About A.D. 360, St. Hilary says: "I am not speaking of things foreign to my knowledge; I am not writing about what I am ignorant of; I have heard and I have seen the shortcomings of persons who are round about me, not of laymen, but of Bishops. For, excepting the Bishop Eleusius and a few with him, for the most part the ten Asian provinces, within whose boundaries I am situate, are truly ignorant of God." *De Syn.* 63. It is observable, that even Eleusius, who is here spoken of as somewhat better than the rest, was a Semi-Arian, according to Socrates, and even a persecutor of Catholics at Constantinople; and, according to Sozomen, one of those who were active in causing Pope Liberius to give up the Nicene formula of the "Consubstantial." By the ten Asian provinces is meant the east and south provinces of Asia Minor, pretty nearly as cut off by a line passing from Cyzicus to Seleucia through Synnada.

16. A.D. 360. St. Gregory Nazianzen says, about this date: "Surely the pastors have done foolishly; for, excepting a very few, who either on account of their insignificance were passed over, or who by reason of their virtue resisted, and who were to be left as a seed and root for the springing

up again and revival of Israel by the influences of the Spirit, all temporized, only differing from each other in this, that some succumbed earlier, and others later; some were foremost champions and leaders in the impiety, and others joined the second rank of the battle, being overcome by fear, or by interest, or by flattery, or, what was the most excusable, by their own ignorance." *Orat.* xxi. 24.

17. A.D. 361. About this time, St. Jerome says: "Nearly all the churches in the whole world, under the pretence of peace and of the emperor, are polluted with the communion of the Arians." *Chron.* Of the same date, that is, upon the Council of Ariminum, are his famous words, "Ingemuit totus orbis et se esse Arianum miratus est." *In Lucif.* 19. "The Catholics of Christendom were strangely surprised to find that the Council had made Arians of them."

18. A.D. 362. State of the Church of Antioch at this time. There were four Bishops or communions of Antioch; first, the old succession and communion, which had possession before the Arian troubles; secondly, the Arian succession, which had lately conformed to orthodoxy in the person of Meletius; thirdly, the new Latin succession, lately created by Lucifer, whom some have thought the Pope's legate there; and, fourthly, the new Arian succession, which was started upon the recantation of Meletius. At length, as Arianism was brought under, the evil reduced itself to two Episcopal Successions, that of Meletius and the Latin, which went on for many years, the West and Egypt holding communion with the latter, and the East with the former.

19. St. Hilary speaks of the series of ecclesiastical Councils of that time in the following well-known passage: "Since the Nicene Council, we have done nothing but write the Creed. While we fight about words, inquire about novelties, take advantage of ambiguities, criticize authors, fight on party questions, have difficulties in agreeing, and prepare to anathematize each other, there is scarce a man who belongs to

Christ. Take, for instance, last year's Creed, what alteration is there not in it already? First, we have the Creed, which bids us not to use the Nicene 'consubstantial;' then comes another, which decrees and preaches it; next, the third, excuses the word 'substance,' as adopted by the Fathers in their simplicity; lastly, the fourth, which instead of excusing, condemns. We determine creeds by the year or by the month, we change our own determinations, we prohibit our changes, we anathematize our prohibitions. Thus, we either condemn others in our own persons, or ourselves in the instance of others, and while we bite and devour one another, are like to be consumed one of another." *Ad Const.* ii. 4, 5.

20. A.D. 382. St. Gregory writes: "If I must speak the truth, I feel disposed to shun every conference of Bishops: for never saw I Synod brought to a happy issue, and remedying, and not rather aggravating, existing evils. For rivalry and ambition are stronger than reason,—do not think me extravagant for saying so,—and a mediator is more likely to incur some imputation himself than to clear up the imputations which others lie under."—*Ep.* 129.

2.

Coming to the opposite side of the contrast, I observe that there were great efforts made on the part of the Arians to render their heresy popular. Arius himself, according to the Arian Philostorgius, "wrote songs for the sea, and for the mill, and for the road, and then set them to suitable music[4]." Hist. ii. 2. Alexander speaks of the "running about" of the Arian women, Theod. Hist. i. 4, and of the buffoonery of their men. Socrates says that "in the Imperial court, the officers of the bed-chamber held disputes with the

[4] The translations which follow are for the most part from Bohn's and the Oxford editions, the passages being abridged.

women, and in the city, in every house, there was a war of dialectics," ii. 2. Especially at Constantinople there were, as Gregory says, "of Jezebels as thick a crop as of hemlock in a field," Orat. 35, 3; and he himself suffered from the popular violence there. At Alexandria the Arian women are described by Athanasius as "running up and down like Bacchanals and furies," and as "passing that day in grief on which they could do no harm." *Hist. Arian.* 59.

The controversy was introduced in ridicule into the heathen theatres, Euseb. v. Const. ii. 6. Socr. i. 6. "Men of yesterday," says Gregory Nyssen, "mere mechanics, offhand dogmatists in theology, servants too and slaves that have been scourged, run-aways from servile work, and philosophical about things incomprehensible. Of such the city is full; its entrances, forums, squares, thoroughfares; the clothes-vendors, the money-lenders, the victuallers. Ask about pence, and they will discuss the generate and ingenerate," &c., &c., tom. ii. p. 898. Socrates, too, says that the heresy "ravaged provinces and cities; and Theodoret that, "quarrels took place in every city and village concerning the divine dogma, the people looking on, and taking sides." *Hist.* i. 6.

In spite of these attempts, however, on the part of the Arians, still, viewing Christendom as a whole, we shall find that the Catholic populations sided with Athanasius; and the fierce disputes above described evidenced the zeal of the orthodox rather than the strength of the heretical party. This will appear in the following extracts :—

1. Alexandria. "We suppose," says Athanasius, "you are not ignorant what outrages they [the Arian Bishops] committed at Alexandria, for they are reported every where. They attacked the holy virgins and brethren with naked swords; they beat with scourges their persons, esteemed honourable in God's sight, so that their feet were lamed by the stripes, whose souls were whole and sound in purity and all good works." Athan *Ap. c. Arian.* 15.

"Accordingly Constantius writes letters, and commences a persecution against all. Gathering together a multitude of herdsmen and shepherds, and dissolute youths belonging to the town, armed with swords and clubs, they attacked in a body the Church of Quirinus: and some they slew, some they trampled under foot, others they beat with stripes and cast into prison or banished. They haled away many women also, and dragged them openly into the court, and insulted them, dragging them by the hair. Some they proscribed; from some they took away their bread, for no other reason but that they might be induced to join the Arians, and receive Gregory [the Arian Bishop], who had been sent by the Emperor." Athan. *Hist. Arian.* § 10.

"On the week that succeeded the holy Pentecost, when the people after their fast, had gone out to the cemetery to pray, because that all refused communion with George [the Arian Bishop], the commander, Sebastian, straightway with a multitude of soldiers proceeded to attack the people, though it was the Lord's day; and finding a few praying (for the greater part had already retired on account of the lateness of the hour), having lighted a pile, he placed certain virgins near the fire, and endeavoured to force them to say that they were of the Arian faith. And having seized on forty men, he cut some fresh twigs of the palm-tree, with the thorns upon them, and scourged them on the back so severely that some of them were for a long time under medical treatment, on account of the thorns which had entered their flesh, and others, unable to bear up under their sufferings, died. All those whom they had taken, both the men and the virgins, they sent away into banishment to the great Oasis. Moreover, they immediately banished out of Egypt and Libya the following Bishops [sixteen], and the presbyters, Hierax and Dioscorus; some of them died on the way, others in the place of their banishment. They caused also more than thirty Bishops to take to flight." Apol. *de Fug.* 7.

2. Egypt. "The Emperor Valens having issued an edict commanding that the orthodox should be expelled both from Alexandria and the rest of Egypt, depopulation and ruin to an immense extent immediately followed; some were dragged before the tribunals, others cast into prison, and many tortured in various ways; all sorts of punishment being inflicted upon persons who aimed only at peace and quiet." Socr. *Hist.* iv. 24.

3. The Monks (1.) *of Egypt.* "Antony left the solitude of the desert to go about every part of the city [Alexandria], warning the inhabitants that the Arians were opposing the truth, and that the doctrines of the Apostles were preached only by Athanasius." Theod. *Hist.* iv. 27.

"Lucius, the Arian, with a considerable body of troops, proceeded to the monasteries of Egypt, where he in person assailed the assemblage of holy men with greater fury than the ruthless soldiery. When these excellent persons remained unmoved by all the violence, in despair he advised the military chief to send the fathers of the monks, the Egyptian Macarius and his namesake of Alexandria, into exile." Socr. iv. 24.

(2.) *Of Constantinople.* "Isaac, on seeing the emperor depart at the head of his army, exclaimed, 'You who have declared war against God cannot gain His aid. Cease from fighting against Him, and He will terminate the war. Restore the pastors to their flocks, and then you will obtain a bloodless victory.'" Theod. iv.

(3.) *Of Syria*, &c. "That these heretical doctrines [Apollinarian and Eunomian] did not finally become predominant is mainly to be attributed to the zeal of the monks of this period; for all the monks of Syria, Cappadocia, and the neighbouring provinces were sincerely attached to the Nicene faith. The same fate awaited them which had been experienced by the Arians; for they incurred the full weight of the popular odium and aversion, when it was observed that their sentiments were regarded with suspicion by the monks." Sozom. vi. 27.

(4.) *Of Cappadocia.* "Gregory, the father of Gregory Theologus, otherwise a most excellent man, and a zealous defender of the true and Catholic religion, not being on his guard against the artifices of the Arians, such was his simplicity, received with kindness certain men who were contaminated with the poison, and subscribed an impious proposition of theirs. This moved the monks to such indignation, that they withdrew forthwith from his communion, and took with them, after their example, a considerable part of his flock." Ed. Bened. Monit. *in Greg. Naz. Orat.* 6.

4 Antioch. "Whereas he (the Bishop Leontius) took part in the blasphemy of Arius, he made a point of concealing this disease, partly for fear of the multitude, partly for the menaces of Constantius; so those who followed the Apostolical dogmas gained from him neither patronage nor ordination, but those who held Arianism were allowed the fullest liberty of speech, and were placed in the ranks of the sacred ministry. But Flavian and Diodorus, who had embraced the ascetical life, and maintained the Apostolical dogmas, openly withstood Leontius's machinations against religious doctrine. They threatened that they would retire from the communion of his Church, and would go to the West, and reveal his intrigues. Though they were not as yet in the sacred ministry, but were in the ranks of the laity, night and day they used to excite all the people to zeal for religion. They were the first to divide the singers into two choirs, and to teach them to sing in alternate parts the strains of David. They too, assembling the devout at the shrines of the martyrs, passed the whole night there in hymns to God. These things Leontius seeing, did not think it safe to hinder them, for he saw that the multitude was especially well affected towards those excellent persons. Nothing, however, could

persuade Leontius to correct his wickedness. It follows, that among the clergy were many who were infected with the heresy: but the mass of the people were champions of orthodoxy." Theodor. *Hist.* ii. 24.

5. EDESSA. "There is in that city a magnificent church, dedicated to St. Thomas the Apostle, wherein, on account of the sanctity of the place, religious assemblies are continually held. The Emperor Valens wished to inspect this edifice; when, having learned that all who usually congregated there were enemies to the heresy which he favoured, he is said to have struck the prefect with his own hand, because he had neglected to expel them thence. The prefect, to prevent the slaughter of so great a number of persons, privately warned them against resorting thither. But his admonitions and menaces were alike unheeded; for on the following day they all crowded to the church. When the prefect was going towards it with a large military force, a poor woman leading her own little child by the hand, hurried hastily by on her way to the church, breaking through the ranks of the soldiery. The prefect, irritated at this, ordered her to be brought to him, and thus addressed her: 'Wretched woman, whither are you running in so disorderly a manner?' She replied, 'To the same place that others are hastening.' 'Have you not heard,' said he, 'that the prefect is about to put to death all that shall be found there?' 'Yes,' said the woman, 'and therefore I hasten, that I may be found there.' 'And whither are you dragging that little child?' said the prefect. The woman answered, 'That he also may be vouchsafed the honour of martyrdom.' The prefect went back and informed the Emperor that all were ready to die in behalf of their own faith; and added that it would be preposterous to destroy so many persons at one time, and thus succeeded in restraining the Emperor's wrath." Socr. iv. 18. "Thus was the Christian faith confessed by the whole city of Edessa." Sozom. vi. 18.

6. SAMOSATA. "The Arians, having deprived this exemplary flock of their shepherd, elected in his place an individual with whom none of the inhabitants of the city, whether poor or rich, servants or mechanics, husbandmen or gardeners, men or women, young or old, would hold communion. He was left quite alone; no one even calling to see him, or exchanging a word with him. It is, however, said that his disposition was extremely gentle; and this is proved by what I am about to relate. One day, when he went to bathe in the public baths, the attendants closed the doors; but he ordered the doors to be thrown open, that the people might be admitted to bathe with himself. Perceiving that they remained in a standing posture before him, imagining that great deference towards himself was the cause of this conduct, he arose and left the bath. These people believed that the water had been contaminated by his heresy, and ordered it to be let out, and fresh water to be supplied. When he heard of this circumstance, he left the city, thinking that he ought no longer to remain in a place where he was the object of public aversion and hatred. Upon this retirement of Eunomius, Lucius was elected as his successor by the Arians. Some young persons were amusing themselves with playing at ball in the market-place; Lucius was passing by at the time, and the ball happened to fall beneath the feet of the ass on which he was mounted. The youths uttered loud exclamations, believing that the ball was contaminated. They lighted a fire, and hurled the ball through it, believing that by this process the ball would be purified. Although this was only a childish deed, and although it exhibits the remains of ancient superstition, yet it is sufficient to show the odium which the Arian faction had incurred in this city. Lucius was far from imitating the mildness of Eunomius, and he persuaded the heads of the government to exile most of the clergy." Theodor. iv. 15.

7. OSRHOENE. "Arianism met with similar opposition at

the same period in Osrhoëne and Cappadocia. Basil, Bishop of Cæsarea, and Gregory, Bishop of Nazianzus, were held in high admiration and esteem throughout these regions." Sozom. vi. 21.

8. CAPPADOCIA. "Valens, in passing through Cappadocia, did all in his power to injure the orthodox, and to deliver up the churches to the Arians. He thought to accomplish his designs more easily on account of a dispute which was then pending between Basil and Eusebius, who governed the Church of Cæsarea. This dissension had been the cause of Basil's departing to Pontus. The people, and some of the most powerful and wisest men of the city, began to regard Eusebius with suspicion, and to meditate a secession from his communion. The emperor and the Arian Bishops regarded the absence of Basil and the hatred of the people towards Eusebius, as circumstances that would tend greatly to the success of their designs. But their expectations were utterly frustrated. On the first intelligence of the intention of the emperor to pass through Cappadocia, Basil returned to Cæsarea, where he effected a reconciliation with Eusebius. The projects of Valens were thus defeated, and he returned with his Bishops." Sozom. vi. 15.

9. PONTUS. "It is said that when Eulalius, Bishop of Amasia in Pontus, returned from exile, he found that his Church had passed into the hands of an Arian, and that scarcely fifty inhabitants of the city had submitted to the control of their new bishop." Sozom. vii. 2.

10. ARMENIA. "That company of Arians, who came with Eustathius to Nicopolis, had promised that they would bring over this city to compliance with the commands of the Imperial vicar. This city had great ecclesiastical importance, both because it was the metropolis of Armenia, and because it had been ennobled by the blood of martyrs, and governed hitherto by Bishops of great reputation, and thus, as Basil calls it, was the nurse of religion and the metropolis of sound

doctrine. Fronto, one of the city presbyters, who had hitherto shown himself as a champion of the truth, through ambition gave himself up to the enemies of Christ, and purchased the bishoprick of the Arians at the price of renouncing the Catholic faith. This wicked proceeding of Eustathius and the Arians brought a new glory instead of evil to the Nicopolitans, since it gave them an opportunity of defending the faith. Fronto, indeed, the Arians consecrated, but there was a remarkable unanimity of clergy and people in rejecting him. Scarcely one or two clerks sided with him; on the contrary, he became the execration of all Armenia." *Vita. S. Basil.*, Bened. pp. clvii, clviii.

11. Nicomedia. "Eighty pious clergy proceeded to Nicomedia, and there presented to the emperor a supplicatory petition complaining of the ill-usage to which they had been subjected. Valens, dissembling his displeasure in their presence, gave Modestus, the prefect, a secret order to apprehend these persons and to put them to death. The prefect, fearing he should excite the populace to a seditious movement against himself, if he attempted the public execution of so many, pretended to send them away into exile," &c. Socr. iv. 16.

12. Cappadocia. St. Basil says, about the year 372: "Religious people keep silence, but every blaspheming tongue is let loose. Sacred things are profaned; those of the laity who are sound in faith avoid the places of worship as schools of impiety, and raise their hands in solitudes, with groans and tears to the Lord in heaven." *Ep.* 92. Four years after he writes: "Matters have come to this pass: the people have left their houses of prayer, and assemble in deserts,—a pitiable sight; women and children, old men, and men otherwise infirm, wretchedly faring in the open air, amid the most profuse rains and snow-storms and winds and frosts of winter; and again in summer under a scorching sun. To this they submit, because they will have no part in the

wicked Arian leaven." *Ep.* 242. Again: "Only one offence is now vigorously punished,—an accurate observance of our fathers' traditions. For this cause the pious are driven from their countries, and transported into deserts. The people are in lamentation, in continual tears at home and abroad. There is a cry in the city, a cry in the country, in the roads, in the deserts. Joy and spiritual cheerfulness are no more; our feasts are turned into mourning; our houses of prayer are shut up, our altars deprived of the spiritual worship." *Ep.* 243.

13. PAPHLAGONIA, &c. "I thought," says Julian in one of his Epistles, "that the leaders of the Galilæans would feel more grateful to me than to my predecessor. For in his time they were in great numbers turned out of their homes, and persecuted, and imprisoned; moreover, multitudes of so-called heretics" [the Novatians who were with the Catholics against the Arians] "were slaughtered, so that in Samosata, Paphlagonia, Bithynia, and Galatia, and many other nations, villages were utterly sacked and destroyed" *Ep.* 52.

14. SCYTHIA. "There are in this country a great number of cities, of towns, and of fortresses. According to an ancient custom which still prevails, all the churches of the whole country are under the sway of one Bishop. Valens [the emperor] repaired to the Church, and strove to gain over the Bishop to the heresy of Arius; but this latter manfully opposed his arguments, and after a courageous defence of the Nicene doctrines, quitted the emperor, and proceeded to another church, whither he was followed by the people. Valens was extremely offended at being left alone in a church with his attendants, and in resentment condemned Vetranio [the Bishop] to banishment. Not long after, however, he recalled him, because, I believe, he apprehended insurrection." Sozom. vi. 21.

15. CONSTANTINOPLE. "Those who acknowledged the

doctrine of consubstantiality were not only expelled from the churches, but also from the cities. But although expulsion at first satisfied them [the Arians], they soon proceeded to the worse extremity of inducing compulsory communion with them, caring little for such a desecration of the churches. They resorted to all kinds of scourgings, a variety of tortures, and confiscation of property. Many were punished with exile, some died under the torture, and others were put to death while being driven from their country. These atrocities were exercised throughout all the eastern cities, but especially at Constantinople." Socr. ii. 27.

16. ILLYRIA. "The parents of Theodosius were Christians and were attached to the Nicene doctrine, hence he took pleasure in the ministration of Ascholius [Bishop of Thessalonica]. He also rejoiced at finding that the Arian heresy had not been received in Illyria." Sozom, vii. 4.

17. NEIGHBOURHOOD OF MACEDONIA. "Theodosius inquired concerning the religious sentiments which were prevalent in the other provinces, and ascertained that, as far as Macedonia, one form of belief was universally predominant," &c. Ibid.

18. ROME. "With respect to the doctrine no dissension arose either at Rome or in any other of the Western Churches; the people unanimously adhered to the form of belief established at Nicæa." Sozom. vi. 23.

"Liberius, returning to Rome, found the mind of the mass of men alienated from him, because he had so shamefully yielded to Constantius. And thus it came to pass, that those persons who had hitherto kept aloof from Felix [the rival Pope], and had avoided his communion in favour of Liberius, on hearing what had happened, left him for Felix, who raised the Catholic standard." Baron. *Ann.* 357. 56. He tells us besides (57), that the people would not even go to the public baths, lest they should bathe with the party of Liberius.

19 MILAN. At the Council of Milan, Eusebius of Vercellæ, when it was proposed to draw up a declaration against Athanasius, "said that the Council ought first to be sure of the faith of the Bishops attending it, for he had found out that some of them were polluted with heresy. Accordingly he brought before the Fathers the Nicene Creed, and said he was willing to comply with all their demands, after they had subscribed that confession. Dionysius, Bishop of Milan, at once took up the paper and began to write his assent; but Valens [the Arian] violently pulled pen and paper out of his hands, crying out that such a course of proceeding was impossible. Whereupon, after much tumult, the question came before the people, and great was the distress of all of them; the faith of the Church was attacked by the Bishops. They then, dreading the judgment of the people, transfer their meeting from the church to the Imperial palace." Hilar. *ad Const.* i. 8.

Again: "As the feast of Easter approached, the empress sent to St. Ambrose to ask a church of him, where the Arians who attended her might meet together. He replied, that a Bishop could not give up the temple of God. The pretorian prefect came into the church, where St. Ambrose was attended by the people, and endeavoured to persuade him to yield up at least the Portian Basilica. The people were clamorous against the proposal; and the prefect retired to report how matters stood to the emperor. The Sunday following St. Ambrose was explaining the creed, when he was informed that the officers were hanging up the Imperial hangings in the Portian Basilica, and that upon this news the people were repairing thither. While he was offering up the holy sacrifice, a second message came that the people had seized an Arian priest as he was passing through the street. He despatched a number of his clergy to the spot to rescue the Arian from his danger. The court looked on this resistance of the people as seditious, and immediately laid considerable fines upon the whole body of the tradesmen of the city. Several were thrown into prison. In three days' time these tradesmen were fined two hundred pounds weight of gold, and they said that they were ready to give as much again on condition that they might retain their faith. The prisons were filled with tradesmen; all the officers of the household, secretaries, agents of the emperor, and dependent officers who served under various counts, were kept within doors, and were forbidden to appear in public, under pretence that they should bear no part in sedition. Men of higher rank were menaced with severe consequences, unless the Basilica were surrendered. . . .

"Next morning the Basilica was surrounded by soldiers; but it was reported, that these soldiers had sent to the Emperor to tell him, that if he wished to come abroad he might, and that they would attend him, if he was going to the assembly of the Catholics: otherwise, that they would go to that which would be held by St. Ambrose. Indeed, the soldiers were all Catholics, as well as the citizens of Milan: there were so few heretics there, except a few officers of the emperor and some Goths. . . .

"St. Ambrose was continuing his discourse, when he was told that the Emperor had withdrawn the soldiers from the Basilica, and that he had restored to the tradesmen the fines which he had exacted from them. This news gave joy to the people, who expressed their delight with applauses and thanksgivings; the soldiers themselves were eager to bring the news, throwing themselves on the altars, and kissing them in token of peace. "Fleury's *Hist.* xviii. 41, 42, Oxf. trans.

20. Christendom generally. St. Hilary to Constantius: "Not only in words, but in tears, we beseech you to save the Catholic Churches from any longer continuance of these most grievous injuries, and of their present intolerable persecutions and insults, which moreover they are enduring,

monstrous as it is, from our brethren. Surely your clemency should listen to the voice of those who cry out so loudly, 'I am a Catholic, I have no wish to be a heretic.' It should seem equitable to your sanctity, most glorious Augustus, that they who fear the Lord God and His judgment should not be polluted and contaminated with execrable blasphemies, but should have liberty to follow those Bishops and prelates who both observe inviolate the laws of charity, and who desire a perpetual and sincere peace. It is impossible, it is unreasonable, to mix true and false, to confuse light and darkness, and bring into union, of whatever kind, night and day. Give permission to the populations to hear the teaching of the pastors whom they have wished, whom they fixed on, whom they have chosen, to attend their celebration of the divine mysteries, to offer prayers through them for your safety and prosperity." *ad Const.* i. 1, 2.

In drawing out this comparison between the conduct of the Catholic Bishops and that of their flocks during the Arian troubles, I must not be understood as intending any conclusion inconsistent with the infallibility of the Ecclesia docens, (that is, the Church when teaching) and with the claim of the Pope and the Bishops to constitute the Church in that aspect. I am led to give this caution, because, for the want of it, I was seriously misunderstood in some quarters on my first writing on the above subject in the *Rambler* Magazine of May, 1859. But on that occasion I was writing simply historically, not doctrinally, and, while it is historically true, it is in no sense doctrinally false, that a Pope, as a private doctor, and much more Bishops, when not teaching formally, may err, as we find they did err in the fourth century. Pope Liberius might sign a Eusebian formula at Sirmium, and the mass of Bishops at Ariminum or elsewhere, and yet they might, in spite of this error, be infallible in their *ex cathedrâ* decisions.

The reason of my being misunderstood arose from two or three clauses or expressions which occurred in the course of my remarks, which I should not have used had I anticipated how they would be taken, and which I avail myself of this opportunity to explain and withdraw. First, I will quote the passage which bore a meaning which I certainly did not intend, and then I will note the phrases which seem to have given this meaning to it. It will be seen how little, when those phrases are withdrawn, the sense of the passage, as I intended it, is affected by the withdrawal. I said then :—

"It is not a little remarkable, that, though, historically speaking, the fourth century is the age of doctors, illustrated, as it is, by the Saints Athanasius, Hilary, the two Gregories, Basil, Chrysostom, Ambrose, Jerome, and Augustine, (and all those saints bishops also), except one, nevertheless in that very day the Divine tradition committed to the infallible Church was proclaimed and maintained far more by the faithful than by the Episcopate.

"Here of course I must explain :—in saying this then, undoubtedly I am not denying that the great body of the Bishops were in their internal belief orthodox; nor that there were numbers of clergy who stood by the laity and acted as their centres and guides; nor that the laity actually received their faith, in the first instance, from the Bishops and clergy; nor that some portions of the laity were ignorant, and other portions were at length corrupted by the Arian teachers, who got possession of the sees, and ordained an heretical clergy :—but I mean still, that in that time of immense confusion the divine dogma of our Lord's divinity was proclaimed, enforced, maintained, and (humanly speaking) preserved, far more by the "Ecclesia docta" than by the "Ecclesia docens;" that the body of the Episcopate was unfaithful to its commission, while the body of the laity was faithful to its baptism; that at one time the pope, at other times a patriarchal, metropolitan, or other great see, at other times general councils, said what they should not have said, or did what obscured and compromised revealed truth; while, on the other hand, it was the Christian people, who, under Providence, were the ecclesiastical strength of Athanasius, Hilary, Eusebius of Vercellæ, and other great solitary confessors, who would have failed without them. . . .

"On the one hand, then, I say, that there was a temporary suspense of the functions of the 'Ecclesia docens.' The body of Bishops failed in their confession of the faith. They spoke variously, one against another; there was nothing, after Nicæa, of firm, unvarying, consistent testimony, for nearly sixty years. . . .

"We come secondly to the proofs of the fidelity of the laity, and the effectiveness of that fidelity, during that domination of Imperial heresy, to which the foregoing passages have related."

The three clauses which furnished matter of objection were these:—I said, (1), that "there was a temporary suspense of the functions of the 'Ecclesia docens;'" (2), that "the body of Bishops failed in their confession of the faith." (3), that "general councils, &c., said what they should not have said, or did what obscured and compromised revealed truth."

(1). That "there was a temporary *suspense* of the functions of the Ecclesia docens" is not true, if by saying so is meant that the Council of Nicæa held in 325 did not sufficiently define and promulgate for all times and all places the dogma of our Lord's divinity, and that the notoriety of that Council and the voices of its great supporters and maintainers, as Athanasius, Hilary, &c., did not bring home the dogma to the intelligence of the faithful in all parts of Christendom. But what I meant by "suspense" (I did not say "suspension," purposely,) was only this, that there was no authoritative utterance of the Church's infallible voice in matter of fact between the Nicene Council, A.D. 325, and the Council of Constantinople, A.D. 381, or, in the words which I actually used, "there was nothing after Nicæa of firm, unvarying, consistent testimony for nearly sixty years." As writing before the Vatican Definition of 1870, I did not lay stress upon the Roman Councils under Popes Julius and Damasus.[5]

(2). That "the *body* of Bishops failed in their confession of the faith," p. 17. Here, if the word "body" is used in the sense of the Latin "corpus," as "corpus" is used in theological treatises, and as it doubtless would be translated for the benefit of readers ignorant of the English language, certainly this would be a heretical statement. But I meant nothing of the kind. I used it in the vague, familiar, genuine sense of which Johnson gives instances in his dictionary, as meaning "the great preponderance," or, "the mass" of Bishops, viewing them in the main or the gross, as a *cumulus* of individuals. Thus Hooker says, "Life and death have divided between them the whole body of mankind;" 'Clarendon, after speaking of the van of the king's army, says, 'in the body was the king and the prince:" and Addison

[5] A distinguished theologian infers from my words that I deny that "the Church is in every time the activum instrumentum docendi." But I do not admit the fairness of this inference. Distinguo: activum instrumentum docendi virtuale, C. Actuale, N. The Ecumenical Council of 325 was an effective authority in 341, 351, and 359, though at those dates the Arians were in the seats of teaching. Fr. Perrone agrees with me. 1. He reckons the "fidelium sensus" among the "instrumenta traditionis." (*Immac. Concept*. p. 139.) 2. He contemplates, nay he instances, the case in which the "sensus fidelium" supplies, as the "instrumentum," the absence of the other instruments, the *magisterium* of the Church, as exercised at Nicæa, being always supposed. One of his instances is that of the dogma de visione Dei beatificâ. He says: "Certe quidem in Ecclesiâ non deerat quoad hunc fidei articulum divina traditio; alioquin, nunquam is definiri potuisset: verum non omnibus illa erat comperta: divina eloquia haud satis in re sunt conspicua; Patres, ut vidimus, in varias abierunt sententias; liturgiæ ipsæ non modicam præ se ferunt difficultatem. His omnibus succurrit juge Ecclesiæ magisterium; communis præterea fidelium sensus." p. 148.

speaks of "navigable rivers, which ran up into the body of Italy." In this sense it is true historically that the body of Bishops failed in their confesson. Tillemont, quoting from St. Gregory Nazianzen, says, "La souscription (Arienne) etait une des dispositions necessaires pour entrer et pour se conserver dans l'episcopat. L'encre était toujours toute prête, et l'accusateur aussi. Ceux qui avaient paru invincibles jusques alors, céderent à cette tempête. Si leur esprit ne tomba pas dans l'heresie, leur main néanmoins y consentit. . . . Peu d'Evêques s'exemterent de ce malheur, n' y ayant eu que ceux que leur propre bassesse faisait negliger, ou que leur vertu fit resister genereusement, et que Dieu conserva afin qu'il restât encore quelque semence et quelque racine pour faire refleurir Israel." T. vi. p. 499. In St. Gregory's own words, *πλὴν ὀλίγων ἄγαν, πάντες τοῦ καιροῦ γεγόνασι· τοσοῦτον ἀλλήλων διενεγκόντες, ὅσον τοὺς μὲν πρότερον, τοὺς δὲ ὕστερον τοῦτο παθεῖν.* Orat. xxi. 24. p. 401. *Ed. Bened.*

(3). That "*general* councils said what they should not have said, and did what obscured and compromised revealed truth." Here again the question to be determined is what is meant by the word "general." If I meant by "general" ecumenical, I should have spoken as no Catholic can speak; but ecumenical Councils there were none between 325 and 381, and so I could not be referring to any; and in matter of fact I used the word "general" in *contrast* to "ecumenical," as I had used it in Tract No. 90, and as Bellarmine uses the word. He makes a fourfold division of "general Councils," viz., those which are approbata; reprobata; partim confirmata, partim reprobata; and nec manifeste probata nec manifeste reprobata. Among the "reprobata" he placed the Arian Councils. They were quite large enough to be called "generalia;" the twin Councils of Seleucia and Ariminum numbering as many as 540 Bishops. When I spoke then of "general councils compromising revealed truth," I spoke of the Arian or Eusebian Councils, not of the Catholic.

I hope this is enough to observe on this subject.

NOTE VI.

CHRONOLOGY OF THE COUNCILS.

(Vide supra, p. 271.)

As the direct object of the foregoing Volume was to exhibit the doctrine, temper, and conduct of the Arians in the fourth century rather than to write their history, there is much incidental confusion in the order in which the events which it includes are brought before the reader. However, in truth, the chronology of the period is by no means clear, and the author may congratulate himself that, by the scope of his work, he is exempt from the necessity of deciding questions relative to it, on which ancient testimonies and modern critics are in hopeless variance both with themselves and with each other.

Accordingly, he has chosen one authority, the accurate Tillemont, and followed him almost throughout. Here, however, he thinks it well to subjoin some tables on the subject, taken from the Oxford Library of the Fathers, which delineate the main outline of the history, while they vividly illustrate the difficulty of determining in detail the succession of dates.

PRINCIPAL EVENTS BETWEEN A.D. 325 AND A.D. 381, IN CHRONOLOGICAL ORDER.

I.

From 325 to 337.

(Mainly from Tillemont.)

A.D.

325. (From June 19 to August 25.) COUNCIL OF NICÆA. Arius and his partisans anathematized and banished,

Arius to Illyricum. The Eusebians subscribe the *Homoüsion.*

326. Athanasius raised to the See of Alexandria at the age of about 30.

328-9. Eusebius of Nicomedia in favour with Constantine.

330. An Arian priest gains the ear of Constantine, who recalls Arius from exile to Alexandria.

331. Athanasius refuses to restore him to communion. Eustathius deposed by the Eusebians on a charge of Sabellianism; other Bishops deposed.

334. Council of Cæsarea against Athanasius, who refuses to attend it.

335. Council of Tyre and Jerusalem, in which Arius and the Arians are formally readmitted. Athanasius, forced by the emperor to attend, abruptly leaves it in order to appeal to Constantine. THE EUSEBIANS DEPOSE ATHANASIUS, AND CONSTANTINE BANISHES HIM TO TREVES.

336. Eusebians hold a Council at Constantinople to condemn Marcellus on the ground of his Sabellianism; and to recognize Arius. DEATH OF ARIUS.

337. DEATH OF CONSTANTINE. The Eusebian Constantius succeeds him in the East, the orthodox Constans and Constantine in the West.

2.

From 337 to 342.

338 — — Exiles recalled by the three new Emperors.
(End of June.) Athanasius leaves Treves for Alexandria.

	(From Valesius, Schelstrate, Pagi, Montfaucon, and S. Basnage.)	*(From Baronius and Petavius.)*	*(From Tillemont an[d] Papebroke.)*
339 — —	Eusebius sends to Pope Julius for a Council	Eusebius, &c. COUNCIL OF ALEXANDRIA DEFENDS ATHANASIUS TO THE POPE.	Eusebius, &c. COUNCIL OF ALEX[ANDRIA], &c. (Sept.) *Athanasius goes to Rome.*[1]
340 — —	COUNCIL OF ALEXANDRIA DEFENDS ATHANASIUS TO THE POPE.	Papal Legates sent to Antioch from Rome. (Early in year) *Athanasius goes to Rome.*	Papal Legates, &c. (End of year) *Athanasius returns to Alexandria.*

[1] The events in italics are grounded on an hypothesis of the authors wh[o] introduce them, that Athanasius made two journeys to Rome, which the[y] adopt in order to lighten the difficulties of the chronology.

341	(Christmas or before Sept.) Council of the Dedication at Antioch (Eusebian), not in order to anticipate the Council at Rome.	Council of Dedication, &c., in order to anticipate the Council at Rome-	(Christmas or before Sept.) Council, &c.
	(Lent) The Arian Gregory in Alexandria.		(Lent.) The Arian Gregory, &c.
	(March — May.) Athanasius escapes to Rome, after the Council of the Dedication, immediately before or after the Papal Legates set out from Rome.	The Papal Legates leave Antioch.	Athanasius escapes, &c. The Papal Legates, &c. The Papal Legates arrive at Rome during the Council there.
		A Roman Council.	(June till Aug. or Sept.) Council of Rome. The Pope's Letter to the Eusebians immediately after the Council.
342	(April or June.) The Papal Legates arrive at Antioch.	(End of year) *Athanasius returns to Alexandria.*	
	(Jan.) The Papal Legates leave Antioch.	(Or beginning Lent.) The Arian Gregory in Alexandria.	
	(March or April.) The Papal Legates arrive at Rome.	The Papal Legates arrive at Rome. Athanasius escapes to Rome shortly after the Roman Council there.	
	Council of Rome. The Pope's Letter to the Eusebians.	Council of Rome. The Pope's Letter to the Eusebians, &c.	

3.

From 342 to 351.

(Mainly from Tillemont.)

345. Council of Antioch (Eusebian), at which the Macrostich is drawn up.

347. Great Council of Sardica, at the instance of the orthodox Constans. Council of Milan against Photinus. Ursacius and Valens sue for reconciliation to the Church.

349. Council of Jerusalem, at which Athanasius is present. Athanasius returns to Alexandria. Ursacius and Valens recant, and are reconciled at Rome. Council at Sirmium or at Rome against Photinus.

350. Death of Constans. The Eusebian Constantius sole Emperor.

351. Great Council of Sirmium, at which Photinus is deposed. First Sirmian creed, &c.

4.

From 351 to 361.

	Baronius.	Petavius.	Valesius.	Pagi.	Basnage.	Tillemont.	N. Alexander	Constant.	Montfaucon.	Mansi.	Mamachi.	Zaccaria
1. GREAT COUNCIL OF SIRMIUM	357	351	351	351	351	351	351	351	351	357-8	351	351
2. Photinus deposed............	357	351		351	351	351	351	351	351	358	351	351
3. First Sirmian Creed (Semi-Arian)......................	357	351		351	351	351	351		351	358	351	
4. Signed by Pope Liberius with a condemnation of Athanasius	357	o	o	o	o	357 or 8	358	357	o	358	o	357
5. Council of Arles (Eusebian) Athanasius condemned	353	353	353	353	353	353 or 4	353	353		354	353	
6. GREAT COUNCIL OF MILAN (Eusebian) Athanasius condemned	355	(	com	mu	niter)		355					
7. Rise of the Eunomians	356	356				356						
8. Syrianus in Alexandria, and George of Cappadocia	356	356	356	356	356	356	355	356	356	356-7	356	
9. Council of Beziers. Hilary deposed and banished	356	355		356	356	356	356	356?		355	356	
10. Fresh Council or Conference at Sirmium	o	357	357	357	357	357	357	357	357	359	357	357
11. Second Sirmian Creed, the blasphemy of Potamius and Hosius (Homœan, if not Anomœan)..	357	357		357	357	357	357	357	357	359	357	
12. Signed by Hosius, but without condemning Athanasius	357	357	357	357	357	357	357	357	357	355	357	357
13. Signed by Liberius, with a condemnation of Athanasius.	o	357							357	o	o	o
14. Another or an altered Creed signed by Liberius with condemnation of Athanasius	o	357	357	o	o	o	o	o	o	o	o	o
15. Council of Antioch in favour of Eunomius................						358	358		358			
16. Its Creed (Anomœan)						358	358		358			
17. Council of Ancyra of 12 Bishops												
18. Its Creed (Semi-Arian) against both the Homoüsian and the Anomœan,	357	358		358	358	358 358	358	358		359		358
signed by Liberius	357	358		358	358			358		359		358
19. Fresh Council or Conference at Sirmium	o		359	358	358-9	358	359	359	359	359	359	
20. Third Sirmian. Creed (Homœan) drawn up by Semi-Arians	357	358	359	358	358-9	359	359	359	359	359	359	359
21. Signed by Liberius	o	o	358?	358	358	o		o	o		o	o
22. BI-PARTITE COUNCIL OF ARIMINUM (Homœan) AND OF SELEUCIA (Semi-Arian)........	359	(	com	mu	niter)							
23. Council of Constantinople (Homœan)			360	359 -60		360	359		360	359	359	
24. Council of Antioch (Anomœan)						361	360		361	361	361	
25. DEATH OF CONSTANTIUS....	361		com	mu	niter)							

5.

From 361 to 381.

(From Tillemont.)

362. Council of Alexandria.
365. Council of Lampsacus (Semi-Arian or Macedonian).
366. Macedonian Bishops reconciled to the Church at Rome.
367. Council of Tyre for the same purpose.
373. Death of Athanasius.
381. Second Œcumenical Council at Constantinople.

NOTE VII.

OMISSIONS IN THE TEXT OF THE THIRD EDITION.

(Vide Advertisement).

Here follow the two sentences, which, as was stated in the Advertisement to this Edition, have forfeited their place in the text :—

1. Supra. p. 11 (p. 12, 1st Ed.), after "external observers," the text proceeded. "Presenting then the characters of a religion, sufficiently correct in the main articles of faith to satisfy the reason, and yet indulgent to the carnal nature of man, Judaism occupied that place in the Christian world, which has since been filled by a corruption of Christianity itself. While its adherents manifested a rancorous malevolence," &c.

2. Supra, p. 393 (p. 421, 1st Ed.), after "his place could nowhere be found," the text proceeded. "Even the Papal Apostasy, which seems at first sight an exception to this rule, has lasted but the same proportion of the whole duration of Christianity, which Arianism occupied in its day; that is, if we date it, as in fairness we ought, from the fatal Council of Trent. And, as to the present perils," &c.

EDITOR'S NOTES

The notes to the text give the full titles of patristic and other ancient works cited by Newman, and also provide translations of his quotations in French, Latin or Greek. In addition, I have attempted to give some idea of where modern scholarship decisively parts company with Newman on historical and interpretative issues, and to amplify allusions to early Christian theology and history for the non-specialist.

p. 1. *the Arian party was ejected*: It is not quite accurate to suggest that after 381 there was a single 'Arian' sect. Local divisions persisted between those who did and those who did not accept the decrees of Nicaea and Constantinople, and the consensus of Mediterranean Christendom certainly shifted decisively towards the acceptance of these decrees after 381. But it is rather misleading to think of the dissidents as a single movement or party, let alone a united parallel church throughout the Empire.

p. 2. *the barbarians of the North*: The Gothic tribes who invaded the empire's territories in increasing numbers in the late fourth and early fifth centuries were predominantly Christians converted by the scholar and missionary Ulfila (*c.* 311–*c.* 383), who had been made bishop by Eusebius of Nicomedia, a major opponent of the Nicene faith. Theological differences embittered the political and ethnic tensions between Goths and Romans in both East and West for several centuries.

p. 2. *a history of the Councils, or of Arianism*: one of the residual marks of Newman's original conception of the work; see Introduction, p. xx.

p. 3. *Paulus*: Little is known in detail about the life of Paul of Samosata; but the connection with Queen Zenobia of Palmyra (p. 4) is treated with caution by modern historians, who commonly give the date of the synods which condemned and deposed Paul as 264 and 268 (Antioch did not come under Zenobia's rule until after 268). He did, however, undoubtedly hold high civic office, and retained control of the main church house at Antioch after his disgrace; Roman imperial authority had later to be invoked to restore it to the orthodox party.

p. 3, n.4. *Vide Euseb.vii.30*: Eusebius of Caesarea, *historia ecclesiastica.*

p. 5. *a kind of Judaism*: Any connection with Zenobia's Judaism is unlikely, but Paul's theology had elements reminiscent of some earlier Jewish Christian thought in resisting the belief that Jesus was from the moment of conception inseparably united to divinity. Even here, though, the connections are tenuous: Paul has nothing in common with the general Jewish Christian interest in the idea of a superior angel descending upon or becoming embodied in Jesus. His is a more economical universe in which the main players are God and the human Jesus.

p. 5, n.8. ... *vide Athan. Tr. p. 175*: As the 'Advertisement to the third edition' (1871) informs us, 'Ath.Tr.' refers to Newman's notes to his translations of Athanasius's *Select Treatises ... in Controversy with the Arians* for the Oxford Library of the Fathers.

p. 5, n.9. *Athan.*: Athanasius, *epistula ad monachos.*

p. 5, n.9. *Theod.*: Theodoret of Cyrrhus, *haereticarum fabularum compendium.*

p. 5, n.9. *Chrysost.*: John Chrysostom, *homilia in Joannem.*

p. 5, n.9. *Philastr.*: Philastrius, *de haeresibus.*

p. 5, n.1. *Athan.*: Athanasius, *oratio quarta contra Arianos* (not by Athanasius, though still assumed to be so at the time of Newman's first edition).

p. 6. *his intimate friend and fellow-countryman, Lucian*: Lucian's association with Paul of Samosata rests on a misunderstanding. (See Introduction, pp. XXXVIII–XXXIX).

p. 7. *the party designation of Collucianists*: The term occurs once only in a letter of Arius to Eusebius of Nicomedia, and is unlikely to mean more than 'fellow-pupil of Lucian'.

p. 7, n.3. *Epiphanius (Anc.)*: *ancoratus.*

p. 7, n.4. *Theod.* Theodoret of Cyrrhus, *historia ecclesiastica.*

p. 7, n.4. *Epiph.*: Epiphanius, *panarion, su adversus lxxx haereses.*

p. 8. *Eusebius the historian*: Eusebius of Caesarea had few real links with Antioch; the Palestinian church had generally looked rather towards Alexandria, which is certainly where Eusebius found his theological heroes.

p. 9. *the heresy recommenced its attack*: In fact, Eustathius, Bishop of Antioch at the time of Nicaea, was one of the fiercest opponents of Arius, and the theological tradition stemming from him remained consistently hostile to the critics of Nicaea. Newman is referring to the Antiochene synod of 341 which repudiated both the creed of Nicaea and the teachings of Arius.

p. 9. *Judaism*: Newman's comments on Judaism reveal an embarrassing ignorance and prejudice (not least in the extraordinary reduction of modern Judaism to a kind of Christian heresy). The relation between Jewish exegesis and the supposed 'Antiochene' tradition as reconstructed here has little to do with the realities of Jewish hermeneutical practice at this period; Newman simply reproduces (here as elsewhere in the book, especially in this chapter) the polemical accounts of Judaism given by early Christian writers, depending particularly on Chrysostom (who wrote towards the end of the fourth century).

p. 11, n.4. *Vide Gibbon*: Gibbon's *Decline and Fall of the Roman Empire*.

p. 11, n.4. *Chrysost.*: John Chrysostom, *adversus Judaeos*.

p. 11, n.5. *ne quis.*: 'let no-one eat the flesh of calves, keeping in mind what is needed for tilling the soil, and correcting the deplorable habits of the *Judaising* crowds'; Jerome, *adversus Jovinianum*.

p. 12. *the Council of Illiberis*: Commonly, in modern works, the Council of Elvira, held in Spain in the first decade of the fourth century.

p. 13. *the quarto-deciman rule*: The Jewish Passover was celebrated on the fourteenth day of the month Nisan; hence the name 'quarto-decimans', 'fourteenthers', for Christians who followed the custom. There is no real evidence that the practice was deliberately adopted at Antioch in the way Newman argues.

p. 14, n.2. *Athan.*: Athanasius, *epistula ad Afros episcopos*.

p. 15. *Audius*: A monk of Edessa, identified by later heresiologists as founder of a sect alleged to hold 'anthropomorphite' views of God (i.e. believing that God had a material form like that of human beings).

p. 15, n.4. *Socr.*: Socrates Scholasticus, *historia ecclesiastica.*

p. 16. *Montanus and Novatian*: Montanus (d. *c.* 170) was one of the founders of the 'new prophecy' movement in Asia Minor, combining rigorous discipline with charismatic enthusiasm; Novatian (flourished mid-third century) was a Roman presbyter who broke away from the Roman Church because of what he saw as a relaxation of its discipline. There is nothing to suggest that he was anything other than Roman by origin: the passage from Philostorgius referred to in n.8 names an otherwise unspecified 'Novatus', and is in any case too late to be obviously reliable evidence. It is quite likely to be a mistake for 'Noetus' (Noetus of Smyrna, a heretical teacher who flourished around 200).

p. 16, n.7. "*ad intelligentiam ... stoliditas barbara*", "slow in understanding, senseless", "barbarous stupidity"; from Jerome, *in epistula ad Galatos*, book 2.

p. 17, n.9. *Sozom.*: Sozomen, *historia ecclesiastica.*

p. 17, n.1. *Tertull.*: Tertullian, *de jejunio adversus Psychicos.*

p. 19, n.6. *Eccles.Pol.*: Richard Hooker, *Of the Lawes of Ecclesiasticall Politie.*

p. 19, n.7. *humanitarianism*: Not in its modern sense of concern for human needs or human rights, but designating a belief in Christ as an exalted human being rather than God incarnate. The use is found early in the nineteenth century as a characterisation of unitarian theology and survived until at least the 1886 edition of the DNB.

p. 19, n.7. *Eusebius*: Eusebius of Caesarea, *contra Marcellum.*

p. 20. *Cerinthians and Ebionites*: There is little reliable information about these groups. Cerinthus appears as a Jewish Christian teacher who held, in common with other gnosticising figures, that the Spirit descended on Jesus at his baptism and left him at the crucifixion. There was no such person as 'Ebion'; the name rests on a misunderstanding by Greek speakers who had no Hebrew. The 'Ebionites' were simply the *ebionim*, the 'poor folk' – a common self-designation for pious Jewish reform groups in the Second Temple period. But the name was used by heresiologists for one specific Jewish Christian sect who denied the virginal conception of Jesus and seem to have shared Cerinthus's Christological views.

p. 20, n.1. *Tertull.*: Tertullian, *de Praescriptione Hereticorum.*

p. 21. *Nazarenes*: Again, there is little dependable information, and the term is almost without practical use. Despite Epiphanius, it is not really possible to identify one sect, heretical or otherwise, under this name. It appears to have been originally a general term for Jewish Christians (c.f. the Hebrew *notsrim* as a designation for Christians). Some writers, especially Jerome, refer to a 'Gospel of the Nazarenes', which seems to have been a rather elaborated version of Matthew in Hebrew or Aramaic.

p. 21, n.3. *Socinianism*: The root of modern Unitarianism, named from the sixteenth-century Italian theologian Socinus, who denied the doctrine of the Trinity and asserted that Jesus was fully and only human.

p. 23. *the great Alexandrian School*: Newman is repudiating the idea that the theology of Clement or Origen should be seen as the seedbed of Arius's thought – a view held by some Protestant writers like Mosheim, and shared in some measure by Anglicans such as Whately, but also highly significant for Roman Catholic scholars influenced by Petavius. It is probably such Catholic writers that Newman has in mind here as enemies of the 'apostolic' claim of the Anglican Church. See Introduction, pp. xxxvii, xxxvi.

p. 24, n.8. *genealogy*: Mostly fanciful: Ebion is a fiction, Artemon or Artemas is known only from such catalogues as this; any direct connection between Paul of Samosata and Diodore of Tarsus is highly improbable. The only point of contact is that the language of Diodore and his followers emphasising the indwelling of the Logos in Jesus (rather than the identification of the Logos with Jesus) distantly echoes some of Paul's idioms.

p. 25. *a General Council*: The exact number of bishops at Nicaea is uncertain (the figure of 318, corresponding to the number of Abraham's servants in Gen. 14, is a later attempt at tidying up), as is the number of Arius's supporters. For discussion, see Williams, *Arius*, pp. 67–68.

p. 26, n.1. ἀναπηδῶαι ... ἄμυναν: 'they leap up like rabid dogs to revenge themselves on their enemies'.

p. 27. ... *A second, and (according to some writers) a third*: Modern scholars agree in recognising only two synods convened to deal with Paul.

p. 27, n.4. σφόδρα ... αὐτῶν: 'Enemies fight more fiercely when their own weapons are used against them.'

p. 28. *the abandonment of the celebrated word*: This is a very complicated question: it is quite likely that Paul had used the word *homousios* to describe the unity of Father and Logos, and that his critics had condemned the use as obliterating the distinction between the divine agents. Some modern scholars would argue that the whole tradition about a discussion of the term at this date is a later invention; but there is enough from Athanasius and elsewhere to suggest that the synods that condemned Paul were an embarrassment to a later generation because of their hostility to his use of this central term in Nicene orthodoxy.

p. 28. *an offender against ecclesiastical order*: Arius is assocated by Sozomen with the schism provoked in Alexandria by Bishop Melitius of Lycopolis in around 306; but there are grounds for doubting the story, and contemporary scholarship has taken it with a grain of salt.

p. 28, n.7. *Philostorg.*: Philostorgius, *historia ecclesiastica.*

p. 28, n.7. *Athan.*: Athanasius, *de decretis Nicaenae synodi.*

p. 29. *the existing Aristotelic school*: Because Aristotle is associated with logic, and the teachings of Arius were regarded in the fourth century as a taking to extremes of logical analysis, the association of the heresy with Aristotle is not uncommon. Any relation to actual Aristotelean commentators of the period is speculative, though not impossible.

p. 29, n.9. "*Omnem . . . destruendi.*": "They put all the force of their poison in dialectical disputation, which is defined in the opinion of philosophers as having no constructive force, but only the studied aim of destruction"; from Ambrose, *de Fide.*

p. 31, n.5. *Vigil. Thaps.*: Vigilius of Thapsus, *contra Eutychen.*

p. 31, n.6. γυμναστικοὶ λόγοι: *gumnastikoi logoi*, 'discursive exercises' as opposed to real contests.

p. 31, n.6. *vide Hypot.*: Sextus Empiricus, *Hypotyposes.*

p. 32, n.8. *Marcellus*: Marcellus of Ancyra (*c.* 280–374) was a prominent opponent of Arius, whose theology inclined towards a conflation of the three persons of the Trinity into a single agency in different modes.

p. 34. *the argument by which Paulus of Samosata baffled the Antiochene Council*: The language of 'unity of substance' for the unity of Father and Son in the Trinity is alien to Greek theology before the fourth century, though Tertullian uses comparable terms in Latin.

p. 35. *symbol*: The conventional patristic term for a credal formula.

p. 36, n.5. "*Solae ... didicit.*": "The divine writings are only brought into disrepute when there is neither school nor teachers [to expound them], and people think they are discussing them expertly when in fact they have learned nothing about them."

p. 36, n.6. "*Non ... postulatur.*": "You who have been fruitful in the spirit have not missed out as far as the letter is concerned ... Where the deeper understanding is risky and uncertain, there the letter of Scripture is needed", from Hilary of Poitiers, *de synodis seu de fide Orientalium*.

p. 39. *new Platonic or Eclectic*: see Introduction, pp. XXXVI–XXXVII, XL–XLI.

p. 39, n.1. *Athan.*: Athanasius, *epistula de synodis Arimini et Seleuciae*.

p. 40. *The Romanists*: see Introduction, p. XXXII, and supra, note on p. 23.

p. 41. *Its catechetical school*: There was certainly a tradition of sophisticated Christian instruction in the early Alexandrian Church, but it is something of an anachronism to speak of a clearly defined 'school' before the fourth century.

p. 42. *Athenagoras*: We know nothing of this second century writers's life or circumstances. Later tradition connects him with Athens, but this may simply be a deduction from his name; some modern scholars have suggested that it is in any case a pseudonym. Any association with Alexandria is speculative and none too probable.

p. 42. *Origen*: Undoubtedly involved in teaching in Alexandria from a very early age, but it is extremely unlikely that we should see his catechetical activity as a young man in terms of a formal appointment, especially as it is associated with a period when the Bishop of Alexandria was absent from the city.

p. 44. *in the system of the early catechetical schools*: What Newman here describes is in broad outline the practice of catechesis in the fourth and fifth centuries, from which periods we have a fairly substantial literature on the order of subjects addressed and the liturgical procedures associated with gradual admission to the Church. As some of Newman's contemporaries pointed out, there is no evidence for such a closely planned scheme from the pre-Nicene age. The reference on p. 45 to St. Cyril of Jerusalem points to one of our main sources for the later period.

p. 45, n.6. τέλειοι: 'perfect'; ἀκροώμενοι, *audienties*, 'hearers'; γονυκλίνοντες, 'those who bend the knee'; εὐχόμενοι, 'those who pray'; *competentes*, 'those who are capable'; *electi*, 'the chosen'; φωτιζομενοι, 'the enlightened'; κατηχέω, 'to instruct'.

p. 46. *As to Scripture*: Newman's chief concern here is polemical, directed against evangelical practice in preaching directly for conversion on the basis of the doctrine of substitutionary Atonement. But he is generally correct in saying that early Christian apologetic and catechesis began with something like 'natural theology' – the evidences of God in creation and in the moral consciousness – and moved only later on to the doctrines of salvation and the sacraments.

p. 48, n.9. στοιχεῖον: 'element'.

p. 48, n.1. *Cyril*: Cyril of Jerusalem, *catecheses illuminandorum*.

p. 49, n.3. "*Bonae . . . pascant.*": "There are in Scripture many good things hidden in the depth of mystery. They are concealed lest they lose their value; they are sought out so that they may exercise the mind; they are opened up so that they may provide nourishment." From Augustine as quoted by Petavius.

p. 50, n.4. *Dr Hawkins*: Hawkins, Provost of Oriel, was extremely unhappy about the use made by Newman of his work, and deliberately distanced himeslf from the latter's interpretation in a sermon of 1838 and his Bampton lectures of 1840. See Nockles, p. 110.

p. 52. *But in truth*: An awkward admission that in fact the pre-Nicene evidence for what Newman assumes is extremely slender. While Clement of Alexandria does indeed work in terms of a graded introduction to faith, and hints at secret doctrines made known only to those who have reached full enlightenment, this does not correspond with what Newman here has in mind and is in any case untypical of the mass of pre-Nicene theology.

p. 53, n.5. *August.*: Augustine, *Contra Adversarium Legis et Prophetarum*.

p. 57. *This method*: In the Hellenistic world, it had become common to offer edifying symbolic readings of classical writers like Homer and Hesiod, or of ancient myths, Greek and Egyptian; this method was associated particularly with the grammatical schools of Alexandria, and was taken up by Hellenised Jews, especially the first century Philo. A little later (p. 62), Newman argues that such interpretation is already part of the way the writers of the New Testament read the Old.

p. 64, n.2. *Heut*: misprint for Huet.

p. 65, n.3. κατ' οἰκονομίαν: 'as a matter of good management'.

p. 65, n.5. Euseubius represents Dionysius, Bishop of Alexandria, as responding to the challenge of the Roman prefect at his trial to worship with gratitude the gods who protect the empire with the words, 'Not all people worship all gods'. The prefect's reply is to ask why Christians cannot worship Christ along with 'the natural gods'.

p. 66. *Theonas, Bishop of Alexandria*: The letter to 'Lucian', described as a chamberlain at the court of Diocletian, is spurious.

p. 66, n.6. "*Insurgere . . . divinitas.*": 'Some mention may arise of Christ; and his unique divine status will then little by little be explained.'

p. 67. *Eclectic*: See above, note to p. 39.

p. 67, n.7. 'Human wisdom we call an exercise for the soul, while divine wisdom is its goal', from Origen's *contra Celsum*.

p. 69, n.3. *Athan.*: Athanasius, *de Sententia Dionysii.*

p. 71, n.5. *Euseb.*: Eusebius, *contra Marcellum.*

p. 74, n.6. 'A person is not necessarily lying even if he says something false', from Plato's *Laws*. Sextus Empiricus, *adversus logicos* (= *adversus mathematicos VIII*). The reference is to Immanuel Bekker's edition, Berlin, 1842.

p. 79. *the divinity of Traditionary Religion*: Newman is appealing to the witness of 'unrevealed' religion as it appears in the heathen world; confused and inconclusive as it is, it nevertheless shows that God deals with human beings through the human institutions of ritual and myth as well as through the direct and infallible means of scriptural revelation.

p. 81, n.7. 'Philosophy was given to the Greeks as a kind of "covenant" suitable to their condition, being a foundation for the philosophy that is according to Christ.'

p. 81, n.8. *Job xxxi. 26–28*: It is a commonplace of patristic and mediaeval interpretation that Job represents the righteous Gentile in the days of the First Covenant.

p. 85. *the overthrow just now of religion in France*: Although by the early 1830s the major onslaught of the French Revolution upon the Catholic Church had spent its force, the condition of the Church in France was still precarious and impoverished, materially and intellectually.

p. 86. *St. Austin*: St. Augustine of Hippo.

p. 87. *the heresy of the Neologians*: 'Neologism' is a contemporary designation for the systems of those nineteenth-century German theologians who retained traditional theological language while radically altering its meaning so as to exclude supernatural agency. Newman almost certainly took this vocabulary from Hugh James Rose's *State of the Protestant Religion in Germany*, Cambridge and London, 1825; see Thomas, pp. 41ff.

p. 90. *Moses was the unknown but real source*: The belief that Plato's philosophy derived from the Pentateuch was a commonplace of patristic apologetic from Justin Martyr onwards. It was the second-century Middle Platonist Numenius (possibly of Jewish origin) who first described Plato as 'Moses speaking Attic Greek'.

p. 90. *Demiurgus*: The usual Platonic term for the creator of this world, first used in Plato's *Timaeus*. In gnostic systems, the demiurge is normally seen as weak, incompetent or malign, but Platonic philosophies debated in detail the relation of this 'creative workman' to the divine mind and the divine ideas.

p. 93, n.2. *the theological language of the Paradise Lost*: A very interesting example, presumably referring to the heavenly dialogue imagined in Book III of the poem: Newman does not make clear whether or not he is aware of Milton's explicit Arian convictions; though it would be fair to say, with C.S. Lewis in his study of the question, that these convictions do not appear unambiguously in the text of *Paradise Lost*.

p. 94, n.3. *Prov.viii.22*: The Septuagint renders Prov. 8.22 as 'The Lord created me at the beginning of his ways'.

p. 94, n.4. *Justin.*: Justin Martyr, *Apologia* and *Dialogus cum Tryphone Judaeo*.

p. 97. *the multitude of grievous and unfair charges*: Origen was accused of heresy in his lifetime; detailed lists of contested teaching were circulating in the first decade of the fourth century (and were answered by Eusebius and Pamphilus in their *apologia* for Origen), and more extensive charge sheets were drawn up in the last quarter of the same century. Attitudes to

Origen's teaching came to be, for some writers like Jerome and Epiphanius, tests of orthodoxy and unorthodoxy. Certain propositions ascribed to Origen were condemned in Constantinople in 553 at the time of the fifth Ecumenical Council, though the Council itself did not issue a formal anathema.

p. 97, n.9. Origen's περὶ ἀρχῶν, *First Principles*, is his major systematic treatise on doctrine. It survives largely in a Latin translation by Rufinus of Aquileia, which tends to smooth out controversial or possible heterodox passages. ἦν ὅτε οὐκ ἦν, 'There was a time when he [the Logos] did not exist'; ἐξ οὐκ ὄντων, 'out of nothing'.

p. 99, n.1. 'Their heresy has about it nothing blessed, nothing provable from Scripture; so they have worked out shameless arguments and plausible sophistries. Now, though, they have even dared to throw out the witness of the Fathers'.

p. 99, n.2. *Apolog.adv.Ruffin.*: Jerome's *adversus Rufinum*.

p. 101. *Potamo ... Ammonius*: The former is no more than a name in chronicles of the history of philosophy; insofar as we can identify a really seminal figure in the evolution of Neoplatonic philosophy (Newman's 'Eclectic' school), it is Ammonius Saccas (*c*. 175–244), teacher of Plotinus. Eusebius (in the passage referred to by Newman on p. 102) quotes Plotinus's pupil Porphyry as evidence for Origen's having studied with Ammonius.

p. 102. *Eusebius, though not without some immaterial confusion*: The matter is much disputed. It is possible that Eusebius has confused Ammonius the philosopher with a Christian writer of the same name; it is generally agreed also that there was a pagan philosopher called Origen roughly contemporary with the Christian Origen. However, the likelihood is that the Christian Origen did indeed study with Ammonius Saccas at some point, and that Ammonius had been brought up as a Christian and later abandoned the faith, though Eusebius was not aware of this. Newman's portrait of a somewhat Machiavellian strategy on Ammonius's part, professing Christianity so as to subvert its teaching from within, is, as the reference to 'Neologism' on p. 103 suggests, as much to do with nineteenth-century anxieties about theological liberalism as with the intellectual history of late antiquity.

p. 102. *he who refused to hear Paulus of Antioch*: Origen died (most probably) in 253–4, and was not involved in the dispute over Paul of Samosata's teaching; nor had he any connection at all with Queen Zenobia. Newman may be thinking of another passage in Eusebius (VII. 27.2) describing the refusal of Bishop Dionysius of Alexandria to attend the first synod called at Antioch to deal with Paul.

p. 103. *St. Austin remarks*: The most famous passage in which Augustine so stresses the similarity of Christianity and Neoplatonism is in Book VII of the *Confessions*, ch. ix.

p. 104. *Instead of viewing them*: Newman probably has in mind the tendency of later Neoplatonism (notably the school of Iamblichus in the fourth century) to make use of ritual magic ('theurgy'), invoking, for example, the gods of the ancient Egyptian pantheon.

p. 106. *Who does not recognize*: Characteristically, Newman sees liberalism as a systematic enemy to the basic idea of revelation (which assumes an authoritative point of reference in the world independent of the individual mind).

p. 106. *The freedom of the Alexandrian Christians*: Newman is insistent that Origen could have had no real influence from Neoplatonism. He is right in saying that Origen cannot have met Plotinus; but the ways in which certain aspects of Origen's thought parallel developments in Plotinus suggest some serious intellectual debt to a common source. Newman's presentation is somewhat skewed by his conviction that Neoplatonism is essentially at this period a matter of concealed apostasy.

p. 108–9. *It went out from the Christians*: The reference is to I John 2.19.

p. 111. *the doctrine of the Chiliasts*: The belief in a literal reign of the saints on earth as a prelude to the Second Coming or to the final end of all things is not specially associated with Antioch or exclusively with Jewish Christianity, though it is undoubtedly opposed by Origen and Dionysius (in the latter case, in response to a local *Egyptian* controversy). See Charles Hill, *Regnum Caelorum*, Oxford, 1992, for a detailed critical discussion.

p. 111, n.4. The reference is to the Benedictine edition of Origen's extant works (Paris, 1733–59).

p. 112, n.6. ἀρχικαὶ ὑποστάσεις: 'principal subsistents'; the three basic, hierarchically ordered principles variously designated in different Neoplatonic systems (as the One, Intellect and Soul, the unparticipated, the participated and the participating, and so on).

p. 114, n.7. *the works attributed to the Roman Clement*: The Pseudo

Clementine *Homilies* and *Recognitions*, of fourth-century composition in their present form, though some have argued for an older stratum of Jewish-Christian tradition behind the existing texts. Newman assumes an early date and an origin in Rome, rather than the Syrian provenance accepted by most modern scholars.

p. 117, n.1. Μοναρχία: monarchia is not exclusively a term used by Sabellians, and its use certainly predates any Neoplatonic doctrine of three ἀρχικαὶ. Theophilus of Antioch in the second century uses it for the sole supremacy of God in the universe. In later fourth-century theology it becomes the usual term (especially in the Cappadocian fathers) for the principle that the Father is the sole source of divine life within the Trinity. Newman discusses this more fully on pp. 182–4.

p. 119. *Aeschines ... openly maintained*: The connection between Montanism and Sabelliansism is mostly a figment of heresiologists' imagination. Hippolytus (at the beginning of the third century) mentions Aeschines as supporting the 'patripassian' view (the idea that the Father suffers in the crucifixion of the Son, or is, indeed, identical with the crucified Son) within the Montanist movement. But on the whole patripassians and Montanists were on opposing sides in the controversies in the Roman Church described by Hippolytus. There is no reason to think that Aeschines was active in Asia Minor.

p. 121, n.1. *Athan.*: Athanasius, *Orationes contra Arianos*. Then, from a fragment of Origen on the Epistle to Titus, 'We define [the divine persons as being] two so that we do not end up believing that the Father was born and suffered (as your perversity deduces)'. Tertullian, *adversus Praxean*.

p. 122. *Ambrosius, the convert and friend of Origen*: According to Eusebius, Ambrosius was a Valentinian (h.e.VI.18.1). Alexander of Alexandria, in his letter to his namesake, Alexander of Byzantium, written in the early stages of the Arian controversy, compares Sabellius and Valentinus in terms of their both teaching a kind of emanation from the first principle, rather than a true distinction of divine persons. The 'Roman Council' of 324 lacks contemporary attestation.

p. 124. *Simon Magus*: Heresiologists' imagination again: Simon Magus was early identified as the fountainhead of gnostic teaching, but (apart from the extreme uncertainty around what he may actually have taught) he cannot be intelligibly linked to a late second-century theological controversy. Throughout this passage, Newman, especially in describing Montanism, is dealing with his own version of 'ideal types' of heresy, or his own sense of the logic that might have led from one error to another, not with anything that can be securely anchored in the actual history of the early Church.

p. 128, n.8. *Tertull.*: Tertullian, *adversus Hermogenem.*

p. 130, n.1. *Athan.*: Athanasius, *apologia contra Arianos* (sometimes *apologia secunda*) and *historia Arianorum ad monachos.*

p. 134, n.1. *Hoc ... doceatur.*: 'It is really absurd for a pupil going to a teacher to turn into an expert before he is taught'; from Jerome, *altercatio Luciferiani et orthodoxi.*

p. 134–5. ... *the Apostolical Tradition, that is, the Creed*: Newman may be presupposing that the Apostles' Creed was the basis of pre-Nicene catechesis; this particular text is in fact exclusively Western and specifically Roman in origin, but it represents fairly accurately the content of the *regula fidei*, the 'rule of faith', which served as a summary of Christian teaching in the Mediterranean churches more generally. For discussion, see R.P.C. Hanson, *Tradition in the Early Church*, London, 1962.

p. 140. *used at table*: Arius's main controversial composition was a verse manifesto which came to be known as the *Thalia*, i.e. 'Songs for a dinner party'; it is not clear whether the title was in fact given to the work by Arius himself, or whether it is a contemptuous nickname invented by his opponents. The actual phraseology of Athanasius tends to support the latter conclusion.

p. 140, n.6. *Athan.*: Athanasius, *orationes contra Arianos.*

p. 140, n.7. *Euseb.*: Eusebius, *vita Constantini*; Gregory Nazianzen, *orationes.*

p. 141, n.8. 'the egregious chorus-leaders in Arius's theatricals', from Eustathius of Antioch as quoted in the *bibliotheca* of Photius.

p. 142, n.2. κίνδυνος ... κύριον: 'There is a danger of betrayal if we do not readily answer questions about God that come from people who love the Lord'.

p. 142, n.2. *Hil.*: Hilary of Poitiers, *de trinitate.*

pp. 149–50. *The clergy, and others in station*: In the light of the discussion in the preceding pages, Newman is arguing the fundamental principle of both the older 'Orthodox' party in the Church of England and of the new

Oxford reformers: the clergy have authority in the formation of souls, and so their own theological and spiritual formation is of first importance. There can be no latitude in doctrinal interpretation for them once it is granted that their charge is as defined here. These pages are of first importance in understanding the whole rationale of Newman's book.

pp. 151–2. This significant passage seems to owe a good deal to Bishop Butler's *Analogy of Religion*, particularly the opening of the second part. But Newman is original in comparing nature interpreted by the history of religions with Scripture interpreted by credal tradition. Quite a bit of Newman's argument throughout the work might be seen as an extension of Butler's principles; it is not only in his *Grammar of Assent* that Newman's debt to the greatest of eighteenth-century Anglican apologists is evident.

p. 152, n.1. *de Principiis* is the Latin name for the *peri archon* (above, on p. 97, n.9).

p. 161, n.9. '. . . to those who call Hermes the Word sent from the presence of God'.

p. 161, n.1. *Euseb.*: Eusebius, *de ecclesiastica theologia.*

p. 162, n.3. *Athan.*: Athanasius, *epistulae ad Serapionem.*

p. 163. *a reiteration of the One Infinite Nature*: The image of 'reiteration' curiously foreshadows Karl Barth's language about God's 'self-repetition' in the trinitarian life.

p. 165, n.7. 'The Son possesses a divinity numerically identical with the Father's, but is different in property. So, as Sonship is in a certain sense less than Fatherhood [the Latin should read *Paternitate quodammodo*] it might be said that the Son, as Son, is less than the Father, as Father, since he is posterior in terms of origin, but not less than the Father as God'.

p. 165, n.7. ἑτεροούσιος: 'of different substance'.

p. 166. *connaturalia instrumenta*: 'instruments sharing the same nature'.

p. 166, n.1. 'service, will (both βούλησις and θέλημα), command or instruction'.

p. 171, n.4. ἐνυπόστατος Λόγος: 'a word given subsistence'.

p. 171, n.6. The second quotation from Athanasius is from *orationes contra Arianos III.* The text from Augustine's *enarrationes in psalmos* means, 'Because he is Word, therefore he is Son'.

p. 173. *coinherence*: The term is more properly used for the interpenetration and interweaving of divine and human activity in the incarnate Christ, but appears in a trinitarian context in Byzantine theology; it was given currency by John of Damascus in the eighth century.

p. 173. *his Christian Instructor*: This is the work usually referred to by its Greek name of the *Paidagogos*.

p. 174, n.9. 'For it is necessary for the divine Logos to be united to the God of all; and the Holy Spirit must indwell God and inhere in him' (the Greek has a misprint, *eudiaitasthai* for *endiaitasthai*). The quotation from Tertullian reads: 'The involvement of the Father in the Son and the Son in the Paracelete makes them three cohering realities, three who are one thing but not one person'.

p. 175, n.1. 'the Father's bosom completely enfolding the Son, the Son nestling and clinging to the Father, resting continually on his breast'.

p. 177, n.7. *agennētos*, 'without origin'; *anarchos*, 'without beginning'.

p. 181. *In process of time*: Prior to the fourth century, little distinction was made between *agenētos* (from *ginomai*, to come into existence) and *agennētos* (from *gennao*, to be born). After Nicaea, it became increasingly necessary to distinguish the two, as the Logos could rightly be said to be without a beginning of existence, yet could not be rightly described as 'unborn'. Some critics of Nicaea insisted that 'unborn' was an intrinsic property of the divine, so that a divine Son was a logical nonsense. In pre-Nicene literature, it is often impossible to distinguish which word was originally used in any given theological discussion.

p. 182, n.4. κεφαλή, 'head'; ἀρχη, 'principle' or 'causal origin'.

p. 183, n.8. 'If we understand the Father as "cause" of the Son, the Son is not *anarchos*, since the Father is the causal principle of the Son.'

p. 186. *it was* not *that in which it is used by philosophers*: In fact, the word *ousia* can refer to an independent subsistent in philosophical usage (Aristotle defined individual existents as 'primary substances' and generic being shared between individuals as 'secondary substance'). But it is certainly correct to say that the initial use of *ousia* in Christian theology was not tied to any specific philosophical definition. The Neoplatonic term *huperousios* (later in this paragraph and in n.2) and the phrase *epekeina tēs ousias*, 'beyond being', originating in Plato's *Republic*, was meant to make it clear that the transcendent Good or god was beyond the definition appropriate to a particular object in the world.

p. 186, n.2. Plotinus, *Enneads*; Origen, *contra Celsum*; John of Damascus, *de fide orthodoxa*.

p. 188. *the Poemander*: Now more usually called the *Poimandres*, the first of the tractates collectively known as the *Corpus Hermeticum*, originating in Egypt in the second and third centuries, and of pagan authorship. It had been a popular text among Renaissance Christian Platonists.

p. 188, n.6. *Archelaus*: The *Acta Archelai* is a work of the mid fourth century, purporting to give the proceedings of a debate between Archelaus, an East Syrian bishop of the third century, and Mani, the founder of the Manichaean movement. It survives in a Latin version, with some Greek extracts preserved by Epiphanius. *De substantia Dei*, 'of [or from] the substance of God'.

p. 190, n.8. 'he sent forth an offspring.'

p. 190, n.9. ὑιοπάτωε: 'Son-Father'.

p. 191, n.3. 'not as an emanation in any sense that would detract from speaking about his generation'.

p. 192. *It is remarkable too*: Undoubtedly the use of *homoousios* was regularly regarded as 'Manichaean' in the later third and early fourth centuries by many, because it suggested that the divine nature could be divided.

p. 193. θελήσει γεννηθὲν: 'born by an act of will'.

p. 196. Λόγος ἐνδιάθετος ... προφόρικος: terms used by second-century apologists to distinguish the 'immanent' divine Logos, within the Father's being, from the 'expressed' Logos, brought forth from the Father's mind for the purpose of creation.

p. 199, n.6. 'His incomprehensible bringing to birth has neither beginning nor end, being without source, without interruption ...'

p. 203. *It concurred with the disciples of Paulus*: The belief that Christ is 'suject to a moral probation' and that his divine status is thus the result of uninterrupted virtue is ascribed to Arius by his opponents; some modern scholarship has made much of this, but nothing in Arius's own recorded work bears it out, and it is entirely inconsistent with other and better attested doctrines of his. As to the denial of the personal being of the Logos (p. 204), this can probably be ascribed to Paul, but Arius's view is more complex: there is certainly a pre-existent personal agent called the Logos, created by God as first and highest of creatures, but his title is derivative from the *logos* and wisdom that are inherent in God's essence.

p. 204, n.4. *the Samosatene doctrine would become identical with Nestorianism*: Antiochene Christology used some of the same language about divine indwelling that had been used by Paul, but was entirely in accord with the trinitarian theology of Nicaea, even fanatically so, and committed to the permanent and total indwelling of the Logos in Jesus. There is no question of any promotion on the grounds of merit.

p. 205, n.7. *Arius's theses, as set down by Socrates*: Nicaea declared that 'those who say that there was a time when he did not exist and that before he was begotten he did not exist and that he came into existence out of nothing, or that he came to be out of some other subsistent reality or substance, or was created, or that the Son of God is variable or changeable – these the Holy Catholic Church anathematises'.

p. 206, n.8 "Those who treat the analogate as having the same force as the prototype are in error. It would not be an analogate if there were not some kind of unlikeness" from Leontius of Byzantium, *contra Nestorianos et Eutychianos*.

p. 208, n.1. "Generation is not the [deliberate] activating of potentiality but a natural matter", from Ambrose, *de incarnationis dominicae sacramento*. "Generation is a work of nature, creation a work of will" (John of Damascus).

p. 209. *Anomoeans*: Insofar as this group stressed the unlikeness in essence of Son and Father, they were at odds with the original theology of Arius, and were in fact critical of his views.

p. 210, n.3. μονογενής, 'only begotten' or 'unique'.

p. 210, n.4. 'A creature, but not like one among creatures; a thing generated, but not like one such thing among others'.

p. 215. *Arius wrote his Thalia*: see above, on p. 140.

p. 224. *The mystery of their creed*: Newman has in mind particularly the Roman Catholic scholars of a slightly earlier generation, who stressed the doctrinal irregularities of pre-Nicene theologians.

p. 244, n.8. 'Their error bears witness to the truth, and, through sharing a common opinion of the faithless, they unite by true faith in a single measured harmony'; from Vigilius of Thapsus, *contra Eutychen*.

p. 226, n.3. 'For if he is from God, and God generates him out of himself, as they say, from his own subsistence or his own essence, then it must be that God suffers division, or else is either extended or contracted in this act of generation, or is subject to some kind of bodily condition' (Epiphanius). 'When they say that he is *homoousios*, which means coming into being out of something, this must be either by division or by discharge or by projection – projection, as a plant comes from a root, discharge, as children from their father, division, as two pieces of gold can be made from one lump. The Son can be none of these, and so what they say cannot be reconciled with the faith' (Socrates).

p. 229, n.5. Athanasius, *homilia in illud*, Omnia mihi tradita sunt (Matt.11.27). 22 in the text is a misprint.

p. 231. *At first it had not scrupled*: See above on p. 203. Arius's own undisputed work does not suggest that he believed the Logos actually capable of change (therefore of sin), though he may well have allowed that in strict principle only God was unchangeable by nature, so that the Son's unchangeability would have to be a contingent matter of fact (he could change in the abstract, but in fact is always totally faithful to God because always totally receptive to God's grace). It is a sticky point.

p. 232. *no firm footing of internal consistency*: The history of theological opposition to Nicaea does not show a steady declension towards a belief in Jesus's humanity only (this belief is associated with only one fourth-century writer, Photinus of Sirmium, whose connection, if any, with Arius or other anti-Nicene groups is entirely obscure), but a steady commitment to the idea of a 'second-order' divinity capable of suffering, and so of involvement in the work of salvation.

p. 234. *The latter should meet with no mercy*: As elsewhere, Newman is pleading for effective doctrinal tests not for all church members but for those in positions of authority.

p. 237. *Arius first published his heresy*: Modern estimates vary, and some scholars (including the present writer) would argue for a slightly later date for the beginning of public controversy (320–1). The earlier history of Arius is, as already indicated, very uncertain, and Newman is right to treat Philostorgius's story with caution. It is not very likely that Arius was ever head of the catechetical school, though his close associate Achillas (not the bishop Achillas mentioned in this paragraph) may have been.

p. 237. *Colluthus, Carponas, and Sarmatas*: Colluthus is identified as founder of a schismatic group in Alexandria, which seems to have grown up in protest at Bishop Alexander's over-lenient treatment of Arius. He later returned to the episcopal fold (no heretical views are associated with his name in the earliest texts), but some of those he had irregularly ordained continued to cause problems in later years for Athanasius.

pp. 238–9. *he had already been supported by the Meletian faction*: This is not borne out by the early literary evidence, though there may have been tactical alliances later against the common enemy, Athanasius.

p. 240. *Asterius*: Evidently one of the really formidable intellectuals among Arius's supporters, he travelled extensively to speak in Arius's support. A layman, he apparently wrote several works of biblical commentary, but there is much dispute as to whether an extant series of homilies on the psalms should be ascribed to him or to another writer of the same name.

p. 242. *Constantine*: Newman is indirectly issuing some cautions about looking to state authority for the resolution of doctrinal disputes; the earthly monarch will always be likely to put social peace above truth.

p. 245. *The Edict of Milan*: Modern historians regard this term as misleading. What happened was that a meeting of eastern and western emperors at Milan in February 313 confirmed the extension throughout the Empire of the already existing western policy that confiscated property should be restored to Christians. Legal toleration for Christians had been guaranteed in the western regions for some years.

p. 245. *Hosius*: Or Ossius, Bishop of Cordova (*c.* 257–*c.* 357), highly influential over Constantine's religious policy in the years leading up to Nicaea. His mission to the eastern Mediterranean in the winter of 324–5 seems to have been decisive in disposing Constantine against Arius.

p. 246, n.8. 'Now the Church is full of secret heretics'.

p. 250. *about 300 Bishops*: see above on p. 25.

p. 251. *Arius was introduced and examined*: In fact, Arius is most unlikely to have attended the Council.

p. 251, n.2. '*the Sotadean Arius*': 'Sotadean' is an adjective with connotations of homosexual behaviour in classical usage; but Athanasius is not making a serious accusation. Because Arius's *Thalia* was written in a metre similar to what was called the Sotadean metre in the prosody of the day, a metre normally used for ribald verse (imagine a purportedly serious religious poem composed in limericks), Athanasius is able to damn the author by association. All the reliable evidence supports Epiphanius's picture of a man with a considerable ascetic reputation.

p. 254. *drawn up by Hosius*: Who drafted the text that was finally accepted by the Council is unknown: Hosius was almost certainly involved, perhaps along with Eustathius of Antioch, who was the object of a fierce hostility among the enemies of Nicaea in the years that followed.

p. 256. *It is said that, some of them*: Again Newman's caution about Philostorgius is well-founded. The term *homoiousios* did not emerge as a compromise formula until some decades later. The course of events after the Council is extremely unclear, with our major sources conflicting. Williams, *Arius*, pp. 71ff. suggests a reconstruction, but others would disagree. It is likely that Arius was exiled to Illyria immediately (along with two Libyan bishops who supported him), but reinstated by a synod a couple of years later, on the basis of a carefully worded statement of faith (but without accepting the creed of Nicaea). The Alexandrian church, however, refused to receive him, and he was unable to return there. He may have spent this period in Libya, probably his native country.

p. 257. *Strictly speaking, the Christian Church*: What follows is a careful statement of broadly High Church theory about the rights of orthodox Christians and the duties of government in a confessional state; see Introduction, pp. XXI–XXVIII.

p. 259. *a secondary object of their exertions*: A strong statement of the fundamentally secular character of Arianism (and, by implication, of other kinds of theological dissent). The history is, predictably, less clear: Arius's supporters cannot be said to have allied themselves uncritically with the Melitians, nor were they uniformly marked by opportunism and inconsistency. Nicene Christians, too, were capable of persecuting and their opponents of suffering. It is true, though, that the methods of some non-Nicenes when in power in Alexandria were particularly violent, if even some part of what Athanasius alleges is accurate.

p. 261. *Alexander's circular epistle*: This is the letter of Alexander to Alexander of Byzantium, which was evidently designed to be circulated among other Asian bishops. Alexander reports that the riots over Arius's teaching prompted the city authorities to repressive measures. The connection with Eusebius of Nicomedia's supposed attitude (itself unlikely) is fanciful.

p. 263, n.5. γοήτεια: black magic.

p. 264. *Wrought upon by a presbyter*: The story is related by Rufinus at the end of the century, and may reflect a real sympathy in the imperial family for the non-Nicene party.

p. 264. *allows the Emperor to style himself "the bishop of Paganism"*: Literally, 'the bishop of those outside [the Church]', a slightly different affair.

p. 266. *It is doubtful*: It is in fact most improbable that Arius ever subscribed the creed of Nicaea. The truth is that the creed itself had become rather rapidly something of a dead letter; hence the lengthy and convoluted attempts in succeeding decades to find another formula without the problems posed by the *homoousios*, which was deeply unpopular even among those who had been persuaded to accept it at the Council.

p. 267. *the orthodox prelates*: Eustathius of Antioch and Asclepas of Gaza were deposed by a local Antiochene synod in (probably) 327 (see also p. 280). Other bishops shared their fate, but it is uncertain which ones. Newman may again be guilty of a faulty recollection of his sources in mentioning a bishop of Hadrianople: Lucius of Hadrianople was indeed deposed and exiled for his support of Athanasius, but not until (probably) 338–9. C.f. p. 312.

p. 269. *the stroke of death*: According to Athanasius, Arius suffered a fatal stroke or rupture in a public lavatory; the parallel with the fate of Judas as recorded in Acts 1 is made much of by pro-Nicene writers.

p. 276, n.4. 'the eunuch'. Leontius was one of those regarded by later non-Nicenes of the Anomoian party as transmitting the true teaching stemming from the martyr Lucian as opposed to the rather inadequate or distorted theology propounded by Arius. Leontius was one of the teachers of the radical Anomoian Aetius.

p. 277. *Eudoxius*: Not actually a pupil of Lucian, but again a significant influence on Aetius and his school.

p. 277, n.5. ἐυσέβεια: 'piety'; ἀσέβεια and δυσσέβεια, 'impiety'.

pp. 277–8, ibid. *Arius also ends his letter to Eusebius*: Arius plays on the bishop's name, addressing him as 'truly pious, *eusebeios*'.

p. 294. *The orthodox majority*: Slightly wishful thinking; the majority, as far as we can ascertain, were confused, and no more sympathetic to Athanasius than to Arius.

p. 294, n.2. *data evectionis copia*: 'under a great deal of forcible pressure', from the *historia* of Sulpicius Severus.

p. 294, n.2. *Cod. Theod*: the Codex Theodosianus (the imperial law code finalised by the Emperor Theodosius I in the late fourth century).

p. 295, ibid. Ammianus Marcellinus, whose *rerum gestarum libri*, a history going up to the 370s, presents a non-Christian perspective on the period.

p. 295, ibid. *Pope John VIII*: 'after the example of pious princes who were always eager to be generous in such matters'.

p. 303. *Constantine, the eldest of the brothers*: Originally ruler of Britain, Gaul and Spain, killed in 340, in the course of his attempt to overthrow his brother Constans; supportive to Athanasius during the latter's exile in the West.

p. 304, n.7. Athanasius, *epistula encyclica*.

p. 306, n.2. κατὰ πάντα ὅμοιον: 'like in all respects'.

p. 307. *The Latin Churches*: A carefully phrased summary, which grants (what is certainly true) that the *homoousion* was not applied as a test of orthodoxy in the West until relatively late in the course of the controversy. The evidence of Hilary of Poitiers, a strong pro-Nicene, suggest that the creed of Nicaea was not well-known in the West generally before the middle of the century. At the same time, it is equally true that the Western churches tended initially to be sympathetic to Athanasius, who worked hard at cementing an alliance with the see of Rome which served him well in his turbulent career.

pp. 309–10. *type, as he really was, and instrument*: again a comment with considerable contemporary force in the 1830s.

p. 312. *the Church of Hadrianople*: c.f. above, on p. 267. As Newman implies, the exact dating of Lucius's second exile and death is not certain, though the mid-40s would be an informed guess.

p. 318. *The history of Liberius*: This does indeed posses a special interest, since Liberius's abandonment under pressure of the Nicene cause was something of a test case for the doctrinal probity of the papacy in the patristic period. The Anglican author of the first edition of this book felt free to be fairly outspoken on the subject; the notes to the later edition show evidence of some slight embarrassment, and a desire to soften the condemnations a little.

p. 322, n.5. *much difference of opinion*: It is generally agreed that, in addition to subscribing to the condemnation of Athanasius at the Council of Sirmium in 351 and later synods at Arles and Milan, Liberius agreed to the creed drawn up at Sirmium in 351, a revision of an earlier creed agreed at the Antiochene synod of 341. Newman assumes that Liberius probably signed the document called the third Sirmium confession, drawn up in 358 (his reference to the 'orthodox Council' of 264 assumes that the enactments of this first council against Paul of Samosata had survived and were identifiable by this date, for which there is no evidence; though it is certain that the 341 creed of Antioch represents a considerably earlier formula, which was widely associated with the martyr Lucian, and no doubt is meant to exclude positions held by Paul and his supporters). It is possible but less likely that Liberius subscribed to the creed of the second synod at Sirmium in 357, the creed known as the 'Blasphemy of Sirmium', which directly condemned the creed of Nicaea. Newman's narrative is here exceptionally compressed and unclear, and the reader is unlikely to have a very satisfactory understanding of the chronology involved. Appendix 3 lays out the problems as understood in scholarship up to Newman's day very thoroughly, but does not come to a firm conclusion about what formula Liberius agreed to. It compounds the confusion of the actual text at this point by using (p. 428) the designation 'Third Sirmian' for the so-called 'dated' creed of 359, normally called the *fourth* confession of Sirmium! The best modern chronological studies make it impossible that Liberius could have signed anything later than the 'Blasphemy' of 357, and strongly suggest that, as Liberius was back in Rome by the spring of 357, prior to the drafting of the 'Blasphemy', the best candidate for the formula that procured his liberty is the 351 document.

p. 323, n.6. The authenticity of some, but not all, of the fragments deriving from Hilary and ascribed to Liberius has been disputed, but scholars generally accept the letters here referred to as genuine.

p. 326. *Meanwhile, the great Egyptian prelate*: A slightly awkward and misleading transition. Newman has just been describing events of 357, by which time Athanasius had for the second time been forced to leave his see. The second exile lasted from 356 to late 361.

p. 334, n.4. Newman is still obviously eager to save the credit of Liberius as far as possible by stressing the unreliability of the documents earlier used and (following Hefele) the relatively innocuous character of the non-Nicene formula he signed. If he did not sign the second Sirmium confession (the 'Blasphemy' of 357), it is true that he did not explicitly repudiate Nicaea; but he certainly agreed to a deliberately non-Nicene formula and supported Athanasius's deposition. Back in office in Rome, he was to reaffirm his support for Athanasius and to work on behalf of the creed of Nicaea.

p. 335, n.1. *Plato made Semi-Arians*: A neat formulation, not without some basis; but we must again be extremely cautious about any assumption of direct Aristotelean influence on Arius. The interesting factor in terms of intellectual history is how Platonic and Aristotelean motifs blend together in Neoplatonism in a way which may be of some significance for the development of Arius's thought. See R. Williams, *Arius. Heresy & Tradition*, London 1987, part B.

p. 344. *Euzoius*: First appears as a signatory with Arius of a statement of faith apparently drawn up in support of a plea for rehabilitation not long after Nicaea.

p. 358, n.5. "*Sanctiores sunt ... sacerdotum*": "The ears of the people are holier than the hearts of the priests".

p. 365, n.9. The reference is to the Benedictine edition of the works of Basil the Great, reprinted in Migne's *Patrologia Graeca*, specifically the biographical introduction, Migne, PG 29; and to the Benedictine edition of Athanasius, with the biographical introduction in PG 25.

p. 367. *Some eminent critics*: The text Newman quotes from the Nicene anathemas certainly suggests that the distinction in meaning between the two words was minimal in normal usage. When Basil the Great distinguishes them later, he has to make a quite fresh case for the grounds of the distinction, and implicitly admits that it is not a matter of current linguistic practice.

p. 369, n.6. ἑτερουσιότης: 'being of another substance or essence'.

p. 372, n.1. Athanasius, *tomus ad Antiochenos*.

p. 379. *As to Semi-Arianism*: 'Semi-Arianism' in fact never designated a coherent party; only a loose alliance of those unhappy equally with Nicaea and with its more aggressive critics. The association with the Macedonian heresy, which denied the full divinity of the Spirit is a little tenuous: Macedonius, regarded as the first propounder of this theology, belonged to the group that historians have called 'Semi-Arian', and attracted support from some others in that group who remained ill at ease with Nicaea. But we cannot speak of a substantial continuity from one 'sect' to another.

p. 380. *Gregory had been placed*: Sasima (as it is now more usually called) was an obscure and unattractive staging post on the imperial highways. Gregory deeply resented his appointment there, and never quite forgave Basil. Anthimus's opposition gave him a reasonable excuse for withdrawal to Nazianzus – though he again tried to evade episcopal duties after his father's death. His call to Constantinople was not initially as bishop, but simply as someone who could defend the Nicene faith for what was at the time the small and beleaguered Nicene group in the capital. By 381, he was acting as *de facto* bishop for this group in much altered circumstances, and played a crucial part in the council of 381; but his position was canonically irregular, and he was pressed to retire. He returned to Nazianzus, but withdrew in 384 from episcopal duties.

p. 392. *The Creed of Constantinople*: Gregory of Nyssa was influential at the Council, and was one of those bishops identified by the Emperor as a touchstone of orthodoxy, but the tradition of his involvement in the drafting of the creed is questionable.

p. 392. *From the date of this Council*: see note on p. 1, above. Although non-Nicene Christianity was the majority faith of the Germanic kingdoms that supplanted the Western Empire, the division cannot be reduced to an essentially ethnic matter.

p. 393. *Then as now*: Newman's most explicit reference to the troubles of the Church of England in the early 1830s.

p. 403. *The Syrian School*: See Introduction, pp. XXXVII ff. Newman brings together a huge variety of theological errors under this one heading, uniting them by their supposed prevalence within what he rather anachronistically calls the 'Patriarchate' of Antioch. This means that he can associate the churches of Palestine, Syriac-speaking Mesopotamia, parts of Asia Minor and Antioch itself as constituting a single unit, and can also assume a homogeneity in the theology of this area from the second to the fifth century.

p. 404. *while Syria was divided*: Only in the fourth century can we begin to identify the emergence of something like a 'Patriarchate' with jurisdiction over local churches, its extent roughly following the boundaries of the imperial province of *Oriens*, 'the East'. Tensions between Antioch and the Syro-Palestinian churches are much in evidence in the fourth century.

p. 404. *its Bishop could banish Origen*: Bishop Demetrius of Alexandria had put pressure on Origen to leave Alexandria, though the root of the trouble was at least as much personal tension as theological disagreement. Origen was subsequently based at Caesarea, very definitely a Palestinian location with little sympathy or connection with Antioch.

p. 405. *Theodore of Heraclea*: We owe to Jerome the statement that he was a literalist in exegesis. His intellectual background is unknown.

p. 405. *a Dissertation upon St. Ephrem*: The quotation from Lengerke shows the awkwardness of Newman's analytical tools. The East Syrian churches, Syriac in language, and culturally distant from Antioch, present a varied pattern of exegesis, which is often at once characteristically 'Semitic' and fiercely anti-Jewish. On the whole question, see D.S. Wallace-Hadrill, *Christian Antioch*, Cambridge, 1982, ch. 2 – though with some caution, as there is something of the same tendency to look for a single 'Syrian' style to cover Greek-speaking Antioch and the Semitic-speaking areas.

p. 406. *Dorotheus*: mentioned in Eusebius's *Historia*, VII.32.2; as Newman hints, it may be misleading to speak of any kind of formal 'school' at Antioch, and Eusebius's report does not suggest such an institution.

p. 406. *Lucian*: see above, p. 6.

p. 407. *the patriarch Marabas*: Mar Aba I (d. 552), head of the (so-called) Nestorian church and a leading scholar and exegete.

p. 407. *Sabarjesus*: Sabr-ishu, head of the Nestorian church at the end of the sixth and beginning of the seventh century.

p. 407. *The original Syrian school*: Newman grants in this paragraph that concern with the literal sense was not at all incompatible with spiritual or allegorical exegesis in the majority of West Syrian writers (he again associates Eusebius with Antioch in a somewhat misleading way; nor would Cyril of Jerusalem (p. 408) fit comfortably into what Newman considers an 'Antiochene' frame).

p. 408. *It would have been well*: There is something of an elision in the argument. It may be that Theodore turned to Jewish commentators, but this cannot easily be linked, as Newman wishes to insinuate, with his Christology.

p. 410. *One other characteristic*: The tendency in some Antiochene writing of the fourth and early fifth centuries to use language suggesting a clear separation in the sacramental elements between the earthly material and the indwelling divine power had been of great interest to polemicists of the Reformation era, especially in Britain; Peter Martyr, Cranmer, Ridley and many others appeal to Theodoret in particular to support alternatives to transubstantiation.

p. 415. *The first act of the exiles of Edessa*: A synod held in 486 permitted clerical marriage for the clergy of the 'Nestorian' jurisdiction in Persia, but it seems that Bar-Sauma (whose career is partly known from some very hostile reports by his theological enemies) did not set out to destroy or suppress monasticism as such – though he did allow professed religious to change their state. This was in part a response to the fierce hostility in the Persian Empire to celibacy.

pp. 417–8. *There can be no doubt*: a clear statement of what Newman found inadequate in the doctrinal histories he had been using. See Introduction, pp. XXXI ff.

p. 421. "*Filii non sine affectu*," "not without the condition of being a Son"; τέλειος λόγος, ὢν μονογενής: 'a perfect Word, being an only-begotten [Son]'.

p. 421. "*in utero Patris*": "in the womb of the Father"; "*non enim foetus . . .*" A foetus is not non-existent before birth; it exists, but in secret. Generation is manifestation. "*Prodivit ex ore . . .*" "he came forth from the mouth of God so that he might create the natural order . . . [having been] an inhabitant of the exalted heart of God", embraced "in the deep hiding place of his holy mind without any unveiling [of the mystery]".

p. 421. τέλειος λόγος υἱὸς ἀτελής, 'perfect as Word, imperfect as Son'.

p. 422. ἀειγεννές, 'eternally generated'; λόγος ἐν τῷ θεῷ ἀτελὴς . . ., 'a word imperfect when it is within God and perfect once it has been generated; ἀτελῆ πρότερον, εἶτα τέλειον ὥσπερ νόμος ἡμέτερος γενέσεως, 'initially imperfect, then perfect, as if it followed the laws of our own processes of coming into being'; *Alia [haeresis] sempiterne natum* . . . "Another sort of heresy fails to understand that the Son is eternally born and thinks that his birth took place in time. Wanting, nevertheless, to confess the Son to be co-eternal with the Father, they hold that he was with the Father prior to this "birth" – i.e., to have been with him always, but not always to have been a Son, beginning to be a Son from the moment of his birth."

p. 423. *Hil. de Syn.*: Hilary *de Synodis.*

p. 425. *Petavius seems to stand alone*: Modern scholarship has dismissed the suggestion of a condemnation of Photinus at Constantinople in 336.

p. 425. *Hilary*: Hilary, *liber contra Constantium.*

p. 430. "*perfidia Ariana*", "Arian apostasy"; "*Solus Valesius* . . ." "Only Valesius thinks that the third [Sirmian confession] is being referred to here."

p. 436. *Origen*: Origen, *commentarii in Joannem*; Ammonius, from *Catenae in evangelia Lucae et Joannis* (ed. J.A. Cramer, Oxford, 1841); Basil the Great, *liber de Spiritu sancto.*

p. 437. *In illud Omnia*: see above on p. 229, n.5.

p. 441. *catachrestically*: to say something *katachrēstikōs* meant to give words an extended (not to say forced) meaning.

p. 442. *nomen Dei*: "the Name of God, since it belongs to the category of words called 'concrete', means a form, not as something abstracted from a set of individual properties but as something subsisting in them. For God is a particular substance possessed of divinity. Just as a human being displays human nature not as a separate or abstracted thing but as something subsisting in a specific individual, yet also representing this human nature not as identical with one fixed and determinate individual or person but exhibiting the nature in a confused and indeterminate way, i.e. (as we say) as a nature existing in something or other . . . so the name of God properly and directly designates divinity, the divine nature, signifying the same concrete reality as it might exist in any particular person and so not designating expressly any one of the three, except in a non-specific or general way."

p. 443. "*Quum hypostasis*": "Since *hypostasis* cannot exist without substance, there is nothing to stop defenders of the doctrine of three *hypostases* taking the word as meaning the same as 'substance', especially where *hypostasis* is being opposed to something that does not subsist or act."

p. 443. *Athanasius*: Athanasius, *de incarnatione contra Apollinarem* (not an authentic work of Athanasius), *de incarnatione*.

p. 444. *Cyril*: Cyril of Alexandria, *Thesaurus de Trinitate*.

p. 444. Εἶδος: 'form'; *neque speciem ejus vidistis*, 'you did not behold his form'. The point is that the word, in Latin, Greek or indeed English, can mean equally the outer appearance of something and the inner structure or essence.

p. 444. *Athan.*: Athanasius, *epistula ad episcopos Aegypti et Libyae*.

p. 448. *Athan. Arian Hist*: Athanasius, *historia arianorum*.

p. 449. *St. Jerome says*: Jerome, *Chronicum* (his translation and continuation of Eusebius's *chronikon*).

p. 450. *St. Hilary speaks*: Hilary, *liber secundus ad Constantium*.

p. 453. "On the week ... flight": Athanasius, *Apologia de Fuga Sua*.

p. 455. *Ed. Bened. Monit*: The preface by the Benedictine editors to Gregory of Nazianzus's sixth oration.

p. 462. *Hilar.ad Const.*i 8: Hilary, *liber primus ad Constantium*.

p. 464ff. An important passage for understanding Newman's nuanced doctrine of the teaching office in the Church (in some respects more nuanced at this later date than in his Anglican years). He has here to defend his view that the common intuition of the baptised can 'carry' the promised infallibility of the Church during periods when, for whatever reason, the majority of the bishops cannot be relied upon. N.5 on p. 467 repudiates the charge that he is denying that the Church is always the 'active instrument of teaching' (*activum instrumentum docendi*). Newman replies: 'I make the distinction: the active instrument of teaching potentially, yes; the active instrument of teaching in actuality, no'. There is always an implicit teaching being conveyed in the Church, even when the actual power in the Church is in the hands of heretics. He appeals to Perrone on the 'common intuition' of the faithful as an 'instrument of tradition', and cites Perrone's example of the dogma 'concerning the beatific vision of God'. The long quotation reads: "There has certainly not been lacking in the Church some kind of divine tradition about this article of the faith; yet it has never been able to be defined. It was not manifest to everyone; the divine utterances of Scripture were not sufficiently clear about it; the Fathers, as we have seen, developed a variety of views on the subject; liturgical practice itself displays no small difficulty in respect of it. The perpetual magisterium of the Church comes to the help of this situation – as well as the common intuition of the faithful."

p. 468. "*La souscription* . . .": "Subscription [to Arian formulae] was one of the necessary conditions for entering and staying in the episcopate. The ink was always to hand; so was the informer. Those who had seemed invincible up to this point gave way before this storm. If their spirit did not fall into heresy, their hand nonetheless consented to it. . . . Very few bishops were exempt from this evil fate; only those whose own obscurity caused them to be overlooked, or those whose virtue bred a generous resistance, and whom God preserved so that there might be some seed, some root to make Israel blossom again."

p. 468. πλὴν ὀλίγων ἄγαν: "Except for a few, all were children of their time [The Greek here has a clause omitted by Newman, corresponding to the last clause – 'only those . . .' – in the immediately preceding quotation from Tillemont, who is paraphrasing Gregory at this point] . . . All that distinguished them from one another was that the same fate overtook some sooner and some later."

BIBLIOGRAPHY

Even by nineteenth-century standards, Newman was rather cavalier in his references. Like his contemporaries in scholarship, he wrote essentially for a readership sharing his intellectual culture, with access to similar libraries, and so did not feel obliged to give full publication details of his literary sources. The notes and citations in his own text can thus be telegraphic in the extreme; and the problem is compounded by the speed and lack of revision in Newman's original composition, so that he does not invariably refer to the same author in the same way. Sometimes he will use the Latinised form of a German or French name, sometimes not. He will also refer to classical and patristic works by abbreviations reasonably familiar to his public (and again is not always consistent about this).

The bibliography attempts to identify all the authors and works referred to by Newman, with the variants of their names as they appear in his work. It has not always been possible to work out which edition of a work he is using; I have normally listed the earliest edition, referring also where appropriate to a major later edition if this may have been available to Newman. He does not seem as a rule to use English translations of his major historical sources, but I have included them as some sort of index of their currency in British Scholarship at the time.

WORKS CITED BY NEWMAN IN TEXT AND NOTES

Alexander, Noel (Natalis), *Selecta historiae ecclesiasticae capita,* 25 vols., Paris, 1677–86.

Assemani, Giuseppe Aloisio, *Bibliotheca orientalis Clementino-Vaticana,* 3 vols., Rome, 1719–1728.

Ballerina, Pietro, *de vi ac ratione primatus Romanorum pontificum*, Verona, 1766.

Baltus, Jean-Francois, *Défence des ss pères accuséz de Platonisme*, Paris, 1711.

Baronius, Caesar, *Annales ecclesiasticae*, Antwerp, 1589, and many subsequent editions.

Basnage, Jacques, *Annales politico-ecclesiastici annorum DCXLV a Caesare Augusto ad Phocam usque*, 3 vols., Rotterdam, 1706.

Idem., *Histoire des juifs depuis Jésus-Christ jusqu'à présent*, The Hague, 1716.

Bayle, Pierre, *Dictionnaire historique et critique*, 2 vols., Rotterdam, 1697 (reprinted 3 vols., 1702; 4 vols., 1720, 1730, 1740; new edition, 18 vols., Paris, 1820); ET *An historical and critical dictionary*, 4 vols., London, 1710; abridged edition, 4 vols., London, 1826.

Beausobre, Isaac de, *Histoire critique de Manichée et du Manichéisme*, Amsterdam, 1734.

Bingham, Joseph, *Origines ecclesiastici*, or, *The antiquities of the Christian Church*, 2 vols., London, 1708 (also, with Bingham's sermons, 8 vols., London, 1834).

Blondel, David, *De la primauté en l'église*, Geneva, 1641.

Bridges, Matthew, *The Roman empire under Constantine the Great*, London, 1828.

Brucker, Johann Joseph, *Historia critica philosophiae*, Leipzig, 1767 (reprinted 1756); ET, *The history of philosophy, drawn up from Brucker's Historia critica philosophiae by W. Enfield*, 2 vols., London, 1791.

Budd (Buddeus), Johann Franciscus, *Isogoge historico-theologica ad thelogiam universam singulasque eius partes*, Leipzig, 1730.

Bull, George, *Defensio fidei Nicaenae*, Oxford, 1685, 1688.

Idem, *Judicium ecclesiae catholicae trium primorum saeculorum de necessitate credendi quod Dominus Noster Jesus Christus sit verus Deus*, Oxford, 1694.

Cave, William, *Scriptorum ecclesiasticorum historia literaria a Christi nato usque ad saeculum XIV*, London, 1688, 1698.

Idem, *Ecclesiastici; or the history of the lives, acts, death and writings of the most eminent fathers of the Church*, London, 1677, reprinted 1683, Burton, Edward, *An inquiry into the heresies of the apostolic age, in eight sermons*, Oxford 1829.

Ceillier, Remy, *Apologie de la morale des pères de l'Eglise contre les accusations de Jean Barbeyrac*, Paris, 1718.

Coleti, Nicolo, *Sacrosancta concilia ad regiam editionem exacta*, Venice, 1728–1733 (new edition, 1759-).

Conybeare, J.J., *The Bampton Lecture for 1824; an attempt to trace the history and to ascertain the limits of the second and spiritual sense of Scripture*, Oxford, 1824.

Cressolles, Louis de, *Theatrum veterum rhetorum, oratorum, declamatorum quos in Graecia nominabant sophistas*, Paris, 1620.

Coustant, Pierre, *Epistolae Romanorum pontificum et quae ad eos scriptae sunt a s. Clemente usque ad Innocentium III*, vol. 1, Paris, 1721.

Cudworth, Ralph, *The true intellectual system of the universe*, First Part, London, 1678.

D'Achéry, Jean Luc, *Veterum aliquot scriptorum spicilegium*, 13 vols., Paris, 1657–77.

Danziger, J.T.L., *de Eusebio Caesariense historiae ecclesiasticae scriptore,* Jena, 1815.

Dodwell, Henry, *Dissertationes in Irenaeum,* Oxford, 1689.

Du Pin, Louis Ellies, *Nouvelle bibliothèque des auteurs ecclésiastiques*, 8 vols., Paris, 1693–1715 (vol. 1, *Auteurs des trois premiers siècles,* Paris, 1693).

Ernesti, Johann August, *Narratio critica de interpretatione prophetiarum messianorum in ecclesia Christiana*, Leipzig, 1769.

Fabricius, Johannes, *Bibliotheca graeca,* 10 vols., Hamburg, 1705; new edition, 14 vols., Hamburg 1708–1728.

Idem (ed.), *Philastrius . . . de haeresibus*, Hamburg, 1721.

Facundus of Hermiane, *Pro definitione trium capitulorum concilii Calchedonensis libri xii,* Paris, 1629.

Fleury, Claude, *Historia ecclesiastica,* 36 vols., Paris, 1719–58 and many further editions; ET, *Ecclesiastical history of . . . abbé Fleury* (1st to 7th centuries), 4 vols., London, 1727–30; also ed. and tr. by Newman (from the Second Council to 456), 4 vols., Oxford, 1842–4.

Galland, André, *Bibliotheca veterum Patrum antiquorumque scriptorum ecclesiasticorum graecolatina*, Venice, 1765–81.

Godefroy (Gothofredus), Jacques (ed.), *Philostorgii Cappadocis ecclesiaticae historiae libri xii a Photio in epitomen contracti*, Geneva, 1643.

Hardouin, Jean, *Conciliorum collectio regia maxima,* 11 vols., 1714–1715.

Hawkins, Edward, *A dissertation upon the use and importance of unauthoritative tradition, as an introduction to the Christian doctrines*, Oxford, 1819.

Hefele, Karl-Joseph von, *A history of the Christian Councils,* and ed. W.R. Clarke, 5 vols., Edinburgh, 1871–1896.

Hoffman, Andreas Gottlieb, *Grammaticae syriacae libr. iii,* Halle, 1827.

Huet, Pierre Daniel, *Origeniana*, Rouen, 1668.

Ittigius, Thomas, *Historia concilii Nicaeni*, Leipzig, 1712.

Idem, *De haeresiarchis aevi apostolici et apostolico proximo*, Leipzig, 1690.

Jortin, John, *Remarks on ecclesiastical history*, 5 vols., London, 1751–1753.

Kestner, Christian August, *Commentatio de Eusebii, historiae ecclesiasticae conditoris, auctoritate et fide diplomatica*, Gottingen, 1816.

Lambeck, Peter, *Commentariorum de augustisissima caesareae Vindobonensia*, 8 vols., Vienna, 1665–1679 (lib. 1, 1665).

Lardner, Nathaniel, *A Large collection of ancient Jewish and heathen testimonies to the truth of the Christian religion*, 4 vols., London, 1764–1767.

Idem, *The credibility of the Gospel history*, 16 vols., 1730–1757.

de Larroque (de la Roque in Newman's text), Matthieu (Larroquanus), *Dissertatio duplex: de Photino heretico; de Liberio pontifice Romano*, Geneva, 1670.

Launoy (Launnois in Newman's text), Jean de, *Epistolae omnes*, ed. W. Saywell, Cambridge, 1689.

Lengerke, Caesar von, *Commentatio critica de Ephraemo Syro s. Scripturae interprete*, Halle, 1828.

Idem, *De Ephraemo Syro arte hermeneutica liber*, Konigsberg, 1831.

Lumper, Gottfried, *Historia theologico-critica de vita, scriptis atque doctrina s. patrum*, 13 parts, Vienna, 1783–1799.

Maimbourg, Loius de, *Histoire de l'Arianisme depuis sa naissance jusqu'à sa fin*, Paris, 1673 (ET, *The history of Arianism*, London, 1728–1729).

Mamachi, Tommaso Maria, *Originum et antiquitatum Christianorum lib.xx* (only 1–5.i published), Rome, 1749–55.

Mansi, G.D., *de epochis conciliorum Sardicensis et Sirmiensis caeterorumque in causa Arianorum*, Lucca, 1746.

Idem, *Collectionis conciliorum synopsis*, Venice, 1768–98, and many later editions.

Maran, Prudent (ed.), *S.P.N., Justini opera*, Paris, 1742.

Idem, *Divinitas Domini Nostri Jesu Christi manifesta in scripturis et traditione*, Paris, 1746.

de Marca, Pierre, *Dissertationes posthumae sacrae et ecclesiasticae*, Paris, 1682.

Marin, Michel-Ange, *Les vies de Pères des déserts d'Orient*, 3 vols., Avignon 1761–4, and many subsequent editions.

Montfaucon, Bernard de (ed.), *S.P.N. Athanasii archiepiscopi Alexandrini opera omnia quae exstant*, 3 vols., Paris, 1698.

Mosheim, Johann Lorenz von, *de causis suppositorum librorum inter Christianos saeculorum I et II*, Helmstadt, 1725.

Idem, *de rebus Christianorum ante Constantinum Magnum commentarii*, Helmstadt, 1753.

Idem, *de turbata per recentiores platonicos Ecclesia commentatio*, Jena, 1733.

Neander, Johann August von, *The history of the Christian religion and the Church during the first three centuries, translated by HJR from vol.1 of Allgemeine Geschichte der christlichen Religion [Hamburg, 1825]*, London, 1831.

Noris, Enrico, *Historica dissertatio de uno ex Trinitate carne passo*, Rome, 1695.

Pagi, Antonio, Critical notes to Baronius, op.cit., included in editions of Baronius from Paris 1689 onwards.

Passaglia, Carlo, *Commentarius de praerogativa b.Petri, apostolorum principis*, Ratisbon, 1850.

Pearson, John, *An exposition of the Apostles' Creed*, London, 1659.

Perrone, Giovanni, *de immaculata Beata Virgine Maria concepta*, Rome, 1847.

Petau (Petavius) Denis, *Appendix ad Epiphanianas animadversiones*, Paris, 1624.

Idem, *Theologicorum dogmatorum tomus primus*, Paris, 1644.

Idem, *de Photino heretico*, no date or place.

Rosenmüller, Johann Georg, *Historia interpretationis librorum sacrorum in Ecclesia Christiana inde ab apostolorum aetate usque ad Origenem*, 5 parts, Hildburghaus, 1795–1814.

Routh, Martin Joseph, *Reliquiae sacrae: sive, Auctores fere jam perditorum IIi et IIIi saeculi fragmenta quae supersunt*, 4 vols., Oxford, 1814–1818.

Schweitzer (Suicer), Johann Caspar, *Symbolum Niceno-Constantinopolitanum expositumet ex antiquitate ecclesiastica illustratum*, Utrecht, 1718.

Idem, *Thesaurus ecclesiasticus*, 2 vols., Amsterdam, 1682; new edition 1728.

Sirmond, Jacques, *Diatribas Sirmitanae II de anno synodi Sirmiensis,* in Petau, D., *Opus de doctrina temporum, vol.III,* Antwerp, 1703.

Tillemont, Louis Sebastien le Nain de, *Mémoire pour servir a l'histoire ecclésiastique des six premiers siècles*, 16 vols, Paris 1693–1712.

Idem, *Histoire des empéreurs*, 8 vols., Brussels, 1692–1693; new edition, 6 vols., Paris, 1700–1738 (to the death of Anastasius).

Valois (Valesius), Henri de, *Eusebii ..., Socratis scholastici ... historiae ecclesiasticae*, 3 vols., Cambrai, 1720).

Idem, *Historia ecclesiastica Eusebii, Pamphili [et al.],* Paris, 1677.

Waterland, Daniel, *Works*, 10 vols., Oxford, 1823.

Wegnern, August Friedrich von, *Theodori Antiocheni quae supersunt omnia,* Berlin, 1834.

Weismann, Christian, *Introductio in memorabilia ecclesiastica historiae sacrae Novi Testamenti*, 2 vols., Stuttgart, 1718; new edition, 4 vols., Halle, 1754.

Whitby, Daniel, *A paraphrase and commentary on the New Testament*, 2 vols., London, 1703.

Zaccaria, Francesco Antonio, *de rebus ad historiam et antiquitates Ecclesiae pertinentibus ... dissertationes Latinae*, 2 vols., Foligno, 1781.